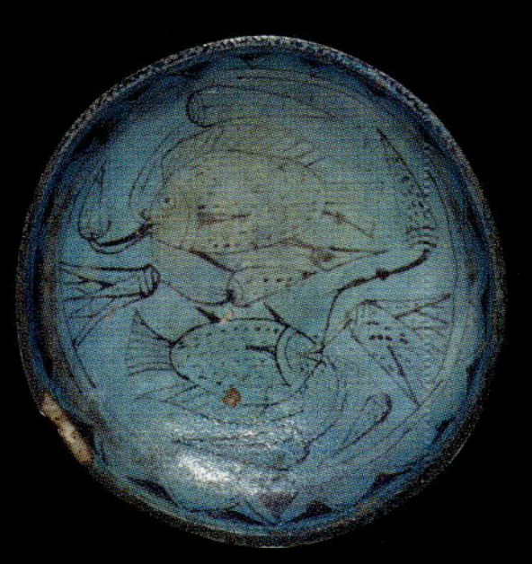

EGYPTIAN ART

The Walters Art Museum

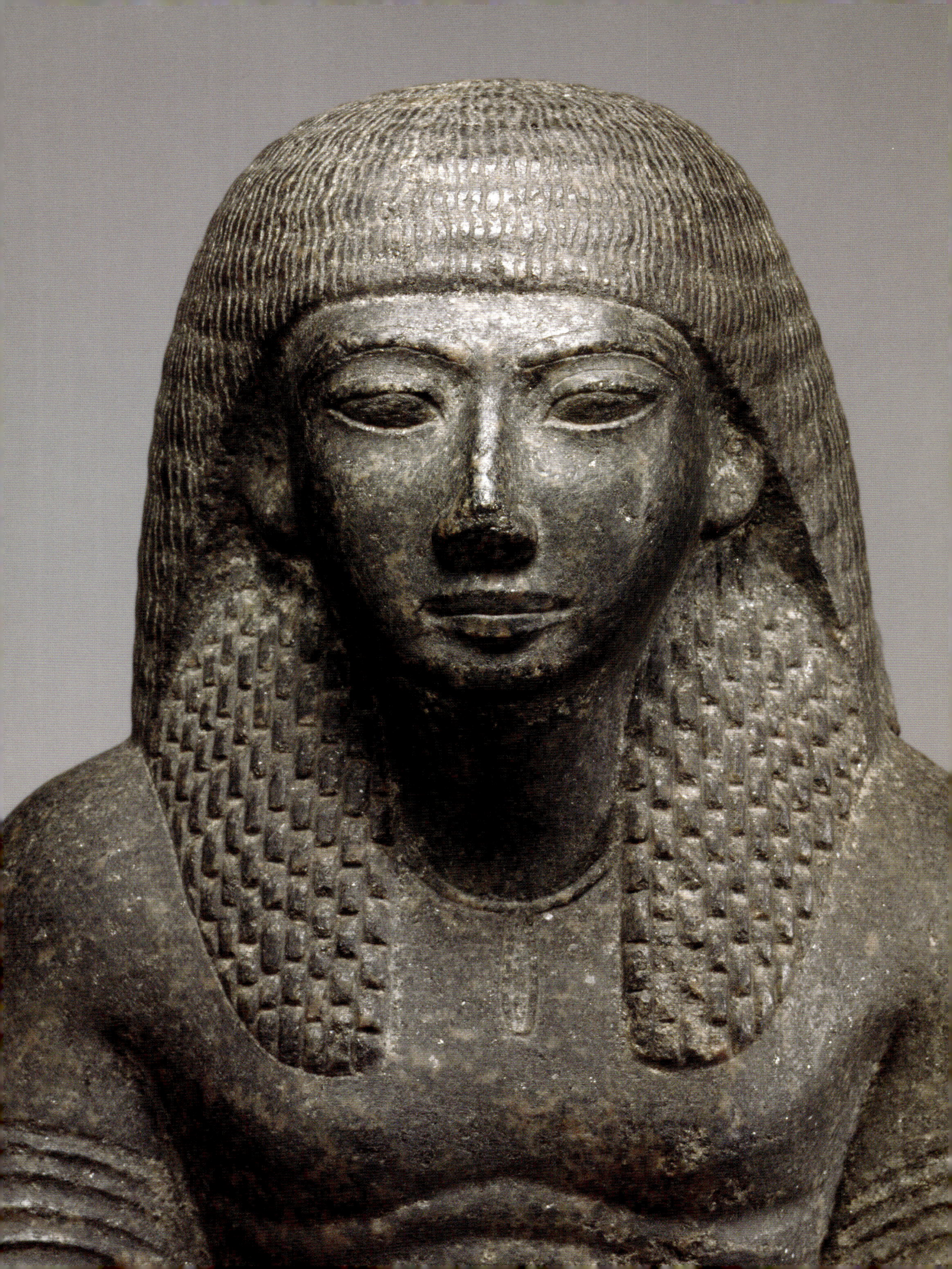

EGYPTIAN ART

The Walters Art Museum

Regine Schulz and Matthias Seidel
with contributions by Betsy Bryan and Christianne Henry

Photography by Susan Tobin

The Walters Art Museum, Baltimore
in association with D Giles Limited, London

This publication has been generously supported by a gift from Clarice and Robert H. Smith

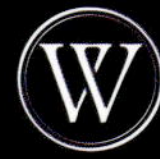

© 2009 The Trustees of the Walters Art Gallery, Baltimore

First published in 2009 by GILES
An imprint of D Giles Limited
2nd Floor, 162–164 Upper Richmond Road
London
SW15 2SL
United Kingdom

ISBN (paperback): 978-0-911886-70-2
ISBN (hardback): 978-1-904832-57-7

All rights reserved

No part of the contents of this book may be reproduced, stored in a retrieval system, or transmitted in any form or by any means, including photocopy, recording, or other information and retrieval systems without the written permission of the Trustees of the Walters Art Gallery and D Giles Ltd.

Library of Congress Cataloging-in-Publication Data

Walters Art Museum (Baltimore, Md.)
Egyptian art / the Walters Art Museum ; Regine Schulz and Matthias Seidel ; with contributions by Betsy Bryan and Christianne Henry ; photography by Susan Tobin.
p. cm.
Includes bibliographical references and index.
ISBN 978-0-911886-70-2 (pbk.) -- ISBN 978-1-904832-57-7 (hardback)
1. Art, Egyptian--Catalogs. 2. Egypt--Antiquities--Catalogs. 3. Art--Maryland--Baltimore--Catalogs. 4. Walters Art Museum (Baltimore, Md.)--Catalogs. I. Schulz, Regine, 1953- II. Seidel, Matthias III. Bryan, Betsy Morrell. IV. Henry, Christianne. V. Title.

N5350.W25 2009
709.32074'7526--dc22
2008045636

All dimensions are in centimeters and inches; height precedes depth precedes width.

Dates, unless otherwise indicated, are regnal dates.

For the Walters Art Museum
Manager of Curatorial Publications: Charles Dibble
Curatorial Publications Assistant: Jennifer Corr
Photography by Susan Tobin
Maps by Jennifer Corr

For GILES:
Copyedited by Sarah Kane
Proofread by John Gilbert
Designed by Mercer Design, London
Produced by GILES, an imprint of D Giles Limited
Printed and bound in China

Front cover: Figures of Tef-ib, nos. 8a, 8b
Back cover: Tile inscribed with the name of Sety II, no. 39
Spine: Bowl with fish and lotus blossoms, no. 21
Frontispiece: Male bust from a group statue, no. 32 (detail)
Facing p. 7 [foreword]: Funerary stela of Tembu, no. 20 (detail)

CONTENTS

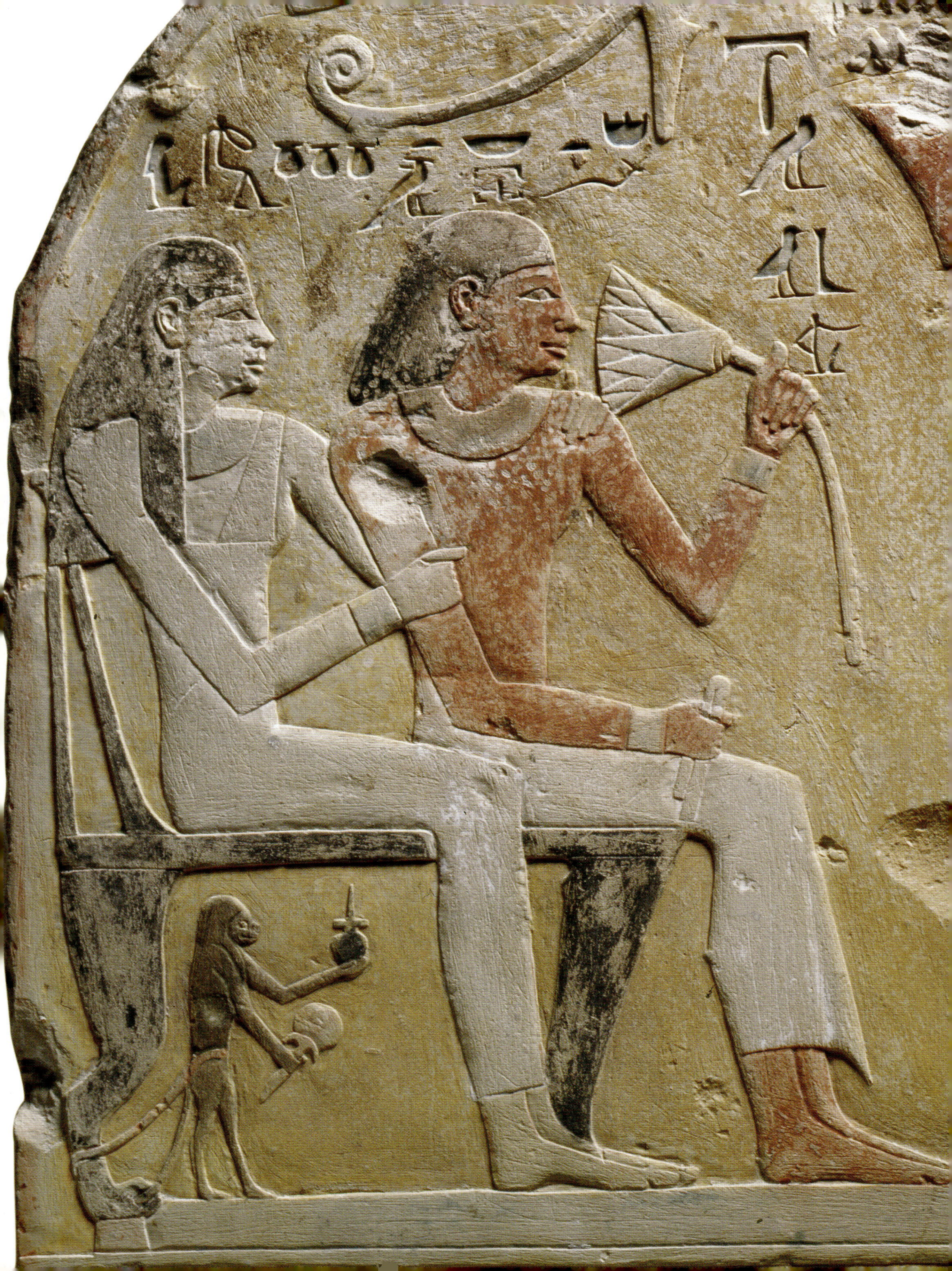

FOREWORD

Henry Walters lived during an era of exuberant collecting, when objects from all corners of the globe and from all ages in human history were valued as worthy of admiration and study. His collection of Egyptian art, bequeathed as part of his gallery to the city of Baltimore at his death in 1931, exemplifies his encyclopedic tastes, ranging from tiny amulets intended to keep sickness at bay to large temple friezes and sculpture that celebrated the divinity of Egypt's pharaohs. Due in part to the arid conditions that preserved fragile materials to an extent not seen anywhere else in the world—wood, papyrus, textiles, glass, and human remains—as well as the more inherently durable media of stone and metal, the collection documents with astonishing, often moving, clarity the daily lives of ordinary people (evidenced most recently in the findings of a CT scan of a mummy in the Walters [no. 41]) as well as the lives of the gods, demigods, and protective deities who presided over them. Henry Walters' collection is both a means of engaging with a distant but vivid past and an object of present wonder.

This title, one in a series of volumes presenting the museum's collections, funded through the extraordinary generosity of Clarice and Robert Smith, is the first publication of the Egyptian collection since George Steindorff surveyed the museum's holdings of Egyptian sculpture more than sixty years ago. Special thanks are due to those who have contributed to the present volume. Foremost among these are the authors: Dr. Regine Schulz, Curator of Ancient Art; Dr. Matthias Seidel, independent Egyptologist; Dr. Betsy M. Bryan, Alexander Badawy Professor of Egyptian Art and Archeology at the Johns Hopkins University; and Christianne Henry, a member of the Walters' curatorial division. Their endeavors were greatly aided by museum conservators Meg Craft and Terry Drayman-Weisser; photographer Susan Tobin, photo services coordinator Ruth Bowler and her predecessor, Jenny Beard, and photography technician Jenny Campbell; chief registrar Joan Elizabeth Reid and associate registrar Betsy Dahl; senior development officer Joy Heyrman; and manager of foundation and government relations Sarah Crowther; and editor Charles Dibble and curatorial publications assistant Jennifer Corr. Dan Giles and Sarah McLaughlin expertly and patiently guided the book through its design and production. For their expert counsel, we are grateful as well to Dr. Abdel Ghaffar Shedid, professor emeritus at Helwan University, Cairo; Dr. Marsha Hill, curator of Egyptian art at the Metropolitan Museum of Art, New York; and Barry D. Daly, MD, FRCR, professor of diagnostic radiology and nuclear medicine at the University of Maryland Medical Center, Baltimore.

Gary Vikan
Director

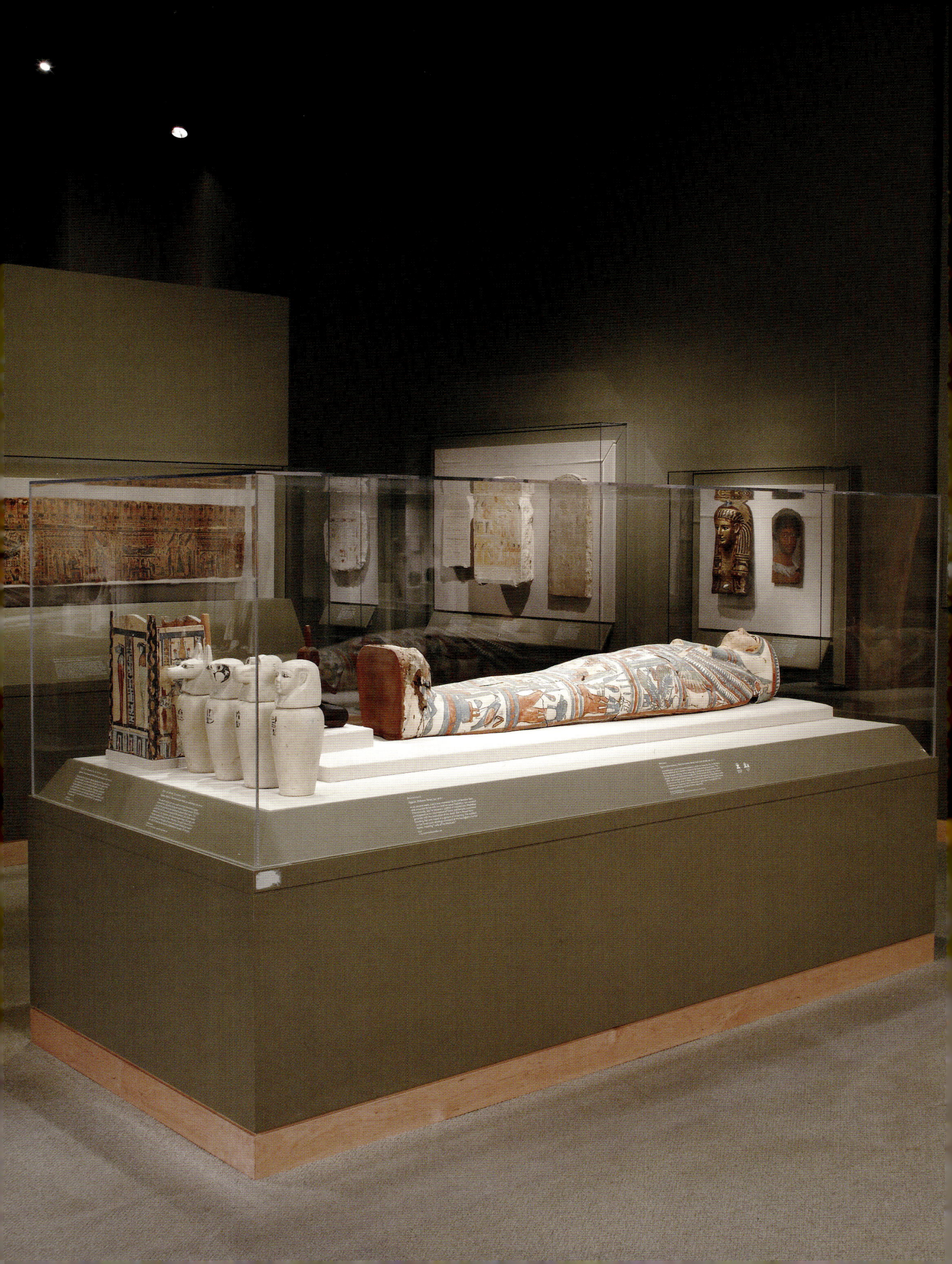

INTRODUCTION

Regine Schulz

The Egyptian collection of the Walters Art Museum (fig. 1) was formed by Henry Walters (1848–1931), between 1899 and 1931. At his death, it was one of the finest private collections in the United States; supplemented in recent years by gifts, acquisitions, and long-term loans, the museum has one of the most important American collections of ancient Egyptian art. Henry Walters (fig. 2) was born in Baltimore and educated in Baltimore, Washington, and Paris. After finishing his college degree at Harvard, he followed in his father's footsteps, both in his business life and as one of the major American collectors of fine art. After the death of his father, William Walters, in 1894, he was elected chairman of the Atlantic Coastline Company Railroad of Virginia, and relocated his headquarters to New York. Whereas William Walters' collecting interests focused on contemporary European painting and sculpture and Japanese decorative arts, Henry was a more expansive collector, extending the collection's holdings in several different areas, including ancient art. He was a supporter of New York's cultural institutions, such as the Public Library, the American Museum of Natural History, and the Metropolitan Museum of Art; he served on the latter's executive committee and was named its second vice president in 1913. Walters was a generous contributor to the Met's acquisition fund, enabling the museum to purchase several objects from the richly appointed tomb of the Twelfth Dynasty Egyptian princess Sat-Hathor-Iunet in 1914, as well as, in 1919, seven large statues of the goddess Sakhmet from the Mut temple area at Karnak (for parallel pieces, see nos. 26a and 26b).

Although Henry Walters had strong connections with several art dealers, his relationships with scholars or curators varied: He never took to Wilhelm Reinhold Valentiner, who had come to America in 1906 as the first curator of decorative arts at the Metropolitan Museum of Art. Indeed, Valentiner wrote to Wilhelm von Bode, the director of the Kaiser Friedrich Museum in Berlin, complaining that "Mr. Walters . . . has enormous influence and buys for his collection in Baltimore more fakes than genuine items."[1] Bode, who had ridiculed the Baltimorean's purchase of the Marcello Massarenti collection of Italian antiquities and Renaissance paintings in 1902, must have been sympathetic to his former colleague's complaint. Fortunately, Walters found Albert M. Lythgoe, the curator of Egyptian art in New York, more sympathetic and subsequently supported the museum's acquisitions of Egyptian art. He also respected other Egyptologists, such as Percy E. Newberry, who compiled a group of scarabs for Henry Walters' collection in 1911.

The scope of Henry Walters' collection, both in Egyptian art and in other areas, was guided largely by his own tastes; he was guarded in discussing his intent to purchase particular objects and particularly secretive about the costs. Whereas institutional and private collectors sought out mummies, papyri, and large objects that reflected the monumental character of Egyptian art, Walters had a predilection for small and precious objects—figurines, amulets, jewelry, and high-quality vanity pieces—but his main focus was Egyptian statuary (fig. 3), and the collection of bronzes is extraordinary both in its range and in its quality. Though he purchased statue fragments, it was important for him that the heads be preserved, and the collection contains an impressive variety of different faces from all periods. In his later years, Walters' interests broadened to include larger works, such as the life-size figure of Nehy (no. 37), purchased in 1925.

The art dealer Dikran Kelekian (1868–1951; fig. 4) became one of Henry Walters' closest consultants; much of Walters' collection of ancient, Near Eastern, and Islamic art was purchased from Kelekian or with his assistance. The son of an Armenian banker from Kayseri (in central Anatolia), Dikran and his brother, Kevork, started their antiquities business in Istanbul, eventually opening branches in New York, Paris, London, and Cairo. Dikran was a specialist in Islamic art, and he was honored with the title "khan" by the shah of Iran in recognition of his promotion of Persian art and culture, particularly in conjunction with the Saint Louis World's Fair of 1904. Kelekian was also interested in and had a good knowledge of ancient art.

Fig. 1 Egyptian Galleries in the Walters Art Museum, 2008

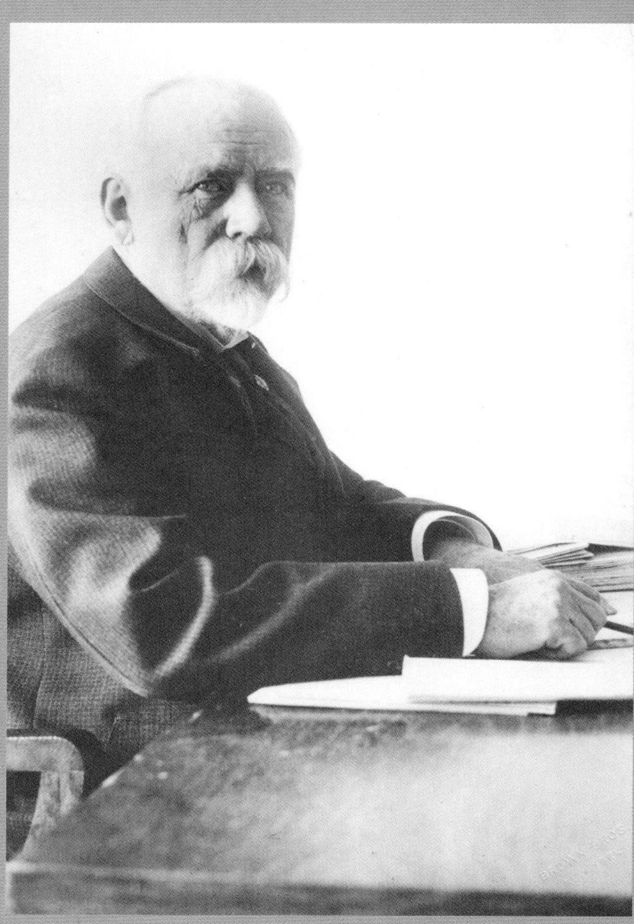

Fig. 2 Henry Walters, ca. 1917–19. Photograph Brown Brothers, New York. Walters Art Museum Archives. (Prelim) RG 11: Records of Henry Walters, series 8: Images relating to Henry Walters

The starting point for Henry Walters' collection of ancient art was a Sotheby, Wilkinson & Hodge auction in London in June 1899 in which the antiquities collection of William Henry Foreman was sold by his nephew and heir, Major Alexander Henry Brown. The British collector William Foreman (1793–1896), who resided in Dorking (Surrey), together with his brother Thomas Seaton, assembled an impressive collection of antiquities and works of art, including many Egyptian items. Dikran Kelekian had known the collection and recommended it to Henry Walters. On Walters' behalf, Kelekian purchased a group of Etruscan, Hellenistic, and Roman statuettes, as well as a large Egyptian bronze cat with inlaid eyes and a scarab on its head (acc. no. 54.403).

Between 1909 and 1931 (the year of his death) Henry Walters bought several hundred Egyptian objects with Kelekian's assistance, but determining the precise number of works purchased from or through Kelekian is hampered by the fact that not all the invoices have been preserved and by the sketchiness of the descriptions in the inventory book of James C. Anderson, the caretaker of Henry Walters' property in Baltimore (fig. 5). Walters purchased at least twenty Egyptian items from Kelekian in 1909, including a temple relief of King Nectanebo II from Sammanud (no. 49); in 1911, he purchased more than thirty, among them an extraordinary piece: a large statue of the hippopotamus goddess Taweret with lion paw-shaped feet, human hands, and a crocodile's tail (no. 69). This statue had belonged to the Lebanese collector Dr. Eddé, who had resided in Alexandria until returning to Lebanon in the 1920s; his collection of Egyptian and Greek antiquities was sold in 1911 at the Hôtel Drouot in Paris.[2]

The largest number of pieces came to Baltimore in the summer of 1912: fifteen crates of antiquities and Islamic art objects. Some came from the collection of Giovanni Dattari, an Italian who lived in Cairo and was a purveyor for the British army in Egypt. Dattari, a well-respected numismatist and specialist in ancient glass, sold his famous glass collection in 1909 to the Freer Gallery in Washington, D.C., and his other antiquities in 1912 in a combined auction with the Greek and Roman art collection of Jean P. Lambros from Athens at the Hôtel Drouot.[3] Forty lots, comprising seventy-four objects, including the bust of a dignitary (no. 50), were sold to Henry Walters and integrated into his collection.

Another important expansion of the Egyptian collection occurred in 1922, when Walters purchased works from the MacGregor collection. William MacGregor (1848–1937) was a vicar at St. Editha's Church in Tamworth (Staffordshire, England), and an important campaigner for the rights of the underprivileged, an influential educationalist, and public health advocate. In 1885 he made his first visit to Egypt to recuperate from a severe illness. There, he started to study the country's ancient culture, became an amateur Egyptologist, a supporter of excavations in Egypt and Nubia (including the excavations of John Garstang at Meroë), and one of the most important British collectors of Egyptian artifacts. He sold

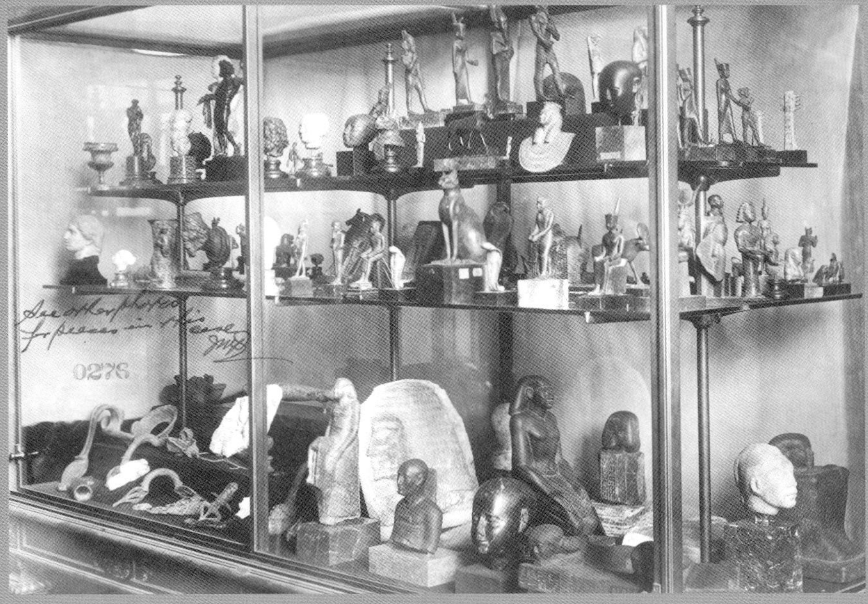

Fig. 3 Case of antiquities in Henry Walters' gallery (1931 or earlier). Visible on the bottom shelf are the base with two prostrate figures (no. 13) and the kneeling figure of Hor-wedja (no. 55) Walters Art Museum Archives. (Prelim) RG 11: Records of Henry Walters, series 8: Images relating to Henry Walters

his Egyptian collection privately in 1921 to support social institutions. One year later, the collection of some eighteen hundred Egyptian artifacts came to auction at Sotheby's London and was sold very successfully to several large museums and collections.[4] Dikran Kelekian was one of the bidders on Henry Walters' behalf, purchasing thirty-nine lots, totaling ninety-three items, for the collection; among the works acquired were a group of elaborate faience objects (see nos. 19, 21, 22, and 60), and a plaque depicting the Nubian king Tanyidamani from Meroë (no. 72).

In 1925 Henry Walters bought one of his most important Egyptian objects, the life-size statue of Nehy from an unnamed French dealer in New York. This statue was once part of the collection of the Château des Aygalades (near Marseille); it may have been purchased in Egypt around 1828–29 by François Champollion, the decipherer of Egyptian hieroglyphs, or even earlier by the officers of Napoleon's Egyptian expedition at the very end of the eighteenth century. The statue, together with a parallel piece, today in the Matsuoka Museum of Art in Tokyo, was almost certainly excavated in the late eighteenth century, probably from a tomb in the cemetery at Saqqara, and sold on the art market.

In the following years, the Egyptian collection was further extended, and Henry Walters also bought objects from other dealers, probably with Kelekian's assistance. One of them was Joseph Brummer (1883–1947; fig. 6), a native Hungarian, and one of the leading New Yorker art dealers of the 1920s and '30s. He and his brother Ernest had started with a gallery of "primitive art" in Paris in 1906; after World War I, Joseph came to New York, where he opened his own gallery of ancient art, as well as Byzantine, medieval, and contemporary art. Joseph Brummer was not only a dealer, but also a passionate collector. Henry Walters had known the Brummers from Paris, and purchased several objects in Paris and New York, including a golden falcon figure with blue enamel work (no. 67).

Henry Walters might have become attracted to ancient Egyptian antiquities during a sailing cruise in the Mediterranean in 1889. He visited Egypt for two days, traveling to Cairo and Giza. The only documentation of this visit is a site-visit permit signed by the Egyptologist Émile Brugsch, who was at that time an employee of the Service des Antiquités de l'Égypte.[5] In Cairo, he bought several pieces from the well-known art dealer Maurice Nahman (1868–1948). Nahman had started his career as an employee of the Crédit Foncier Égyptien, operating an antiquities business as a sideline. In 1913 he opened a shop on Madeberg Street (present-day Sharia Sherif), where he welcomed collectors and scholars from all over the world (his visitors' book is in the Egyptian collection of the Brooklyn Museum). Henry Walters bought twenty-seven antiquities in Nahman's shop, including two extraordinary statuettes of high Middle Kingdom officials, one in graywacke (no. 17) and the other in ivory (no. 12). He also visited the shop of the Abemayor family on Sharia Kamel in Cairo, founded by Michel Abemayor in 1888 and run in the 1920s by Elie Albert and Joseph Abemayor. Here he bought the Middle Kingdom statue of Intef (no. 15) as well as amulets, jewelry, and smaller figurines. In addition, he purchased objects from the renowned Khawam Brothers' shop in Cairo. The most important pieces that he purchased, with advice from Dikran Kelekian, were the reliefs from the tomb of Ankh-ef-en-Sakhmet (no. 53). A few items purchased from Sheikh Ismael, who had a shop in Giza, are identified in James Anderson's register as "bought

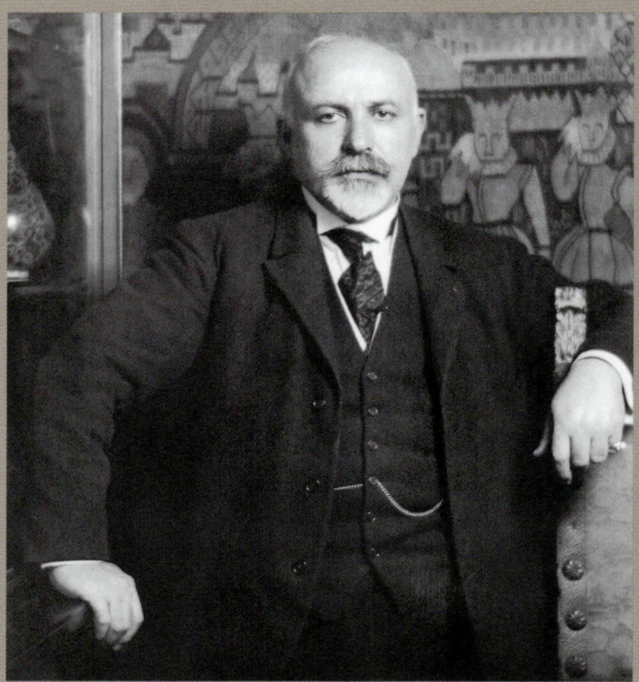

Fig. 4 Dikran Kelekian, 1921. Photo Arnold Genthe. Arnold Genthe Collection, Library of Congress Prints and Photographic Division ([DLC] 94837677)

from a sheikh at the pyramids."

As so often with private collectors, a quite accidental and lucky opportunity opened up for Walters to purchase a very important group of objects, again through his valuable connection to Dikran Kelekian. By doing so, Walters participated in one of the most significant archeological discoveries in Egypt. Under the direction of the famed French Egyptologist Gaston Maspero, then director of the Service des Antiquités Égyptiennes, his countryman Georges Legrain began excavating the courtyard of the Seventh Pylon in the temple of Amun at Karnak in 1901. In December of 1903, the first royal statue emerged from the ground; when the excavations concluded in the summer of 1905, a total of eight hundred stone statues and approximately seventeen thousand bronzes had been recovered from the cachette of Karnak—the largest single collection of royal and private figures found to date. Accommodating such a vast corpus of statues challenged the resources of the Egyptian Museum; ultimately several of the smaller, less important figures were sold by the museum, a happy meeting of opportunity and Henry Walters' particular collecting interests. (Among American museums, the Walters owns the largest group of statues from the cachette.)

Henry Walters wanted to share his entire collection with the people in his hometown of Baltimore and built a special museum for this purpose, which he opened to the public in 1909. In his will he bequeathed the building and its contents to the mayor and city council of Baltimore "for the benefit of the public." When he died in 1931, the Walters Art Gallery became a museum of the City of Baltimore.

The outstanding collection of Egyptian antiquities that Henry Walters bequeathed to the city, defined as it was by the collector's interests, had weaknesses in certain areas, particularly mummies, funerary equipment, objects of daily life, and papyri. During the fifty years since the collection was bequeathed to the city, the museum

OBJETS DE COLLECTION

DIKRAN KELEKIAN

MEMBRE DU JURY

Exposition Universelle de 1900

Commissaire Général de Perse à l'Exposition de St. Louis

2, Place Vendôme, 2

252, Fifth Ave. NEW-YORK.

Adresse Télégraphique: KELEKIAN-PARIS

Paris, le 25 Août 1907

Monsieur H. Walters Doit

1	Statue grecque P	3500 –
1	" P	3500 –
2	petites statues	700 –
2	faïences Egyptiennes	250 –
1	bague	600 –
1	Tablette	300 –
1	Statue	800 –
2	faïences	550 –
2	bagues	750 –
1	bague Egyptienne	1100 –
3	pierres	3250 –
26	Cylindres et pierres gravés	4550 –
13	Philippus en or	2200 –
1	Statue Egyptienne en pierre dure. P	15000 –
	francs	37050 –
		7500
		44,550

Payment authorized through Hallgarten's Paris House 44550 fcs

Fig. 5 Kelekian invoice to Henry Walters, Paris, 25 August 1907, for a purchase of antiquities, Kelekian Documents, Walters Art Museum Archives. (Prelim) RG II: Records of Henry Walters, series 2: Vertical file by subject

Fig. 6 Henri Rousseau (French, 1844–1910). Portrait of Joseph Brummer, 1909. Oil on canvas. © National Gallery, London / The Bridgeman Art Library

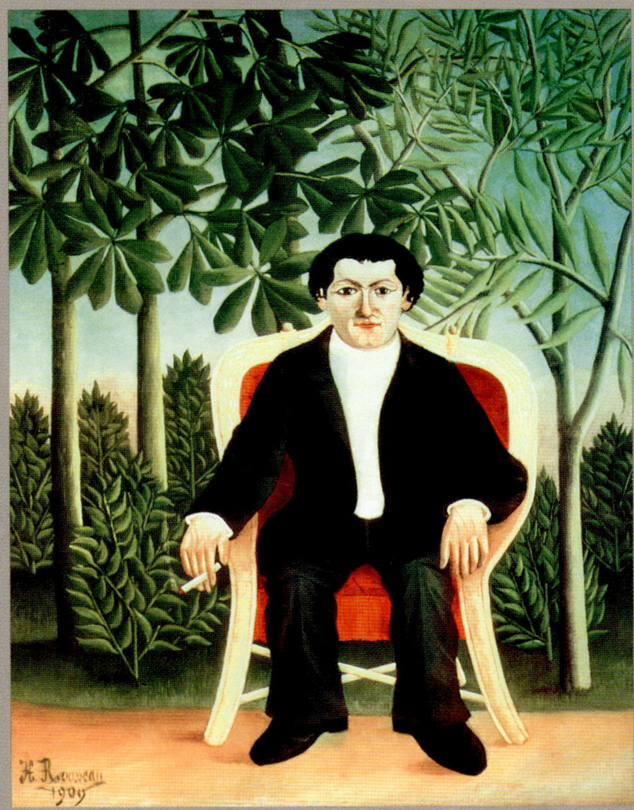

has sought to enrich the Egyptian display through purchases, exchanges, and loans in order to present a holistic view of ancient Egyptian culture.

One such opportunity arose in 1941 with the acquisition of a mummy from the Metropolitan Museum of Art in New York as part of an object exchange. The mummy (no. 41) was excavated in 1930–31 at Deir el-Bahari (western Thebes) and came to the United States as part of an official division of finds. This mummy of a woman, together with its beautiful cartonnage case, became one of the main attractions of the Walters Art Gallery. Another mummy of the Roman Period arrived later as a long-term loan from Goucher College in Baltimore, and animal mummies were presented to the museum as gifts from individual donors. In 2004 a so-called corn-mummy, an ancient mummy imitation used for rituals, was also added to the display as a long-term loan.

To strengthen the Walters collection of works relating to the afterlife, the Metropolitan Museum of Art agreed to a long-term loan of an entire coffin set (no. 42), consisting of an outer and an inner coffin as well as a mummy board. In addition a mummy mask from the former Jozef Nestor collection was purchased in 2001. One of the earliest mummy masks of the Middle Kingdom (ca. 1980 B.C.), the mask complements a Greco-Roman example, representing the end-point in the development of funerary masks, purchased by Henry Walters in 1913 (no. 70).

To enrich the daily life collection, ancient Egyptian tools came to the museum as loans from the Oriental Institute of the University of Chicago, and a pair of ancient leather soles of sandals as a gift from the Royal Scottish Museum in Edinburgh. A wonderful addition was a small group of ostraca (limestone flakes carrying inscriptions or drawings) with artists' sketches, given to the museum in 1998 by the family of Donald N. Wilber, who purchased them in Luxor in the 1930s.

An unusual opportunity to acquire a papyrus arose after Joseph Brummer's death, when his collection was sold in a Parke-Bernet Galleries sale in May 1949. The Walters Art Gallery purchased several objects, including an Old Kingdom tomb relief (no. 4); the most important object from the collection, however, was a large papyrus, called "The Book of the Faiyum" (no. 66).

In 2000 and 2001, when the reinstallation of the ancient galleries took place, the museum sought out pieces that could mark the entry into the Egyptian galleries. The Sakhmet figures that Henry Walters had helped purchase for the Metropolitan Museum of Art would have been perfect for such a purpose, but they were already spoken for in the museum's installation. Ultimately, the Walters is extremely fortunate in the long-term loan of two statues of the lion-headed goddess Sakhmet from the British Museum (nos. 26a and 26b). These loans are important for Baltimore in a double sense, since they not only introduce the visitor to the ancient Egyptian world, but also link the museum to the excavations of Johns Hopkins University in the Mut temple area at Karnak, the place of origin of the two statues.

Notes

1. Foreman Collection 1899.
2. Eddé Collection 1911.
3. Dattari Collection 1912.
4. MacGregor Collection 1922.
5. Johnston 1999, 119 and n. 14.

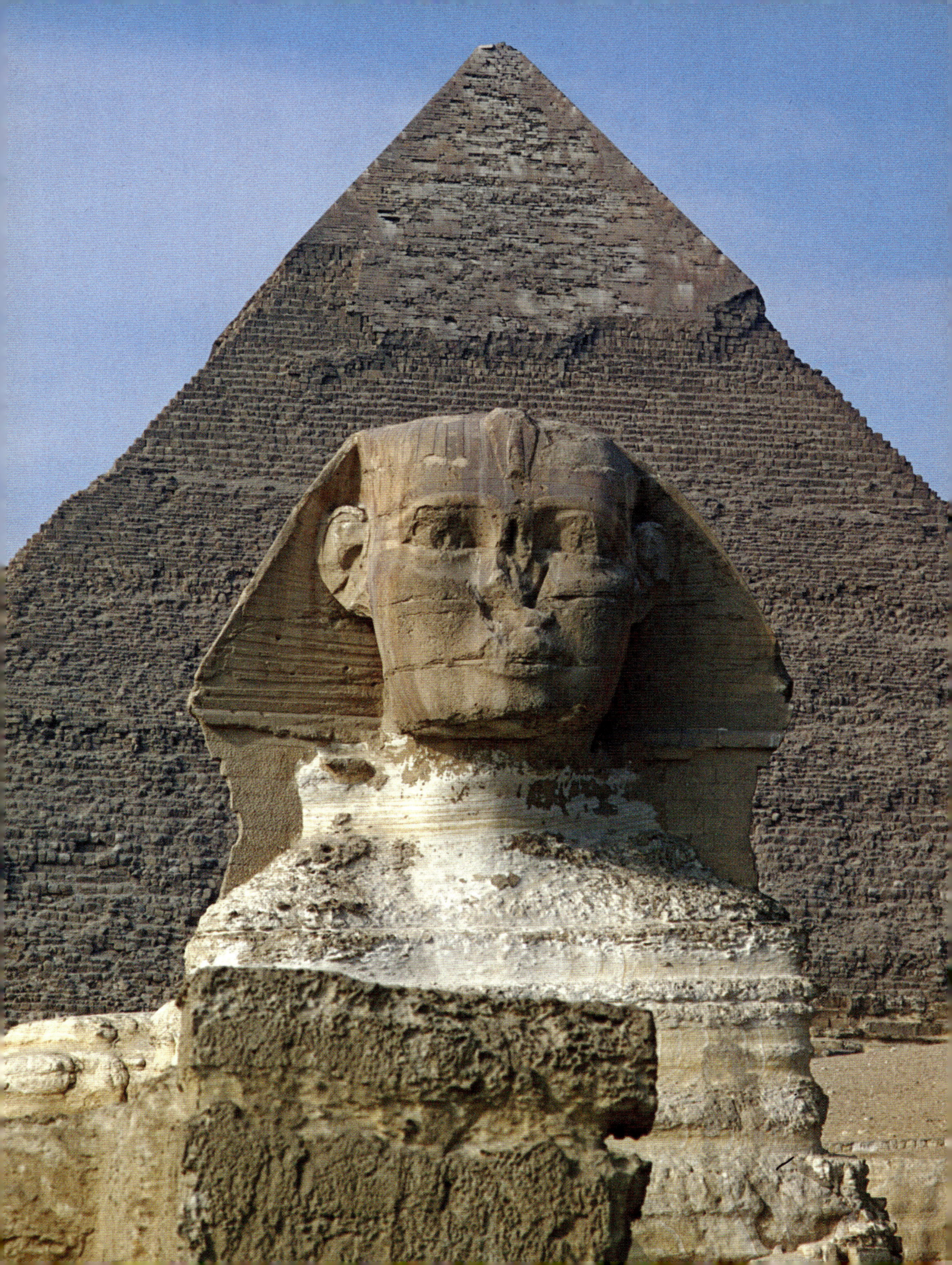

THE EARLY DYNASTIC PERIOD (ca. 3000–2686 B.C.) AND THE OLD KINGDOM (2686–2181 B.C.)

Around 3150 B.C. the final phase of the Naqada culture (Naqada III) started a process that ended the rich predynastic period in Egypt and saw the first unification of Upper and Lower Egypt into a large territorial state (ca. 3000 B.C.). Archeological evidence has demonstrated that the birth of pharaonic history was the result of an indigenous development based in Egypt's south. During the course of the early dynastic period (First and Second Dynasties, ca. 3000–2686 B.C.), most of the basic elements of Egyptian culture had already emerged. Agriculture, especially the cultivation of wheat and barley, was the economic core of the new state. The efficient distribution of the huge quantity of cereals that the Nile floodplain yielded required an elaborate administrative apparatus. Soon a highly effective bureaucracy had organized the entire state through a system of taxation that supported the most important institution in Egypt: the divine kingship embodied in the person of the pharaoh. The ideology of a ruler connecting the world of the living with that of the gods, endowed with spiritual and temporal power to secure the state's welfare, endured for several millennia; indeed, it was never effectively challenged until the advent of the Ptolemies. The various needs of the state administration also spurred the development of hieroglyphic writing, already in its infancy before the country's unification.

Although New Kingdom traditions name the legendary Menes as Egypt's first ruler, present evidence identifies Horus Aha as the actual founder of the First Dynasty. The nation's capital was established at Memphis, some twenty-five kilometers south of present-day Cairo, strategically situated at the border between Upper and Lower Egypt. The royal cemetery remained in the south at Abydos; early tombs contain subsidiary burials, marking the only instance in Egypt's history when humans were sacrificed for the afterlife of the deceased pharaoh. Internal conflicts at the end of the Second Dynasty were put to rest with the accession of Djoser (2667–2648 B.C.), the only outstanding ruler of the Third Dynasty. Erected at the dawn of the Old Kingdom (Third–Sixth Dynasty, 2686–2160 B.C.), his Step Pyramid at Saqqara was the first important stone structure in the history of mankind, constructed by Imhotep, the high priest of Heliopolis, deified by later generations as the son of the god Ptah. The "Age of Pyramids" began with the reign of Sneferu (2613–2589 B.C.), founder of the Fourth Dynasty, who abandoned Saqqara as a royal burial ground and built two pyramids further south at Dahshur: the so-called Bent Pyramid and a second, constructed at a shallower angle, that served as the king's tomb. A third pyramid, built at Meidum, is also attributed to Sneferu, making this pharaoh one of the greatest builders in Egypt's history. The process of pyramid building was perfected with the erection of three structures on the desert plateau at Giza, where the pharaohs Khufu (Cheops), Khafre (Chephren), and Menkaure (Mykerinos) constructed what is surely the most iconic of architectural ensembles. The tallest of the three, the Great Pyramid of Khufu (2589–2566 B.C.), rising to a height of 146.5 meters (450 ft.), constitutes the extraordinary achievement of an administrative apparatus in the service of religious faith. Nor were these efforts limited to the pyramid itself: large cult temples were built on its eastern side; hundreds of mastaba tombs were erected for the state's officials; smaller pyramids housed the tombs of queens; and the Great Sphinx—at 72 meters (236 ft.), the largest statue in antiquity—was carved out of the limestone bedrock.

The ongoing demands for large-scale building projects, however, put enormous pressure on the economy and society; it might have been for that reason that the kings of the Fifth and Sixth Dynasties constructed much smaller pyramids, now at the sites of Abusir and again at Saqqara. A sea change in religious practice was mirrored by a new temple type: the sun-temple, dedicated to the particular worship of the sun god Re, and each built separately by six rulers of the Fifth Dynasty (2494–2345 B.C.). The Sixth Dynasty witnessed a steady decline in royal power, fueled by the increasing independence of provincial officials (see no. 5), whose office and attendant benefits often became hereditary. During the extraordinarily long reign of Pepy II (2278–2181 B.C.), economic pressures and the breakdown of the central administration signaled the end of the once mighty state, further weakened by famine and natural disasters.

After the final collapse of the Old Kingdom, Egypt experienced a period of political instability during which the country was divided into smaller geographical units under the leadership of local rulers. During this so-called First Intermediate Period, the monarchs of Herakleopolis, a town south of the Faiyum, consolidated their power in Lower Egypt and ruled as the Ninth and Tenth Dynasties (2160–2025 B.C.).

MS

Giza, Pyramid of Khafre and the Great Sphinx (Fourth Dynasty, ca. 2550 B.C.). Photo © Dr. Abdel Ghaffar Shedid, Munich

1a

Gaming piece: Figure of a lioness

Said to be from Abydos

Hippopotamus ivory; 2.9 x 5.3 x 2.35 cm (1 1/8 x 2 1/16 x 15/16 in.)

Late First/Second Dynasty, ca. 2850 B.C.

Provenance: Arthur Sambon, Paris; Henry Walters, 1926; Walters Art Museum, by bequest, 1931 (71.623)

1b

Gaming piece: Figure of a dog

Hippopotamus ivory; 3.0 x 6.5 x 2.1 cm (1 1/8 x 2 9/16 x 13/16 in.)

Late First/Second Dynasty, ca. 2850 B.C.

Provenance: Henry Walters, before 1931; Walters Art Museum, by bequest, 1931 (71.622)

The economic strength of early dynastic Egyptian society resulted in a wide range of artistic production of considerable quality. Equally remarkable was the ability of the early residents of the Nile Valley to establish long-distance trade routes that enabled them to exploit the natural resources of the hostile regions of the desert. Ivory was a particularly prized medium, and ivory artifacts have been recovered in great abundance from graves and tombs throughout Egypt, including the elite and royal cemeteries at Abydos, the seat of royal power during the early dynastic period and a major cult center until the Ptolemaic dynasty.

Ivory was also used, from predynastic times forward, to create luxurious practical objects such as combs, hair pins, amulets, spoons, and knife handles.[1] Around 3000/2900 B.C., a distinctive class of ivory objects—gaming pieces in the form of animals—emerged. These small statuettes represent recumbent lions (both male and female) and hounds. The broad collar and absence of a mane indicate that the subject of one of the pieces illustrated here is a female lion;[2] the rectangular pectoral on the figure's breast is the result of modern recarving, and the high polish was not original to the figure. The dog wears a tripartite collar decorated with a rectangular pattern and a semicircular neck protector. Such figurines were probably used in the game of *mehen* ("coiled one"),[3] played on a round board in the form of a coiled serpent with a trapezoidal projection (fig. 7). The game was popular until the end of the Old Kingdom; the reasons for its demise thereafter are unknown, although it resurfaces twice in Late Period tomb decorations.

MS

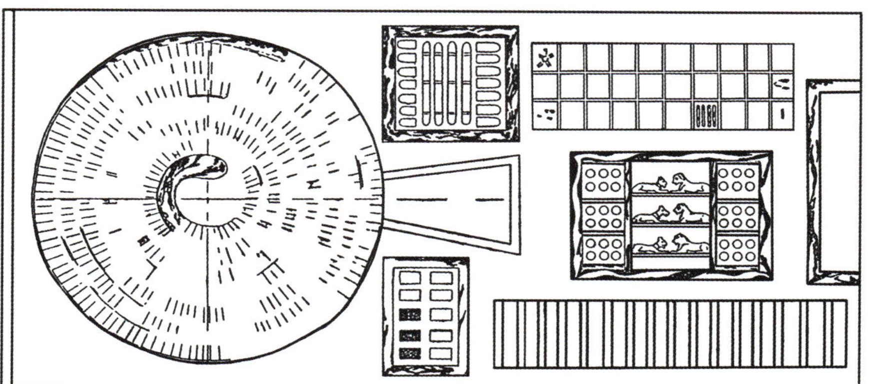

Fig. 7 Box with game boards and six gaming pieces in animal form. Wall painting from the tomb of Hesy-Re, Saqqara, Third Dynasty (ca. 2650 B.C.). Drawing after J.C. Quibell, *Excavations at Saqqara, 1911–1912: Tomb of Hesy* (Cairo, 1913) 18–20, figs. 2–3

Bibliography

Steindorff 1946a, 19–20 (nos. 6 and 7), pl. I; Canby 1985, 44 (nos. 20 and 21).

Notes

1. Drenkhahn 1986.
2. For the typology of lion figures, see Adams 1992, 69–76; for parallels, see Petrie 1903, pl. III, 26 and 28; Davis 1981, 41; and Needler 1984, 355, 356.
3. Piccione 1990, 43–52.

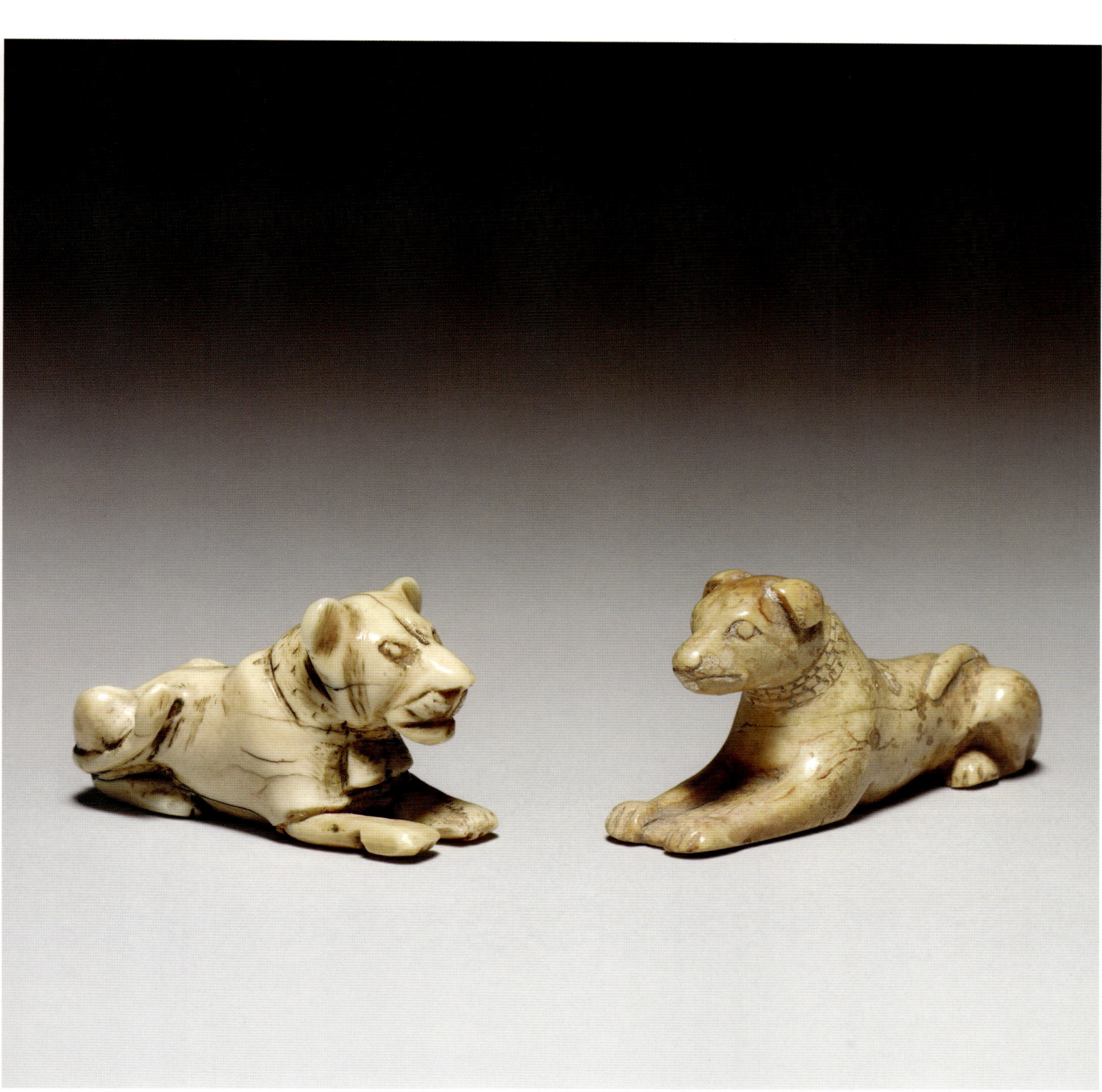

2

Head from a male statue

Anorthosite gneiss; height 13 cm (5 in.)

Early Fifth Dynasty, ca. 2490 B.C.

Provenance: Dikran Kelekian, New York / Paris; Henry Walters, 1912; Walters Art Museum, by bequest, 1931 (22.58)

In addition to statues representing pharaohs, an extraordinary number of statues depicting individuals of high status have survived from Old Kingdom tombs; excavations in the cemeteries at Giza, Dahshur, Abusir, Meidum, and Saqqara since the mid-nineteenth century have yielded thousands of such figures. The statues served an important function in funerary rituals. Placed in a concealed room within the tomb (called the *serdab*) separated from the main cult chapel by a wall pierced by a small slit or hole, these "living images," revived by offerings of incense in rites carried out by special priests, secured the existence and welfare of the deceased in the afterlife.

The elaborate wig, popular during the Old Kingdom, composed of curls radiating from the top of the head to the shoulders, identifies the individual represented in this fragment as a government official.[1] The head was broken off from either a standing or seated statue—the attitudes in which males of high status were most often depicted. The hard stone used in its manufacture, from a distant quarry in Upper Egypt or Nubia, indicates that the statue's owner held a particularly high rank.[2] The well-balanced features of the round face—full cheeks, naturalistic eyes, and a straight mouth—give the subject a serious, nearly ageless expression, but the work is not a portrait.

MS

Bibliography

Steindorff 1946a, 22, no. 23, pl. III.

Notes

1. Ziegler 1997, 268–69.
2. Wildung 1972, 145–60.

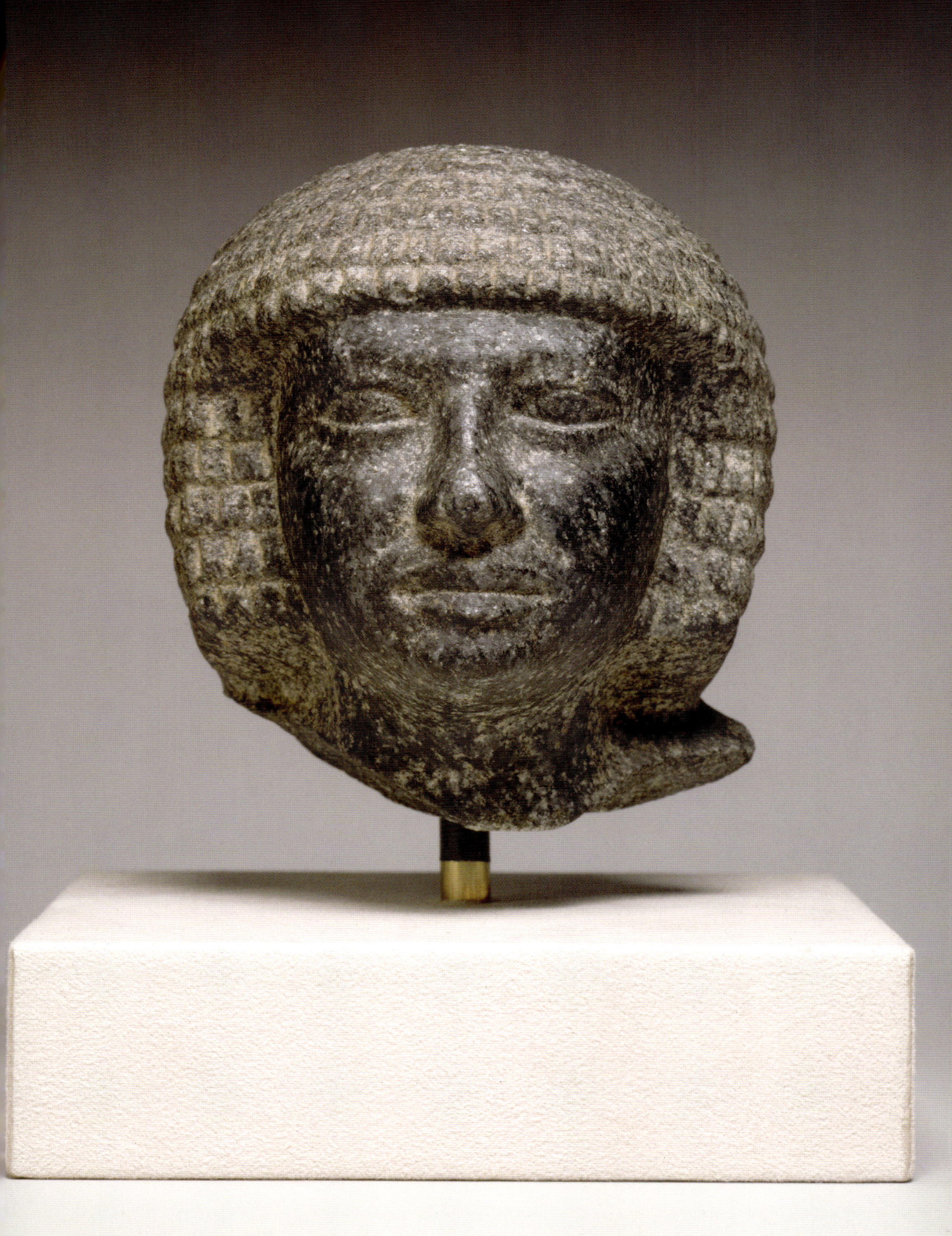

3

Tomb relief: Ships on the river

Probably from Saqqara

Limestone, remains of red paint; 35.5 x 28.1 cm (14 1/16 x 11 in.)

Late Fifth Dynasty, ca. 2370–2345 B.C.

Provenance: Henry Walters, 1922; Walters Art Museum, by bequest, 1931 (22.87)

The Nile with its branches and network of canals was an essential artery in the transport of people, raw materials, and manufactured goods in ancient Egypt, and ships figured prominently in daily life as well as in religion. The bows of ships were often ornamented, carved in the form of a papyrus blossom or an animal head. Ships with hedgehog's-head bow ornaments that faced the stern, seen on the lower right of this fragment of a tomb relief, are common in Fourth to Sixth Dynasty contexts: in tomb reliefs and paintings (most often in Giza and Saqqara), on boat models (found in Elephantine, Abydos, and Dahshur), and on offering plates and basins. Such ornaments are not associated with particular kinds of boats: indeed, the hedgehog occurs on sailing and rowing ships, vessels used for travel or for transporting cargo, pilot- and tug-boats, as well as small boats used in the papyrus thickets. The captions of the tomb scenes describe either the destination and purpose of the journey, or contain remarks on navigation or warnings against collisions.

The variety of contexts in which ships with hedgehog's-head bows appear makes it difficult to determine their meaning. Some scholars have discerned an apotropaic function in such ornaments;[1] others associate them with renewal.[2] The presence of the hedgehog ornament on model boats found in the sanctuary of Satet (the goddess associated with Nile floods) in Elephantine might also suggest an association with the tutelary god of the cataracts, Khnum, and with the funerary boat mentioned in the Pyramid Texts.[3]

This fragment of a tomb relief depicts three river vessels. The upper register shows part of the boat's hull and the heads of five crewmen, facing right. The first crewman holds the handle of an oar, and behind the fourth crewman the ship's mast is visible. Therefore, it is likely that the boat was represented sailing upstream. Two standing and two kneeling oarsmen are visible on the left of the lower register.

RS

Bibliography

Steindorff 1946a, 78, no. 263, pl. L;
von Droste zu Hülshoff 1980, 105, no. 55;
Altenmüller 2007.

Notes

1. Junker 1941, 72; von Droste zu Hülshoff 1980.
2. Hornung and Stähelin 1976, 117–18.
3. Altenmüller 2007.

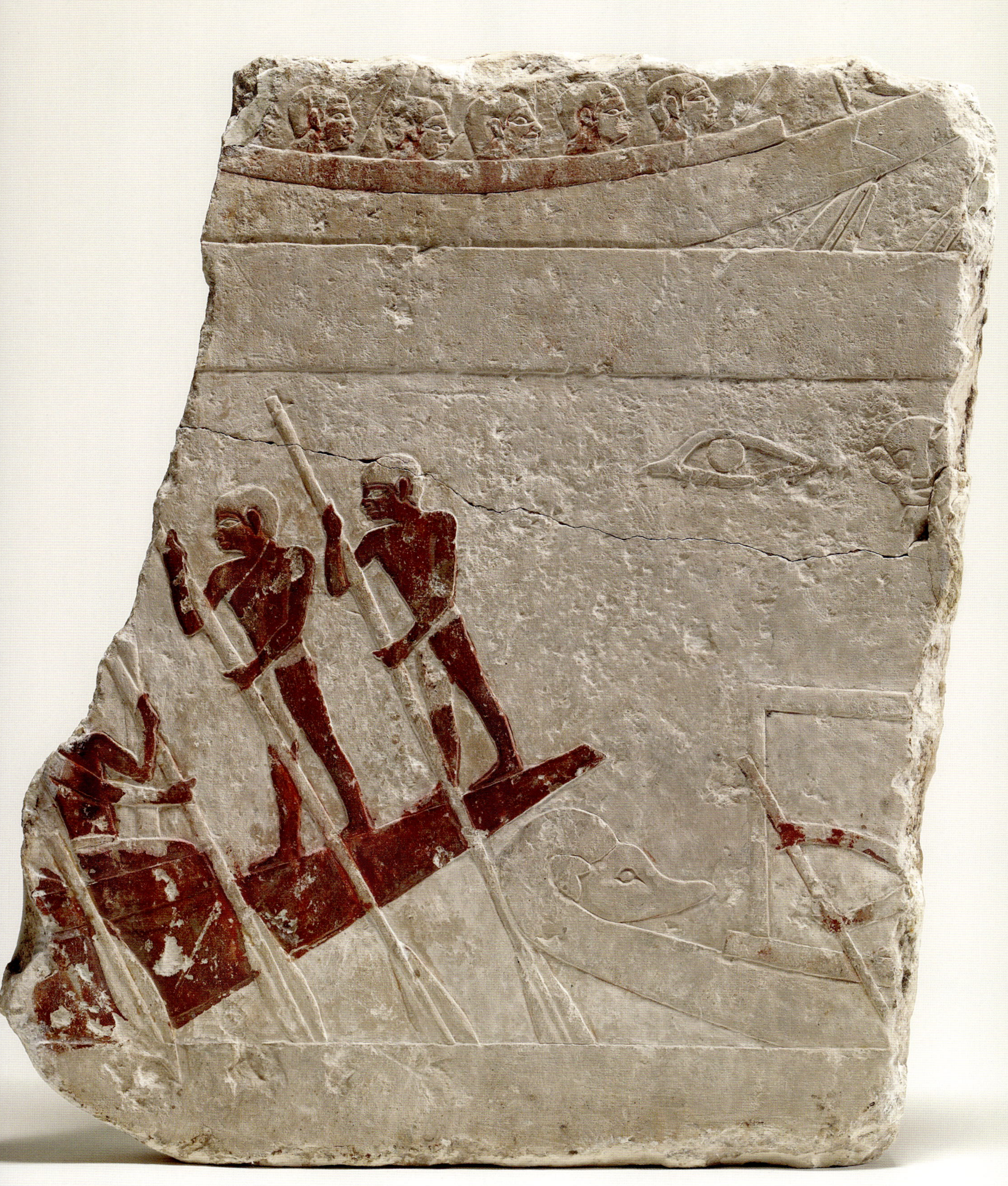

4

Tomb relief: A dog facing a herdsman

Probably from Giza

Limestone; 43.8 x 101.6 cm (17 1/8 x 40 in.)

Fifth Dynasty, ca. 2400 B.C.

Provenance: J. Brummer, New York/Paris; sale, Parke-Bernet Galleries, New York, 9 June 1949 (lot 474); Walters Art Museum, museum purchase, 1949 (22.422)[1]

This scene combines two familiar subjects in Egyptian funerary art: a man accompanied by his dog, and a herdsman driving a reluctant calf. Carved in raised relief and originally painted, the scene is divided among four limestone blocks that were once part of the lower register of a tomb's interior wall. Only the left foot and the staff of the dog's master have been preserved. The dog stands upright, its head raised and ears alert. The herdsman leans forward to hold the calf by its rope bridle, pushing it toward the dog and his master—probably the tomb owner—for inspection. The text in front of the herdsman describes the action depicted: "Bringing a calf." An inscription above the dog's back gives his name: Beha, possibly an abbreviation of *behkai* (oryx antelope), a dog's name known from other contexts.[2]

The disproportionate scale of the master and his dog relative to the herdsman and calf signals their higher status, and their close relation is expressed by their overlapping forms. Mastiffs and hounds are the most frequently depicted dogs in Egyptian art. Hounds normally have collars around their necks to indicate that they are domesticated; they were used for hunting in the desert, as retrievers for fishing and hunting wildfowl, and as watchdogs. In predynastic times such dogs were associated with the ruler, but they later came to be associated with the nobility; they are often depicted in front, behind, or under their master's chair. Sometimes they are depicted in the company of monkeys and dwarves, but dogs were more than pets; they were a status symbol and, in tomb contexts, emblems of vigilance and protection.

Beha's slender proportions, his elongated snout, and his collar, composed of several rows with a large loop at the end below his throat, suggest that this relief originates from Giza's eastern cemetery. The dog resembles that in a relief in the Fifth Dynasty tomb of the palace officer Kha-ef-Ra-ankh at Giza;[3] the Walters relief might have come from the same tomb, or it might have been carved by artists of the same workshop for a nearby tomb.

RS

Bibliography

Weill 1914, 85–87; Parke-Bernet Galleries 1949, 101, lot 474; Schulz 2006.

Notes

1. The blocks were mentioned by the French Egyptologist Raymond Weill (1914, 85), who saw them in Paris before 1914, thus establishing a terminus for their presence outside of Egypt.

2. The explanation of the name is given on the famed Eleventh Dynasty "dog-stela" of Intef II; see Aufrère 2000, 35–40.

3. G 7948 (Lepsius 1897, 75). The dating of the tomb follows Harpur 1981, 24–35. For the re-excavation and documentation of the tomb, see Kormyschewa 2001, 23–37, and Kormyschewa 2003, 91–130.

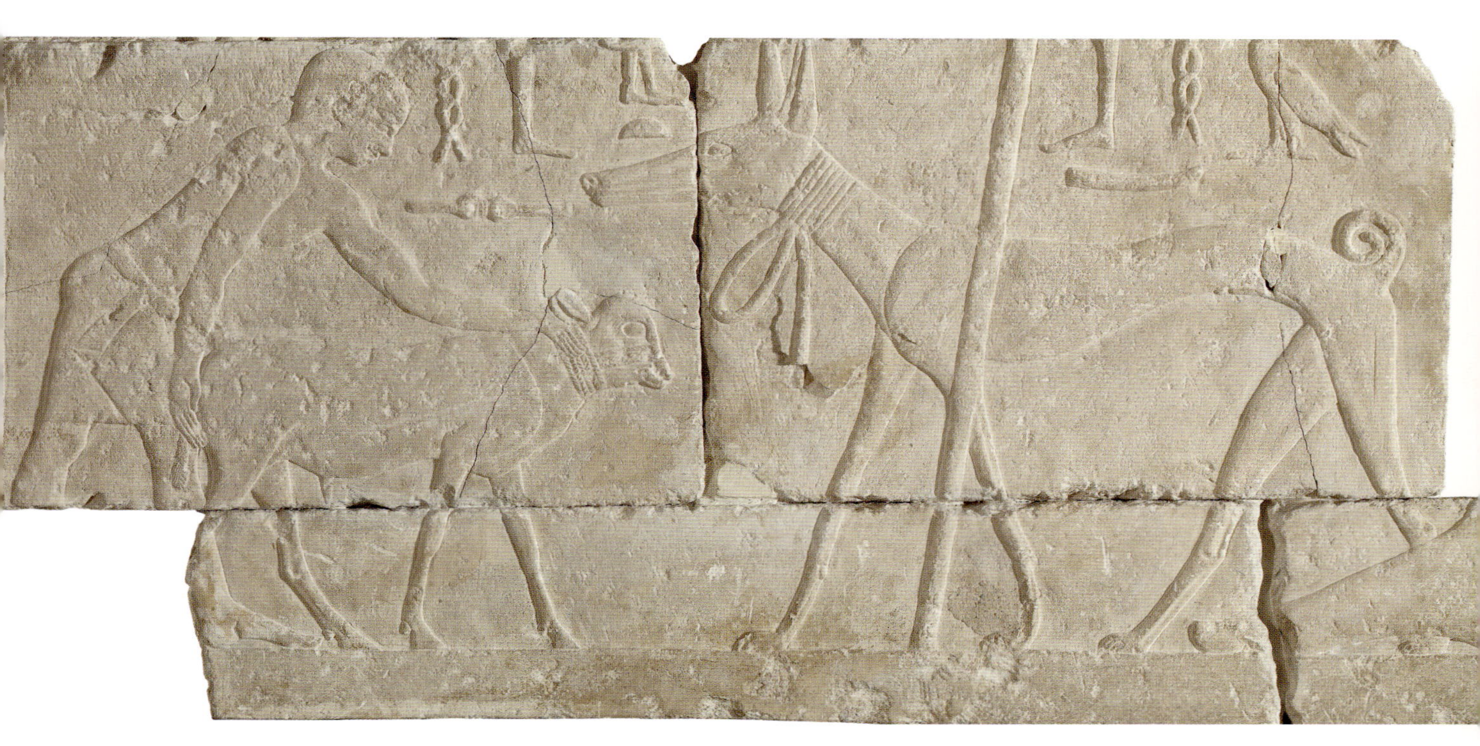

5

Statue group of Nen-kheft-ka and his wife, Nefer-shemes

From Deshasheh, mastaba of Nen-kheft-ka
Limestone, traces of paint; height of male figure: 49.5 cm (19½ in.);
height of female figure: 38.1 cm (15 in.)
Late Fifth Dynasty, ca. 2350 B.C.
Provenance: Museum of Fine Arts, Boston (Egypt Exploration Fund)
(97.1092); Walters Art Museum, by exchange, 1973 (22.425)

These statues were found in 1897 by the British archeologist Flinders Petrie in the *serdab* (statue room) of the tomb of Nen-kheft-ka at Deshasheh, about 115 kilometers (70 miles) south of Cairo. Although the superstructure of the mastaba had been severely damaged in antiquity by tomb robbers, Petrie recovered twelve limestone statues, some in fragments, from the tomb. Situated near Egypt's capital, Memphis, Deshasheh was part of the twentieth nome (district) of Upper Egypt. The tombs there are clear evidence that the administration of districts in this part of the country was decentralized by the late Fifth Dynasty. Nomarchs such as Nen-kheft-ka were local authorities, who lived and ruled in their nome rather than in the country's capital, and were consequently also buried in their local cemetery.

These two standing figures were not originally intended as a dyad,[1] which in part explains their considerable difference in size. They were joined in antiquity by being inserted into two slots carved at the back of a rectangular slab. The male is a classical example of the standing male figure type, a standard form of representation in the Old Kingdom.[2] In striding position with left foot set forward, both arms hanging down at his sides and gazing straight ahead, the high official is destined for eternity. He wears a short, partially pleated kilt secured by a knotted belt at his waist, and a tightly fitting curled wig. In each fist he clutches a rolled cloth amulet, whose specific character and function remains uncertain. Nefer-shemes, her feet together, wears an ankle-length gown that leaves the form of her body clearly visible, and a longer parted wig with a strip of her natural hair exposed directly over the brow. Both hands rest flat against her thighs. The two figures, once completely painted, share the same idealized, roundish faces; their uniformity of style suggests that they were produced in the same workshop.

MS

Bibliography

Petrie 1898, 12–15, pls. 31, 32; Smith 1946, 81, 89; Vandier 1958, 73, 78, 80; Walters Art Gallery 1997, 20 (S. Harvey).

Notes

1. Cherpion 1995, 33–47, pls. 2–8.
2. Ziegler 1999, 57–71.

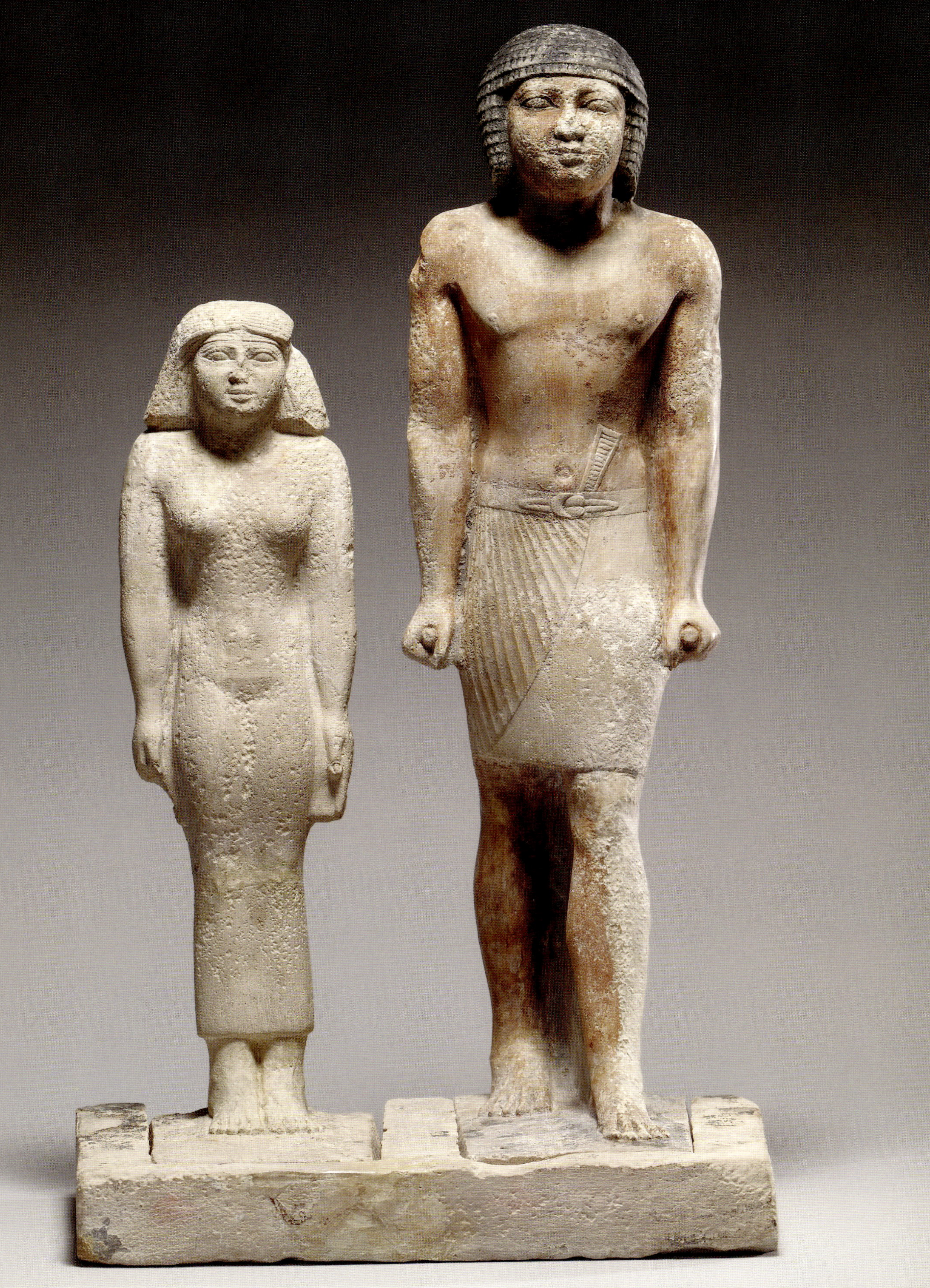

6

Jubilee vessel of Pepy I

Probably from Saqqara
Egyptian alabaster (calcite) and pigment; height 14.5 cm (5 ¾ in.);
diameter 14.4 cm (5 ⅝ in.)
Sixth Dynasty, ca. 2290 B.C.
Provenance: Dikran Kelekian, New York/Paris; Henry Walters, 1914;
Walters Art Museum, by bequest, 1931 (41.28)

Vessels such as these, with a wide foot and rim and slightly concave sides, were used as containers for perfumed oils and unguents. This jar would originally have had a flat lid made from the same stone. The rectangular hieroglyphic inscription is incised and filled with pigment (probably calcium copper silicate: so-called Egyptian blue), elegantly offset by the cream color of the stone. The text's frame, like those that enclose royal temple reliefs, has a substantive import: two lines above and beneath the inscription represent the heavens and earth, separated and supported by two *was* scepters, the hieroglyph that visually represents "dominion" or "power." The text includes the names (inscribed in a cartouche) of the Sixth Dynasty pharaoh Pepy I (2321–2287 B.C.) and refers to the festival marking the first thirty years of his reign:

> The Horus, Mery-tawy; king of Upper and Lower Egypt, Mery-re [Pepy I], first occasion of the Sed Festival. Given life and dominion forever [twice].

Many similar inscribed calcite unguent jars alluding to the celebration of the Sed Festival have been found, both in Egypt and abroad (some as far away as the Phoenician city of Byblos in present-day Lebanon).[2] Although examples are widely dispersed, dating from the late Old Kingdom to the Eleventh Dynasty, they were probably all produced in the royal workshops at Memphis.

Such commemorative vessels, together with their precious contents, were liberally handed out to courtiers and other members of the administration. They were, however, more than luxurious souvenirs from the pharaoh. The first Sed Festival was an occasion to demonstrate the awesome power of the king. Pepy himself (who adopted the throne name Mery-re: "beloved of Re") reigned over Egypt for at least forty-four years (forty-nine, according to one account), although his rule, like that of other pharaohs, faced very human obstacles: one of his queens led an unsuccessful conspiracy to murder him.

MS

Bibliography

Detroit Institute of Arts 1963, no. 117.

Notes

1. For the stone, see Harrell 1990, 37–42; Klemm and Klemm 1991, 57–70; for the distribution of festival jars, see Eichler 1993, 299–307.
2. Aston 1994, 104.

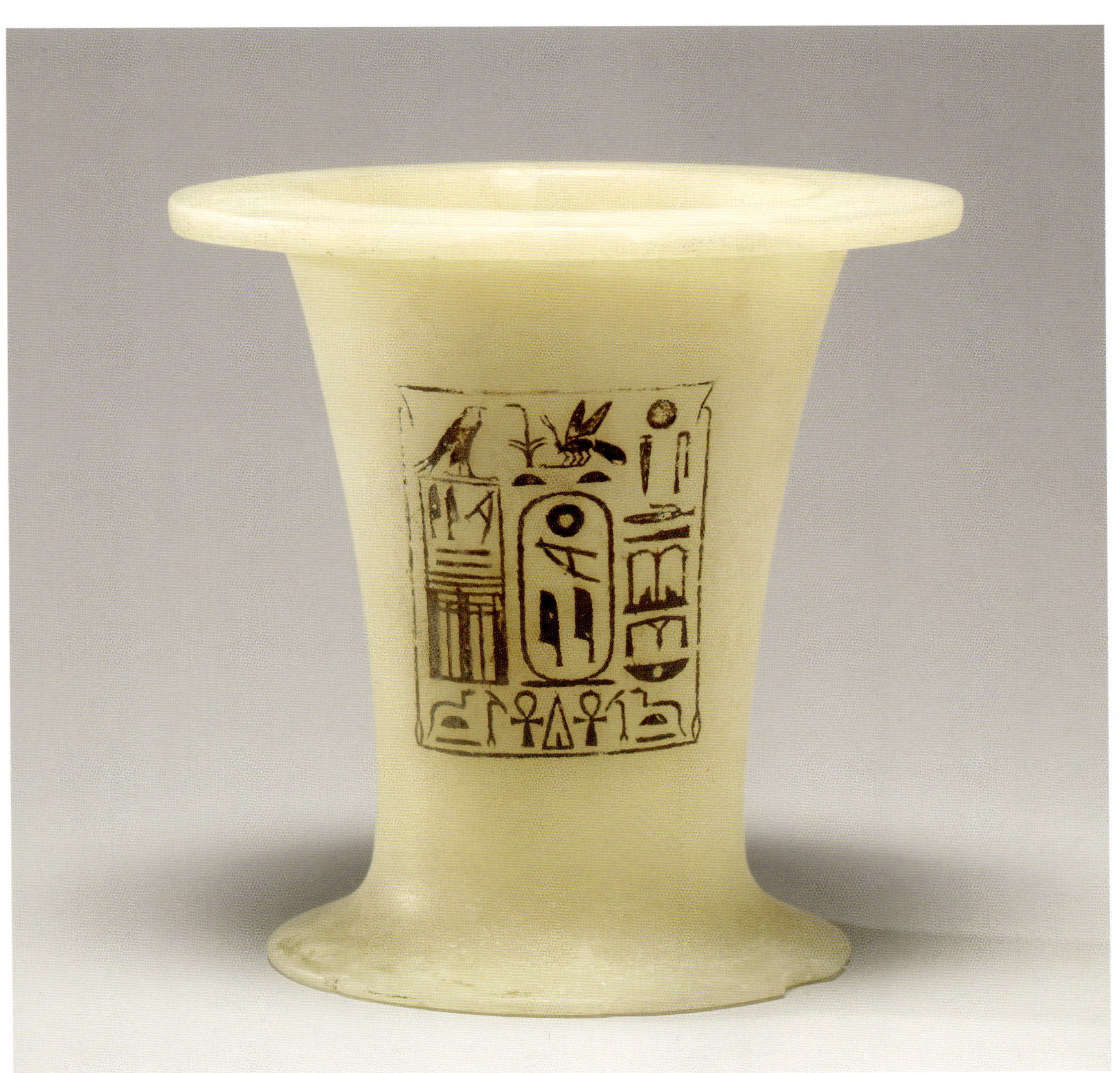

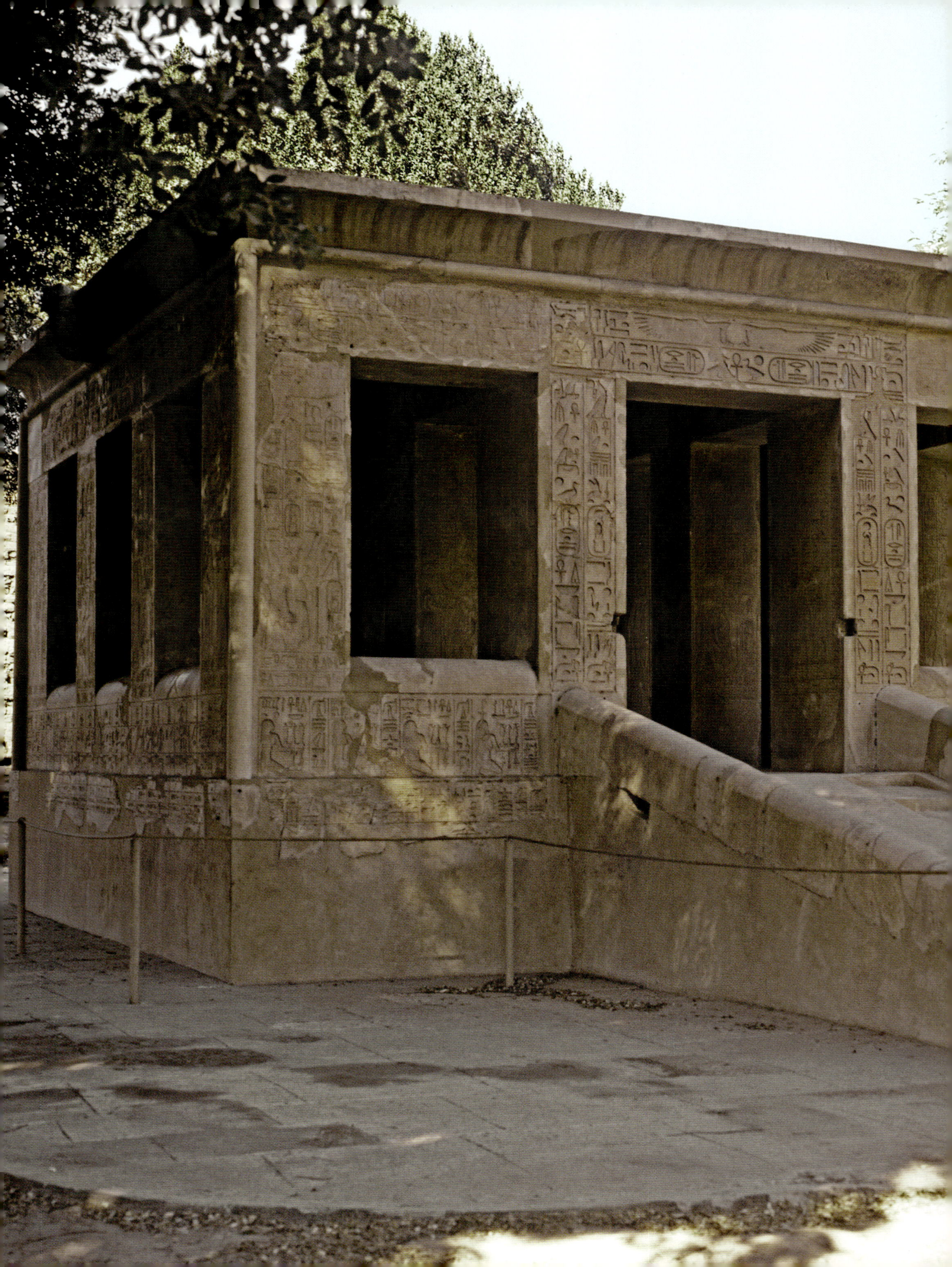

THE MIDDLE KINGDOM (2055–1650 B.C.)

At about the same time that the Herakleopolitan kings ruled the north, a new family of rulers emerged at Thebes in Upper Egypt. These local nomarchs, alternately named Intef or Mentuhotep, assumed the royal titles and initiated building activities at Karnak in honor of Amun. Nebhepetre Mentuhotep II (2055–2004 B.C.) prevailed in the struggle for supremacy between north and south, defeating the Herakleopolitans and reuniting Egypt. His dynamic character is evident in the innovative design of his mortuary complex at Deir el-Bahari, the new religious center of western Thebes (see no. 7). The massive building combined a temple edifice with the king's rock-cut tomb, as well as several unprecedented Osirian installations, such as the "garden of resurrection": a grove of sycamores in the temple's courtyard. For unknown reasons, his two successors, Mentuhotep III and Mentuhotep IV (2004–1985 B.C.), were unable to hold on to power. Instead, the vizier of the last ruling Mentuhotep seized the throne and ruled as Amenemhat I (1985–1956 B.C.), the first pharaoh of the famed Twelfth Dynasty.

Language, literature (notably, the *Story of Sinuhe*), and the fine arts (see nos. 8–13) of the subsequent two hundred years were enshrined as a cultural high point by later generations of Egyptians as late as the Ptolemaic Period. Early in his reign, Amenemhat I left Thebes and moved the capital, named Itj-tawy, northward to the Faiyum region (its precise location remains unknown). He constructed his pyramid in the nearby cemetery of el-Lisht, evoking the traditions of the Old Kingdom; whereas the sheer monumentality of such structures had formerly offered protection against theft, mazes of internal corridors and chambers now secured the royal burials. Amenemhat I was assassinated and followed by his son Sesostris I (1956–1911 B.C.), credited as the true founder of the Twelfth Dynasty; during his long reign Sesostris embellished the country with a huge construction program that included nearly every major cult site. Particularly noteworthy are the construction works undertaken at the temple of Karnak; among these, the most important is the so-called White Chapel—a shrine of white limestone erected to celebrate the sed-festival, marking the thirtieth year of the king's reign. Territorial incursions extended Egyptian influence in Nubia as far as the Second Cataract at Buhen, whereas northern trading routes to Syria across the Sinai Peninsula supplied Egypt with cedar wood, silver, and turquoise. The reign of Sesostris II (1877–1870 B.C.), in contrast, focused on domestic affairs, notably the development of new farmland in the Faiyum oasis through the construction of a network of dams and irrigation canals. Under the powerful kings Sesostris III (1870–1831 B.C.) and Amenemhat III (1831–1786 B.C.), the Middle Kingdom reached its political and cultural zenith. Sesostris III (see no. 14) shored up Egypt's southern boundary in Nubia and mounted an expedition to the Levant. Domestically, he concentrated power in a centralized government by curtailing the independence of the nomarchs. At Abydos, the pharaoh commissioned a second funerary complex, although a pyramid had already been erected for him at Dahshur, leaving the location of his true resting place unsettled. His son Amenemhat III, the last major ruler of the Middle Kingdom, concentrated his efforts in the Faiyum region, where he completed the hydraulic projects; his association with the region is commemorated in a wealth of shrines, including the mortuary temple in front of his pyramids at Hawara, the fabled labyrinth recorded by Herodotus, Strabo, and Pliny the Elder. The Twelfth Dynasty saw profound changes in religious and funerary beliefs as well. Private individuals could now donate stelae and statues (see nos. 15–17) in the temples of the gods in order to participate in the offering rituals on a regular basis. The growing cult of the god Osiris ushered in a modified assemblage of grave goods such as shabtis and various magical objects (see nos. 18, 19). Following the brief reign of Queen Sobekneferu (1777–1773 B.C.) at the close of the Twelfth Dynasty, a succession of undistinguished kings ruled as the Thirteenth Dynasty (1774–ca. 1650 B.C.), doing little more than maintaining the traditions of their predecessors. The true Second Intermediate Period started around 1650 B.C. and was marked by the loss of the country's territorial integrity. In Nubia the kingdom of Kerma rose to power, and in Upper Egypt the Seventeenth Dynasty emerged at Thebes. The power vacuum in the Delta and Middle Egypt was filled by the Hyksos ("rulers of foreign lands"), tribes of Semitic origin who reigned from their capital at Avaris in the Delta as the Fifteenth and Sixteenth Dynasties (1650–1550 B.C.). A sophisticated military culture, the Hyksos introduced the Egyptians to horse and chariots, the most effective weaponry of the time. Eventually the foreign overlords were driven out of Egypt by the sibling rulers of Thebes, Kamose and Ahmose, the latter of whom reigned as the first pharaoh of the New Kingdom.

MS

Karnak, "White Chapel" of Sesostris I (Twelfth Dynasty, ca. 1930 B.C.). Photo © Dr. Abdel Ghaffar Shedid, Munich

7

Woman carrying a sunshade

Western Thebes, Deir el-Bahari, tomb of Queen Nefru (TT 319)
Limestone, traces of paint; 12.5 x 15 x 2.5 cm (4 15/16 x 5 7/8 x 1 in.)
Eleventh Dynasty, ca. 2040 B.C.
Provenance: Dikran Kelekian, New York / Paris; Henry Walters, 1924; Walters Art Museum, by bequest, 1931 (22.325)

The small relief fragment formed part of the wall decoration in the rock-cut tomb of Nefru, sister and chief queen of King Nebhepetre Mentuhotep II (2055–2004 B.C.), founder of the Middle Kingdom. The façade of the tomb, located at the northern edge of Mentuhotep's mortuary temple at Deir el-Bahari, was blocked by the construction of the large and complex funerary temple of Queen Hatshepsut (1473–1458 B.C.) in the early Eighteenth Dynasty. Five hundred years after its construction, and despite its hidden location, Nefru's tomb, accessible through a narrow tunnel, was still visited, as attested by numerous ink graffiti left on its walls during the New Kingdom. Robbed in antiquity, the tomb was rediscovered by Auguste Mariette in 1858; it was cleared and the site restored in 1925–26 by the Egyptian Expedition of the Metropolitan Museum of Art.[1]

Nefru's tomb consists of a short passageway (its decoration executed in sunk relief) leading to a cult chapel (decorated in raised relief), from which a tunnel descends to two more rooms and the burial chamber. The raised relief of the Walters fragment associates it with the chapel,[2] and comparison with other examples from the tomb dates it to early in Mentuhotep II's reign. The face of the woman depicted is dominated by a large almond-shaped eye, pointing downward at the tear duct, and the long eyebrow situated directly above it. Equally noteworthy are the long stylized ear with a large circular lobe and the distinctive broad lips of the squared mouth. The woman wears a tripartite wig composed of narrow striations and holds a staff in her right hand; other, more complete reliefs from the same tomb indicate that the staff is that of a sunshade (fig. 8), and that the Walters relief formed part of a procession of at least ten women carrying sunshades, together with one male, all facing right.

MS

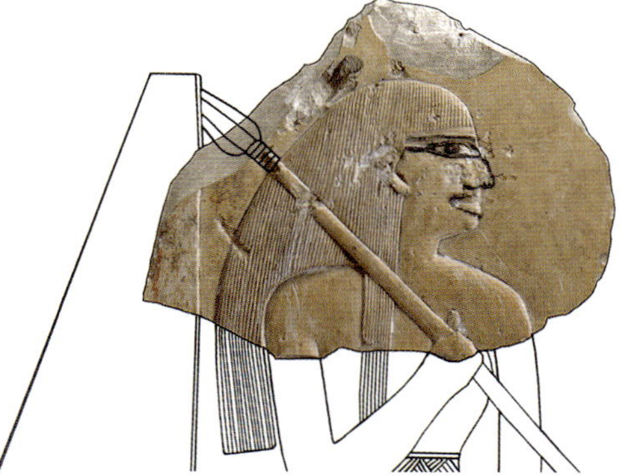

Fig. 8 No. 7 (22.325) superimposed on a line drawing of relief from the tomb of Queen Nefru (TT 319), Yale University Art Gallery, acc. no. 1956.33.87 (Gift of Mr. and Mrs. Fred Olsen). Rendering by Regine Schulz

Bibliography

Steindorff 1946a, 72, no. 239, pl. XLVIII; Fischer 1958, 36 n. 5; Simpson 1974b, 106 and 115–16 n. 13; Scott 1986, 59.

Notes

1. For the archeology of the tomb, see Ward 1986, 103–5.
2. For further fragments, see Scott 1986, 59.

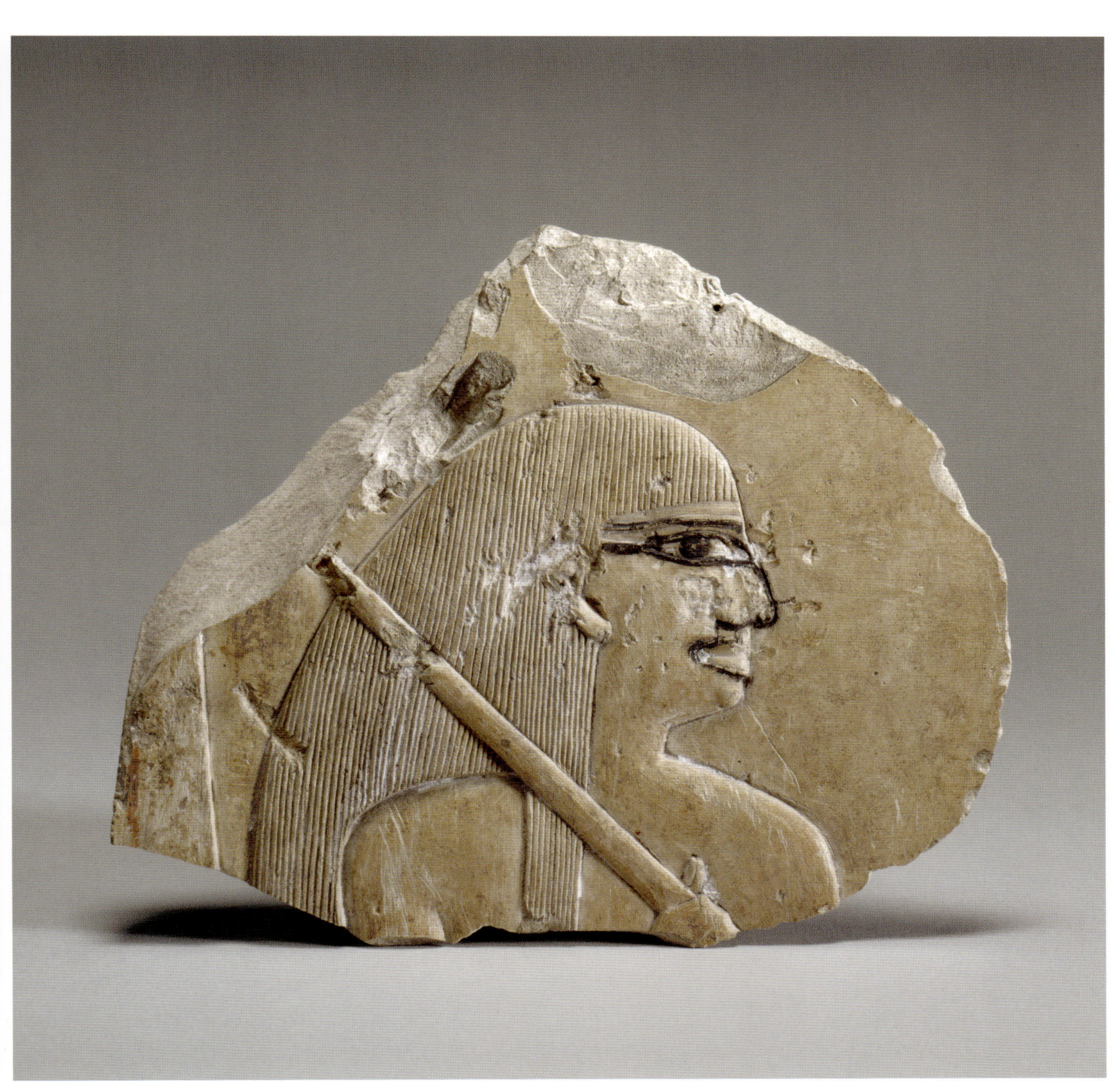

8a, 8b

Two figures of Tef-ib

Asyut, tomb of Tef-ib (?)

Wood, polychrome paint; *8a* (22.11): 37 x 8.9 x 17.8 (14 1/2 x 3 1/2 x 7 in.); *8b* (22.12): 37.5 x 8.7 x 17.2 cm (14 1/16 x 3 7/16 x 6 3/4 in.)

Early Twelfth Dynasty, ca. 1980 B.C.

Provenance: Dikran Kelekian, New York/Paris; Henry Walters, 1924; Walters Art Museum, by bequest, 1931 (22.11, 22.12)

The city of Asyut is located about 375 kilometers (250 miles) south of Cairo on the west bank of the Nile. This important settlement served as the capital of the thirteenth nome (district) of Upper Egypt. Inscriptions in the tombs of the nome's governors recount that they formed an alliance with the rulers of Herakleopolis in a war against Thebes during the First Intermediate Period (2160–2055 B.C.). Many tombs in the necropolis at Asyut had already been looted in the late nineteenth century and their contents sold on the art market. The French Egyptologist Émile Chassinat undertook the first systematic excavations at Asyut in 1903, but the contents of many tombs were subsequently plundered in unsystematic and underdocumented excavations carried out on behalf of Sayed Khashaba Pasha, a wealthy Egyptian landlord and collector.[1] Four wooden male statuettes in the Walters (acc. nos. 22.10–22.13), including these two, most probably came from Sayed Khashaba's stockpile, which contained hundreds of objects from Asyut. Each standing figure bears a single line inscription running down the kilt. Without further evidence or documentation of their excavation, the owner's identity remains elusive: the name Tef-ib inscribed on each of the statues was a common Middle Kingdom name in Asyut, as was his title of "steward."

Although the two figures illustrated here are very similar in size, they are clearly differentiated by wigs and kilts, as are the other two statues from the set. The facial features of the statuettes, youthful in this pair, more mature in the other two, attest to their maker's attempt to individualize the works, despite the prevailing style of the early Twelfth Dynasty, characterized by the "hieroglyphic" structure of the physiognomy. The inscriptions on the statues each invoke the protection of one of the four Sons of Horus, the four deities that protected the inner organs of the deceased: Imset (22.11), Hapy (22.12), Duamutef (22.10), and Qebehsenuef (22.13). The figures were likely originally placed in the burial chamber near the chest containing the canopic jars (see no. 43) to reinforce the assurance of the body's completeness in the afterlife.

MS

Bibliography

Steindorff 1946a, 32–33, nos. 66, 67, pl. XIII; Vandier 1958, 227, 249, 252, 270, pl. LXXXVII, 6, 7; Detroit Institute of Arts 1963, no. 52; Porter and Moss 1994, 58.

Notes

1. For recent investigations, see Kahl et al. 2005, 159–76; Kahl et al. 2006, 241–49; Kahl 2008.

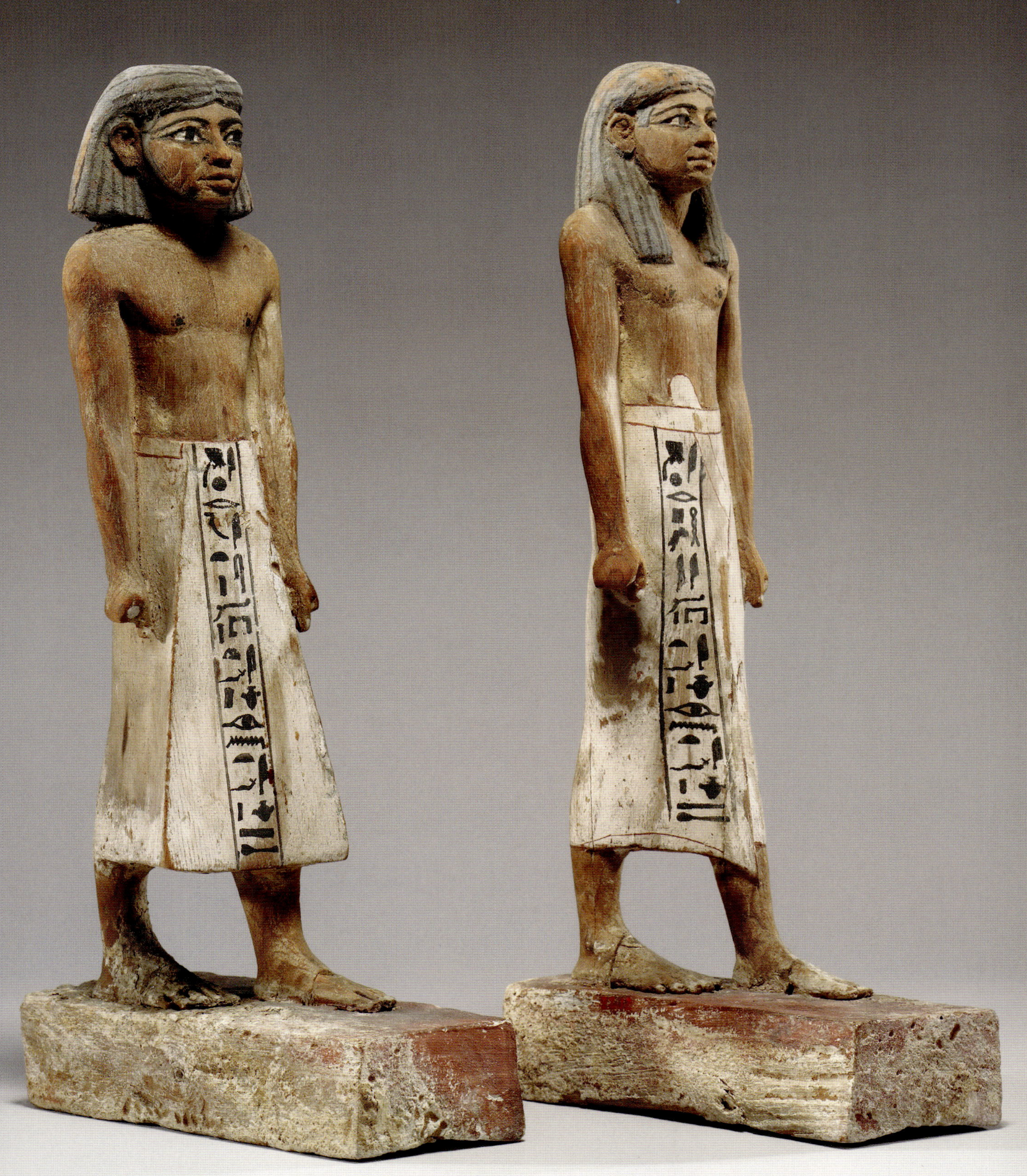

9

Model of a riverboat

Probably from Asyut or Meir

Wood, polychrome paint, and cloth; length (without rudder oar): 45 cm (17 3/4 in.); width: 10 cm (3 15/16 in.)

Eleventh Dynasty, ca. 2050 B.C.

Provenance: Dikran Kelekian, New York/Paris; Henry Walters, 1913 (22.19: rudder oar; 22.225: rudder post), and 1916 (22.18: boat); Walters Art Museum, by bequest, 1931

Wooden boat models have often been found among the burial objects in the Middle Kingdom rock-cut tombs of Middle Egypt (the area south of Memphis to Asyut). These models had several purposes: to assist the deceased in navigating the underworld Nile in the afterlife; to transport the deceased on their pilgrimage to the holy city of Abydos, considered to be the burial site of the god Osiris; or to enable the deceased to traverse the sky, like the sun god Re, in the company of the gods. Water was the most important means of transport in Egypt. Harnessing the prevailing northerly winds in Egypt, skiffs sailed upstream to southern destinations, while rowing boats traveled downstream with the current to northern ports.

This model rowing vessel is manned by twelve oarsmen in white painted kilts (six wear linen garments); a kneeling helmsman (in white kilt and linen garment) in the stern, who operates the large rudder oar; and a standing leadsman, or lookout (in white kilt), in the bow. The head, torso, and legs of the figures are each carved from a single piece of wood; the separately carved arms were attached with wooden pegs at the shoulders.[1] The figure near the stern represents the boat's owner, the deceased, wrapped in a white garment, his hair and beard, as well as facial cosmetic lines, rendered in blue paint.[2] The boat's stern sweeps back at a steeper angle than the bow.[3] The oar and rudder post are not original to this boat, but were acquired by Henry Walters in 1913, three years earlier. The rudder oar is ornamented with lotus flowers, a symbol of rebirth and regeneration, and *wedjat* eyes, the eyes of the falcon-god Horus, a protective device. Such decorated oars[4] are commonly found in papyrus-form funerary boats,[5] differing from this rowing vessel.

CH

Bibliography

Hill 1951, 3–4.

Notes

1. The figures of the crew resemble those in another model boat from Meir in the British Museum (BM EA 25361); see Glanville 1972, 22, fig. 20 and pl. IVa.
2. A similar figure appears on another boat from Meir (BM 25360): see Glanville 1972, 19, fig. 18a and pl. IIIc (25360).
3. This is consistent with the riverboat typology of Reisner Type II; see Reisner 1913, ix–xvi.
4. See Glanville 1972, 10, fig. 10 and pl. IIIa.8 (9524).
5. Reisner's Type V riverboat typology; Reisner 1913, ix–xvi.

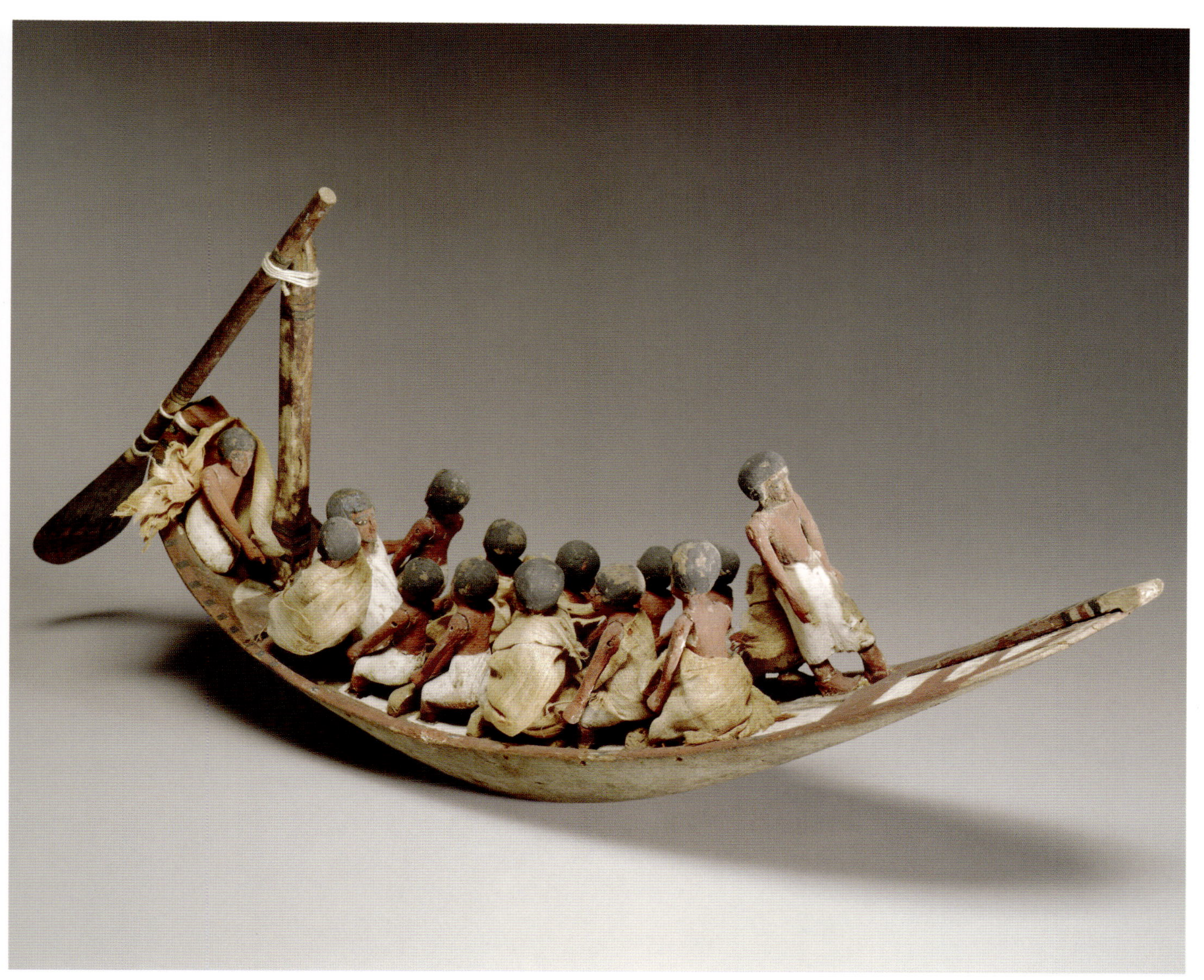

10

Mummy mask

From Asyut

Cartonnage, polychrome paint; height 62.9 cm (24 3/16 in.)

Eleventh / early Twelfth Dynasty, ca. 2000–1980 B.C.

Provenance: Possibly Sayed Khashaba Pasha, Asyut excavations 1913–14; P. Jozef Nestor, Belgium, 1920–30; sale, Christie's, New York, 5 December 2001 (lot 289); Walters Art Museum, museum purchase, 2001 (78.4)[1]

The earliest Egyptian funerary face and body coverings—made of painted linen, plaster, or cartonnage (layers of linen and gesso)—date to the Old Kingdom (ca. 2480 B.C.).[2] Masks sheathing the entire head and upper chest appear predominantly in the Eleventh Dynasty (ca. 2125–1985 B.C.). Cartonnage masks were molded to the form of the deceased before the gesso set; once dry, they were painted in bright colors and sometimes also gilded. These masks were not intended as portraits of their subject; rather, they represented the idealized features of the deceased following his resurrection as a divine being in the afterlife. The gilded or yellow-painted faces in many of the masks convey this divine aspect; the Egyptians believed that the flesh of the gods was made of gold.

Although this mask lacks an archeological context, its style and iconographic details unambiguously associate it with the necropolis of Asyut. The similarity of two other masks in Boston and Hildesheim[3] to this example suggests that they were produced in the same studio in the late Eleventh Dynasty. This mask was probably discovered during the poorly documented excavations of Sayed Khashaba Pasha (see no. 8); much of the excavated material was later sold on the international art market.

Because of their fragility, few Middle Kingdom funerary masks have survived in as good a state of preservation as the Walters mask.[4] The physiognomy of the subject is formal and stylized, giving the face a somewhat stiff expression. Even so, details are carefully indicated, such as the bristles of the full beard, the mustache and the eyebrows, all stippled in black over a blue ground. The man wears a voluminous wig with long, rounded frontal lappets that extend down to the chest and have rimmed edges. A broad collar composed of several rows of beads features falcon-headed terminals and is held in position by strings that emerge under the wig on the mask's back. A simple necklace with a large rhomboid bead completes the adornment. The most striking of his jewels is the richly ornamented diadem with a floral motif over the forehead. The prototype of such a diadem would have been made in gold and silver inlaid with semiprecious stones, such as carnelian, lapis lazuli, and turquoise.

RS

Bibliography

Christie's New York, 2001, 60–61, lot 289; Seidel 2002–3.

Notes

1. Plaisant Jozef Nestor (Belgian, 1886–1950) began to collect Egyptian art in 1910, and it is almost certain that he purchased the mummy mask before 1930.
2. The earliest known cartonnage masks, which covered only the face, date to the reign of Niuserre (2445–2421 B.C.); see Tacke 1996, 311, 334–36.
3. Boston, Museum of Fine Arts, 1987.54; and Hildesheim, Roemer- und Pelizaeus-Museum, 6226.
4. Also from Asyut are, besides the two masks mentioned in note 3, the mask of a woman in Hildesheim, Roemer- und Pelizaeus-Museum, 6227, the mask of Ankhef in London, British Museum, EA 46631, and the mask of Nakhty in Paris, Musée du Louvre, E 11995.

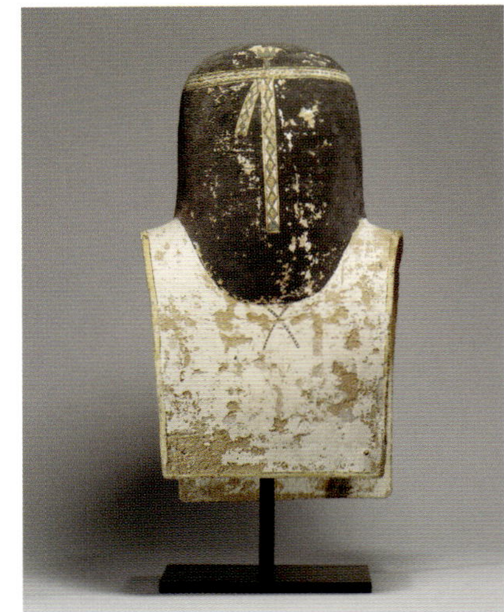

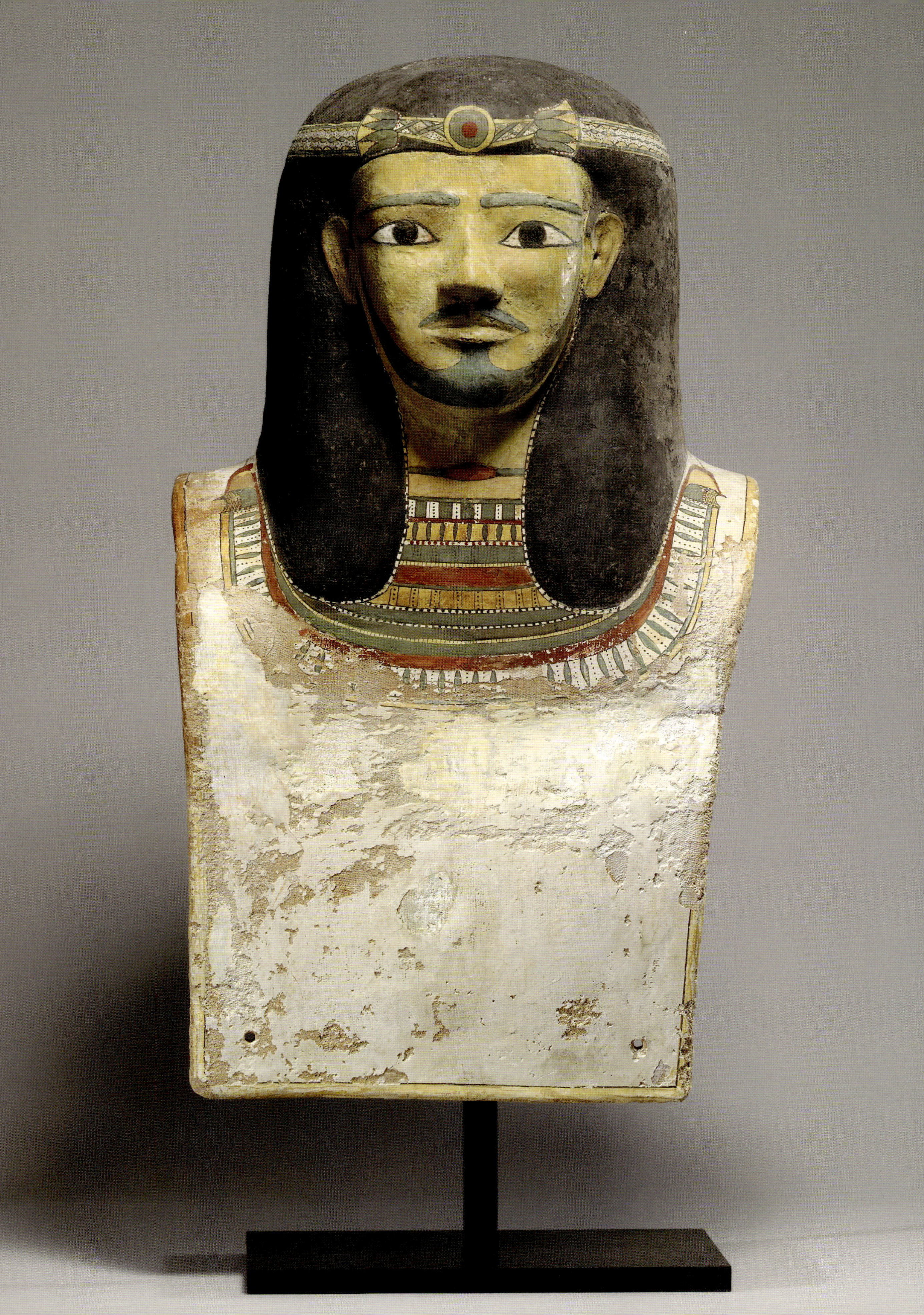

11

Statuette of a woman

Probably from Asyut

Wood, remains of polychrome paint

25 x 6.8 x 4.6 cm (9 3/16 x 2 11/16 x 1 3/16 in.)

Twelfth Dynasty, ca. 1930 B.C.

Provenance: Dikran Kelekian, New York/Paris; Henry Walters, 1912; Walters Art Museum, by bequest, 1931 (22.16)

This wooden statuette of a standing women is one of the finest surviving examples of small-scale Egyptian sculpture. The quality of the craftsmanship is evident in the fine modeling of the body and the carefully executed details. With the loss of the figure's base, the subject's name and identity are unknown; her accoutrements, however, indicate a woman of status rather than a servant. Nor is it certain whether the figure was paired with a male statuette; in that instance, the pendant figure would have represented her husband. Single wooden statuettes like this example, representing males and females, have been found in the burial chambers of Middle Kingdom private tombs, sometimes even within the coffin next to the mummy.

The figure is depicted standing, her feet close together and her unnaturally long arms hanging straight down at each side; the open hands add to the elongated proportions,[1] as does the figure's high waistline. She is dressed in a traditional tight-fitting linen garment held up by shoulder straps; much of the white paint that defined the dress has faded, but the details, marked by simple red lines, are still visible. The figure is richly adorned with jewelry: pairs of wrist- and ankle-bracelets and a necklace composed of a single large central bead, probably intended to represent carnelian. Under a massive wig, composed of thick pigtails terminating in short curls that cascade onto the back and breasts and divided into two large plaits by bands at each side of the temple, the woman's natural hair is visible on her forehead.

Together with the arms, the wig was separately carved and affixed to the figure with wooden pegs. The woman's fresh and confident expression, together with the style and manufacture of the statuette, date this work to the early Twelfth Dynasty, probably the reign of Sesostris I (1956–1911 B.C.).

MS

Bibliography

Steindorff 1946a, 36–37, no. 86, pl. XVII; Hill 1960, 2–4; Vandier 1958, 159.

Notes

1. For the style, see Delange 1987, 173–74; Fay 1996, 115–41; Wildung 2000, 121, no. 129.

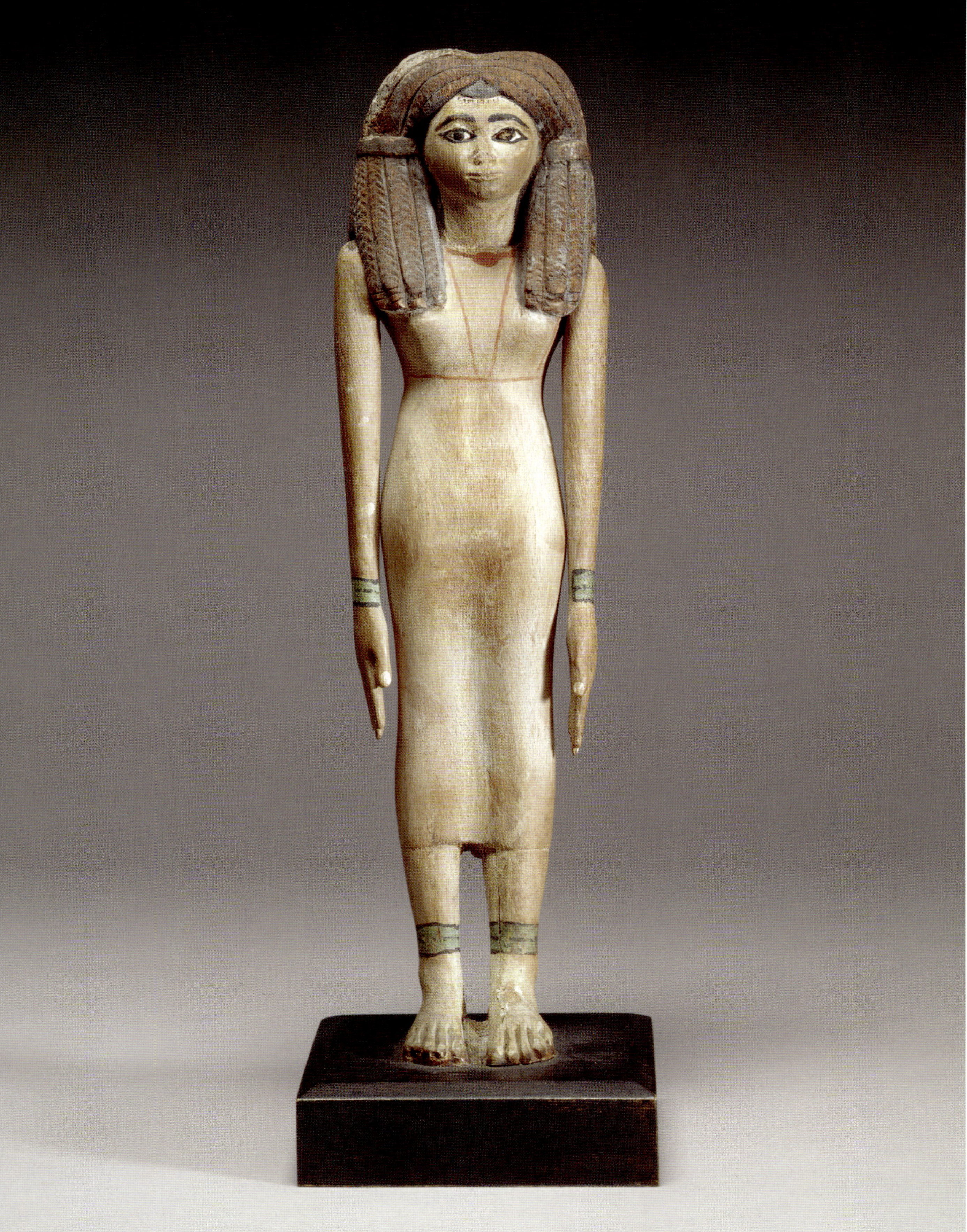

12

Standing figure of a male dignitary

Said to be from Asyut

Elephant ivory; 21.2 x 6.8 x 5.3 cm (8 3/8 x 2 11/16 x 2 1/16 in.)

Early Twelfth Dynasty, ca. 1970 B.C.

Provenance: Maurice Nahman, Cairo; Henry Walters, ca. 1930; Walters Art Museum, by bequest, 1931 (71.509)

Both elephant ivory and hippopotamus ivory were highly valued commodities in Egypt from the predynastic era forward. The costs of obtaining ivory (due to the danger of the hunt and, in the case of elephant ivory, to the considerable distances that the materials traveled to reach artisanal centers) limited its use to luxury goods made for the pharaoh, his family, and high officials. Royal temple inscriptions and biographical data on the walls of private tombs often record details of its transport and delivery. An inscription in the tomb of the Sixth Dynasty nomarch Harkhuef (ca. 2215 B.C.) in Aswan, for example, recounts his expedition to Nubia, from which he brought incense, ebony, oils, leopard hides, and elephant tusks on the backs of three hundred donkeys.[1] An inscription on an obelisk base of Queen Hatshepsut (Eighteenth Dynasty, ca. 1470 B.C.) at Karnak describes an unprecedented tribute of seven hundred elephant tusks from Libya. A royal elephant hunt undertaken by Thutmose III on the upper reaches of the Orontes River in northern Syria is recorded in the Eighteenth Dynasty tomb of Amen-em-heb, an officer who saved the king's life when he was charged by a mighty bull elephant.

Sadly, this small figure of a standing official has lost its original base, which would have provided information on his identity, but the outstanding quality of its workmanship and the material used indicate that it was made for an individual of very high status. The man is represented with his upper body bare, striding forward on his left foot; his head is shaved, but the hairline is visible. The curious ankle-length kilt with a starched trapezoidal apron was introduced in the late Old Kingdom[2] and remained in fashion, albeit with variations, until the Twelfth Dynasty. The single and double lines that form horizontal bands on the garment indicate the crease lines that result from folding. The official grasps a fold of the apron in his right hand; the placement of the left hand on the breast is a sign of reverence to a god.

MS

Bibliography

Steindorff 1946a, 27–28, no. 46, pl. XI; Vandier 1958, 228, 249; Bochi 1996, 230–31, fig. 9; Ziegler 1998, 410, fig. 4.

Notes

1. Lichtheim 1975, 23–27.
2. For an early example, also in ivory, see Ziegler 1997, 201–3, no. 57.

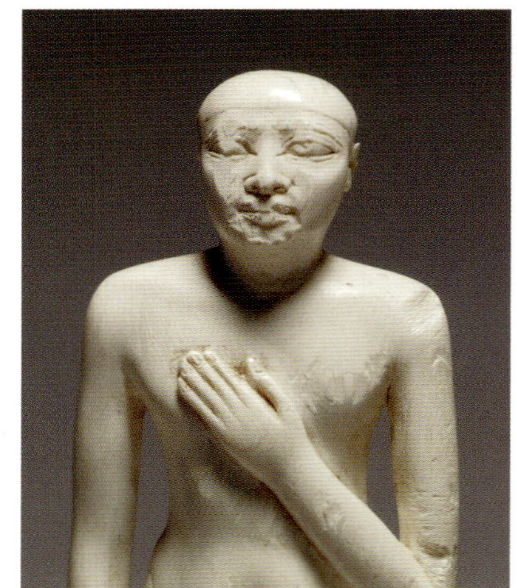

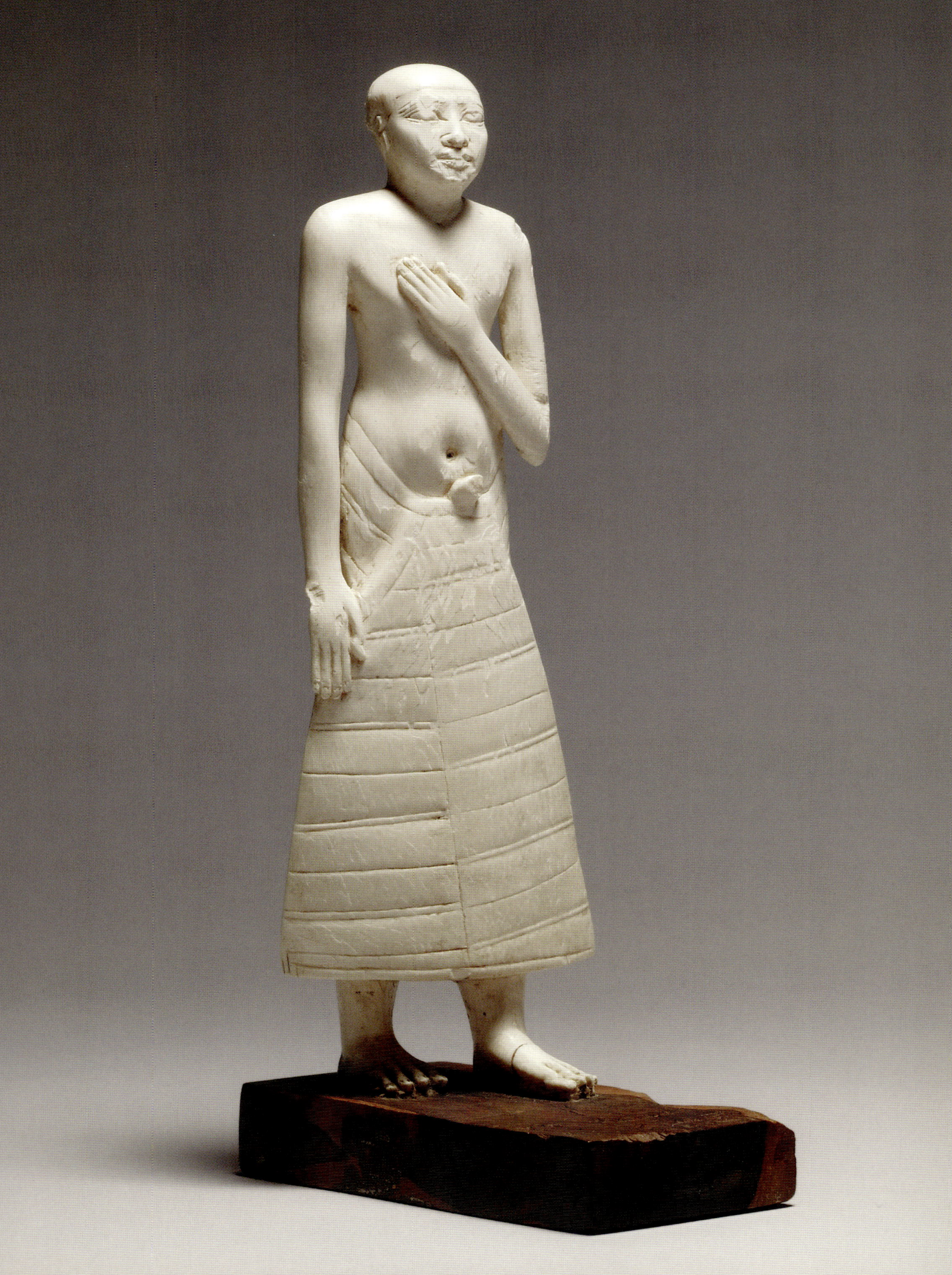

13

Base with two prostrate figures

Probably from Dahshur or Faiyum region

Red-brown quartzite; 27.5 x 28 x 11 cm (10 13/16 x 11 x 4 5/16 in.)

Twelfth Dynasty, ca. 1880 B.C.

Provenance: Henry Walters, before 1931; Walters Art Museum, by bequest, 1931 (22.373)

This unusual sculpture may be the most challenging object in the Walters Egyptian collection for the simple reason that it is a unique work, with no known parallels. Two male figures lie prostrate at left and right of a flat base in a position that the ancient Egyptians called *senj ta*—"kissing the earth"—a demonstration of absolute obedience and submission to a king or god. A third figure originally lay at the center of the base but was meticulously erased in antiquity, together with his names and titles. The intact inscriptions below each of the remaining figures identify the individuals for whom the object was made; on the left:

> The hatj-a [governor or nomarch, mayor] Hat-ankh, born of Sat-wsret

and on the right:

> The hatj-a Nekht the Elder, born of Maket

Each man wears an ankle-length kilt, a short chin-beard, and an unusual elongated bulging wig. The workmanship and the style of the figures' facial features[1] date the work almost certainly to the mid-Twelfth Dynasty.

The identity of the individual in the center, why he was removed, and the object's purpose, however, remain tantalizing mysteries. Despite their unusual wigs, we know, on the basis of their iconography, titles, and names, that the individuals depicted are not foreigners but high officials in Egypt's provincial administration. It is likely that the individual originally at the center had at least the same status as the other two, but the fact that the space he occupied was slightly wider may indicate a higher status. We can only speculate as to why his memory was so deliberately and systematically eradicated.

It is certain, however, that to fulfill its function as the representation of a hierarchical political/religious order, the base was part of a larger assemblage—perhaps joined in a larger base with the enthroned figure or a king or god and the prostrate figures in front.[2] The open courtyard of a temple is the most likely site in which such a meaningful work would have been displayed.

MS

Bibliography

Ziegler 2002, 197, fig. 2, 438, no. 124 (C. Henry).

Notes

1. Compare Seipel 1992, nos. 57–61.
2. The disposition of the figures is complicated in detail because the inscriptions on the front would have had to remain visible.

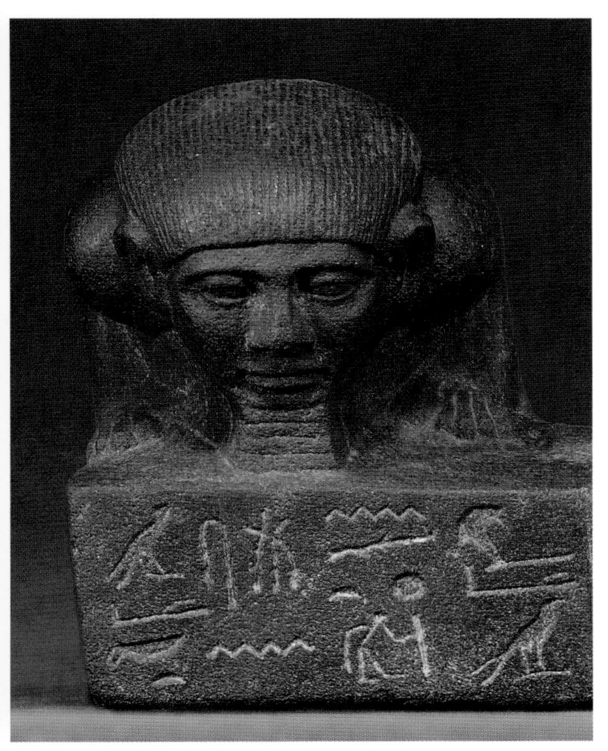

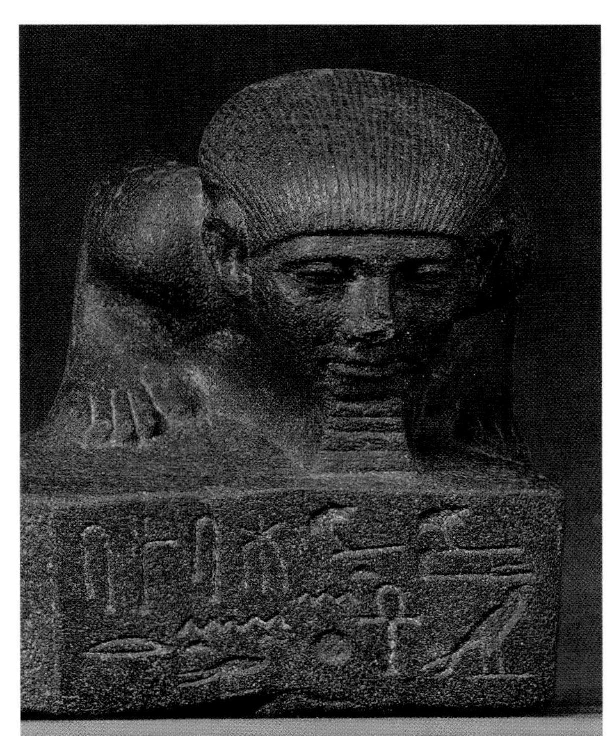

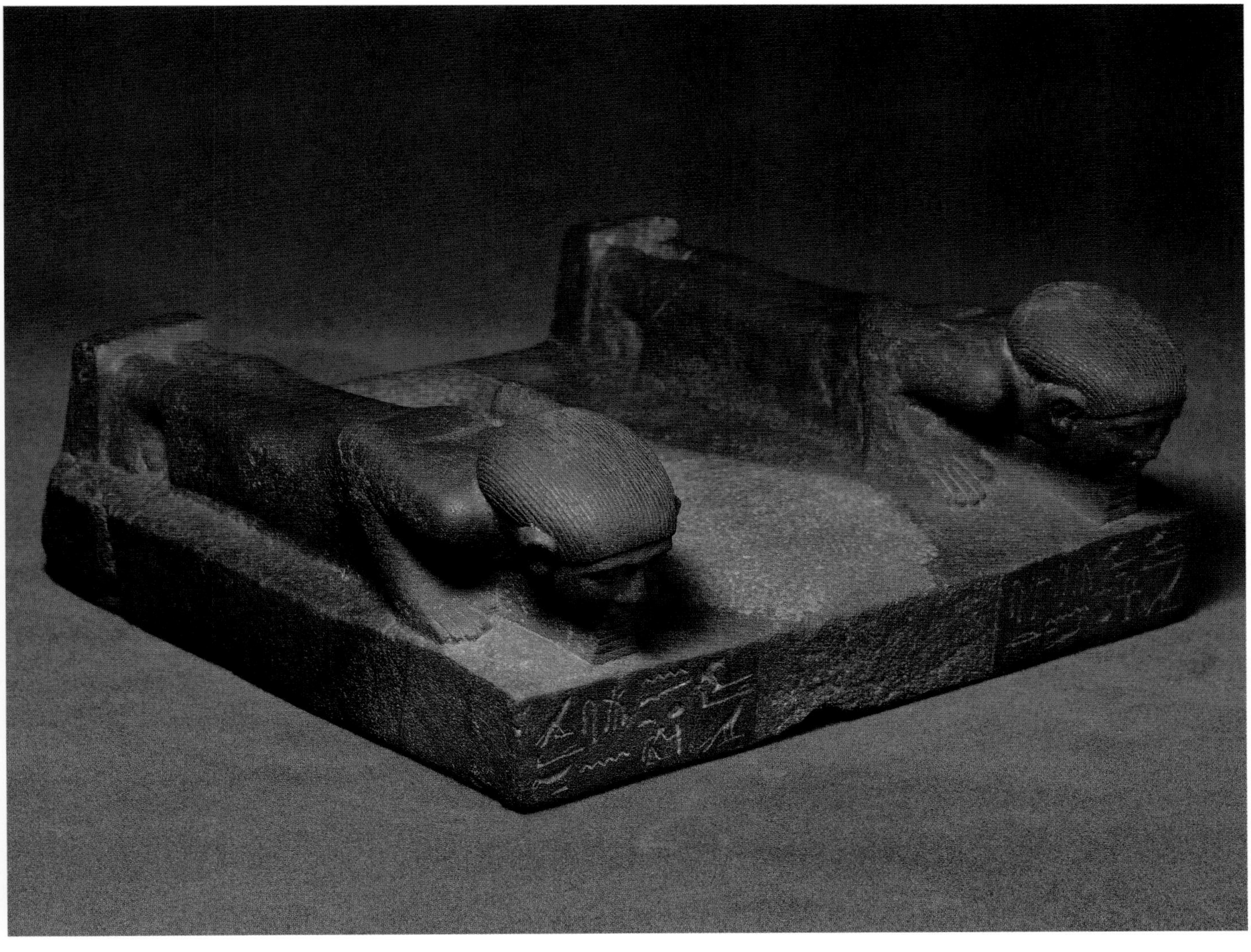

14

Seated statue of Sesostris III

Probably from Upper Egypt

Black granite; 61 x 18.5 cm (24 x 7 5/16 in.)

Twelfth Dynasty, ca. 1850 B.C.

Provenance: Dikran Kelekian, New York/Paris; Henry Walters, 1925; Walters Art Museum, by bequest, 1931 (22.115)

The important position of Sesostris III (1870–1831 B.C.) among the pharaohs of the Twelfth Dynasty is clearly signaled by the vast number of royal statues he erected in temples throughout Egypt. The actual count will never be known, but more than a hundred such figures, varying in size from modest statuettes to colossal statues, are documented today. The seated statue in the collection of the Walters Art Museum is unusual in that it is one of very few surviving statues of intermediate size,[1] considerably smaller than life-size but larger than most statuettes. Its size suggests that the Walters statuette was likely placed in a chapel or a minor temple, of which there were many throughout Egypt. A richer line of inquiry, however, may lie in the inscription, in front of the throne on each side of the legs, that twice names him:

> Beloved of [the god] Wasty, lord of the Oasis.

The god associated with this surname is probably Montu, by tradition the local deity of Thebes, the fourth nome of Upper Egypt. His unusual link to the western desert oasis region can be understood only by the true presence of the royal figure there, perhaps as ritual protector of the caravan route south to Nubia.

This statue depicts Sesostris III seated on a block throne with low back and a tapering back pillar. His right fist (lost) rests on the knee, while his left hand is extended palm-down on his thigh. The king wears the *nemes* headcloth, a *uraeus* serpent, and the short *shendyt* kilt with an undecorated belt and the ceremonial bull's tail between the legs. The necklace with an amulet pendant is characteristic of statues of Sesostris III; no examples of the actual amulet have ever been found, and its meaning remains uncertain. Although the mouth is quite damaged, the face bears the unmistakable features of Sesostris III framed by a pair of large, protuberant ears.[2] This facial landscape, dominated by naturalistic lidded eyes and deep furrows running down the cheeks, conveys the image of an aged ruler, fully aware of the responsibilities of his office. This psychological approach to representation was not intended as realistic portraiture, but rather to fulfill the needs of royal ideology.

MS

Bibliography

Steindorff 1940, 42–53; Steindorff 1946a, 23, no. 30, pl. V; Vandier 1958, 190, pl. LX, 2; Detroit Institute of Arts 1963, no. 2.

Notes

1. For another example, see Fazzini et al. 1989, no. 21 (J.F. Romano).
2. See Polz 1995, 227–54.

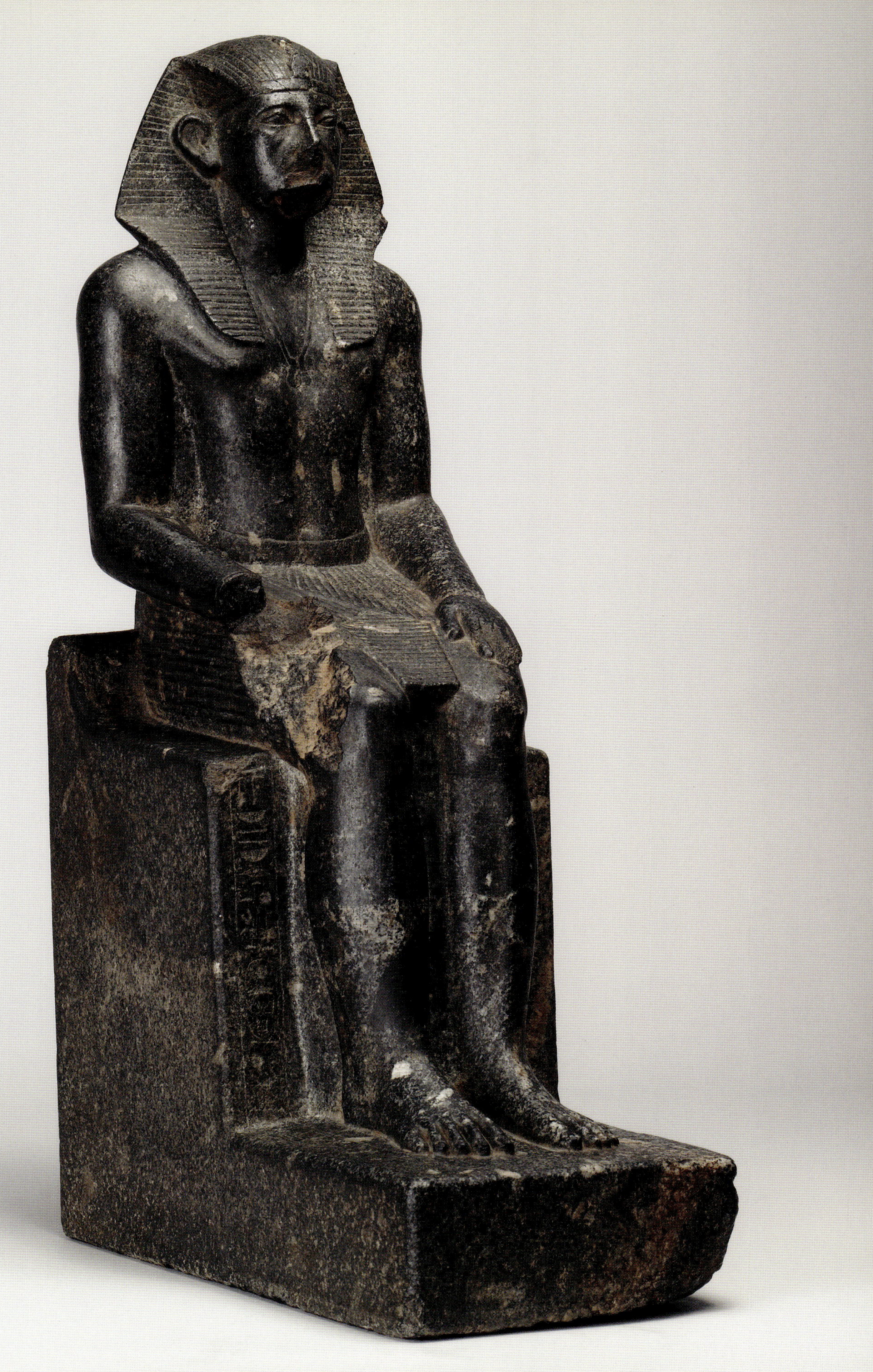

15

Squatting figure of Intef

Granodiorite; 17.5 x 11.4 x 13.3 cm (6 7/8 x 4 1/2 x 5 1/4 in.)

Twelfth Dynasty, ca. 1870 B.C.

Provenance: E.A. Abemayor, Cairo; Henry Walters, 1928; Walters Art Museum, by bequest, 1931 (22.197)

This small figure shows a man seated on the ground with crossed legs, a characteristic position in private statues of the Middle Kingdom.[1] He wears a shoulder-length unparted wig, leaving the ears uncovered. A short chin-beard and kilt complete the outfit of this official; the lower body is unarticulated. Both hands, palms downward, rest on his thighs, a posture of concentration associated with scribe figures during the Old Kingdom but with prayer and worship during the Middle Kingdom. Despite the statue's small scale and the extreme hardness of the stone, its details are finely executed. The facial features, with naturalistic eyes and prominent large ears, date the work to the second half of the Twelfth Dynasty.

On the rectangular base and the kilt a short inscription reads:

> An offering that the king gives [to] Osiris, the great god, may he give an offering of bread, beer, ox and fowl, everything good to the revered, the steward Intef, born by Sat-ipet [?], lady of reverence.

The use of the traditional offering formula, as well as the general figure type, suggests that statues like these functioned differently than did earlier tomb statues, such as no. 2 above. They were no longer confined in a special statue room (*serdab*) in the mastaba tombs of the Old Kingdom, but placed in the open courtyard of temples by the courtiers and other members of the royal administration. There, the statues guaranteed the subjects' eternal presence under the gods' protection and ensured their participation in the daily offering rituals. Statues such as these were by and large dedicated in temples of local gods, of which the Middle Kingdom witnessed a remarkable efflorescence. They were erected during the subject's lifetime as well as posthumously. The large number of figures of modest size that have survived demonstrates that the opportunity to establish new forms of interaction between mankind and the gods was not limited to individuals of high status, but was available as well to officials of middle and lower rank.

MS

Bibliography

Steindorff 1946a, 30, no. 56, pl. VIII; Vandier 1958, 233.

Notes

1. For this type with variations, see Delange 1987, 131–32, 136–41, 178–79; Seipel 1992, 186–95, nos. 57–61.

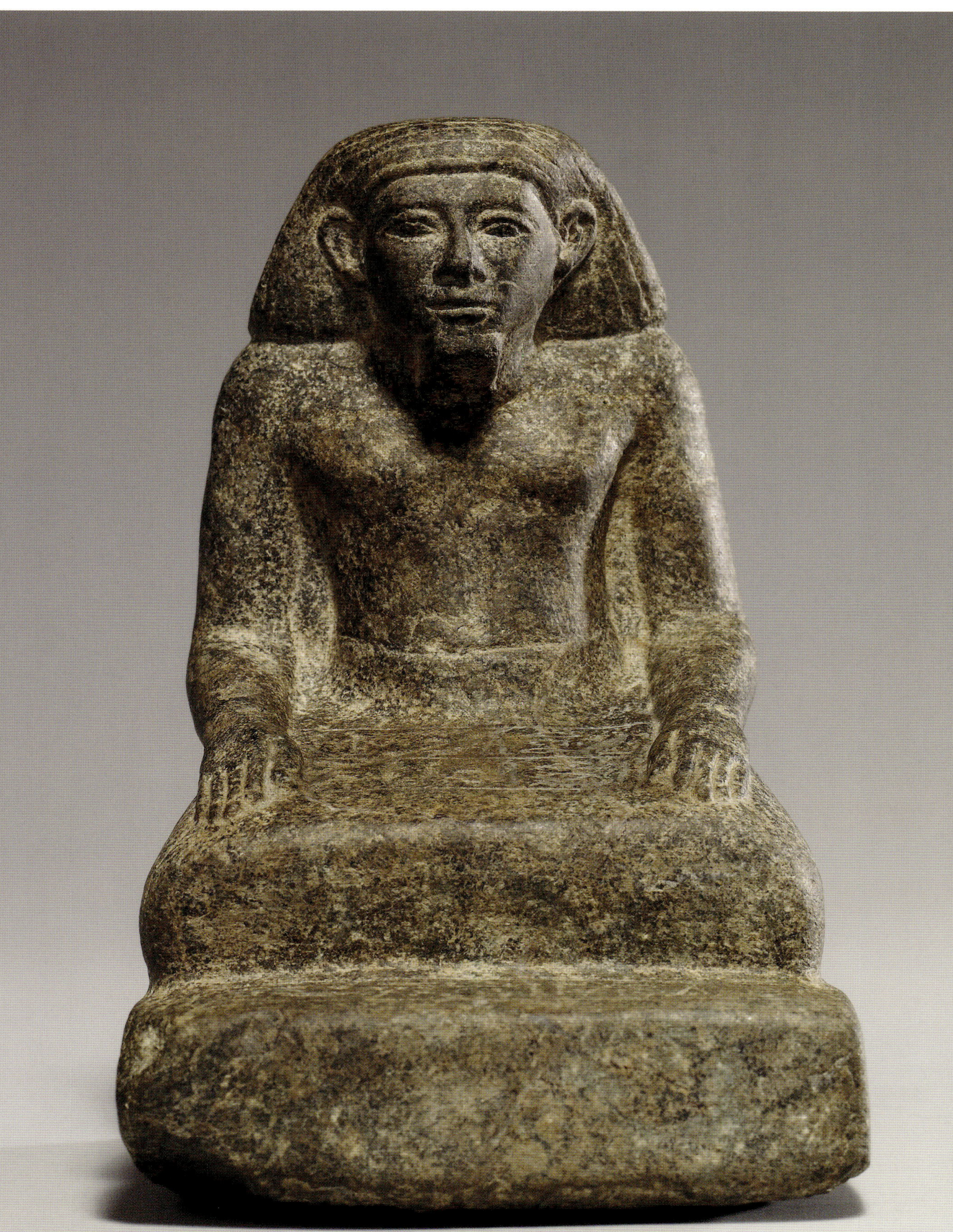

16

Family group

Limestone; 20 x 15.1 x 8.7 cm (7 7/8 x 5 15/16 x 3 7/16 in.)

Twelfth Dynasty, ca. 1850–1800 B.C.

Provenance: Dikran Kelekian, New York/Paris; Henry Walters, before 1931; Walters Art Museum, by bequest, 1931 (22.349)

Statue groups representing families, in various combinations and sequences, were a common theme in ancient Egyptian art. Whereas in Old Kingdom statues the sizes of the individuals signaled their relative importance and their relationship, Middle Kingdom statue groups are characterized by more naturalistic depictions.

This family group consists of three individuals: a man flanked by two women—a well-attested sequence in Middle Kingdom sculpture. The front right corner of the base is missing, and with it the name of the statue's male subject and owner; the remainder of the inscription names the two women but does not describe their relation to one another or to the man; they may be his wives.[1] It reads:

> A mortuary offering [granted by the king, and composed of] bread, beer, oxen, and fowl for the Ka [i.e., the creative and sustaining life power] of [. . .] -Sobek [. . .] born of Dedet-Sobek and [for] Aw, born of Senet.

All three figures stand upright; the man's hands rest flat on the front of his kilt, whereas the women's arms hang at their sides; the hands of all three are disproportionately large. The women's feet are parallel, while the man strides slightly forward. The man wears a heavy, shoulder-length, striated wig; the women wear so-called Hathor-wigs, named for the distinctive hairstyle, with thick curling side plaits, associated with the cow-goddess Hathor (see no. 54). The man wears a typical Middle Kingdom kilt that is wrapped around the waist, calf-length and with a slightly sloping vertical edge, and overlapping end-folds. The women wear ankle-length, sheath gowns with broad shoulder straps.

The round faces of the three figures are very similar, with eyes deeply set into the sockets, naturalistic brows, short noses, mouths with protruding lips and drooping corners, and large, prominent ears—characteristic features of sculpture from the second half of the Twelfth Dynasty.

Statue groups such as this have been discovered in tombs, as well as ritual areas in temple precincts, for example in the Osiris temple at Abydos,[2] which was an important center for pilgrimage to secure the support of Osiris in the afterlife.

RS

Bibliography

Steindorff 1946a, 29, no. 52, pl. XII; Vandier 1958, 242 and 258, Simpson 1977, 24, no. 12.

Notes

1. It resembles the family group of Ukh-hotep II (Boston, Museum of Fine Arts, 1973.87, formerly Baltimore, Walters Art Museum, 22.170).
2. See, for example, the Thirteenth Dynasty high-relief sculpture and offering table of Senpou and his family: Paris, Musée du Louvre, inv. no. E 11573, in Simpson 1974b, pl. 75.

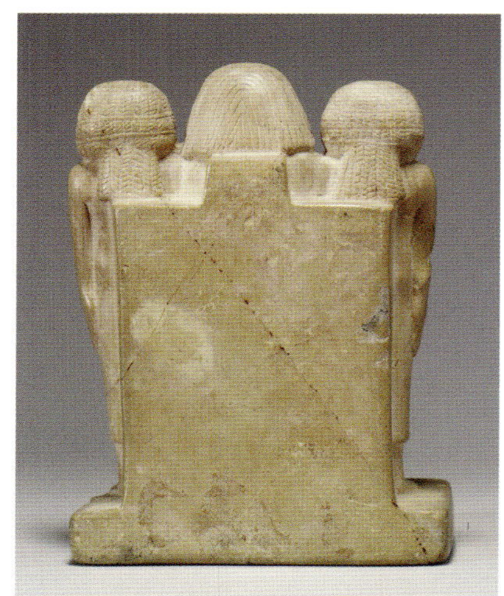

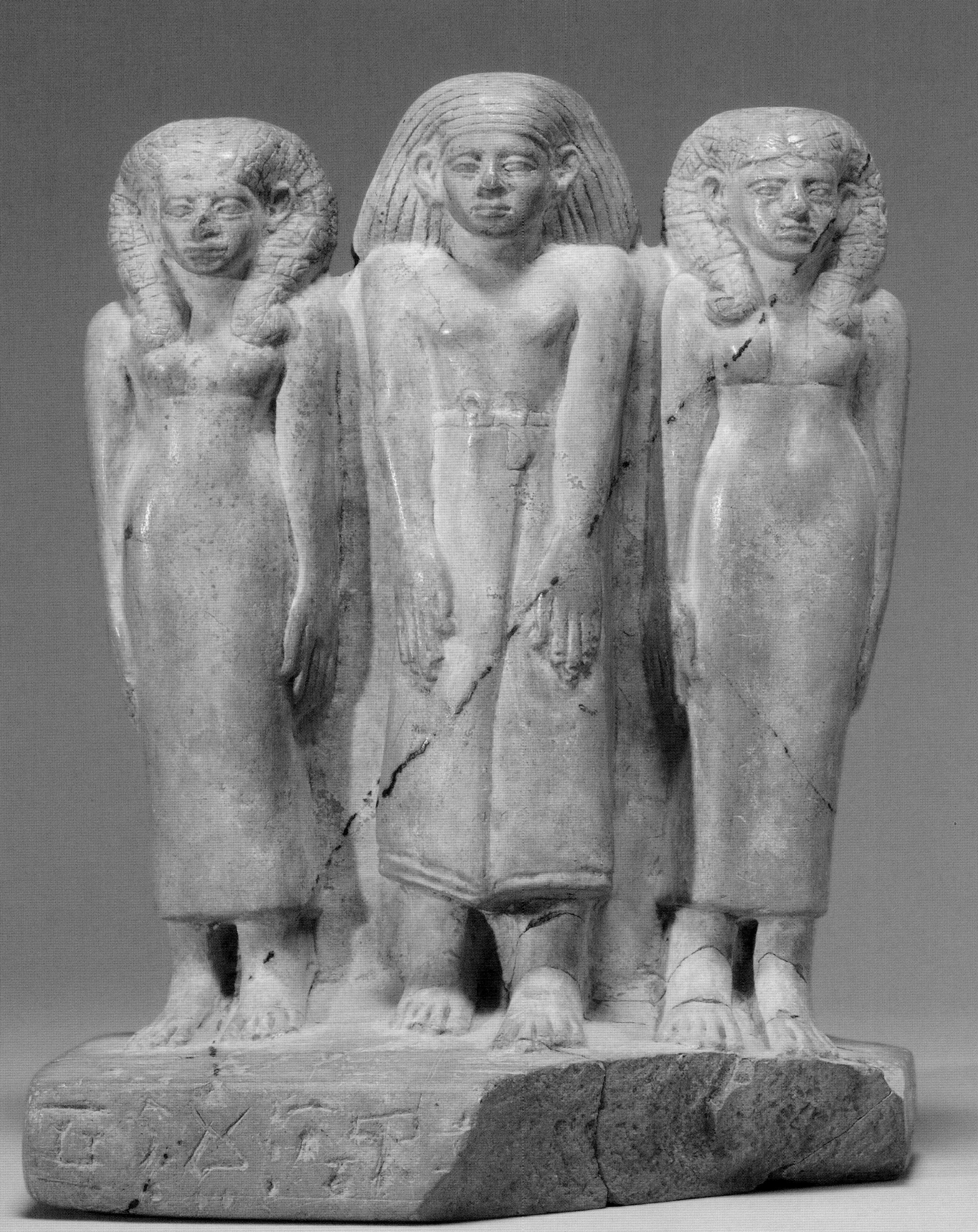

17

Statue of a vizier usurped by Pa-di-iset

Nile Delta (?)[1]

Graywacke; 30.5 x 10.2 x 11.5 cm (12 x 4 1/16 x 4 1/2 in.)

Statue: Late Middle Kingdom, Thirteenth Dynasty, ca. 1780–1700 B.C.;

Inscription and relief: Third Intermediate Period, Twenty-second Dynasty, ca. 900–850 B.C.[2]

Provenance: Maurice Nahman, Cairo; Henry Walters, 1928; Walters Art Museum, by bequest, 1931 (22.203)

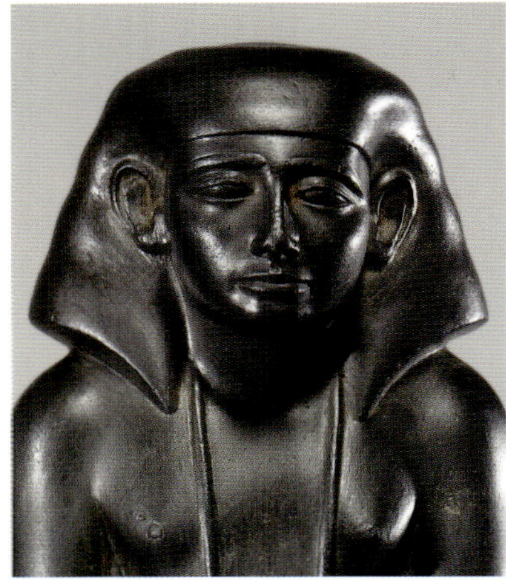

The statue represents a high official of the late Middle Kingdom, standing before a back pillar that ends at his neck, his hands resting flat on the front of his calf-length kilt. The man wears the typical slightly waved wig of the late Middle Kingdom, with short triangular frontal lappets, that leaves the ears uncovered. Two long cords extend from the neck to the waist, and disappear under his calf-length kilt. Although similar cords are familiar in representations of the long, chest-high vizier's kilt, they are less frequently seen, as here, with shorter kilts.[3] The cords in such statues have been construed as suspenders; while that reading is plausible in the case of the long and (presumably heavy) viziers' robes, short kilts or skirts would not have needed them. One indication as to their significance may be the fact that the cords appear exclusively in representations of viziers, named in accompanying inscriptions. Therefore, these cords may represent the viziers' insignia;[4] if so, this statue's original owner would have been the highest official of the state, subordinate only to the king.[5] Certainly, the statue's superb quality, evident in the figure's meticulously executed details, such as the nipples, the navel, and the fingernails, and the high polish of the surface, supports such an association.

Nearly a thousand years after its creation, the statuette was reused, the original inscriptions on the back pillar removed, and a new inscription added. A vignette was carved in sunk relief into the lower part of the kilt, depicting the new owner kneeling in a posture of adoration before the divine family: Osiris, Horus, and Isis. The relief's interior was left slightly rough, an indication that it might have originally been painted or gilded.

The caption of the scene on the kilt names the new owner: "Ka of Osiris: Pa-di-iset, the justified, son of Apy." The two columns on the back pillar contain an offering formula to the god Osiris Wen-nefer and the name and title of the beneficiary, the statue's owner: "The only renowned one, the impartial envoy of Philistine Canaan, Pa-di-iset, son of Apy."

Although Pa-di-iset (probably pronounced *Peteese*) is a plausibly Egyptian name, it appears as well in Phoenician contexts.[6] The name Apy, Pa-di-iset's father, has a Semitic origin,[7] and it is written on the statue with the character for "foreign land." These elements suggest that Pa-di-iset was in fact an envoy or ambassador from Philistine Canaan—a district of Gaza[8]—to Egypt, and not an Egyptian ambassador to that region. During the Third Intermediate Period, the Egyptian pharaohs sought to form alliances with the cultures of the Levant. It may be that the Egyptian authorities extended the extraordinary privilege of using the statue of a vizier of the Middle Kingdom, Egypt's "Classical Age," for the burial of a respected foreign envoy or ambassador.

RS

Bibliography

Chassinat 1901, 98–100; Steindorff 1939, 30–33; Steindorff 1946a, 49, no. 145, pl. XXV; Alt 1952, 163–64; Porten 1981, 36–52; Valloggia 1976, 188–89, no. 147; Nibbi 1989, pl. VI; Walters Art Gallery 1997, 20 (S. Harvey); Schipper 1999, 193–97.

Notes

1. Purchase records in the Walters Art Museum's curatorial files associate the statue with an unnamed findspot in the Nile Delta. The usurpation of the statue by a foreign consul or ambassador in the Twenty-second Dynasty suggests that it came either from Bubastis or Tanis (Egypt's northern capitals) or that the statue was taken to Gaza (Pa-di-iset's possible place of origin), and then returned to Egypt.
2. For the dating of the inscription, see Schipper 1999, 194.
3. For examples, see Fay 2008, 98, figs. 9 (Boston, Museum of Fine Arts, 11.1484) and 10 (formerly Stoclet collection).
4. Biri Fay (2008, 89–91) proposes that these cords represent a necklace with a cylindrical seal at the end, similar to that displayed in the tomb reliefs of the vizier Dagi (see Davies 1913, pls. 32, 34). That interpretation, however, raises the question of why the seal is concealed in a three-dimensional sculpture.
5. Fischer 1974, 17.
6. Vittmann 2003, 57–59, fig. 21.
7. Schipper 1999, 194–95.
8. Schipper 1999, 194f.

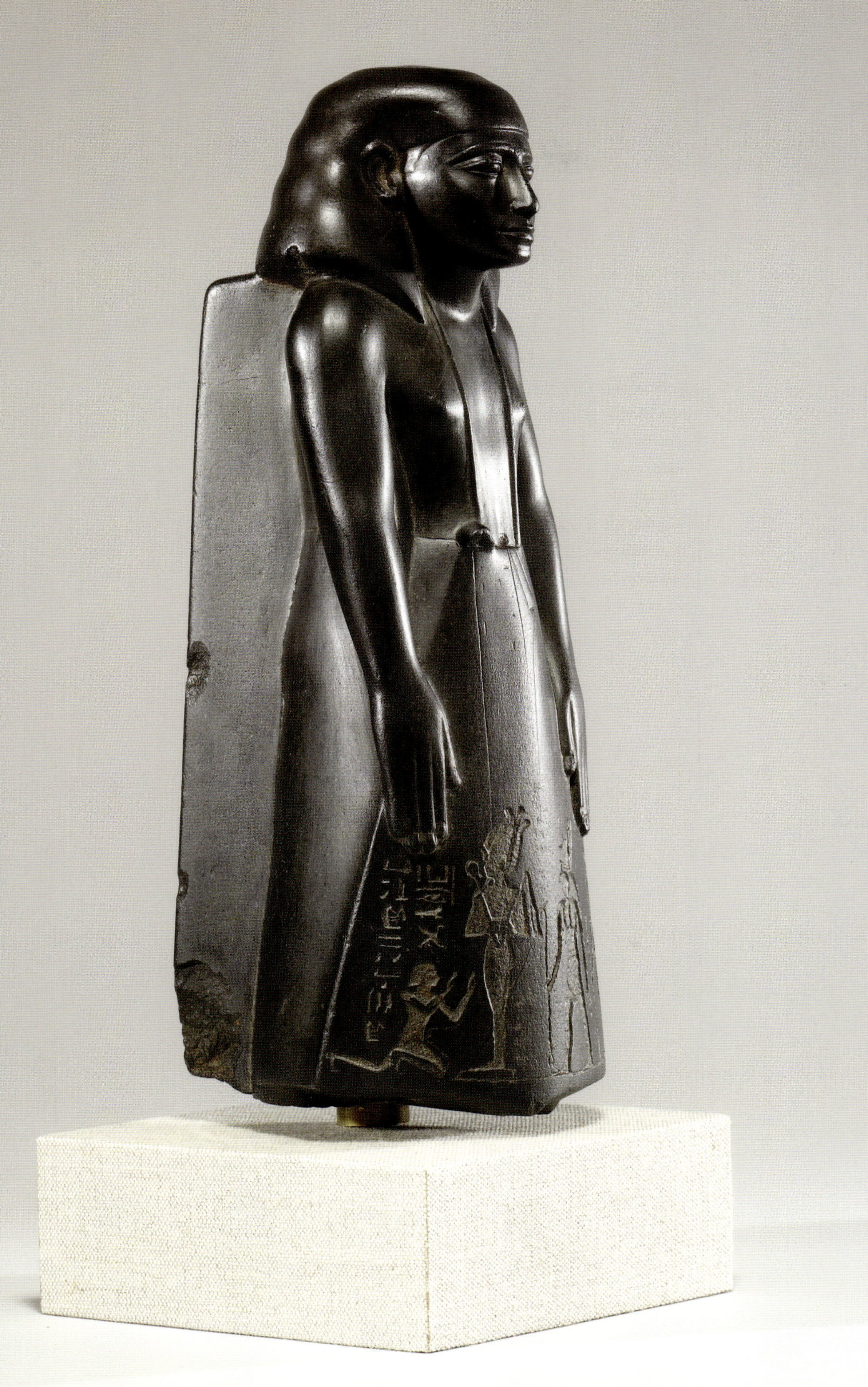

18

Magical wand

Hippopotamus ivory; 36.5 x 16 x 0.7 cm (14 3/8 x 6 5/16 x 1/4 in.)
Late Twelfth or Thirteenth Dynasty, ca. 1880–1700 B.C.
Provenance: Dikran Kelekian, Paris; Henry Walters, 1914;
Walters Art Museum, by bequest, 1931 (71.510)

Objects such as these resemble throw-sticks used for hunting wildfowl; their decoration, however, indicates that they were not utilitarian objects but apotropaic instruments, intended to ward off evil. Wands are generally carved from hippopotamus tusk, as is this example, to intensify their magical properties. They have been found in tombs, but signs of use and repair evident on many examples (this wand is broken into five pieces, and the narrow end is heavily damaged) indicate that they were not intended exclusively for burial. During the owner's lifetime, they might have protected him or her against demons, nightmares, curses, or illnesses. Vigorous handling or throwing during a special ritual would explain the extensive damage evident on many apotropaic wands. Such a ritual might have taken place after the death of the wand's owner and before the object's interment.

The layout of the decoration varies slightly, but all examples depict powerful animals, mythic creatures, and protective deities. Some of the figures wield knives, snakes, or powerful symbols; short captions, spells, or the name of the owner sometimes complete the scenes. On the evidence of inscriptions, as well as the presence on the wands of the hippopotamus goddess Taweret (see no. 69) and the god Aha (see no. 19), the protection of mother and child was clearly one of their functions.[1] Excavated examples originate from Lisht, Middle Egypt, Thebes, and Kerma and date to the Middle Kingdom and the Second Intermediate Period. The owners of objects made of such precious material were undoubtedly of the upper class.

This throw-stick has one convex and one flat side, both of which are decorated. On the convex side are eleven figures, all facing left, with the exception of the god Aha, depicted frontally, in the center. The sequence depicts, from left to right: a jackal with a lotus flower between its ears; a spotted feline with an extraordinarily long neck and the hieroglyphic sign for "protection" on its back; the hippopotamus goddess Taweret; a griffin with a serpent-tail and a human head between its wings; a baboon carrying a protective *wedjat* eye, a feline (with a leopard's body and male lion's head) crushing a human enemy under its left front paw; Aha grasping two snakes; a frog seated on a base; a jackal head with a wig, supported on the legs of a lion; a male lion walking upright with an *ankh* symbol in front of him; a solar-disk with a *uraeus* serpent on human legs; a vulture; and a feline head (with attributes of both a cheetah and leopard) at the thicker end.[2] All the creatures, except Aha, brandish knives and snakes in their mouths.

The flat side of the throw-stick depicts two winged cobra-serpents oriented to the center between the jackal and the feline head. Figures of two frogs, a lion, Taweret, a vulture, and a sphinx, as well as *wedjat* eyes appear among the undulating coils of the serpents' body. Two empty columns in the center may have been intended to carry an inscription.

RS

Bibliography

Steindorff 1946b, 41–51, 106–7, figs. 1–2; Canby 1979a, no. 2; Altenmüller 1986, 1–27, pl. 3; Capel and Markoe 1996, 64, no. 12.

Notes

1. A good example is the magic throw-stick for "the child Min-hotep," excavated in Lisht, New York, Metropolitan Museum of Art, 08.200.19.
2. Creatures with the attributes of two or more animals are common in Egyptian art; the composite leopard and cheetah, both of which have spotted pelts, alludes to the body of the sky deity, spotted with stars.

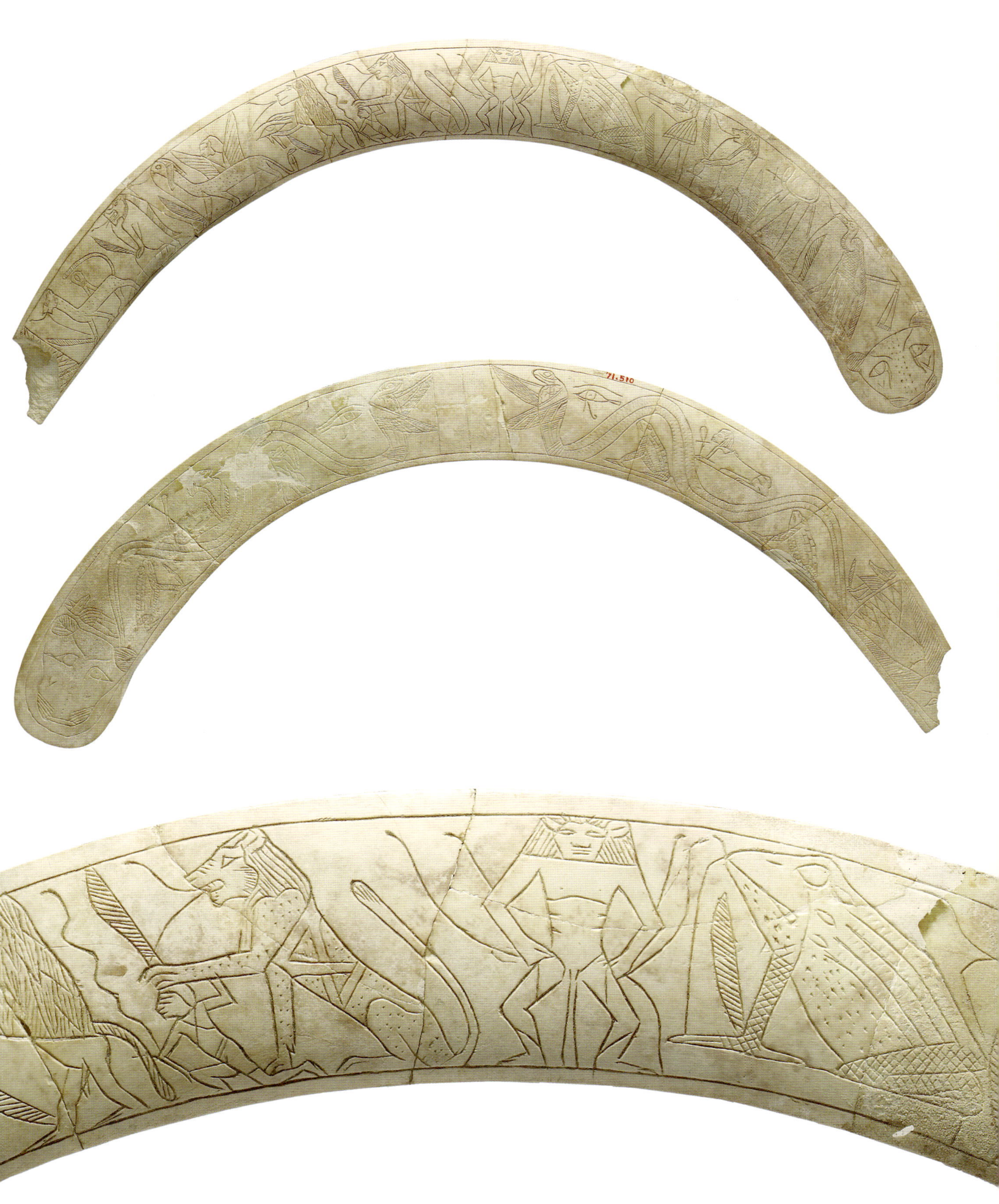
71.510

19

Magical figure of Aha-Bes

Western Thebes, Dra abu'l Naga[1]

Glazed faience; height 17.2 cm (6 ¾ in.)

Thirteenth Dynasty, ca. 1800–1750 B.C.

Provenance: William MacGregor, Tamworth, Staffordshire; sale, London, Sotheby, Wilkinson & Hodge, 26–29 June and 4–6 July 1922; Henry Walters, 1922; Walters Art Museum, by bequest, 1931 (48.420)[2]

The belief in the existence of demons and the conviction that evil could be warded off through divine intervention were essential elements of Egyptian religion. In representing apotropaic powers as manifestations of the divine, the Egyptians used characteristic features of dangerous animals (such as lions, crocodiles, hippopotamuses, or snakes) as well as protective and magical symbols.

The first depictions of Aha or Bes date from the early Middle Kingdom (ca. 2000 B.C.) and appear on apotropaic "wands" (no. 18) or as figurines.[3] These early images represent the god nude, with the mane, tail, and sometimes the skin of a lion. He is depicted frontally and in a unique posture: his knees bent and hands resting on the hips. It is possible that the nude juvenile represents Aha, whereas the more dwarfish form represents Bes. Both gods were deemed to be effective against demons and the illnesses they cause, as well as powerful protectors of mothers and infants in childbirth. Aha's and Bes's lion characteristics associate them with the celestial sphere—perhaps a special manifestation of the sun god—and their frontal depiction symbolizes their readiness to face all evil.

Dwarf gods such as Bes or Pataikos—the latter is a manifestation of the creator god Ptah—were thought to have special magic powers. Some depictions show Bes dancing or playing the flute or harp, as part of a divine protective ritual. The bent knees of the early representations may indicate a dancing posture, and it is likely that priests wearing Aha or Bes masks executed these ritualistic dances. The mask itself became a powerful magic symbol that was used as an amulet or a protective device on Horus stelae (no. 64).

This figurine depicts Aha–Bes as a young, nude male with a lion's mane, ears, and tail.[4] The representation seems to assimilate the two deities: the proportions of the body clearly signal Bes's characteristic dwarfism, whereas the snakes clenched in the figure's hands are attributes of Aha. The statuette is glazed an intense turquoise-blue, a color associated with life and rebirth that may also signal the god's youth. The mane, the ears, the eyes and brows, the nipples, and the toes, as well as the snakes in the god's hands are painted in black underglaze. The large painted eyes dominate the juvenile face; his nose and lips are modeled but not painted.

Later representations of the god show Bes with a full beard. This beard became so iconic that it is present even in depictions of Bes as a child.[5]

RS

Bibliography

Wallis 1900, 47: 313; MacGregor Collection 1922, 37, lot 265; Steindorff 1946a, 143, no. 624, pl. XCIV; Dasen 1993, pl. 3.3.

Notes

1. Mentioned in the Sotheby's London sales catalogue of June–July 1922.
2. This statuette is probably the same figure mentioned by Henry Wallis in his pamphlet on Egyptian ceramic art in the MacGregor Collection; see Wallis 1898.
3. Although inscriptions naming Bes do not occur before the New Kingdom, the god's characteristic dwarf-leonine shape supports the identification with Middle Kingdom representations of Aha (named on apotropaic throw-sticks of the Middle Kingdom), but also of Bes.
4. A close parallel was excavated by John Garstang in 1905–6 from tomb 275 at Esna. See Bourriau 1988, 112–13, no. 99.
5. One such example is in the Roemer- und Pelizaeus-Museum, Hildesheim, inv. no. 0248; see Kayser 1973, 110. For a photograph, see www.globalegyptianmuseum.org/record.aspx?id=10466.

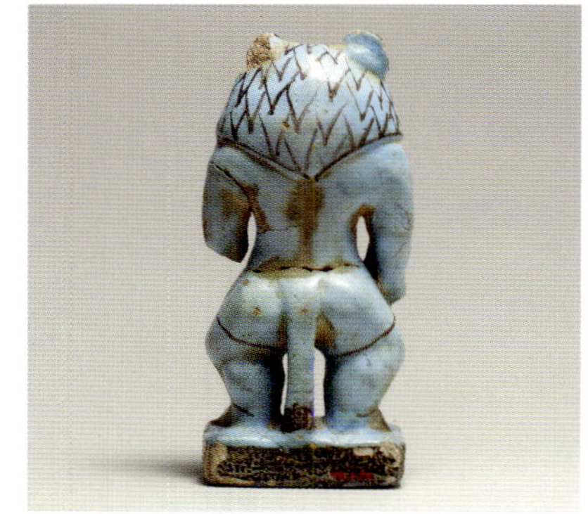

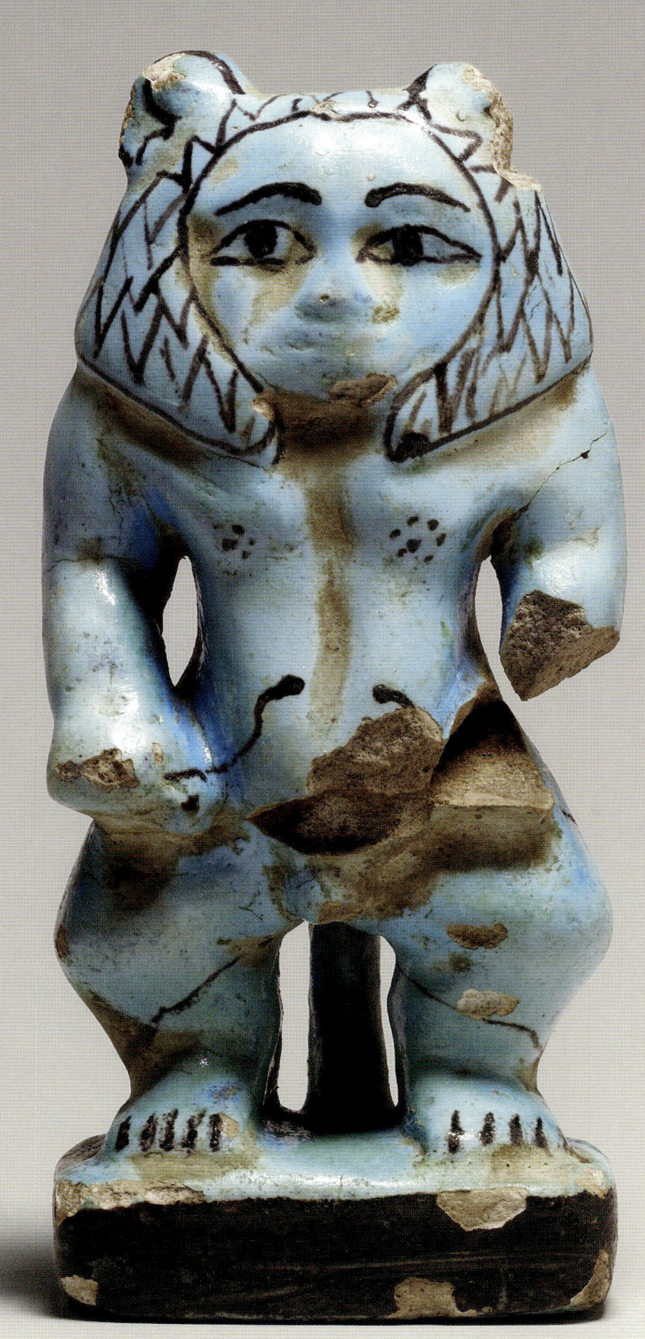

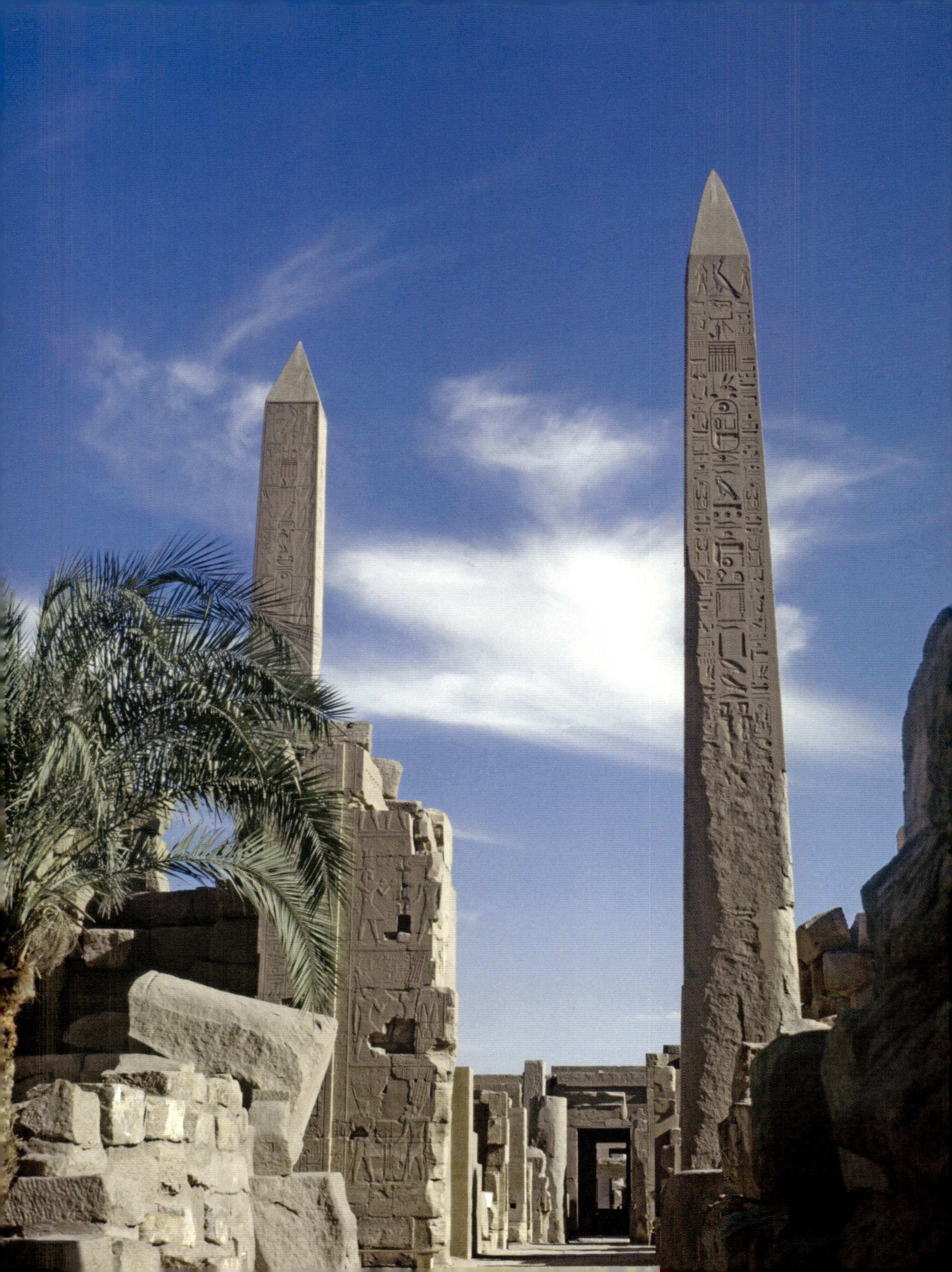

THE NEW KINGDOM (1550–1069 B.C.)

The period of the New Kingdom is unquestionably the high point—the Golden Age—of ancient Egyptian culture. As often happened in Egypt's history, change came from the south. The struggle to expel the Hyksos from Egypt, led by the local rulers of Thebes, started around 1555 B.C.; ultimate victory was achieved by King Ahmose (1550–1525 B.C.), who is regarded as the founder of the Eighteenth Dynasty. At Avaris (Tell el-Dab'a), Ahmose and his immediate successors erected a new palace complex on the ruins of the Hyksos rulers' razed capital. Minoan-style wall paintings in some of the palaces, resembling those at the palace of Knossos in Crete, attest to close connections between the Aegean civilizations and Egypt, although their implications have not been fully explored. By the reign of Amenhotep I (1525–1504 B.C.), most of the cultural markers for the Eighteenth Dynasty were already well established. The new state was based on military power under the control of the reigning pharaoh, who was enshrined in dogma as the son of the god Amun-Re. This Theban local deity was elevated to supreme status in the pantheon and venerated at his main sanctuary at Karnak, a temple city that grew to unprecedented dimensions by continuous building over the centuries to come. The success of Egypt's foreign policy was matched by a highly efficient state administration executed by a small circle of officials with close relations to the royal court. The fact that most of the kings ascended to the throne at a very young age meant that extraordinary power was vested in administrative officials, such as viziers, high priests, and army generals. Thutmose I (1504–1492 B.C.) decisively crushed the Kushite empire of Kerma; Nubia with its material riches (notably gold) fell entirely under Egyptian control, the exploitation of its resources administered by the new office of a viceroy, the so-called King's Son of Kush. The same pharaoh launched also a brief campaign in the Levant, although he saw little direct military confrontation. The actual conquest of Syria and Canaan is credited to Thutmose III (1479–1425 B.C.), when he came into his maturity as pharaoh (see nos. 20–23) following the death of Queen Hatshepsut (1473–1458 B.C.). Through more than a dozen campaigns on Egypt's northern front (the Levant and Syria) and deep into Nubia to the south, he led Egypt to its maximum territorial extent and unprecedented regional hegemony. As a result of his victories, a seemingly endless stream of booty and tributes from the conquered territories reached Egypt and boosted the economy. Supported by stable political conditions, Egypt's material culture soared to previously unknown levels of sophistication, mostly associated with the reign of Amenhotep III (1390–1352 B.C.). Beside stunning artistic and architectural achievements (see nos. 25–29), the conception of the pharaoh increasingly focused on his divine nature. This pattern was sustained by Amenhotep IV (see no. 30), who changed his name to Akhenaten (1352–1336 BC), left Thebes to found a new capital, Akhetaten, in Middle Egypt, and declared the sun disk Aten as the sole god. This revolutionary change to the religious landscape, with the king and his wife Nefertiti as the deity's sole prophets, was short-lived. After Akhenaten's death, one of his successors, Tutankhamun (1336–1327 B.C.), left Amarna and restored the traditional cult of the former state god Amun at Karnak. With the death of the boy king, most famous for the treasures of his tomb in the Valley of the Kings, the royal bloodline of the Eighteenth Dynasty was extinguished. A general—Horemheb (1323–1295 B.C.)—seized power and served as the epoch's last pharaoh (see nos. 31, 32), entrusting his succession to another general, Paramessu, who initiated the Ramesside period by ruling as Ramesses I (1295–1294 B.C.). The Nineteenth Dynasty was dominated by two kings (see nos. 33, 34): Sety I (1294–1279 B.C.) and his son, Ramesses II (1279–1213 B.C.). The latter was venerated as a living god during his extraordinarily long reign in the vast number of temples (see no. 35) he commissioned. The kingdom's political center shifted to Pi-Ramesses (Qantir), a new capital in the western Delta, while Thebes remained the country's religious nucleus. In the fifth year of his reign, Ramesses faced off against the emerging superpower of the Hittites. The battle of Qadesh (northen Syria) ended in a lucky draw for the Egyptians; some years later, a peace treaty regulated relations between the two powers. In the following Twentieth Dynasty, ruled by a succession of Ramesses, the territorial integrity of Egypt was defended for the last time by Ramesses III (1184–1153 B.C.) in several battles against the Libyans and the Sea Peoples (a confederation of tribes from the eastern Mediterranean). The final reigns of the Ramesside period were rather troubled, beset by a weak economy, public unrest, and the gradual breakdown of the central administration. Under Ramesses XI (1099–1069 B.C.), the last pharaoh of the New Kingdom, the country was badly shaken by famine and civil war, leading to the breakup of the state from within.

MS

Karnak, Temple of Amun, obelisks of Thutmose I and Queen Hatshepsut (Eighteenth Dynasty, ca. 1500–1465 B.C.).
Photo © Dr. Abdel Ghaffar Shedid, Munich

20

Funerary stela of Tembu

Probably from Western Thebes

Limestone, polychrome paint; 68.1 x 46.2 cm (26 ¾ x 18 ¼ in.)

Early Eighteenth Dynasty, ca. 1500–1470 B.C.

Provenance: Henry Walters, before 1931; Walters Art Museum, by bequest, 1931 (22.92)

In its spacious arrangement of scenes and crisply executed faces, the artistic style of this funerary stela, carved from a slab of fine limestone, is characteristic of the early Eighteenth Dynasty, suggesting that it was made during the reign of Queen Hatshepsut (1473–1458 B.C.), or even slightly earlier. The curved top, or lunette, was introduced at the beginning of the Middle Kingdom and remained a standard feature of Egyptian stelae until the Roman Period. The composition of the pictorial space follows artistic conventions: the subject making the offering is depicted in one or more registers, framed at the top by magical symbols inscribed in the lunette and at the bottom by an inscription. The figural elements are in raised relief, whereas the inscriptions are sunk. The stela was commissioned for an otherwise unknown official with the uncommon name Tembu, who held the title of overseer; it does not elaborate on who Tembu was or what he did. The colors are unusually well preserved.

The group of hieroglyphic signs in the lunette includes two *wedjat* eyes (the sacred eyes of Horus) flanking the central group with a *shen* ring of eternity at top, three water lines and *wseh* vessel below.[1] An offering scene is placed beneath this protective composition with cosmic quality.

Accompanied by his wife, "the Mistress of the House, Ta-nenw," the stela's owner sits on a broad chair smelling a large lotus blossom. A small monkey stands under her chair, holding a mirror upside down.[2] In front of the couple, a lavishly stocked offering table provides nourishment for the afterlife. The ritual is conducted by one of Tembu's daughters, Maha, presumably the eldest, who stands behind the table and presents a small dish of water to her parents. In the lower register, six more children are depicted, some of whom bring offerings. Their title suggests that the four sons held an undisclosed position in the navy. This male group is divided from the two younger daughters at the left by an enormous beer jar with a pointed stopper. The stela closes with two lines of the traditional offering formula, assuring the provision of food and drink for the deceased.

MS

Bibliography

Ranke 1939, 19–23; Steindorff 1946a, 84, no. 281, pl. LII; Hill 1958, 278.

Notes

1. Westendorf 1966, 74–75.
2. For the iconography and meaning of the monkey under the chair, see Hornung and Bryan 2002, 93, no. 12 (E. Sullivan).

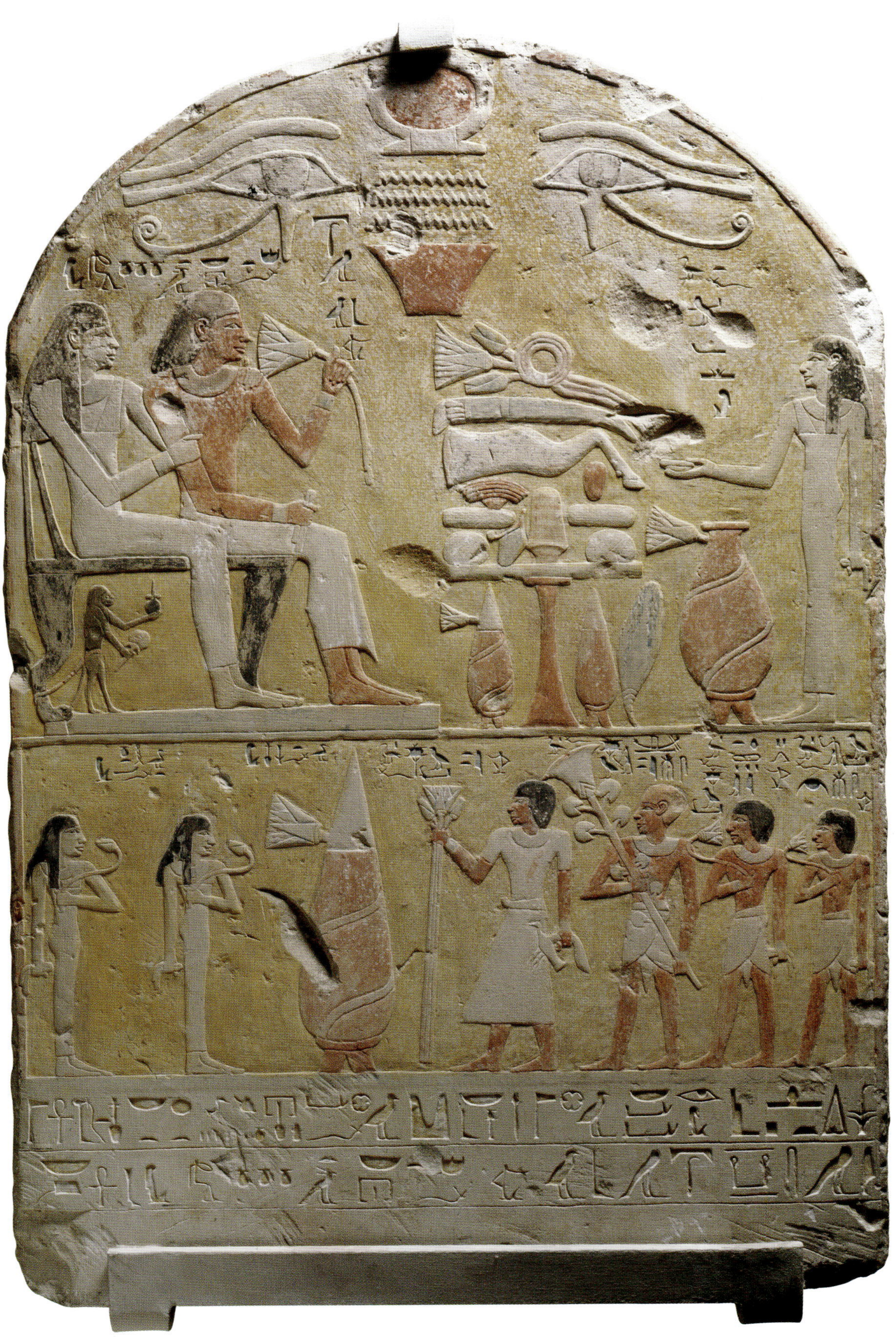

21

Bowl with fish and lotus blossoms

Probably from Western Thebes
Glazed faience; height: 5 cm (1 15/16 in.); diameter: 14.2 cm (5 9/16)
Eighteenth Dynasty, ca. 1450–1400 B.C.
Provenance: William MacGregor, Tamworth, Staffordshire; sale, Sotheby, Wilkinson & Hodge, 26–29 June and 4–6 July 1922, London; Dikran Kelekian, New York / Paris, 1922; Henry Walters, 1923; Walters Art Museum, by bequest, 1931 (48.400)

Shallow faience bowls of this type were particularly popular during the early to middle Eighteenth Dynasty. Faience was a commonly used material in Egypt; it was made from silica—found in quartz pebbles, sand, or lime—mixed with a binder into a paste and formed in molds. Its blue or turquoise color came from the inclusion of copper as colorant. This bowl was molded over a hemispherical form and then glazed and fired. The dark purple decoration, often added to monochrome faience pieces, was painted before firing with a manganese-based pigment.

These vessels (sometimes described as "marsh bowls") are typically embellished with aquatic imagery alluding to fertility, such as tilapia fish, lotuses, papyrus umbels, buds on stems, and pools of water. The bright blue of faience, as well as the aquatic motifs adorning these bowls, is associated with the life-giving qualities of cool, fresh water. The blue lotus (*Nymphaea caerulea*) and the tilapia fish (*Tilapia nilotica*) are emblematic of such imagery. Here, two fish carry lotus stems with buds and opened blossoms in their mouths. The ornamentation relates to the powerful themes of rebirth and regeneration.

The lotus flower symbolizes rebirth, the opening and closing of the blossom corresponding to the rising and setting of the sun. It was believed that the sun god was reborn each day as a young child from the primordial waters of Nun (a personification of the formless ocean of chaos),[1] and the lotus became associated with the self-generative powers of the sun deity. The fragrant lotus is frequently depicted on funerary equipment or on commemorative objects dedicated to the deceased and placed in temples.

Regeneration is suggested as well by the unusual spawning behavior of tilapia. The female lays her eggs and she or the male stores them in its mouth, from which the hatchlings appear, conveying the notions of fertility and spontaneous generation. The regenerative imagery of the lotus and tilapia fish reinforces the possibility that these types of bowls were offering gifts for the temple[2] and tomb and not intended for use in daily life; they are associated predominantly with female burials.[3]

A decorative scalloped border painted on the interior rim is an embellishment rarely seen on these vessels. On the exterior, lotus petals, drawn in fine outline, rise up from the bowl's base in imitation of the underside of the lotus flower. The variety of decoration on the interior of such bowls resulted in no two being exactly alike in the arrangement of the motifs represented.[4]

CH

Bibliography

Wallis 1898, pl. 7, 1; MacGregor Collection 1922, 35, no. 257, pl. VIII.

Notes

1. Strauß 1974, 70–76.
2. Such offerings are primarily associated with sanctuaries dedicated to the goddess Hathor, as in Deir el-Bahari or Serabit el-Khadim (Sinai); see Pinch 1993, 308–15.
3. Friedman 1998, 211, no. 76.
4. For examples, see Brovarski et al. 1982, 141–43, nos. 138–40; Spurr, Reeves, and Quirke 1999, 28–29, nos. 26–30; Caubet and Pierrat-Bonnefois 2005, 69–71, nos. 164–67; Roehrig 2005, 176–80, nos. 100–105.

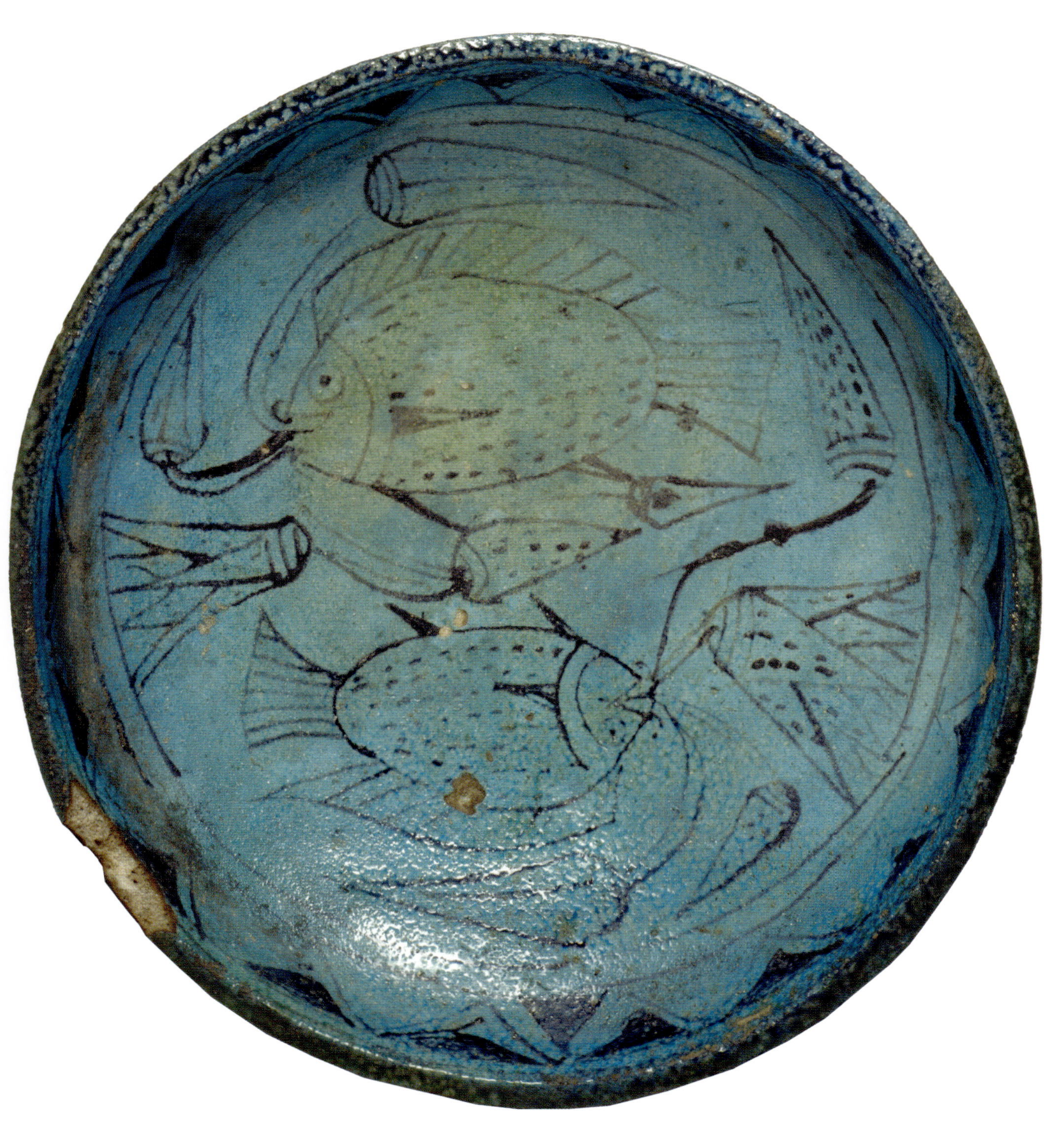

22

Lidded vessel

Probably from Tuna el-Gebel

Glazed faience; 19 x 11.1 x 9.8 cm (7 1/2 x 4 3/8 x 3 13/16 in.)

Eighteenth Dynasty, ca. 1400–1300 B.C.

Provenance: William MacGregor, Tamworth, Staffordshire; sale, London, Sotheby, Wilkinson & Hodge, 26–29 June and 4–6 July 1922; Dikran Kelekian, New York / Paris, 1922–23; Henry Walters, 1923; Walters Art Museum, by bequest, 1931 (48.426a, b)

This finely modeled faience lidded vessel imitates basketry.[1] It was hand-modeled over a form; when the paste was almost dry, the artisan carved out the surface. The domed lid would have been secured to the vessel by string threaded in a decorative net pattern through holes pierced in the faience. The lively painted decoration, executed in freehand style, was applied before firing. It may have been added by another artist, a common practice in traditional Egyptian workshop production, which was highly specialized. The lid is divided into four sections, inscribed with jackal-like animals (possibly allusions to Anubis) and triangles of uncertain meaning. The body is decorated with vegetal imagery (floral sprays and branches), rosettes, triangles, and animals. The presence of lotuses and jackals would suggest that the vessel had a funerary function.

Especially during the New Kingdom, elaborate objects in faience were produced to mimic other media, such as woven baskets, wood, stone, or bronze. This vessel is the finest of three known examples of faience baskets.[2] Faience workshops were probably in operation from the fourth millennium B.C. but little is known about where they were located or how they were organized. Nor have any visual records of faience production survived, as they have for other crafts; this may be due to the medium's association with magic and religion.[3]

The volume of material found at Tuna el-Gebel, the cemetery for Hermopolis, and the high quality of the ware suggest that it was an important manufacturing center during the New Kingdom. This basket may well have originated from this site, as did a lidded basket of lesser quality in the Eton Collection, purchased in the nineteenth century.[4]

The elaborate closure suggests that the container held valuable or particularly cherished objects, such as cosmetics, jewelry, or charms.

CH

Bibliography

Wallis 1900, pl. 14; Burlington Fine Arts Club 1921, 85, no. 16; MacGregor Collection 1922, 37, no. 270, pl. VIII; McDonald 1982, 151, no. 157; Rogers 1982; Friedman 1998, 120, 218, no. 92.

Notes

1. McDonald 1982.
2. Friedman 1998, 218 no. 92.
3. Friedman 1998, 17.
4. Spurr, Reeves, and Quirke 1999, 3–37, nos. 47 and 48 (Eton College, Myers Collection, ECM 845 and 494).

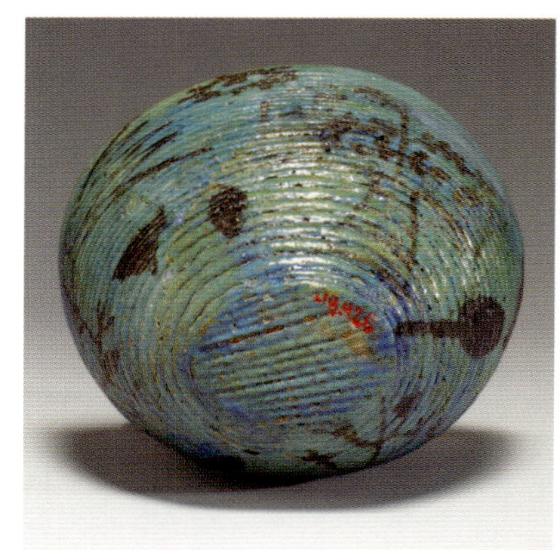

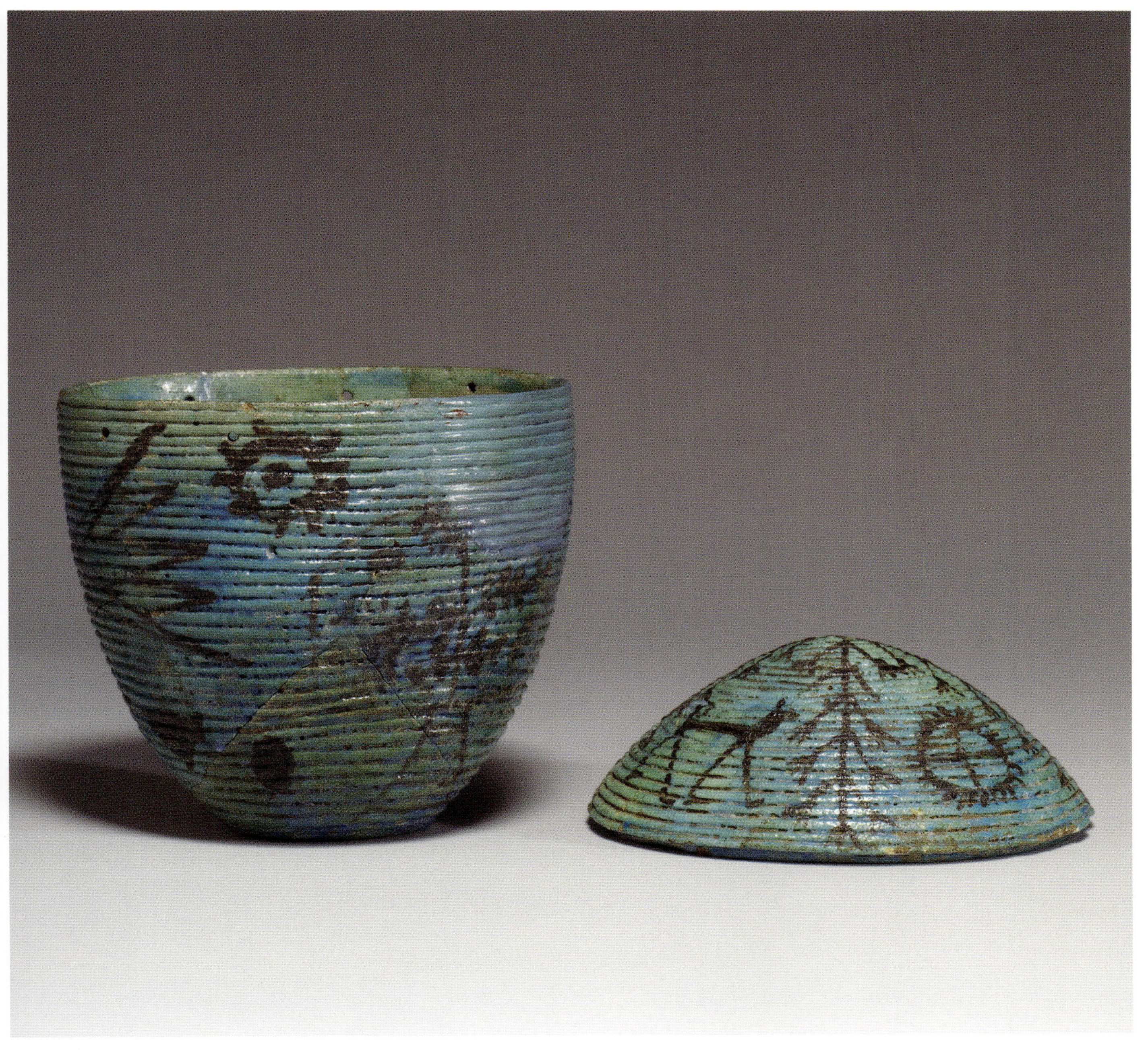

23a, 23b

Two glass vessels

Probably from Western Thebes

Polychrome glass; 23a (47.31): height 11.4 cm (4 7/16 in.), width, including handles 7.8 cm (3 in.), diameter 5.9 cm (2 3/8 in.); 23 b (47.32): height 8.2 cm (3 1/4 in.), width, including handles 5.6 (2 1/4 in.), diameter 4.8 cm (1 15/16 in.)

Both Eighteenth Dynasty, ca. 1450–1350 B.C.

Provenance: 23a (47.31): Dikran Kelekian, New York / Paris; Henry Walters, 1912; Walters Art Museum, by bequest; 23b (47.32): Henry Walters, before 1931; Walters Art Museum, by bequest, 1931

Although the manufacture of faience can be traced back to the predynastic period (the fourth millennium B.C.), the production of true glass did not emerge in Egypt until the early Eighteenth Dynasty,[1] around 1500 B.C. Recent excavations and technical analysis support the hypothesis that the technology of glassmaking was imported from western Asia.[2] Both raw glass, in the form of large ingots, and finished vessels were likely imported at an early stage, as were the artisans themselves. Within a short time, however, the Egyptians had developed a highly sophisticated industry that flourished under Amenhotep III (1390–1352 B.C.) and his successor, Akhenaten (1352–1336 B.C.). Polychrome glass seems to have been particularly esteemed by the court; large numbers of vessels have been found in the tombs of Eighteenth Dynasty pharaohs. The contents of many glass flasks—fragrant essences dissolved in plant-based oils—confirm their status as objects of high luxury.

In addition to its use in jewelry, amulets, inlays, and architectural decoration, glass was used for vessels, particularly distinctively shaped perfume bottles. The two most common shapes take their names from specific types of Greek pottery: *amphoriskos* ("little amphora") and *krateriskos* ("little krater"). The Walters *amphoriskos* (23a), broad-shouldered with a rounded base, has an opaque white ground; the *krateriskos* (23b) has a cobalt blue body decorated with white, yellow and light blue bands, two horizontal handles, applied to the shoulder, and a wide foot. Both are core-formed vessels; the technology of blown glass was as yet unknown.[3] The molten mass, composed of silica and natron (heated to a temperature of around 1000°–1150° C), was wrapped around a clay or dung core that was later removed. Decorative bands were formed by pressing threads of colored glass onto the molten surface; combing the threads with a metal tool created decorative patterns.

MS

Bibliography

23a (47.31): Burlington Fine Arts Club 1895, 107, no. 10; Hilton-Price 1897, 147, no. 1483 (ill.); Nolte 1968, 139, pl. 30.13; Walters Art Gallery 1982, no. 14; *23b (47.32)*: Froehner 1903, pl. XXIII, 3; Nolte 1968, 83, pl. III, 3; Kozloff and Bryan 1992, 385, no. 93.

Notes

1. Lilyquist and Brill 1993.
2. Oppenheim et al. 1973, 259–66.
3. Stern and Schlick-Nolte 1994, 130, no. 5; Shaw and Nicholson 1995, 112–13.

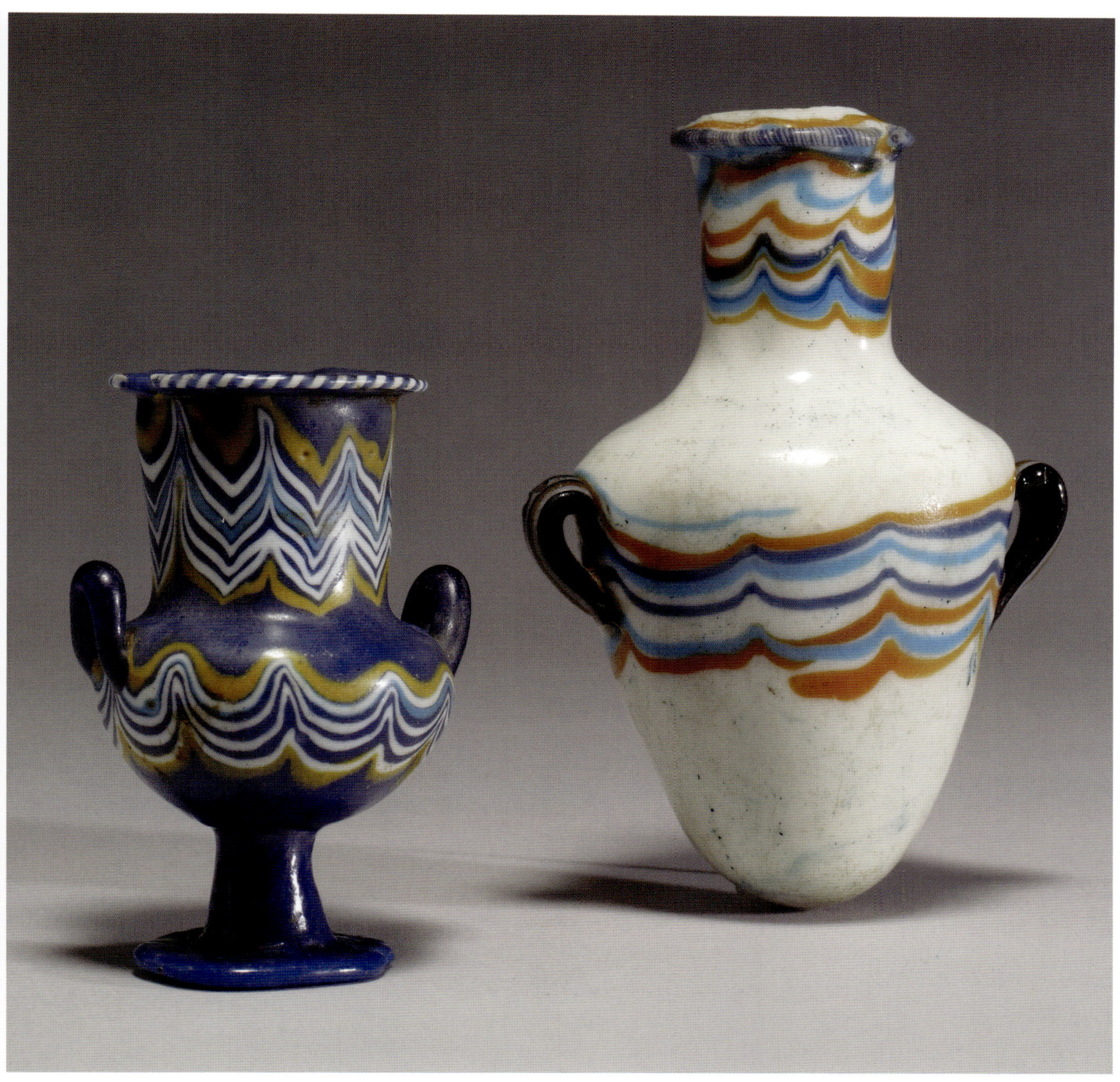

24

Priest Teti with his parents

Possibly from Memphis

Granodiorite; 54.6 x 35 x 18.5 cm (21 ½ x 13 ¾ x 7 ¼ in.)

Eighteenth Dynasty, ca. 1390 B.C.

Provenance: Dikran Kelekian, New York/Paris; Henry Walters, 1926; Walters Art Museum, by bequest, 1931 (22.163)

The familiar conventions of Egyptian sculptural art are stretched to a near-breaking point in this work of the Eighteenth Dynasty. Neither "statue" nor "relief" can describe this family group of Teti and his parents. Rather, the highly unusual leaning position of the father on the left results from an attempt not to flatten all three figures against the back pillar but instead to create a three-dimensional curve around the surface of the monument.[1] The back support, extended above Teti's head, and the angle of the inscriptions right and left suggest that it terminated in a rounded or sharpened point. The overall height of the sculpture would have approached 130 centimeters (50 inches); as a monument, it would have been quite imposing, since the curvature indicates that it was placed to be seen both for its decoration and its rounded hill shape.

A precise date for the sculpture may be arrived at by studying its physical traits. The faces are most similar to those of the square-chinned portraits of Amenhotep II (1427–1400 B.C.) and his son Thutmose IV (1400–1390 B.C.). The almond-shaped eyes accord more comfortably with the prevailing artistic styles in the latter's reign and that of his son Amenhotep III (1390–1352 B.C.). It is finally the heavy upper-body type of the male figures that lends most support to a date in the reign of Thutmose IV, for during the reign of Amenhotep III this athletic type was less in fashion.[2] We may thus be confident that Teti was active in the very early fourteenth century B.C. Teti's inscription requests that he be fed from the offering table of the god of Memphis, Ptah, also called "he who is south of his wall," a reference to the wall of Memphis itself.[3] Granodiorite was often used for temple statues in the Eighteenth Dynasty, so this monument perhaps once stood in the Ptah precinct, but its association with a tomb is also possible.

Teti carries a single title that is rather unusual and may be translated as "pure priest of the tomb or the cemetery," although an association with the Ptah temple itself has also been suggested.[4] Teti's father, shown smaller than he, is termed "dignitary and priest" but, due to breakage, without name or temple assignment. Teti's mother, equally small, is named "the Mistress of the House, Maket." The parent figures each extend an arm behind Teti's kilt, in a gesture both of familial attachment, typical of Thutmoside-era group statues, and of protection toward their son. Teti's gesture, with outstretched arms, is a prayerful stance, as if he eternally praises god.

The unusual rounded nature of this sculpture may be intended to evoke the nearby cemeteries of Saqqara, particularly that of Teti's namesake, King Teti of the Sixth Dynasty (2345–2323 B.C.). The stone shape recalls the pyramids of the great royal tombs and also the original round-topped *benben* stone in the sun god's home city. Shown eternally emerging from the solar hill, Teti's image embodies his role as priest, constantly available to his family and all those at rest in the cemetery.

BB

Bibliography

Steindorff 1946a, 28, no. 49, pl. XII; Vandier 1958, 343; Vernus 1969, 93–101; Vernus 1971, 7–9.

Notes

1. The Egyptian artistic canon relied strongly on frontality as an organizing principle, but here, although the figure of Teti is nearly frontal and flat against the stone, the figures of the father and mother or wife are not, due to their adaptation to the stone surface. For general principles of Egyptian art, see Robins 2000. For an in-depth discussion, see Schäfer (ed. Baines) 1986.

2. Bryan 1987, 3–20, for the facial features and eye types of the period. For the body type, see Bryan 1990, 65–80.

3. Herman Te Velde (1982, 1177–80), notes that the epithet places the temple of Ptah south of the city of Memphis. Jaromír Málek (1997, 90–101), suggests that the original "white walls" of Memphis were located near Abusir, with Ptah's sanctuary south of it.

4. Violaine Chauvet (1999, unpublished entry for the Walters Art Museum Egyptian collection reinstallation project) reinterpreted Vernus's 1969 discussion of the title to mean "pure priest of the cemetery," rather than of the "roofed part of a temple." The connection with the Teti cemetery at Saqqara may be highly appropriate to this Teti's priestly service.

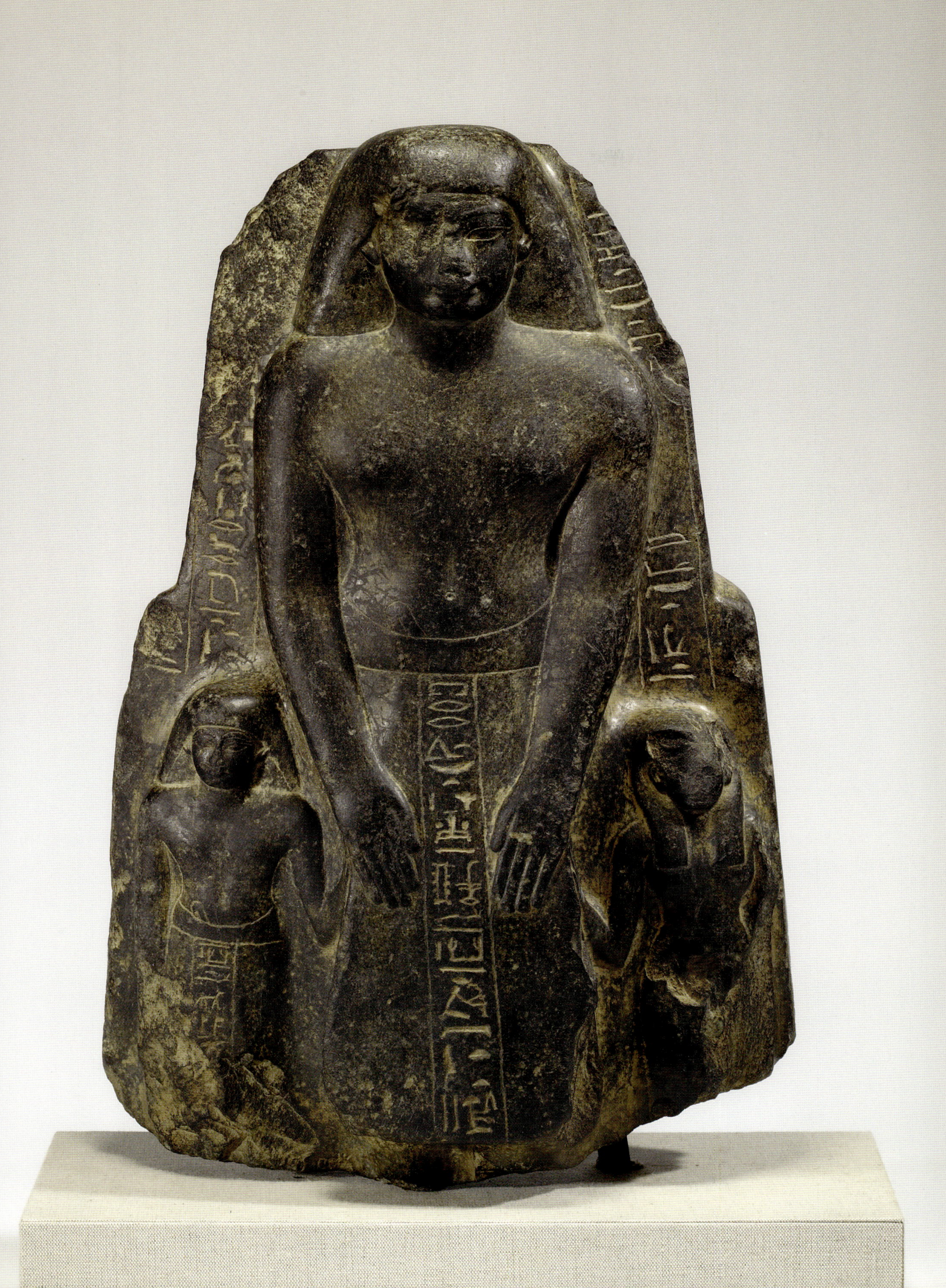

25

Head of Amenhotep III

Probably from Thebes

Granodiorite; 43.2 x 28.6 x 32 cm (17 x 11 1/4 x 12 5/8 in.)

Eighteenth Dynasty, ca. 1360 B.C.

Provenance: Dikran Kelekian, New York/Paris; Henry Walters, 1923; Walters Art Museum, by bequest, 1931 (22.107)

This head from a statue represents a king identified as Amenhotep III (1390–1352 B.C.). Yet the image is more complex than this, and the face that we now view also represents Ramesses II (1279–1213 B.C.). A careful observer will notice some lighter coloration around the eyes that resulted from recarving without polishing of the finish on the original surface. The round face has a stubby chin and a damaged but visible mouth with a raised line around the thick and pursed lips. These features are hallmarks of the face of Amenhotep III, for whom dozens of granodiorite statues were made in Thebes during the latter part of his reign.[1] Ramesses II and his son Merenptah (1213–1203 B.C.) reused the statuary of Amenhotep III in a number of locations, but most particularly at Luxor Temple and at their mortuary temples, both of which were adjacent to that of Amenhotep III.[2] The original eyelids of Amenhotep III were carved to show a surface that rounded outward above the eyes, while those of Ramesses II were normally made to show a hollowed lid area. In addition, until the last reign of the Eighteenth Dynasty, kings did not have the traditional hieroglyphic cosmetic lines, as here, when they wore this type of crown.[3] The rough marks and profile views indicate that the area from the top of the browband to the bottom of the eyes was cut back and recarved with hollowed lids and new eyebrows and cosmetic bands. The face was thereby brought closely into connection with original images of Ramesses II. Two lines were also added on the neck, a feature introduced into statuary during the reign of Akhenaten (1352–1336 B.C.).

The king is wearing the "blue crown," so called because of its frequent coloration in ancient depictions. The actual name of this crown in ancient Egyptian was the *khepresh*, and its helmetlike shape may not be altogether coincidental. Kings wore this headgear in nearly every military representation from the Eighteenth Dynasty onward, but they might also wear it whenever their role as earthly representative of the gods was to be understood, in contrast to their more sacred position among the gods themselves.[4] At present it is not possible to be certain of the king's pose, but examples of the king striding, kneeling for coronation, and enthroned (only after the reign of Amenhotep III) are known for rulers wearing this crown.

BB

Bibliography

Steindorff 1946a, 48, no. 139, pl. XX; Sourouzian 1989, 170–71; Bryan 2007, 154–56, figs. 7 and 8.

Notes

1. Kozloff and Bryan 1992, 128, for the features of Amenhotep III; 172–75, for marks of recutting for Ramesses II.
2. Sourouzian 1989, 159–72, for examples of reuse of Amenhotep III's statuary.
3. Hardwick 2003, 117–41.
4. Bryan 2007, 156–58.

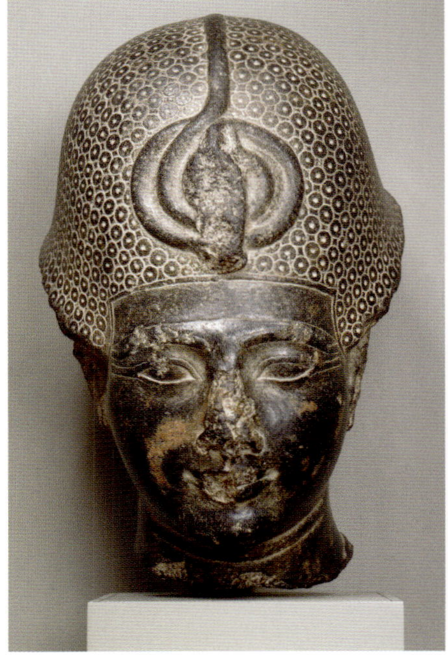

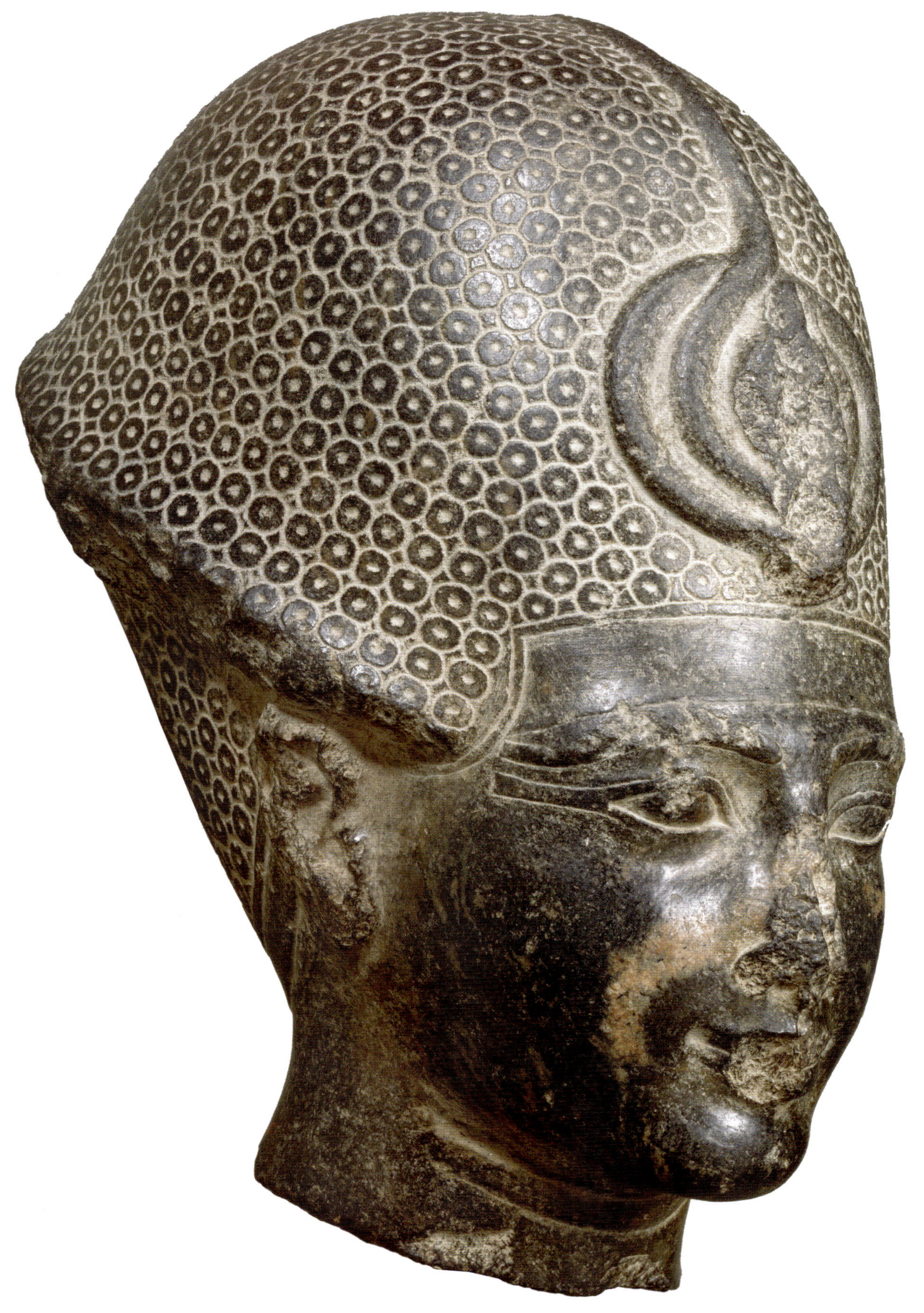

26a, 26b

Statues of Sakhmet

Karnak, temple of Mut

Granodiorite; 26a (IL.2001.1.1): 206 x 53 x 98 cm (91 1/8 x 20 7/8 x 38 9/16); 26b (IL.2001.1.2): 187 x 48 x 102 cm (73 5/8 x 18 7/8 x 40 3/16 in.)

Eighteenth Dynasty, reign of Amenhotep III, ca. 1380–1360 B.C.

Provenance: British Museum, London (EA 63 and EA 37); long-term loans to the Walters Art Museum (IL.2001.1.1 and IL.2001.1.2).[1]

Sakhmet (literally: "the powerful one") was one of several protective goddesses with ferocious attributes that gave them particular power to ward off danger and evil.[2] Sakhmet could both visit and avert catastrophes such as wars, storms, or plagues. She was also linked to the myth of the fire-spitting eye of the sun god Re, punishing humanity for its rebellion. As daughter of Re, and divine consort of the god Ptah in the Lower Egyptian city of Memphis, she was one of the most important goddesses in the Egyptian pantheon. But Sakhmet was a prominent deity in Thebes as well, where Amun emerged as the preeminent god of the pantheon during the New Kingdom. With his ascent the members of his divine family were also brought into focus, and the role of Amun's spouse in particular had to be redefined. Mut became his divine consort, and it is likely that the motherhood and sexuality aspect was taken over from the royal patroness Hathor. For the aspect of warding evil Sakhmet was integrated into the Mut concept. She rose to particular prominence under Amenhotep III, who commissioned more than seven hundred life-size statues for the Theban temples,[3] many of them for his mortuary temple at Western Thebes and for the precinct of the Mut temple at Karnak. The enormous scale of the commission raises myriad questions as to what provoked it: was Amenhotep seeking succor for his own illness or for an epidemic among his people?

The statues, depicting the goddess with the body of a human female and the head of a lioness, either seated or standing, conform to a standardized iconography. She wears an ankle-length, close-fitting dress, usually with rosettes on the breast, and a long wig that joins the leonine head to the female body. She is adorned with anklets, bracelets, and a broad collar necklace; the seated form holds an *ankh* sign in her left hand. The presence of a male lion's mane symbolizes the leonine character in general, not a gender-specific aspect.

The two Sakhmet statues exhibited at the Walters are of the seated type. Both seats have a short backrest and an emblem on their sides symbolizing the union of Upper and Lower Egypt. The statue without a sun disk (26b) preserves the original inscription, carefully incised on the front of the seats beside the goddess's lower legs. A rectangular border that transitions into the hieroglyphic sign for "sky" at the upper end frames the inscription. The text to her right side reads:

> Perfect God, Lord of Joy, Lord of the Two Lands: Neb-maat-Re, beloved of Sakhmet, Lady of Seheret,[4] who may give life.

The text to her left reads:

> Beloved Son of Re, [son] of his body: Amenhotep, ruler of Thebes, beloved of Sakhmet, Lady of Seheret, who may give life.

The name Amenhotep was erased under the reign of Akhenaten, when the worship of Amun was suppressed, and restored in the late Eighteenth or early Nineteenth Dynasty.

The second Sakhmet (26a) has a sun disk on her head. It was broken off in antiquity and repositioned;[5] the erect cobra, the *uraeus*, that one would expect to see above the forehead, is lost.

The inscription of the second statue was usurped by Sheshonq I, first king of the Twenty-second Dynasty (945–924 B.C.). The stonemasons effaced the original text in its entirety, inserting the birth and throne name of the king. Next to the goddess's right leg, the inscription reads:

> Perfect God, Lord of the Two Lands: Hedj-kheper-Re, setep-en-Re

and to the left:

> Son of Re, Lord of the Crowns: Sheshonq, beloved of Amun.

RS

Bibliography

26a (IL.2001.1.1 [EA 63]): Porter and Moss 1994, 290 with further references; *26b (IL.2001.1.2 [EA 37])*: Gauthier 1920, 188; Porter and Moss 1994, 265 with further references.

Notes

1. No. 26a (IL.2001.1.1 [EA 63]) was purchased by the British Museum from the Henry Salt collection in 1823. The provenance of no. 26b (IL.2001.1.2 [EA 37]) is less certain: it may have been among the group of Egyptian antiquities that were confiscated from the defeated French army of Napoleon in 1801 by the British army, or purchased from the Henry Salt collection in 1823 together with its pendant, or have come from the Belmore Collection in 1857; see Gauthier 1920, 177–82.
2. For the nature and meaning of the goddess Sakhmet, see Germond 1981, 188, no. 32.
3. No convincing estimates have yet been advanced for the total number of statues in the various temples at Thebes. Recently discovered Sakhmet figures are surveyed by Hourig Sourouzian in *Egyptian Archaeology* 29 (2006): 21–24.
4. For the epithet, see Gauthier 1920, 188.
5. Whether the sun disk is original to this piece or whether it belonged to another Sakhmet statue is uncertain.

Photo © The Trustees of the British Museum

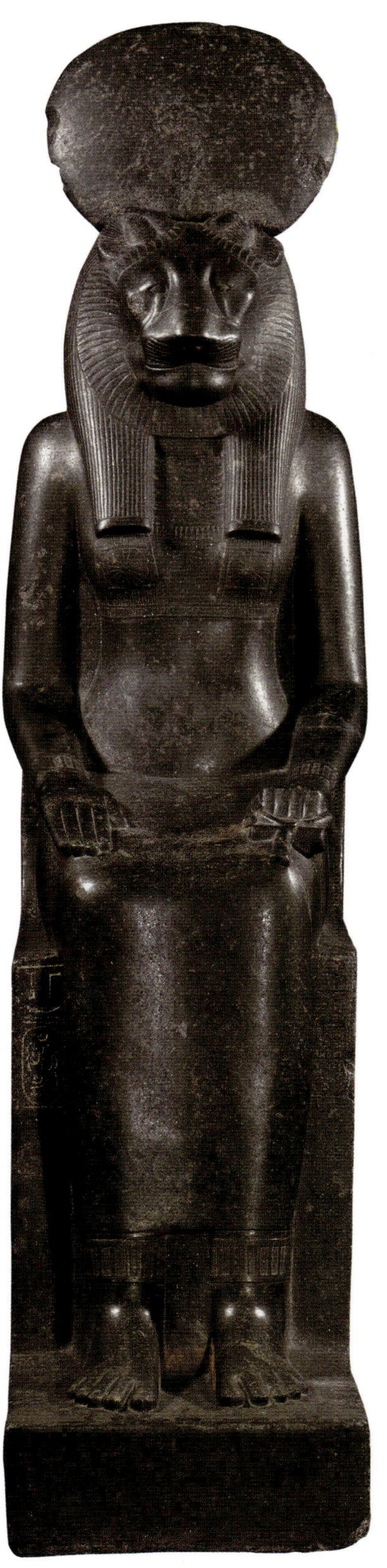

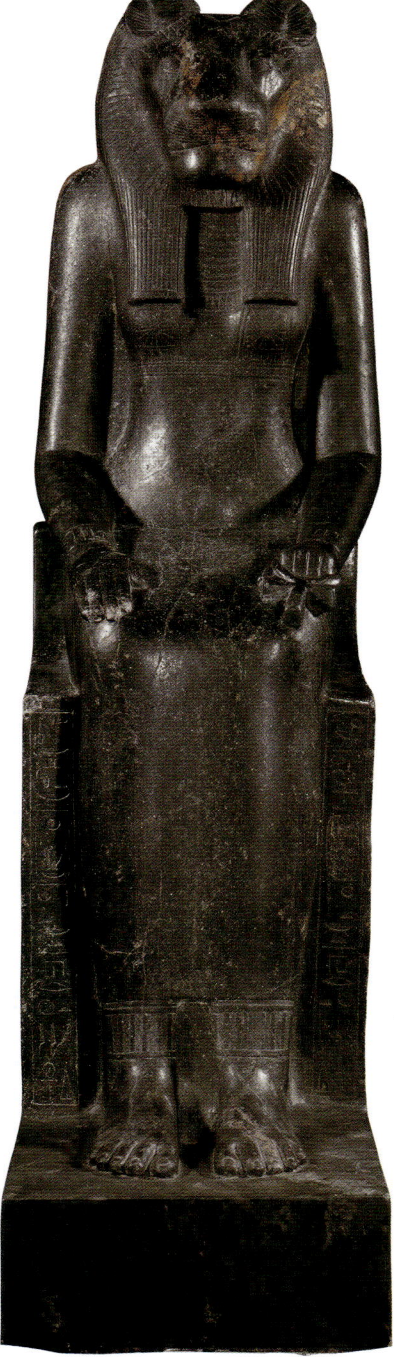

27

Block statuette of Kha-em-Waset

Probably from Karnak

Black serpentine; 8.6 x 4.1 x 6.1 cm (3 3/8 x 1 5/8 x 2 3/8 in.)

Eighteenth Dynasty, reign of Amenhotep III, ca. 1370–1360 B.C.

Provenance: Dikran Kelekian, New York / Paris; Henry Walters, before 1931; Walters Art Museum, by bequest, 1931 (22.68)

Egyptian block, or cuboidal, statues depict a person (usually a man; more rarely a woman)[1] in a specific squatting position: the knees drawn up in front of the chest and the arms crossed and resting on the knees. This compact statue-type emerged in the early Twelfth Dynasty to represent a male attending the daily rituals for a deity or king, the squatting pose and the crossed arms being signs of respect. Most of these statues were placed in temples, to ensure provisions, both material and spiritual, in this world and the afterlife.[2] The idea of representing an honored person, with personal access to the king or god, emerged in the New Kingdom, and the block statue became one of the most popular statue types, remaining in use until the Greco-Roman Period.

During the Twenty-second Dynasty, a special hieroglyphic character depicting a block statue was introduced, which illuminates the meaning of the statue type. This character, attached to the term *hesiu* ("the praised one"), refers both to a person and to his or her representation.

This well-preserved statuette represents Kha-em-Waset: the "chief of works in the temple of Amun" and "fan-bearer of the troop 'The Recruits Are Perfect'"[3] He is seated on a small rectangular base and supported by a neck-high back pillar. His body forms are well defined; the right arm crosses the left, the hands are outstretched on the knees, and the feet protrude under the seam of the ankle-length kilt. He wears a short beard and a tripartite wig (waved at the top and curly at the bottom) that leaves the earlobes uncovered.

The base and back pillar, as well as the front of the kilt, are inscribed. The text contains a royal offering formula for Amun-Re, names Kha-em-Waset as the beneficiary, and praises him as "the excellent unique one, of good character, friendly, not negligent and evasive." The characters on his right shoulder name the "Temple of Amun."

The dating of the statuette is based on iconographic and stylistic criteria. Block statues with well-modeled body forms, a small seat and a back pillar came into use in the middle of the Eighteenth Dynasty, the same period when elaborate tripartite wigs became popular. However, the best dating criterion may be the style of the statuette's facial features, which closely follow the model of Amenhotep III.

The statue probably comes from the temple of Amun-Re at Karnak, where it would have been placed, together with other small statuettes, on an offering platform in the court or in the temple precinct.[4] The quality of the workmanship, as well as Kha-em-Waset's title, suggests that the statuette might have been produced in one of the temple's workshops.

RS

Bibliography

Steindorff 1946a, 44, no. 121, pl. 26; Schulz 1992, 59, pl. 3c; Porter and Moss, ed. Málek, Magee, and Miles, 2008, 600, no. 801-643-050; Schulz 2008, 216–22.

Notes

1. See Schulz 1992, 779–82.
2. See Schulz 1992, 783–85.
3. The figure's left elbow is missing; there are some losses to the corners of the base and minor damage to the body.
4. Schulz 2008, 219.

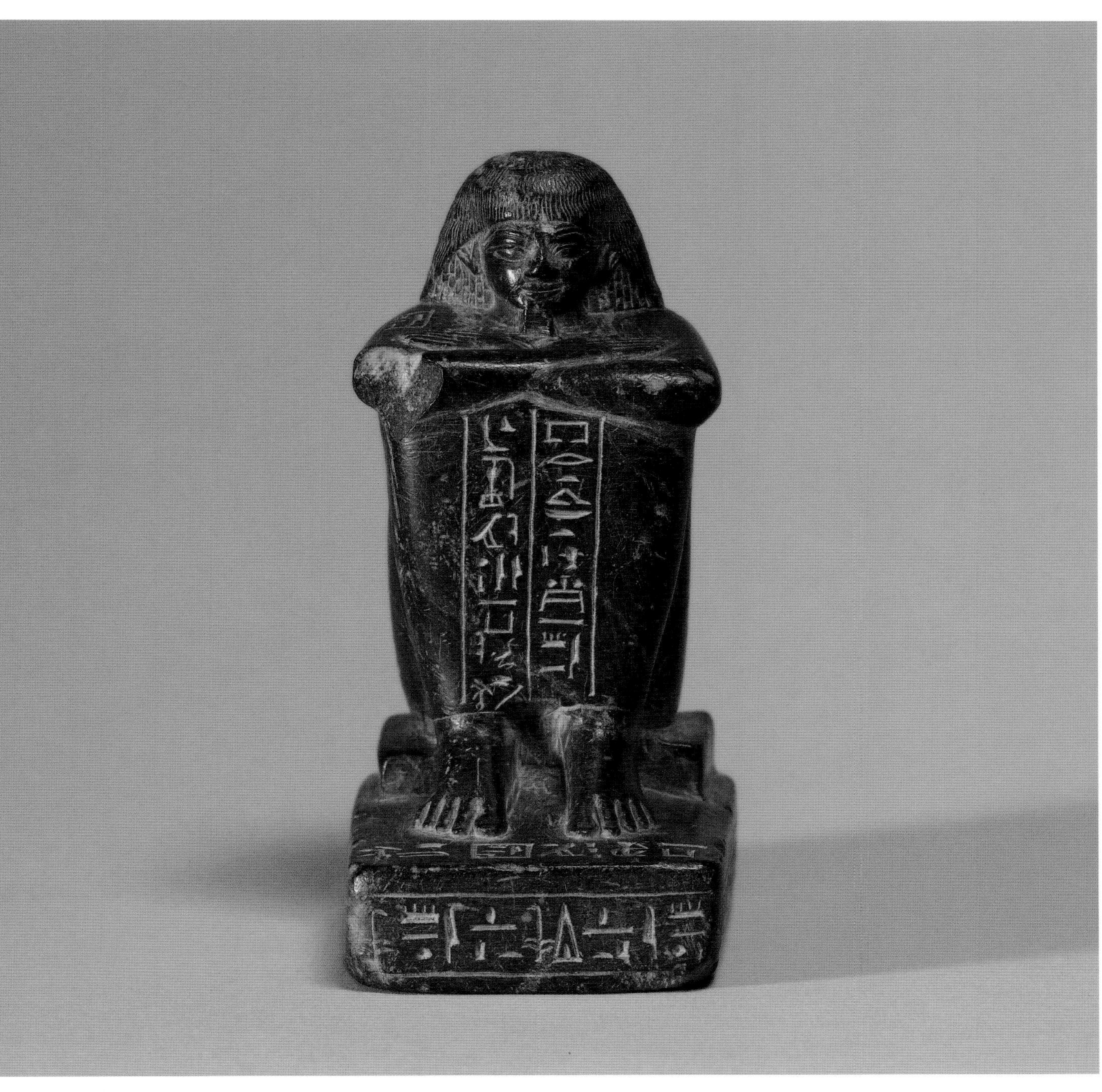

28

Commemorative scarab of Amenhotep III

Steatite, traces of glaze; 8.5 x 5.6 x 3.8 cm (3 3/8 x 2 3/16 x 1 9/16 in.)
Eighteenth Dynasty, ca. 1380 B.C.
Provenance: Dikran Kelekian, New York / Paris; Henry Walters, 1914; Walters Art Museum, by bequest, 1931 (42.206)

The reign of Amenhotep III (1390–1352 B.C.) was the apogee of Egypt's political efficacy, at home and abroad. One of the more remarkable commemorative acts undertaken on Amenhotep's behalf was the production and distribution of a series of large scarabs, of which more than two hundred have been found—some at a great distance from his capital: as far as Soleb (Nubia) to the south and Ras Shamra (Syria) to the northeast.[1] The texts on the bases of these scarabs record five milestones in the first decade of his reign: the lion hunt of Year 2; a wild bull hunt in the same year; Amenhotep's marriage to Queen Tiye (in an unspecified year); the embassy of Gilukhepa, a princess from the kingdom of Mittani in northern Mesopotamia, in Year 10; and the building of a lake for Queen Tiye in Year 11.

The purpose of these scarabs and the circumstances of their issuance are still debated. Most Egyptologists maintain that the scarabs were issued sequentially in or soon after the year that they record, but others argue that they were issued collectively much later. Why the practice abruptly ceased at Year 11 and why it was not revived by other New Kingdom rulers remains unclear. The distinct differences in quality,[2] iconography, and style of the scarabs seem to support the argument that they were manufactured in several workshops.

This scarab is one of the "marriage scarabs," in number the second most common of the group after the "lion hunt scarabs." On the base, following Amenhotep's titles, ten lines read:

> The great royal wife, Tiye, may she live. The name of her father is Yuya, the name of her mother is Tjuiu. She is the wife of a mighty king; the southern border at Karoy, the northern border at Naharina.

The texts on the commemorative scarabs are not uniform, but all name the king's wife, underscoring the important role she played in the royal dogma as formulated by Amenhotep III. Here, in an entirely unique instance, even the parents of the queen are explicitly named, leaving no doubt that Tiye was of nonroyal origin. The pharaoh's decision to grant a tomb in the Valley of the Kings to his wife's parents reflects Tiye's unprecedented position in the court. This new power constellation was most likely the true import of these scarabs, distributed in the hundreds—perhaps even thousands—among the bureaucracy of the state.

MS

Bibliography

Blankenberg van Delden 1969, 40, no. A 28, pl. V; Schulz and Seidel 2007, 40–42, no. 23, pl. 3.

Notes

1. Kozloff and Bryan 1992, 67–72; Gundlach 2002, 31–46; Baines 2003, 29–43.
2. Compare, for example, Wiese 2001, 101, no. 62.

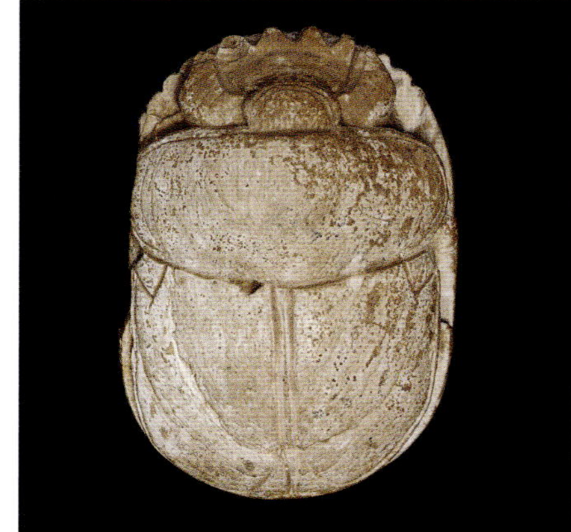

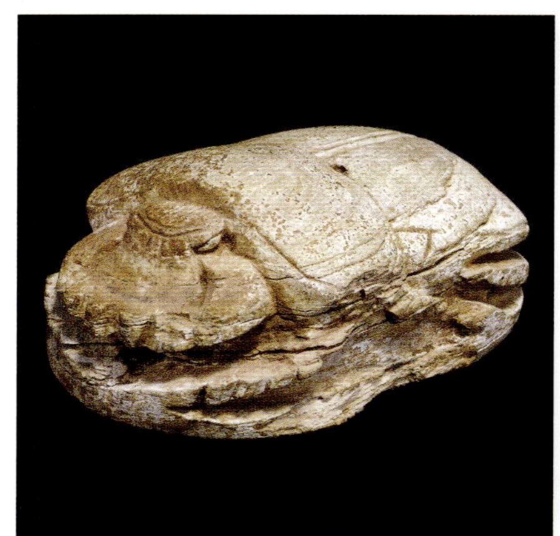

29

Jar with names of Amenhotep III and Queen Tiye

Faience, dark blue glaze; height 7.2 cm (2 13/16 in.); diameter 5.8 cm (2 5/16 in.)
Eighteenth Dynasty, ca. 1370 B.C.
Provenance: Dikran Kelekian, New York / Paris; Henry Walters, 1923;
Walters Art Museum (48.403)

His contemporaries and successors deemed Amenhotep III's reign of nearly forty years to be Egypt's artistic zenith. The nation's economic prosperity and stable political conditions created a climate for works of exquisite quality, ranging from colossal statues to the smallest amulets. In the medium of faience, craftsmen introduced new colors and glazing techniques to create objects of previously unseen beauty and brilliance.[1] Indeed, some shades of blue and green are specifically associated with the time of Amenhotep III and the subsequent Amarna period.[2] This small ointment jar with its pear-shaped body exemplifies one of the most common vessel types of the New Kingdom, executed in various media in addition to faience, including stone, clay, painted wood, and glass. Such ointment jars typically have a flat bottom (or shallow base) and a large dishlike lip. The lid of this jar has not survived, but other examples indicate that it would have been round and flat. A dark residue inside the vessel is probably the remains of a scented ointment.

The rich dark blue glaze was achieved by soaking the faience paste in a cobalt pigment; the glossy finish and saturated color might be due to the mixture of crushed glass powder into the paste. The rectangular inscription field shows perfectly inlaid hieroglyphs in a light blue color (a copper oxide pigment). The fusion of the inlays and the vessel's body was an exacting process, of which only the most experienced artists would have been capable. The short inscription contains the names of Amenhotep III and his wife, Queen Tiye:

> Perfect god, Neb-maat-Re, son of Re, Amenhotep-Ruler of Thebes, may he live like Re; Royal wife, Tiye, may she live.

MS

Bibliography

Burlington Fine Arts Club 1922, 91, no. 43, pl. XLII.

Notes

1. Friedman 1998, 183, no. 23; 261, no. 195.
2. Caubet and Pierrat-Bonnefois 2005, 73–79.

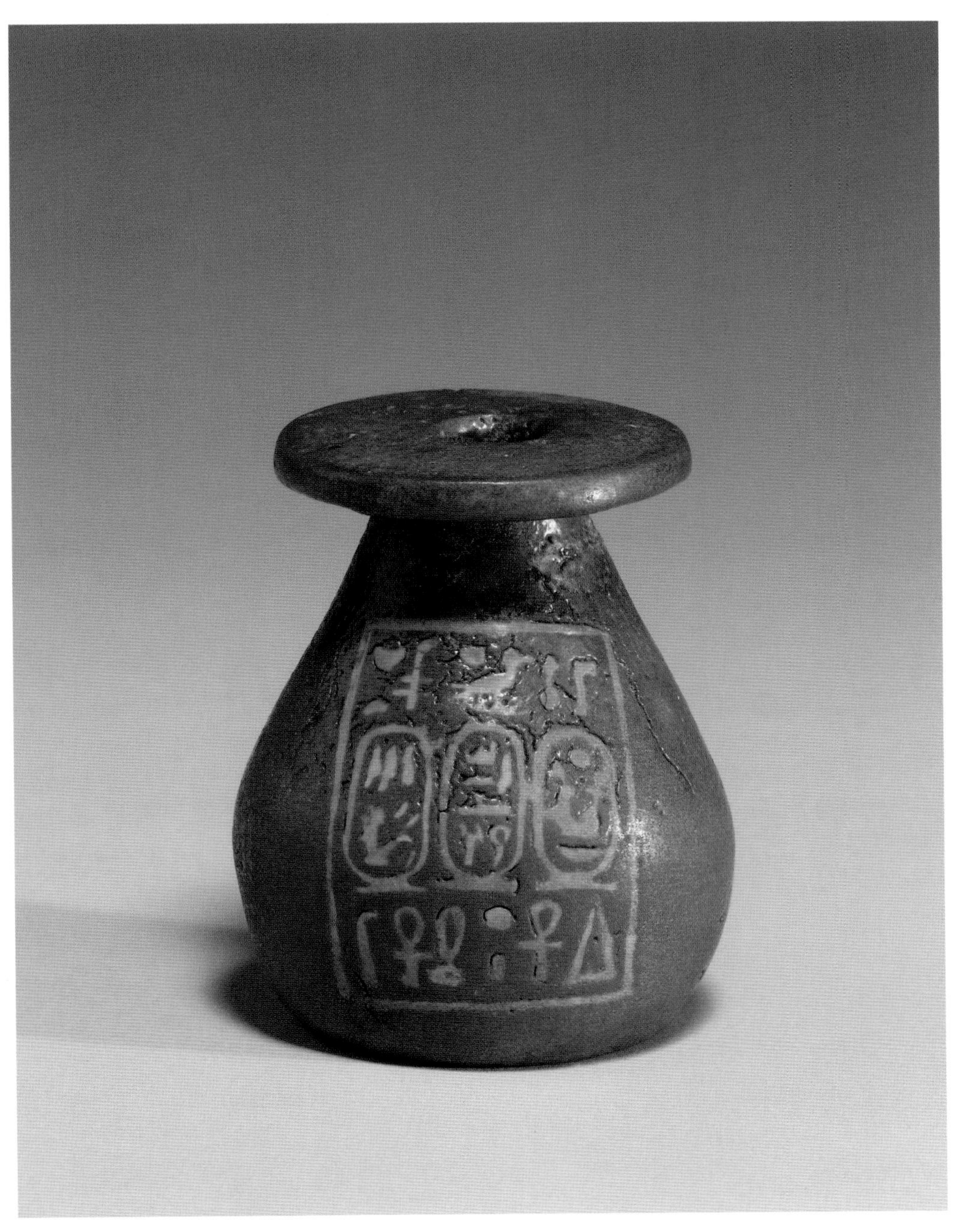

30

Standing Amarna king

Said to be from Medinet Gurob

Bronze; 10.4 x 2.7 x 1.9 cm (4 1/8 x 1 1/16 x 3/4 in.)

Eighteenth Dynasty, ca. 1345 B.C.

Provenance: Henry Walters, 1927; Walters Art Museum, by bequest, 1931 (54.406)

This small and somewhat ungainly figure of a king is indicative of that remarkable period of religious revolution when Akhenaten (1352–1336 B.C.) introduced the worship of his personal god, the Aten, the orb of the sun. Although the ruler represented in this tiny bronze image is not known, the details of dress and body confirm the dating. The so-called Nubian wig that slants from back to front was popular in this era, as was the pleated kilt that hugs the thighs and features a long front sash. The body type is also of the period, when the king's figure was deliberately elongated at the torso and enlarged in the chest and hip region. Most characteristic of all is the crescent shape of the navel, which narrows to a point at the bottom. The shape recalls one that naturally appears when a stomach is distended by plumpness and wrinkling, and the art of the Amarna era was above all naturalistic.[1] The figure's broad collar establishes a date for the work; such collars were not shown covering the shoulders until this precise epoch, when the fashion for draping the necklace onto the arms emerged. Numerous images of Amarna kings wearing this collar exhibit the same detail.[2]

The small bronze king is solid cast; while the arms and legs are poorly modeled, the necklace and kilt are carefully detailed. Study of this piece has demonstrated that the bronze was gilded; the present appearance of the statuette is much simpler than it would have been originally.[3]

The image of a golden king, standing with feet together, is particularly evocative of divinities and recipients of cultic offerings, since offering bearers were represented in striding rather than standing poses. The suggestion has been made that this small figure was part of a diverse group of votive offerings placed in a chapel at Medinet Gurob in the Faiyum oasis, where the family of King Amenhotep III (1390–1352 B.C.) and his widow, Queen Tiye, were worshiped after his death.[4] The statuette's provenance from a famous cache of small images found at Medinet Gurob was established early in the twentieth century, making this recent interpretation all the more plausible.[5]

BB

Bibliography

Steindorff 1946a, 47, no. 134, pl. XXII; Hill 2004, 171, no. 43; Hill and Schorsch 2007, 27–29, 203, no. 10, fig. 14.

Notes

1. Marianne Eaton-Krauss (1981, 245–64) and Marsha Hill (Hill and Schorsch 2007, 29) note the dating criterion of the navel.
2. See, for example, the paired statuettes of Akhenaten and Nefertiti from Amarna. Musée du Louvre, inv. no. E. 15593, in Aldred 1973, 63, figs. 39 and 40. Marsha Hill (2004, 171, no. 43) notes the breadth of the collar in the Walters bronze.
3. Hill 2004, 20, 171.
4. Hill and Schorsch 2007, 28–30; Arnold 1996, 27–28, 34–35. The existence of family cults at sites such as Malqata and Gurob was also suggested earlier with regard to the wooden "Gurob figures"; Bryan in Kozloff and Bryan 1992, 194.
5. Borchardt 1911, 16.

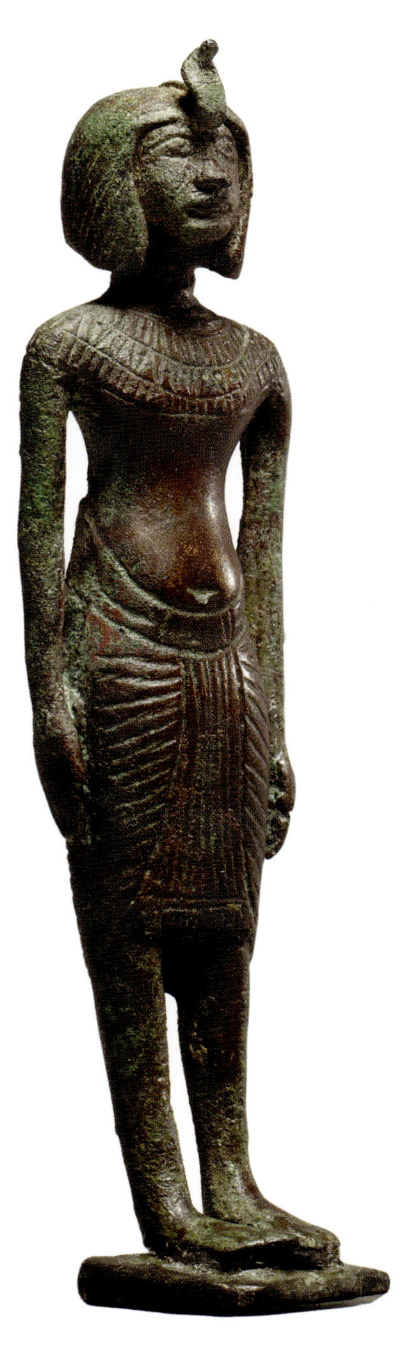

31

Fragment of a tomb relief

Saqqara, tomb of Horemheb

Limestone, painted; 41.9 x 36.7 cm (16 ½ x 4 ⅜ in.)

Eighteenth Dynasty, ca. 1325 B.C.

Provenance: Dikran Kelekian, New York / Paris; Henry Walters, 1925;

Walters Art Museum, by bequest, 1931 (22.128)

Deriving from one of the most beautifully sculpted New Kingdom tombs, this small relief exemplifies the best artwork of the era of Tutankhamun (1336–1327 B.C.).[1] A scribe of the general (and later king) Horemheb is shown standing behind a chair, which is represented on a scale far larger than he. Though the scribe's social status is obviously below that of the tomb's owner, his curling, echeloned wig and his upturned nose are characteristic features favored in the period immediately following Akhenaten's death in 1336, as is the somewhat slight body, which is punctuated by a spreading belly and hips.[2] The delicately carved and clearly defined pleating of the scribe's garments reveals that the body type is a deliberate fashion and not artistic ineptitude.

The bureaucrat grasps his far wrist with his near hand in a gesture of deference to the unseen tomb owner seated before him. Tucked under his near armpit is the man's scribal palette, which identifies his profession, despite the absence of any inscription. The vertical bar behind the official indicates the end of this composition, but these features are not the end of what we know about this highly interesting fragment, due to more recent archeological research.

The tomb of Horemheb was "lost" for over more than a century after many of its sculptures were transferred to museums in Europe and the United States. The work of British Egyptologist Geoffrey Martin resulted in the rediscovery of the tomb in 1975;[3] soon thereafter the excavators also found the exact original location of this relief fragment: in the doorway to the tomb's central statue niche.[4] The lower legs of the scribe (very likely named Sementawy, on the basis of his other appearances in the tomb) and the lion foot of Horemheb's chair are still to be seen in the tomb in Saqqara.[5] The fragment in the tomb also shows a pair of feet beside the chair, belonging most likely to a kneeling figure, perhaps Horemheb's wife. In two other places in the tomb, the scribe Sementawy stood behind his master, but in those instances his name and title had been changed to those of the scribe Ramose, who succeeded him. Whether that was the case here too is uncertain, but because of the research done to relocate the tomb of Horemheb, this small relief is now known to have been part of the small room in which the enduring cult for the tomb owner was centered.

BB

Bibliography

Steindorff 1946a, 79, no. 269, pl. XLVIII; Martin 1989, 121–22, pls. 131, 135; Ertman 2000, 112–19.

Notes

1. Donald Spanel (in Fazzini et al. 1989, no. 55) dates the tomb's construction after the reign of Akhenaten, despite the presence of the Aten's name. Jacobus van Dijk (1992) identifies several stages of decoration in the tomb.

2. Dorothea Arnold (1996, 121–25) discusses in great detail distinctions between Amarna and early post-Amarna facial elements, the latter particularly reasserting elements of the pre-Akhenaten era. See also Eaton-Krauss and Graefe 1985 for descriptions of specifically Tutankhamun-period style.

3. Martin 1975, 73–75.

4. Martin 1989, scene 113, pp. 121–22, pls. 131, 135.

5. Beatrice Arnst (1991, 5–30) analyzes scene types to identify several more reliefs from the Horemheb tomb.

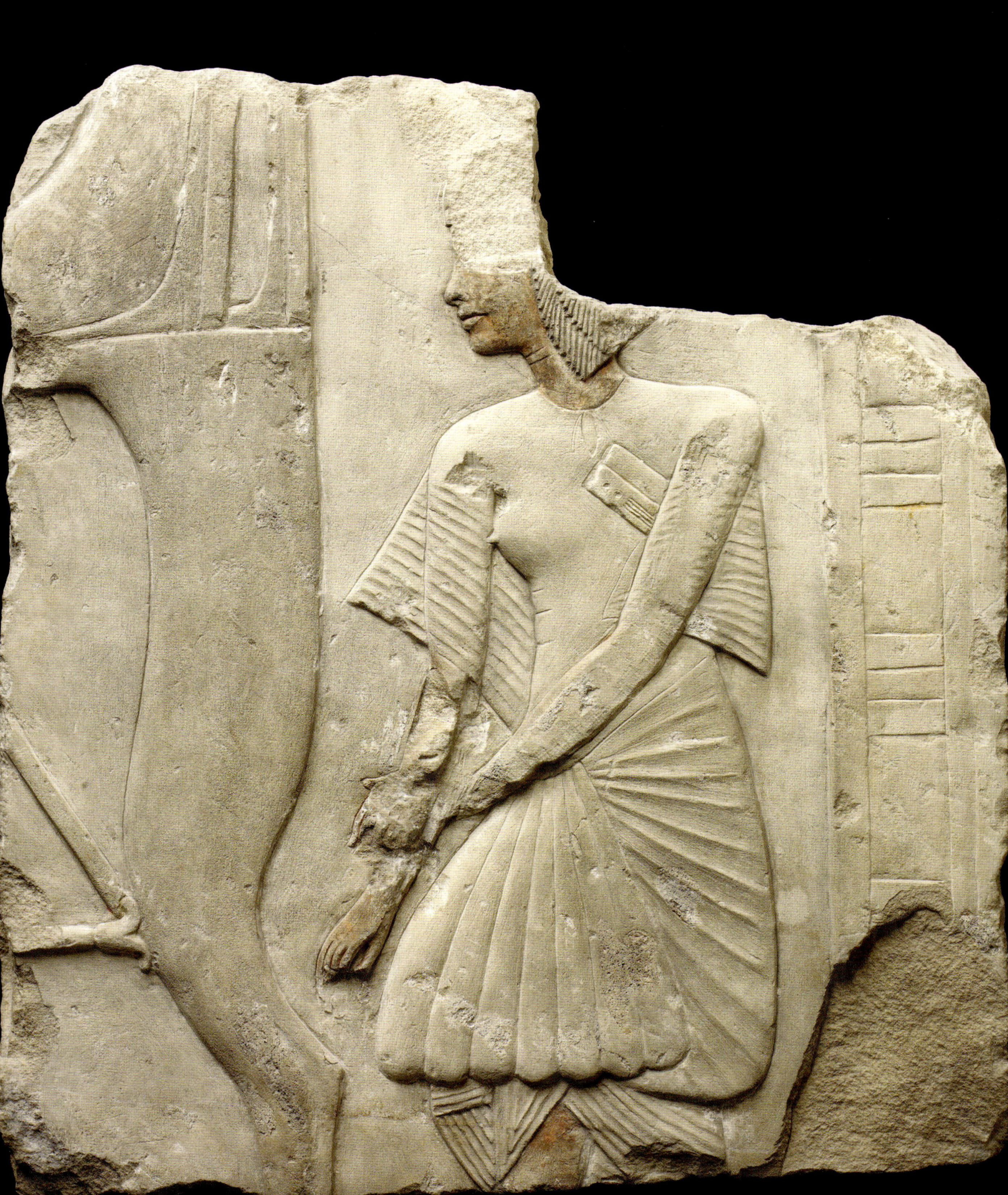

32

Male bust from a group statue

Probably from Memphis
Granodiorite, 43.5 x 37.5 x 18 cm (17 1/8 x 14 3/4 x 7 1/16 in.)
Late Eighteenth/Nineteenth Dynasty, ca. 1300–1290 B.C.
Provenance: Dikran Kelekian, New York / Paris; Henry Walters, 1929;
Walters Art Museum, by bequest, 1931 (22.111)

This very fine figure of a nonroyal man is part of a double statue of a husband and wife seated together. The lady's hand (partly concealed by the back pillar) rests on the shoulder of her spouse in a gesture of support and protection.[1] The four carved wavy lines across the man's chest are an impressionistic means of indicating rolls of fat, alluding to wealth and ease of lifestyle. An inscription on the rear of the statue indicates that the man was a royal scribe, a position of some dignity, but his name and that of his wife have not survived.

The scribe's wig is long and consists of crimped, tapering tresses beneath which are long cylindrically curled extensions that were worn behind and in front of the shoulders, creating the illusion of lappets resembling those on cloth headdresses. The length of the wig was fashionable and common in the era that began in the late Eighteenth Dynasty and continued through the mid-Nineteenth Dynasty.[2] The wide pleated sleeves of the garment match this dating, but precision is somewhat elusive.

Five partial columns of text on the rear suggest the statue's original location. The dedication was to "Ptah, the lord of Truth, the noble pillar, the one foremost of the Tjennet sanctuary, and Sokar..." Ptah and Sokar were gods associated with the ancient capital of Memphis in Lower Egypt. The inscription also mentions "his traveling around the walls," and this too places us in Memphis, where a festival in honor of Sokar included going around the walls of the city.[3] The epithets of Ptah also expand our knowledge, since they associate him both with sovereignty as a god but also with the afterlife and the cemetery,[4] where Sokar was most at home. At least one statue dating to the reign of Ramesses II and dedicated in the Ptah temple at Memphis referred to both the "noble pillar" and "the foremost of Tjennet," so this statue could have been the gift of the royal scribe in that great national religious center. This is only a surmise, however, since granodiorite was used for statuary in both temples and tomb chapels, its black color alluding to the fertility of Egypt's rejuvenating Nile silt brought by the annual flood.

BB

Bibliography

Steindorff 1946a, 43, no. 117, pl. XXIII; Vandier 1958, 442; Málek (Porter and Moss 8, part 2) 1999, 496.

Notes

1. Parallels of gesture and date include Berlin, Ägyptisches Museum, inv. no. 2303, New York, Metropolitan Museum of Art, 15.2.1, and Cairo, Egyptian Museum, CG 597, all illustrated in Vandier 1958, pl. CXLIV.
2. Showing parallel details from the late Eighteenth Dynasty, see Freed, Markowitz, and D'Auria 1999, 277, nos. 251 and 279, no. 256, figs. 148, 153.
3. The early name of Memphis itself was "the White Walls," and Ptah's most common epithet was "south of his wall."
4. For Ḫnty-Ṯnnt, "foremost of the Tjennet sanctuary," compare Leitz 2002, V. 876, and for Ḏd-šps "the noble pillar" compare idem, VII, 678–80.

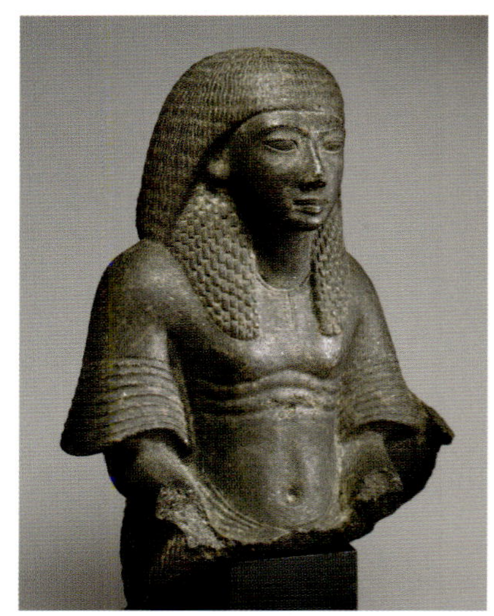

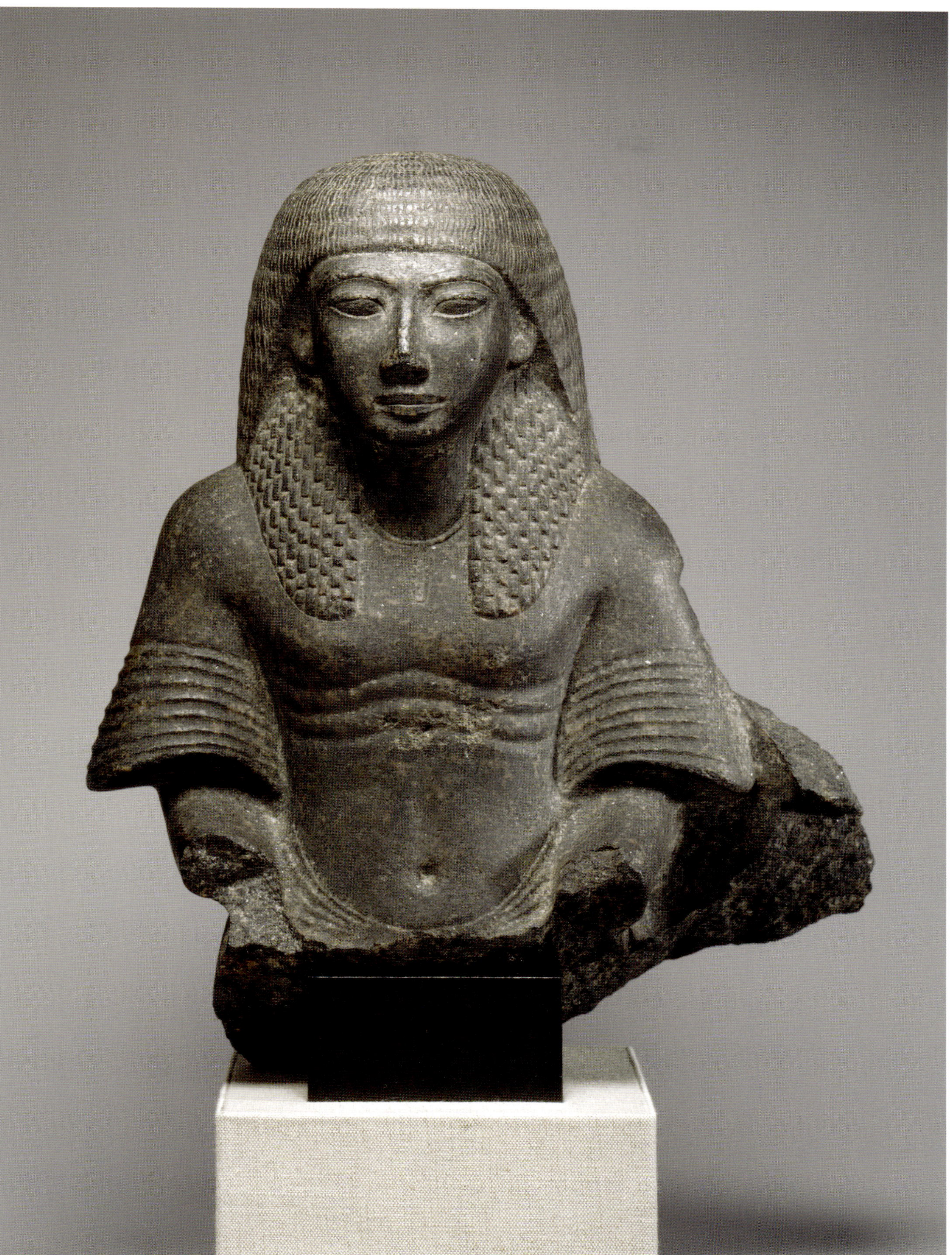

33

Conjoined jars

Faience, traces of glaze; height 3.7 cm (1 7/16 in.), width of conjoined jars 8.5 cm (3 5/16 in.), depth 4.3 cm (1 11/16 in.)

Nineteenth Dynasty, ca. 1285 B.C.

Provenance: Dikran Kelekian, New York / Paris; Henry Walters, 1926; Walters Art Museum, by bequest, 1931 (48.457)

Multivessel ensembles are documented in ancient Egypt during all periods, but they are particularly abundant in New Kingdom and Late Period contexts.[1] Each of these conjoined vessels has a squat conical form tapering upward, a flat bottom, and a protruding lip. The vessels are joined at their lower halves; traces of breakage on the side opposite the inscriptions indicate that they may have been part of an ensemble of four or more vessels.[2]

Inscriptions of dark blue faience paste are inset on the front of the vessels. Each inscription is composed in three columns in a rectangular frame containing the throne and birth name of Sety I: "Men-Maat-Re; Sety, beloved of Re," as well as the epithet "beloved of Maat," who is named "Daughter of Re" on the right vessel and "Mistress of the Two Lands" on the left vessel. A line below each frame gives the name and titles of the owner of the ensemble, "Paser"; the title mentioned on the right is "priest of Maat" and, on the left, "governor of the city and vizier."

Paser was appointed vizier under Ramesses I (1295–1294 B.C.),[3] and held the office during the reign of Sety I (1294–1279 B.C.), and for more than twenty-five years under Sety's successor, Ramesses II (1279–1213 B.C.). He was one of the most influential officials in the court and the main power behind the throne. Paser accompanied the king on his campaign to Syria and participated in the famous battle of Qadesh between the Egyptians and Hittites. He was a leading figure in Egypt's foreign relations, representing the king in the negotiation of a peace treaty between Egypt and the Hittite state (in Year 21 of the reign of Ramesses II, 1258 B.C.); his letter to the Hittite king Hattushili III (1265–1238 B.C.)—inscribed on a cuneiform tablet found in the Hittite capital, Hattusha—is the oldest preserved treaty between two countries.

Records and monuments of Paser have been discovered throughout Egypt, as well as in Nubia and in Serabit el-Khadim on the Sinai Peninsula. Paser's male ancestors originated in the Near East,[4] but they soon became part of the Egyptian upper class. His father, Neb-netjeru, held the important position of high priest of Amun, and his mother came from an Egyptian family of priests of Amun in Memphis. His many responsibilities in Egypt's domestic and foreign policy over a long career (he died at age 70) apparently so occupied Paser that he probably never married; no children are recorded in his tomb (TT 106) in Western Thebes.

This ensemble of small vessels was produced during the reign of Sety I; it may originally have been placed in Paser's tomb or within his commemorative chapel at Saqqara.

RS

Bibliography

Donohue 1988, 109, no. VII.1; Raedler 2004, 329, Q 4.65.

Notes

1. For a New Kingdom example, see Philadelphia, University of Pennsylvania Museum of Archaeology and Anthropology, acc. no. E 597a–d, in Capel and Markoe 1996, 80–81, no. 231; for Late Period examples, see Caubet and Pierrat-Bonnefois 2005, 149 and 151, nos. 399–404.
2. A group of four faience vessels of similar shape but joined by a shared base is in Florence, Museo Archeologico Nazionale/Museo Egizio, inv. no. 3081, see www.globalegyptianmuseum.org/record.aspx?id=9554.
3. See Brand 2000, 341.
4. Raedler 2004, 345, with further references.

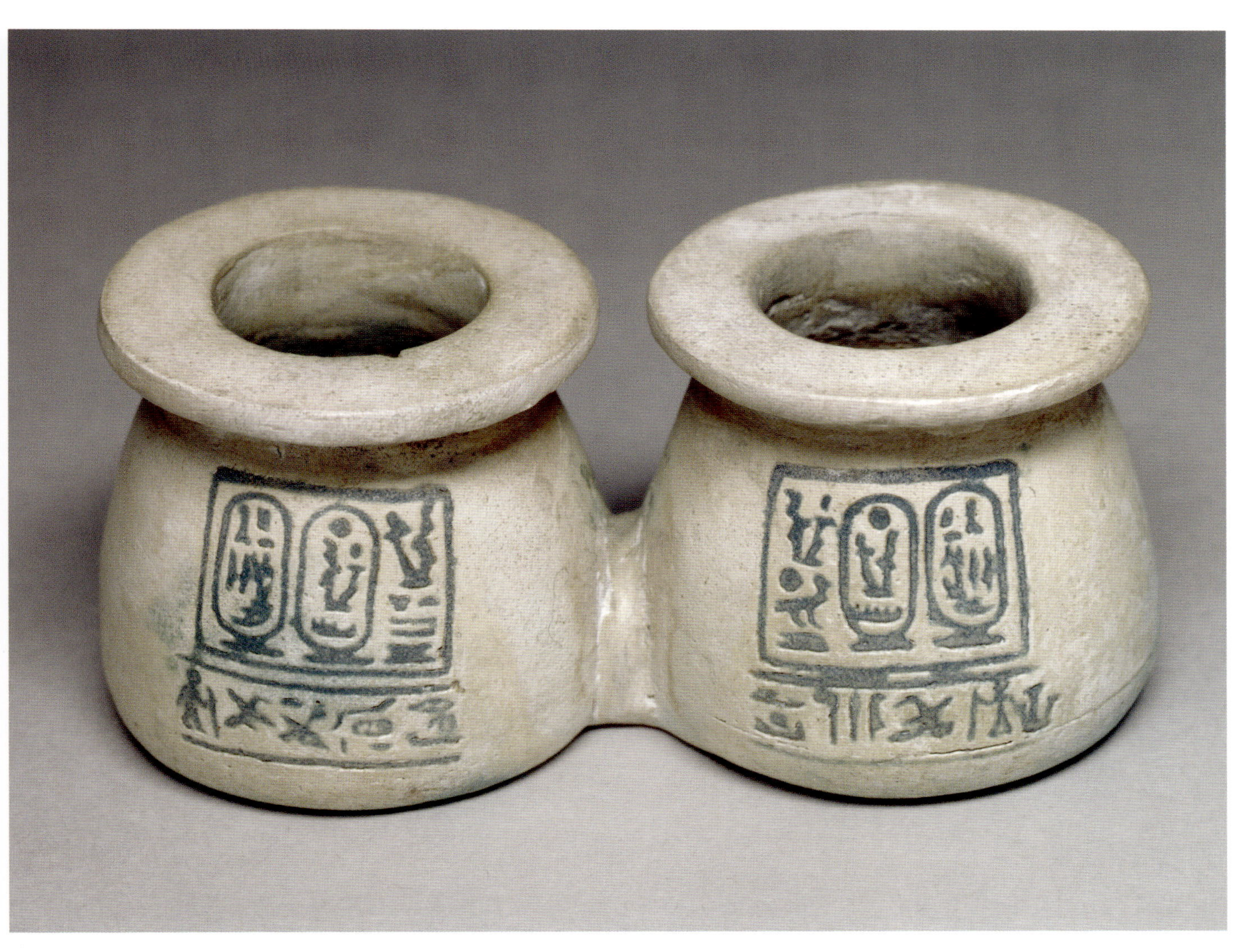

34

Figure of Ramesses II from a group statue

Probably from Upper Egypt

Greenish brown granite; 53.5 x 14 x 9.5 cm (21 1/16 x 5 1/2 x 3 3/4 in.)

Nineteenth Dynasty, ca. 1250 B.C.

Provenance: Dikran Kelekian, New York/Paris; Henry Walters, 1925; Walters Art Museum, by bequest, 1931 (22.114)

Group figures showing the king with one or more deities are known from the early Old Kingdom (ca. 2650 B.C.) onward.[1] The statue type, though of long standing, was particularly favored by the powerful pharaohs of the Eighteenth and Nineteenth Dynasties. Celebrating the king's union with a local god or goddess or his connection to the state god Amun at Karnak,[2] such group figures were erected within temples in strategically important places such as the courtyards beside the main aisle, the central rooms near the sanctuary or within the sanctuary itself. The king's divine status was often formally expressed by his being depicted on the same scale as an accompanying deity.[3] More elaborate group statues were issued for occasions such as the coronation or the Sed Festival, marking a reign of thirty years. For the most part we have just a faint idea about the religious-dogmatic conception of larger installations, in particular of the placement of movable objects such as statues.

No other pharaoh commissioned more group statues for his temples than Ramesses II (1279–1213 B.C.), who saw himself as a god among gods. He apparently reckoned early in his long reign that the many possible group configurations were the ideal way to convey the message of his own divinity in life to men and gods. In temples throughout the country, and particularly in the Nubian temples (such as Abu Simbel) and those of the Nile Delta, group sculptures represented the myriad interactions of the divine Ramesses with the gods.

The figure of the king is all that remains of this group sculpture, its larger original form attested by the off-center inscription columns, which contain the royal name set in cartouches; such inscriptions were invariably placed at the sculpture's center. To Ramesses' right stood a deity (either a god or a goddess) that grasped him by the right hand.[4] The king, holding the *ankh* sign (now lost) in his left hand, wears the *nemes* headcloth topped by the double crown, the ceremonial beard, and the short royal kilt with a belt buckle containing his throne name: "User-Maat-Re setep-en-Re."

MS

Bibliography

Steindorff 1946a, 39, no. 100, pl. XVIII; Vandier 1958, 397, 399, 407, 409–10, 414, pl. CXXVIII, 3.

Notes

1. See generally Seidel 1996.
2. El-Saghir 1992, 62–68.
3. See, for example, Seidel and Schulz 1998, no. 107.
4. See, for example, Wiese 2001, 128, no. 86.

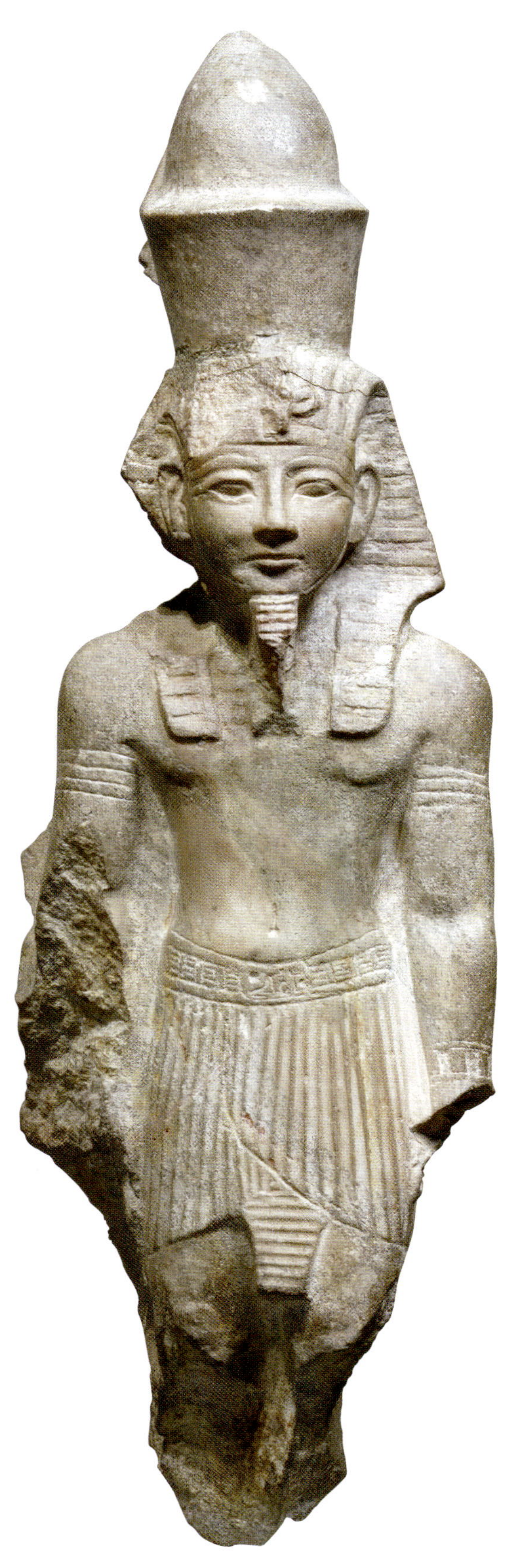

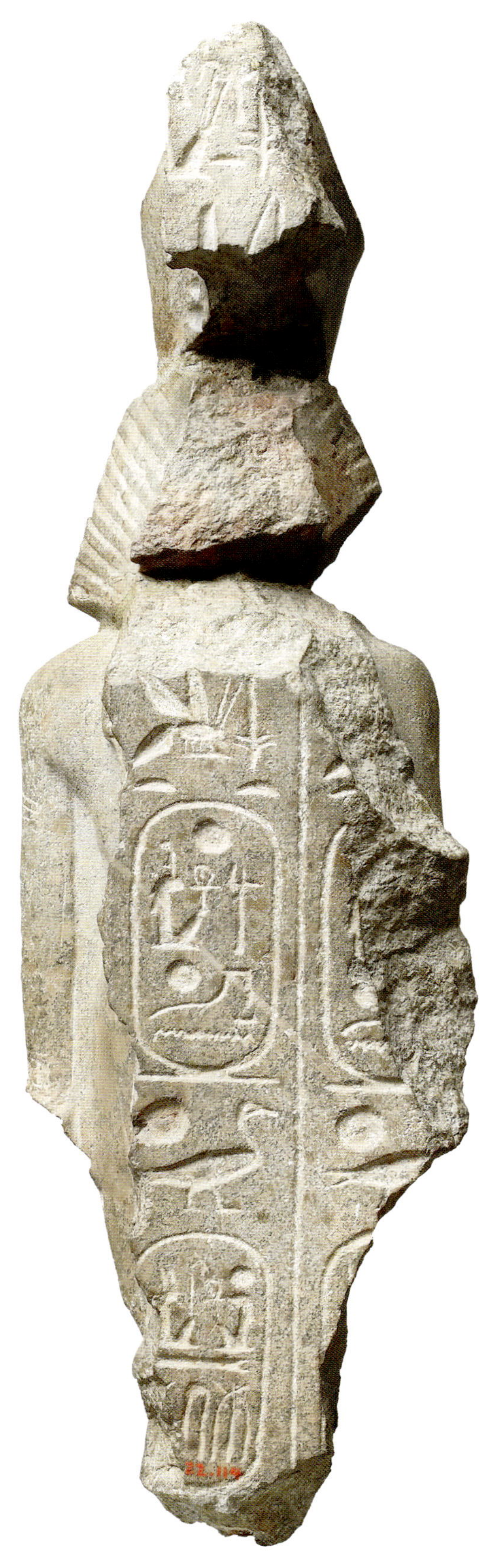

35

Fecundity figures bearing offerings

Abydos, temple of Ramesses II

Nineteenth Dynasty, ca. 1270 B.C.

Limestone, painted; right fragment (22.93): 28 x 32 x 5.5 (11 x 12 5/8 x 2 3/16 in.);

left fragment: (22.100): 26 x 36 x 5.5 cm (10 1/4 x 14 3/16 x 2 3/16 in.)

Provenance: Dikran Kelekian, New York / Paris; Henry Walters, 1912;

Walters Art Museum, by bequest, 1931 (22.93 and 22.100)

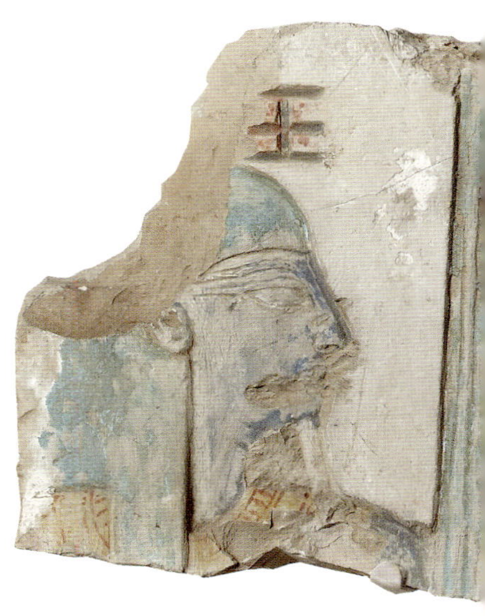

These two associated wall fragments, carved in sunk relief, with well-preserved pigment, were once in the temple of Ramesses II at Abydos, the main cult center of the god Osiris. Both reliefs come from the same single block of stone. They were situated along the base of the southern wall of the temple's first octostyle hall (a room with eight pillars).[1] During the New Kingdom, the lower sections of temple walls were adorned with sequences of fecundity figures bringing food offerings, emblematic of the abundance of the Nile Valley, for the monarch or the main god of the temple.[2] The procession of deities in the Ramesses II temple comprises male and female figures, representing the regions of Upper Egypt.[3]

The fragments depict a male and a female figure, both facing right. The male is shown bearing offerings for the temple's patron god, Osiris, in Ramesses II's name. The female's offerings are not visible in the fragment. The bottom sections displaying the lower part of the deities' bodies remain in situ at Abydos and portray both as kneeling figures (fig. 9). The carving is executed in sunk relief, which accentuates the play of light and shadow on the figures, but it is not very detailed. The neck creases of both figures are reminiscent of the Amarna style.

The male figures represent Egypt's administrative nomes, or districts (of which there were forty-two: twenty in Lower Egypt, twenty-two in Upper Egypt). Each nome's patron deity was identified by the distinctive standard on the top of his head. The emblem sits atop a pole rising from the hieroglyphic sign *sepet* (meaning nome). Such figures are depicted with a

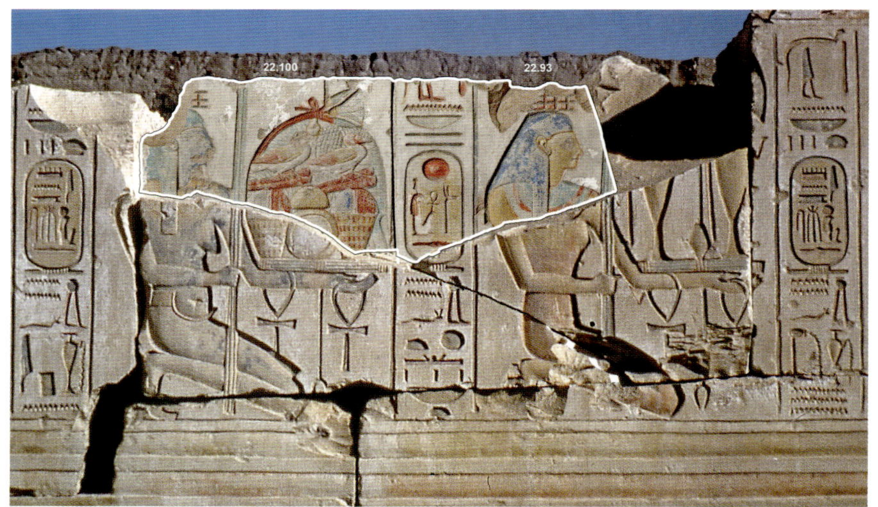

Fig. 9 No. 35 (22.93 and 22.100) superimposed on the remains of a frieze of fecundity figures, temple of Ramesses II, Abydos. Photo by J.J. Shirley, rendering by Regine Schulz

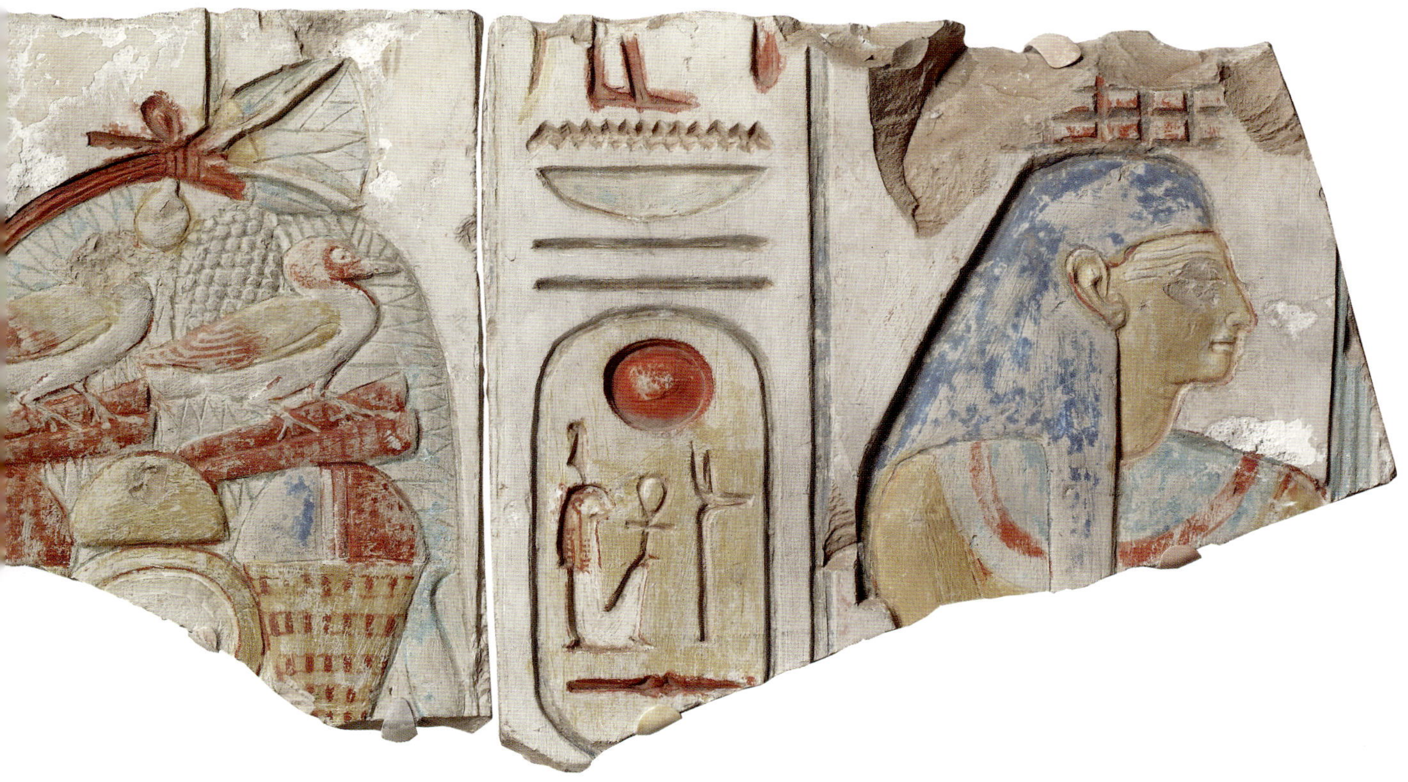

paunch and pendulous breasts, like the Nile god Hapy, symbolizing the bounty and fertility of the land. The blue-skinned male personification on the left (22.100) retains only a small portion of the *sepet*. His missing right hand holds plant stalks (possibly papyrus) directly in front of his face. The unseen left arm balances a reed mat or tray piled with food offerings: two ducks, a pomegranate, small baskets with grapes, round loaves of bread, onions, and a leek or cucumber. At the top of the offerings is a bouquet of blue lotus flowers.

The yellow-skinned female personification on the right (22.93) retains a portion of the *sepet* sign on her head. The lower part of her body, which remains in the temple, is clad in a red tunic, and her right arm grasps a bundle of plant stalks, which she faces in the fragment. She wears a *wesekh* collar of light green and red. Her unseen left arm balances a reed tray with two tall offering vessels. The kneeling divinities are separated by vertical columns of hieroglyphic inscriptions enclosed within register lines. To the left of the goddess, the preserved inscription in the column reads "of the lord of the Two Lands, User-Maat-Re," referring to the throne name of Ramesses II contained in the cartouche.[4]

Two other fragments from the same frieze are in the Egyptian collections in Brooklyn and Moscow.[5]

CH

Bibliography

Steindorff 1946a, 79–80, nos. 268, 271, pl. LIII; Cooney 1967, figs. 2, 4; Baines 1985, 371–73.

Notes

1. For the reliefs in this hall and further references, see Kuhlmann 1982, 355–62, pls. 102–4; for the significance of the temple, see Ullmann 2002, 179–200.
2. Cooney 1967, 279.
3. Baines 1985, 374.
4. Steindorff 1946a, 79, no. 268.
5. Brooklyn Museum, acc. no. 11.670; see Fazzini et al. 1989, no. 61; Moscow, Pushkin Museum of Fine Arts, inv. no. 1.1.a5650; see Hodjash and Berlev 1982, 130 and 134, no. 73.

36

Ostracon with a royal head

From Western Thebes

Limestone with ink; 18.5 x 14.6 x 2.9 cm (7 5/16 x 5 3/4 x 1 1/8 in.)

Nineteenth Dynasty, ca. 1280 B.C.

Provenance: Dikran Kelekian, New York / Paris; Henry Walters, 1923; Walters Art Museum, by bequest, 1931 (32.1)

This rare example belongs to the well-documented class of objects known as figural ostraca—flakes of limestone used as a drawing surface for informal or preparatory sketches. The findspot is unrecorded, but it was likely either the village of Deir el-Medineh or the Valley of the Kings, both of which have yielded ostraca in great abundance. The larger sketch, drawn in black and red ink, shows the head and shoulders of a Ramesside king, wearing the high version of the *khepresh*, the so-called blue crown, with an elaborately coiled *uraeus* above the forehead and fluttering bands at the back. The figure's broad collar and double-stranded necklace of beads are cursorily sketched. A slightly aquiline nose dominates the face; the almond-shaped eye is elongated, with a curving brow; the earlobe is pierced. The most intriguing feature, however, is the king's stubble beard, which is seldom represented and only on ostraca; the field of bristles gives the impression of an unshaven face rather than an attempt to depict a natural beard. Such an unconventional image may well have been understood as a depiction of mourning; other images of the king unshaven show tears streaming from his eyes.[1]

Two human forearms flank the royal head,[2] one with the palm flat, the other with the hand forming a fist. The difference in quality between these sketches, executed with thick brushstrokes, and the finely rendered representation of the king is evident. The curious combination of styles raises the question of this ostracon's function. The most plausible explanation is that a sketch for a scene in a Ramesside royal tomb was subsequently used as a student exercise in proportions. It would seem unproblematic to date this piece to the Nineteenth Dynasty, and quite reasonable to assign it to the reign of Sety I or even to the early years of his son Ramesses II.

MS

Bibliography

Peck 1978, no. 31;
Ziegler 2002, 228–29, fig. 6.

Notes

1. Vandier d'Abbadie 1937, 99, 116–17, pl. LXXII, no. 2568.
2. Compare, for example, a drawing board in the British Museum, EA 5601; see Russmann 2001, 153–54, no. 66.

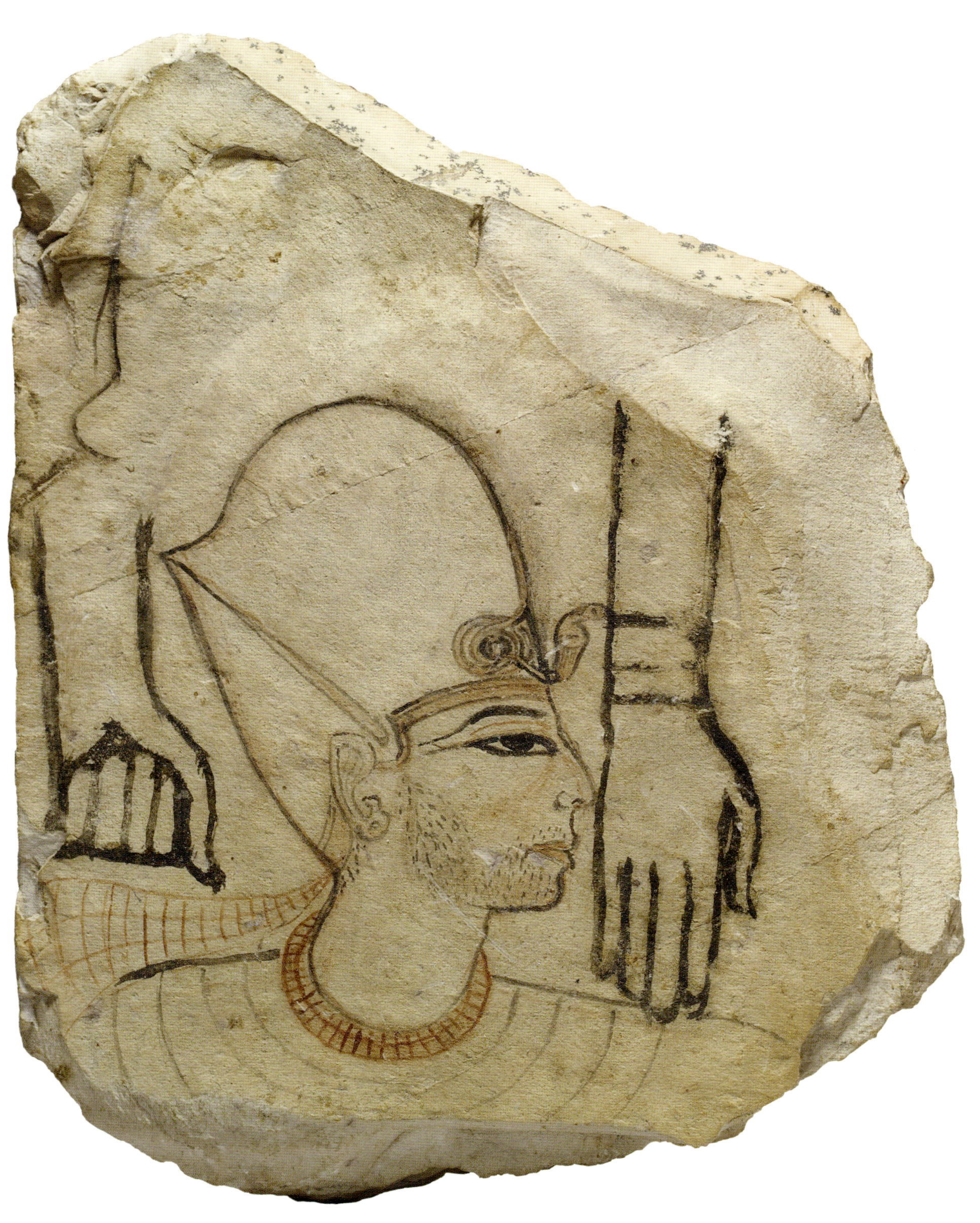

37

Statue of Nehy

Probably from Saqqara

Limestone; 132 x 45.1 x 87.8 cm (51 15/16 x 17 3/4 x 34 9/16 in.)

Nineteenth Dynasty, ca. 1250–1230 B.C.

Provenance: Reportedly from the collection of the Château des Aygalades (near Marseille);[1] unnamed Marseille dealer, 1917;[2] sold between 1917 and 1921 by Jacques Seligmann to Henri Daguerre and Joseph Brummer, and later, in New York, to Samuel Untermeyer; Henry Walters, 1925; Walters Art Museum, by bequest, 1931 (22.106)

The life-size statue of Nehy was probably discovered at the very end of the eighteenth century or early in the nineteenth century in the Memphite necropolis of Saqqara together with a very similar companion piece representing the same woman.[3]

The Walters statue presents a woman seated on a chair with leonine legs and a high backrest that has a small back pillar extension behind her head. She wears an elaborately pleated, full-length gown with fringed edges; it crosses over her chest, leaving only the front of the feet, the lower right arm, and the left hand uncovered. The V-shaped neckline of an undergarment is visible below her neck. Her very long, plaited wig extends down to the waist, and strands of hair terminating in long curls frame her face. The hair of the wig is tied back with filets of leaves, and a lotus flower filet encircles her head at the temples. In her left hand, Nehy holds a sistrum in front of her chest, while her right hand rests flat on her thigh. The handle of the hoop-type sistrum is adorned with the head of the goddess Hathor, symbolizing her divine presence. The use of clappers and rattles was an important part of the temple rituals, intended to invoke and delight the gods.

The front of the woman's gown displays a column with hieroglyphic text containing a standard offering formula benefiting the deceased subject and names her

> Osiris: Mistress of the House, Musician of the Mistress of the Heaven, She of the Southern Sycamore, Nehy, true of voice.

These titles not only confirm Nehy's status as mistress of the house but also mention her active role in musical performances for the goddess Hathor. Although the goddess is not named directly, the epithet of celestial goddess and the association with the "Southern Sycamore" (a reference to the Hathor sanctuary at Memphis) clearly point to this deity. The description of her as an "Osiris" and the epithet "true of voice" defines her status as a deceased worthy of revival in the afterlife.

The sides of the chair and the back of the statue are roughly carved and bear deep chisel marks, which may indicate that the statue had been intended to reside in a niche in the superstructure of Nehy's tomb, where the sides would have been barely visible. The modeling of the figure is more carefully executed, but the surface is not polished. The summary execution is less an indicator that the statue was unfinished, but rather that the details were once painted in. The statue has lost all its paint, and also displays some damage in the nose and chin area, as well as minor chipping all over the body. Damage to the figure's right upper arm was squared and repaired with a fill in antiquity; today, this fill is lost.

The iconography of Nehy's statue, particularly the full-length pleated gown, calls to mind late Eighteenth Dynasty sculpture from Saqqara;[4] but the style, particularly the very round face, the elongated body and wig,[5] and the schematic carving of the details makes a later date under the reign of Ramesses II more likely.

On the evidence of the size of her two statues, her elaborate costume and wig, and the privilege of serving as a "musician" in the important Hathor sanctuary at Memphis, Nehy belonged to the upper class. Although we do not know the name and title of Nehy's husband, we may know her father and mother. A stela of the same period in the Museo Egizio in Turin documents a "Priest of Ptah" named Ptah-may,[6] and mentions his wife (Hatshepsut) and two daughters, both named Nehy, one of whom was a musician of Amun and the other a musician of Hathor; the latter may be the same Nehy depicted in the Walters statue.

RS

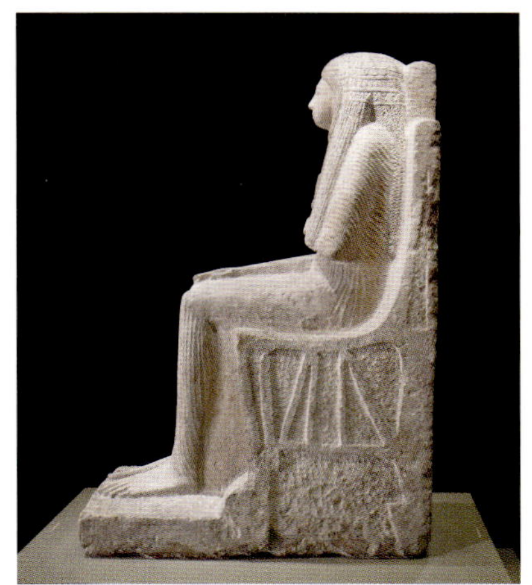

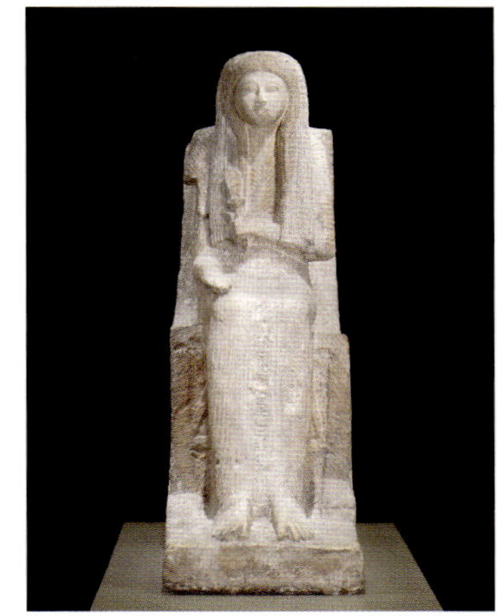

Bibliography

Catalogue des livres du feu M. l'abbé de Rothelin (Paris, 1764), no. 456; Steindorff 1942, 9–17; Steindorff 1946a, 40, no. 106, pl. XXI; Steindorff 1947, 57–59, fig. 1; Walters Art Gallery 1997, 20–21; Capel and Markoe 1996, 96–98, no. 35.

Notes

1. The statue's modern history can be traced as far back as the early nineteenth century. It may have been purchased, together with a companion piece, from François Champollion in 1828–29 and brought to France, or by the French collector Sebastien Saulnier (see Steindorff 1942, 11); another possibility is that the two statues were brought to France by officers of the Napoleonic expedition (see B.V. Bothmer, cited by Steindorff 1947, 58). At some point in the nineteenth century they came to the Château des Aygalades.
2. See Steindorff 1947, 58.
3. This statue was purchased by the American theologian and collector Theodore Pitcairn, and became part of his collection in Philadelphia. In July 1976 it was sold in a Christie's auction in London to the Matsuoka Museum of Art in Tokyo.
4. See, for example, the statue of Meryt and Maya at Leiden, National Museum of Antiquities, AST 2; in Martin 1991, 147–88; Capel and Markoe 1996, 96.
5. See, for example, Turin, Museo Egizio, C 7352, in Vassilika 2006, no. 43.
6. Maspero 1883, 141.

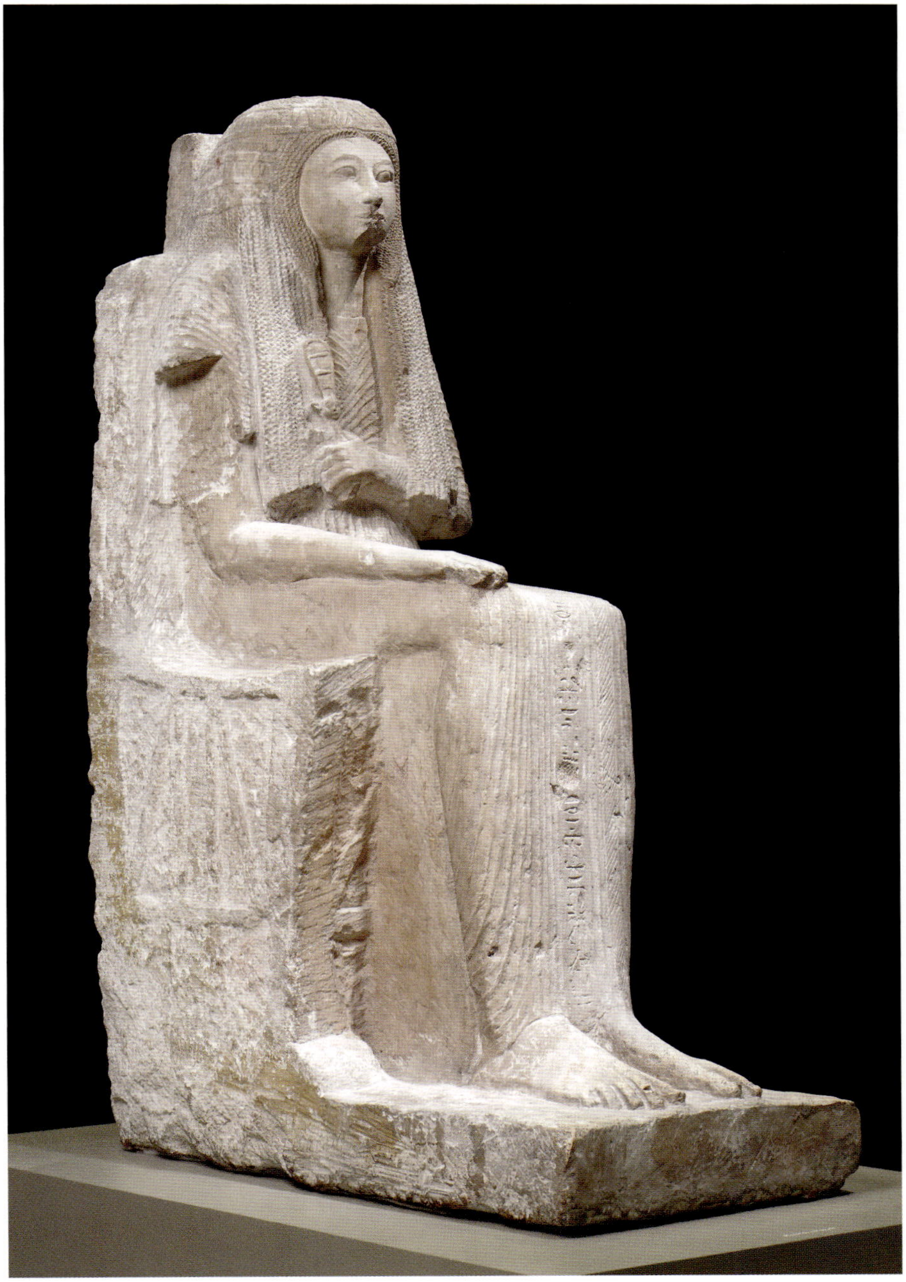

38

Hor-nakht as standard-bearer

Probably from Tell el-Belamun (Delta)

Granodiorite; 78 x 21.5 x 33.5 cm (30 11/16 x 8 7/16 x 13 3/16 in.)

Nineteenth Dynasty, ca. 1220 B.C.

Provenance: Henry Walters, before 1931; Walters Art Museum, by bequest, 1931 (22.105)

The owner of this statue, Hor-nakht, is represented in a striding position holding a long staff with his left hand. The head that crowns the standard is damaged, but it can be identified with some assurance as that of a ram because of the reference to the god Amun-Re on the pole's inscription. The type of the standard-bearer was introduced into the program of royal statuary in the middle of the Eighteenth Dynasty[1] but was soon used by nonroyal individuals as well.[2] Common during the Ramesside period—the Nineteenth and Twentieth Dynasties—the statue type vanished with the end of the New Kingdom.

In the fist of his right hand the official grasps the unusual combination of an *ankh* sign and a rectangular object, perhaps a scribal kit. He wears an ankle-length, elaborately pleated kilt with a characteristic trapezoidal front panel; a shawl over an open-necked tunic; a curled wig parted in the center that covers the ears; and sandals. Also noteworthy are the short, artificial beard of dignity (now broken) and a large bracelet on each of the wrists. Behind the forward left foot the plane is engraved with the figure of Hor-nakkht's wife, the "Mistress of the House" Shepses-Isis, as the inscription informs us. She is holding in each of her hands a sistrum, the rattle used in the temple cult; and she wears an elegant garment, which spreads down to ankle level.

The inscriptions, composed mostly of simple offering formulas, give the titles of this high-ranking dignitary. As "colonel of the troops and overseer of foreign countries," Hor-nakht[3] served in the state administration for military affairs. Even though we have no further written evidence of him,[4] we can date the figure with some certainty to the Nineteenth Dynasty (probably the late reign of Ramesses II or his successor, Merenptah [1213–1203 B.C.]) on the basis of art historical determination; the figure's full cheeks, the wig, and the clothing are characteristic for this period. The somewhat stocky proportions and the simple modeling of the details may indicate a provincial origin and manufacture. It is possible that the statue of Hor-nakht was created for the temple of Amun-Re at Tell el-Belamun (Delta), an interpretation depending entirely on the reading of the defective written toponym [Sema]-Behedet in the invocation on the staff of the statue.

MS

Bibliography

Steindorff 1946a, 40, no. 107, pl. XXI; Schulman 1964, 53–56, doc. 406 k, 516a; Satzinger 1981, 33, doc. C. 2; Chadefaud 1982, 104–5; Petschel and von Falck 2004, 77–78, no. 66.

Notes

1. See Kozloff and Bryan, 1992, 141, figs. V.21, V.22.
2. See Tiradritti 1998, 346.
3. Schulman 1964, 53–56.
4. Chadefaud 1982, 105.

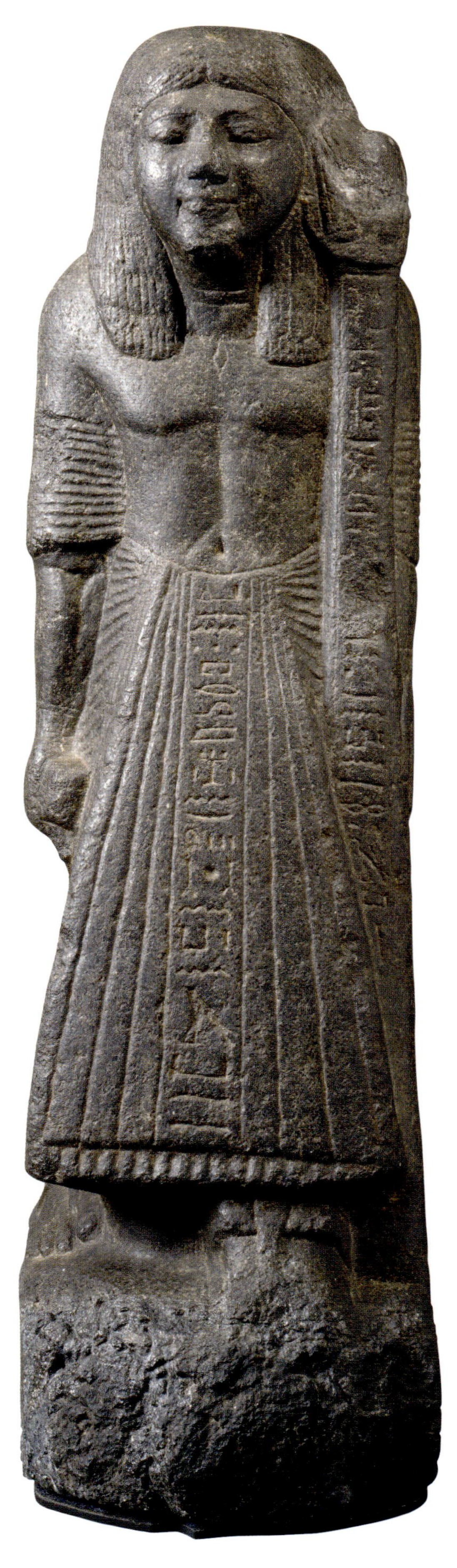

39

Tile inscribed with the name of Sety II

Probably from Qantir (eastern Delta)

Glazed faience; height 13.3 cm (5 ¼ in.)

Nineteenth Dynasty, ca. 1200 B.C.

Provenance: Dikran Kelekian, New York/Paris; Henry Walters, 1924; Walters Art Museum, by bequest, 1931 (42.85)

Unlike the many well-preserved pyramids, temples, and tombs that were erected for the pharaohs during Egypt's long history, their splendid palaces have survived only as ruins—if at all. The extensive use of mud brick and wood undoubtedly made the royal quarters comfortable, but these materials provided scant assurances of permanence in the face of catastrophes such as fire or flooding or the abandonment of the palaces for political or dynastic reasons. Accordingly, we know little about their inner decoration. Some New Kingdom sites, however, have preserved enough archeological evidence to enable us to imagine the original splendor of the royal residences. The ruins of Tell el-Amarna,[1] founded as Egypt's new capital around 1345 B.C. by Akhenaten (1352–1336 B.C.), and the vast city of Pi-Ramesse/Qantir (in the eastern Delta) from the early Nineteenth Dynasty under Sety I (1294–1279 B.C.) and Ramesses II (1279–1213 B.C.) are particularly important sources for palace architecture. Although decorative elements in precious metals and other reusable materials have vanished, some of the wall and floor paintings remain fairly well preserved, with their bright, original colors.

Another way to enhance the official rooms of a palace (for example, the throne-room) was through the use of polychrome faience tiles for inscription bands and figurative representations. Such work was extensively used in the many Ramesside palaces at Qantir, where most of the known material has come to light. Two methods were employed to manufacture tiles that were assembled to compose inscriptions. The simpler method involved rendering the hieroglyph in a glaze distinguishable from the color of the background;[2] a more laborious technique used inlays of whitish calcite set into the fired faience tile to form the character. The fine example in the Walters is a royal cartouche crowned by a double feather and sun disk presenting the throne name of Sety II: "Wser-kheperu-Re meri-Amun." The tile probably originated in one of the king's palaces[3] when he reigned at Qantir in the late Nineteenth Dynasty.

MS

Bibliography

Schulz 2003a, 20, no. 43.

Notes

1. Freed, Markowitz, and d'Auria 1999, 228, nos. 78–30, fig. 97.
2. Caubet and Pierrat-Bonnefois 2005, 95–97, no. 255.
3. Caubet and Pierrat-Bonnefois 2005, 79, 81, no. 234.

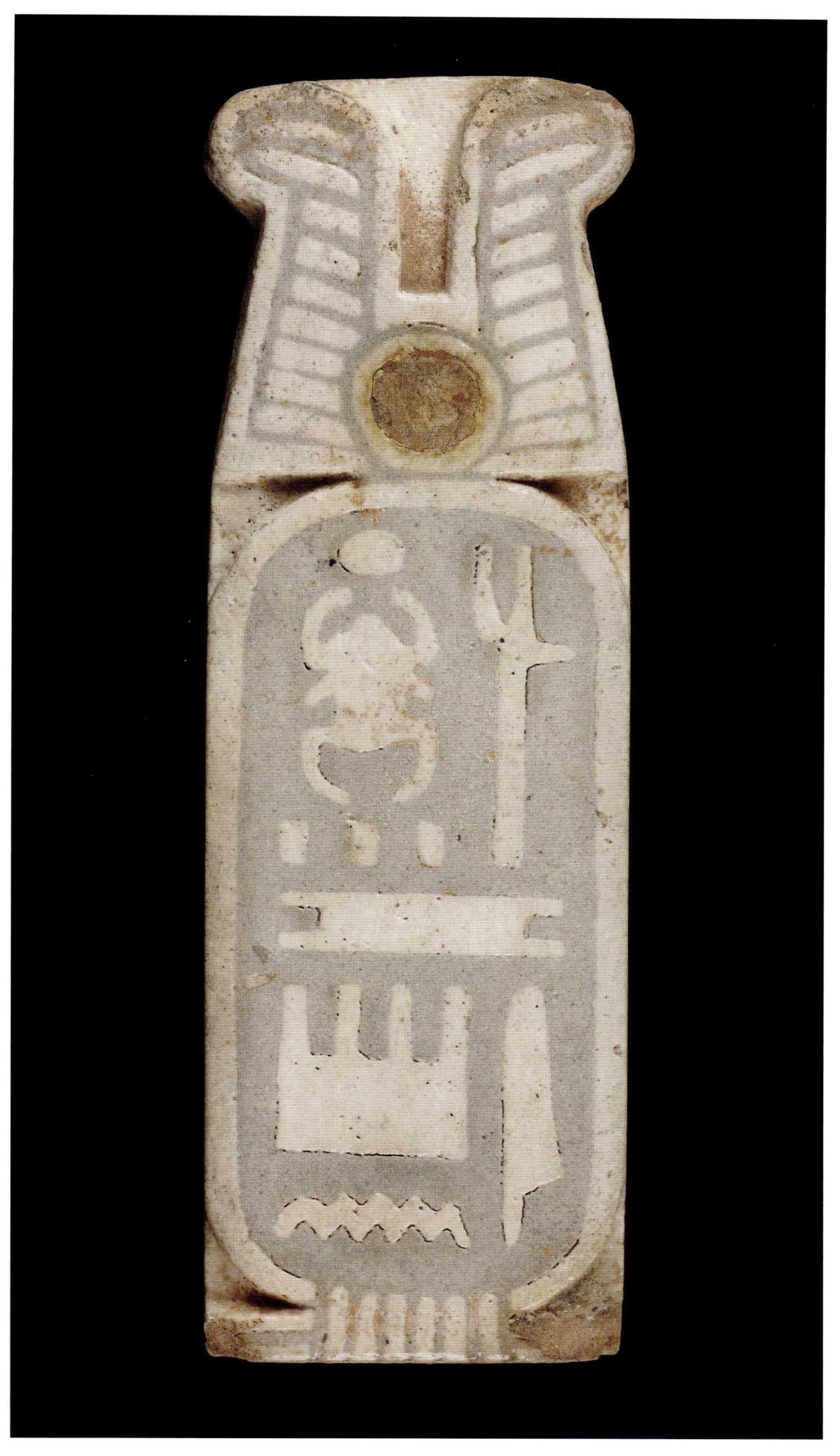

40

Shabti of Amen-em-ipet

Dark gray serpentine; 30.5 x 11.2 x 6.5 cm (12 x 4 3/8 x 2 9/16 in.)

Nineteenth Dynasty, ca. 1260 B.C.

Provenance: Dikran Kelekian, New York/Paris; Henry Walters, 1923; Walters Art Museum, by bequest, 1931 (22.177)

This little statuette belongs to a specific class of burial equipment called a *shawabti* or *shabti*. Used in burials from the later Middle Kingdom forward, by the New Kingdom these figurines had become essential accoutrements for any tomb, royal or private, and they remained so until the Ptolemaic Period. Varying considerably in number and size, and made of faience, wood, stone, or bronze, *shabtis* also evince varying qualities of workmanship, ranging from crude and simple manufacture to highly sophisticated examples.

The basic purpose of a *shabti* was to assist the tomb owner in the netherworld, especially to do heavy tasks, such as cultivating the fields and clearing the irrigation canals. For that reason, most *shabtis* carry farming implements such as hoes, axes, or seed bags. To ensure their efficacy, they were frequently inscribed with a specific spell (spell 6) from the Book of the Dead: on demand, the *shabti* had to answer the call of the god and work for the deceased.[1] Since they were used universally, *shabtis* were often prefabricated, leaving room for the name of the future owner to be inscribed.[2] When a customer intended to buy some examples for his burial, a short contract of sale was issued, the proper name was inscribed on the *shabtis*, and the agreed number were delivered after payment.[3]

Unlike commonly seen mummiform examples, the finely rendered *shabti* of Amen-em-ipet, who held the office of "chief of the doorkeepers,"[4] wears an elegant, long, pleated robe, knotted around the hips, and furnished with a long apron at the front. Such figurines in everyday dress served as overseer-*shabtis*, heading a group of conventional, mummiform examples. A single column of inscription gives the name and title of the official, who served in a larger, unknown temple. The text from the Book of the Dead is written in six lines over the back of the garment. An elaborate bipartite wig with curled hair that leaves the earlobes uncovered, a double-string necklace, and a short, squared beard complete the costume. The dating of this *shabti* to the early Nineteenth Dynasty (in the reign of Ramesses II) is established by the general style of the face with a broad shape and full cheeks, a light smile of the mouth, and the delicately formed eyes.[5] That date is further supported by the position of the arms (crossed over the chest) and the attributes: the *shabti* holds a Djed-pillar, the main cult fetish of the god Osiris, in the right hand and the *Tyet* symbol of the goddess Isis in the left.

MS

Bibliography

Steindorff 1946a, 159, no. 717, pl. CVII;
Simpson 1977, no. 32.

Notes

1. For the different versions of the text, see Schneider 1977, 81–158.
2. See, for example, Wildung and Schoske 1985, no. 84.
3. For a text with price statement, see Edwards 1971, 120–24.
4. For doorkeepers in Deir el-Medineh, see Črný 2001, 161–73.
5. For the same type, see Seipel 1989, 202–3, no. 171; Schneider 1977, no. 3.1.5.5 (pl. 17), 3.2.5.1 (pl. 30), and 3.2.5.10 (pl. 31).

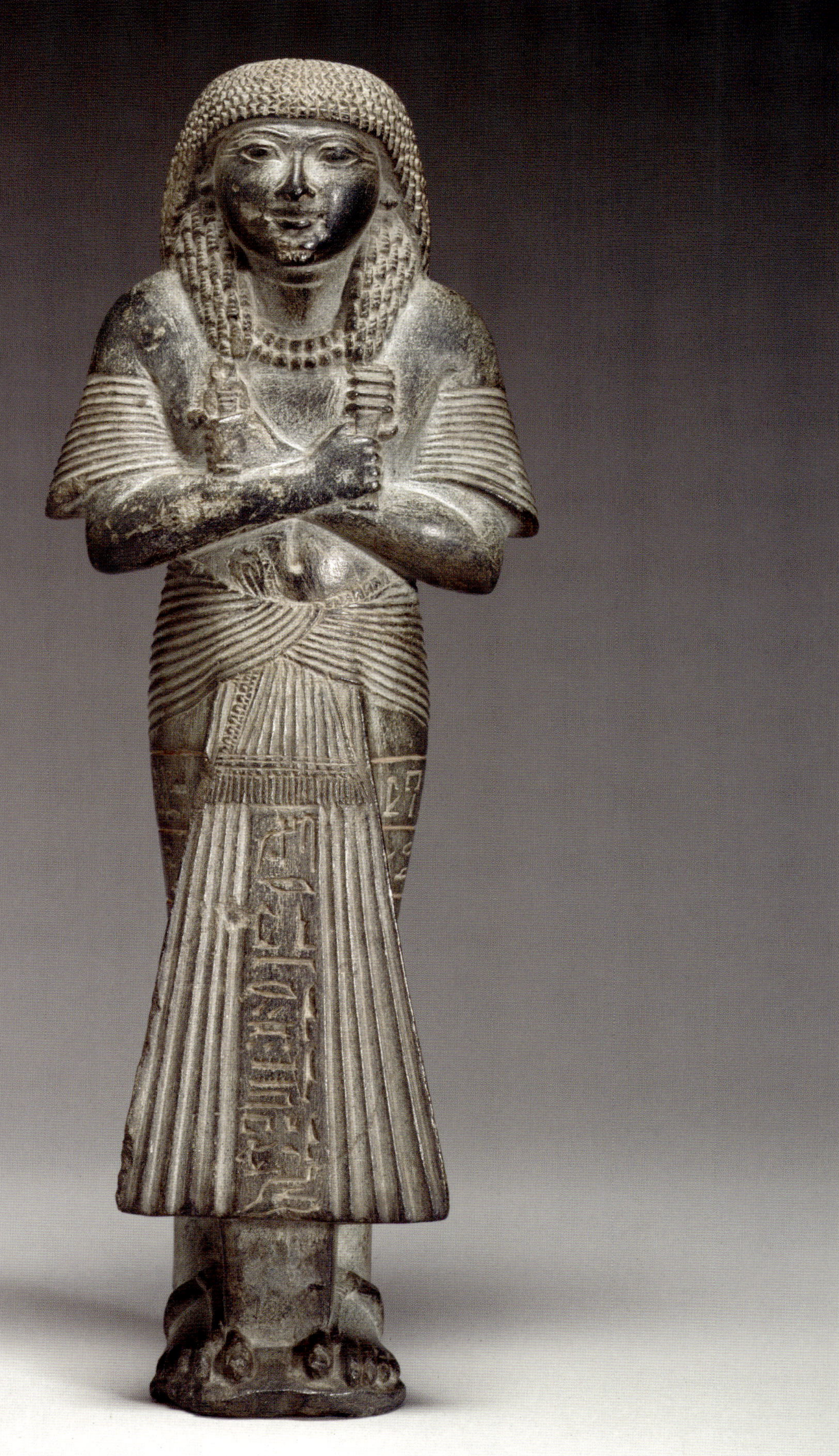

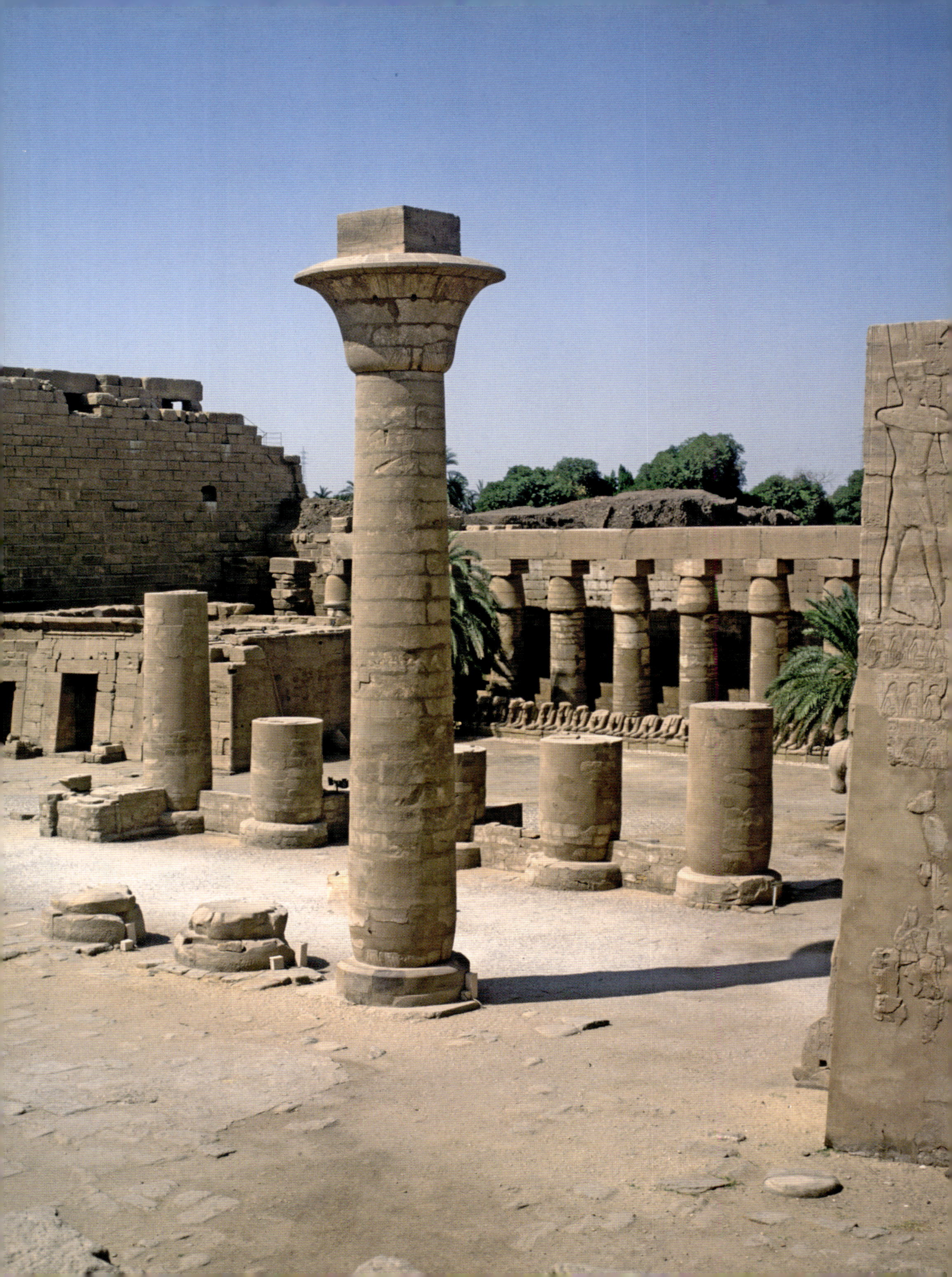

THE THIRD INTERMEDIATE PERIOD (1069–664 B.C.) AND THE LATE PERIOD (664–332 B.C.)

The death of Ramesses XI marked the eclipse of the glorious New Kingdom and the start of substantial changes that would come to affect Egypt in its entirety. Under the Twenty-first Dynasty, the country was in effect divided into two spheres of influence: King Smendes (1069–1043 B.C.) and his successors controlled the north as nominal pharaohs, whereas in Middle and Upper Egypt a line of high priests of Amun ruled from Thebes as a theocracy of sorts. The northern kings built their religious center at Tanis in the eastern Delta, an enormous site with several temples and royal tombs located within the enclosure walls. Several of these burials, such as that of Psusennes I (1039–991 B.C.), were discovered intact with their precious contents in 1939–40 by the French Egyptologist Pierre Montet, stunning evidence of an otherwise underdocumented era. The unexpected wealth of the royal tombs at Tanis was second only to the treasures from the tomb of Tutankhamun, but clear evidence of rather troubled times emerges from the reuse of the granite sarcophagus of the Nineteenth Dynasty pharaoh Merenptah, found with the burial equipment of Psusennes I, the outstanding ruler of his era, who reigned for almost fifty years. The state was in fact fiscally weak, as attested by the cessation of private tomb constructions (see nos. 41 and 42) and the plundering, at the state's instigation, of the New Kingdom royal burials in the Valley of the Kings at Thebes in order to retrieve the precious metals accumulated there.

The long-resident Libyan component of the population in the Delta and around Memphis came to prominence when the chief of the Meshwesh (a Berber tribe with Libyan origins) from Bubastis claimed the throne as Sheshonq I (945–924 B.C.) and founded the Twenty-second Dynasty (945–715 B.C.). Sheshonq I, the first and most capable of the Libyan pharaohs, is credited with revitalizing Egypt's standing as a regional power by launching a campaign in 925 B.C. against Israel and southern Palestine. The Bible (1 Kings 14: 25–26) records the invasion and attributes the looting of Jerusalem's riches to "Shishak, king of Egypt." Toward the end of the Twenty-second Dynasty (after ca. 825 B.C.), the power of the court had weakened, and the government of the now-fragmented country was divided among several local rulers. The last of these petty kings was Tefnakhte of Sais (727–720 B.C.), who with his successor, Bocchoris, formed the elusive Twenty-fourth Dynasty. Tefnakhte's territorial ambitions with regard to Upper Egypt were swiftly thwarted by the kingdom of Kush. From their capital at Napata, not far from the Fourth Cataract (in present-day Sudan), the so-called black pharaohs established a dynasty (the Twenty-fifth) that ruled over the union of Kush and Egypt. Under King Piy (747–716 B.C.), the Kushites crushed the local princes of the Delta and dominated the country. Memphis became the seat of the Nubian rulers' Egyptian court, whereas Thebes remained Upper Egypt's administrative center. There, power was vested in the God's Wife of Amun, most often an unmarried princess of the royal family who came into office through adoption by her predecessor. The reign of Taharqo (690–664 B.C.) marked the cultural and political apogee of the Kushite dynasty; it also founded the dynasty's decline as a result of growing conflict with Assyria. The second invasion of Egypt and sack of Thebes in 663 B.C. by the army of Ashurbanipal forced the last Kushite king, Tanutamani, to retreat to Nubia for good.

The subsequent reunification of the country was achieved by one of the Assyrians' vassal rulers, Psamtek of Sais, who founded the Twenty-sixth Dynasty and ruled Egypt as Psamtek I (664–610 B.C.). The Saite state enjoyed a stable economy, attested by extensive building campaigns and an efflorescence in the visual arts (see nos. 50, 53, 55–57). In the Delta, the Greek city of Naukratis prospered under Apries and his successor, Amasis (570–526 B.C.; see no. 47). Within a year of Amasis's death, however, Egypt was conquered by the Persians, led by their king, Cambyses II, whose victory at the battle of Pelusium in 525 B.C. proved decisive. For more than a hundred years, Egypt was a province of the Persian Empire, which ruled Egypt as the Twenty-seventh Dynasty (525–404 B.C.). After the short-lived Twenty-eighth and Twenty-ninth Dynasties, of only local importance, Egypt enjoyed its last period of independence under the native rulers Nectanebo I (380–362 B.C.) and Nectanebo II (360–343 B.C.; see no. 49). The two kings, who came from military backgrounds, tried to regain lost glory for the country by associating themselves with their Twenty-sixth Dynasty pre-decessors and honoring Egypt's religious cults by building or refurbishing temples. In 343 the Persian ruler Artaxerxes III again established the Achaemenid Empire's control of Egypt, only to cede it in 332 B.C. to Alexander the Great. The pharaonic history of Egypt had ended once and for all.

MS

Karnak, Temple of Amun, first court: column of Taharqo (Twenty-fifth Dynasty, ca. 680 B.C.). Photo © Dr. Abdel Ghaffar Shedid, Munich

41

Mummy and painted cartonnage of an unknown woman

Western Thebes, Deir el-Bahari, temple of Hatshepsut
Human remains, cartonnage (linen and plaster), paint; 167 x 46 x 27.5 cm (66 x 18 ⅛ x 10 ⅞ in.)
Second half of Twenty-second–Twenty-third Dynasty, ca. 850–750 B.C.
Provenance: The Metropolitan Museum of Art, New York; Walters Art Museum, by exchange, 1941 (79.1)

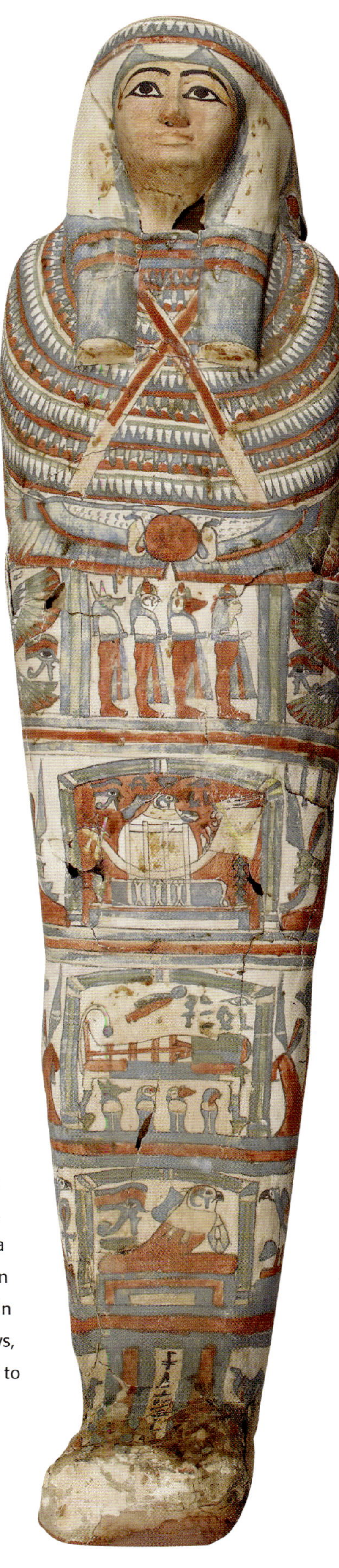

This mummy with a cartonnage case was excavated at Deir el-Bahari during the winter of 1930–31 by Ambrose Lansing, director of the Metropolitan Museum of Art's Egyptian Expedition. It came from one of four burials entombed in the rubble of the southern part of the middle terrace of the Hatshepsut temple, which by the Twenty-second Dynasty was no longer in use. The mummy and its cartonnage were found in an anthropoid coffin made of sycamore and undecorated, with the exception of the eyes and brows, which were painted in black. No indication of the deceased's name, social, or family status was discovered in the excavation; such information would probably have been written on the walls of a chapel associated with the burial, a stela, or even a label, none of which have survived.

The mummy is that of a woman who was between 50 and 60 years old when she died; at 145.7 cm (57 ⅜ in.), she was quite small, even by the standards of her time. Her body is largely intact, with the exception of some postmortem fractures. Computed tomography scans of the mummy show signs of osteoarthritis and infirmities associated with ageing (fig. 10). She had severe dental problems, though, with no fewer than sixteen abscesses, and must have been in terrible pain during her later years. One tooth has a prosthesis, probably made of resin. The treatment would not have alleviated the underlying infection, however, and her death probably resulted from septicemia caused by the abscesses.

The mummification technique is typical of the Third Intermediate Period. The woman's brain tissue was removed through the nose; her eyes are preserved and in good condition. All the viscera, with the exception of the heart, were removed, and the cheeks, throat, and the concavity of the torso packed with linen.[1]

The mummy's cartonnage consists of several layers of linen and plaster molded over a core. The back was split, the core removed, and the two edges were pierced with holes so that the cartonnage could be laced shut after the body had been inserted. The wooden footboard, on which the mummy would have been placed upright during a part of the funeral ritual, is a modern re-creation (the original was lost before the cartonnage arrived at the Metropolitan Museum of Art).[2] The exterior of the cartonnage was painted white; the scenes were outlined in black and subsequently filled with colored paint. Orpiment (arsenic sulfide), used for the yellows, is sensitive to light, and the yellow passages have faded considerably, which makes it difficult to distinguish what would originally have been white or yellow (fig. 11).[3]

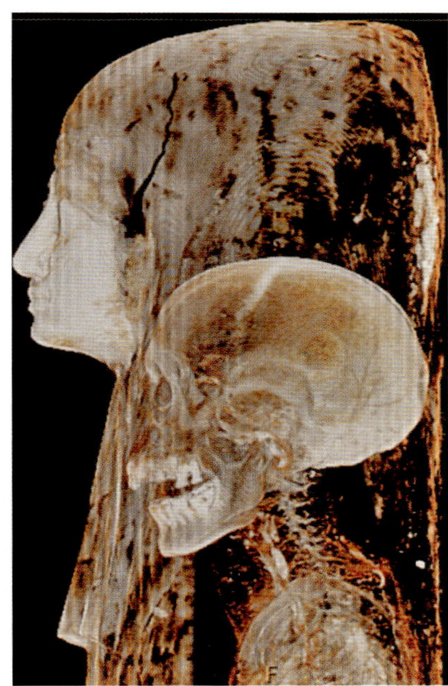

Fig. 10 CT scan of no. 41, mummy and painted cartonnage. Courtesy Department of Diagnostic Radiology, University of Maryland School of Medicine, Baltimore

The decoration covers the front and the sides. The long, blue painted wig is adorned with a headband of red and blue with a wreath of white lotus petals. Vultures' wings at the bottom edge extend down to the neck,[4] and the talons hold *shen* rings, symbolizing eternity. Above the forehead appears the lower part of a sun disk, the upper part seems to disappear under the headband. The sun disk; and vultures' wings were originally painted yellow, the color that most closely resembled gold and stood for divinity.

A large multirow collar with petal motifs covers most of the chest, and long bands cross over the collar, imitating the straps sometimes found over linen mummy bandages. A winged sun disk flanked by *uraeus* serpents separates the collar from four stacked registers of scenes on the lower body; these depict, reading from top to bottom: the four sons of Horus—protectors of the deceased and in particular of the internal organs—flanked by erect, winged cobra serpents with sun disks on their heads; the barque of the Memphite necropolis god Sokar; the mummy of the god Osiris lying on a lion bed with canopic jars beneath; and the Sokar falcon. The three lower scenes are enclosed in reed shrines, flanked by protective deities. In the foot section the painted feet are visible, flanked by recumbent jackals on shrines, representing the funerary god Anubis. The cartonnage bears few inscriptions: one,

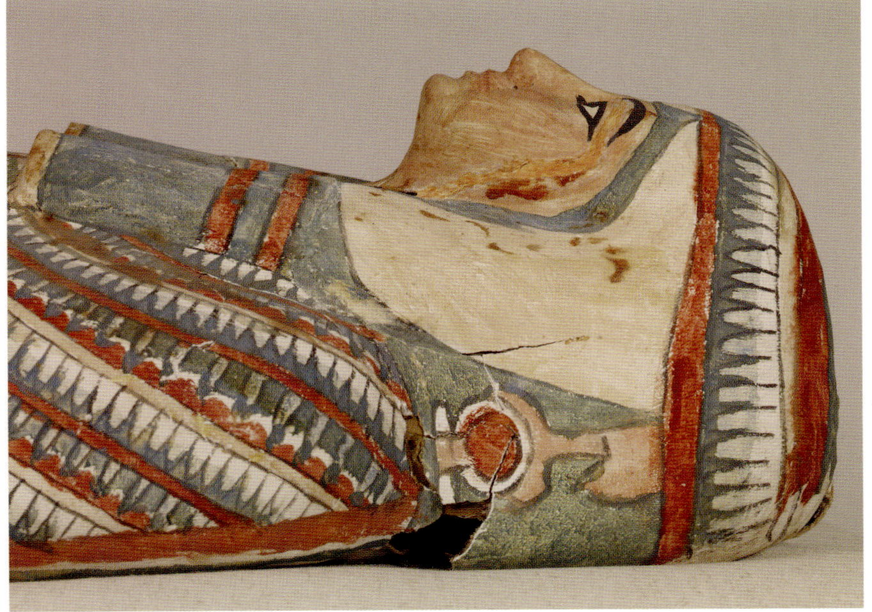

Fig. 11 Reconstruction of original pigments in no. 41. Rendering by Regine Schulz

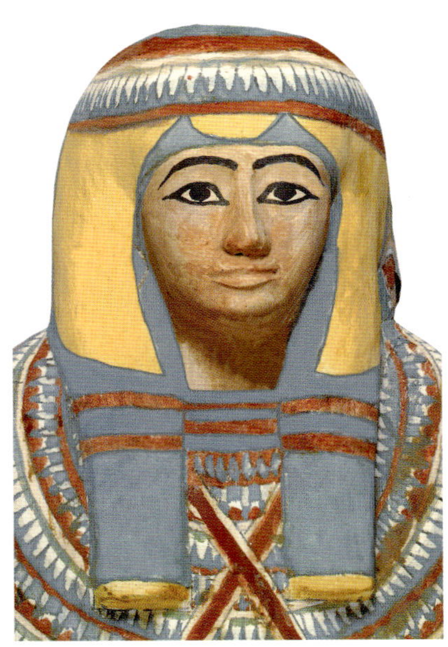

above the recumbent figure of Osiris, names him "Osiris, Lord of the Underworld;" the other, at the feet, is the abbreviated version of the standard offering formula. This formula set in motion the presentation of offerings in the name of the king to Osiris, who would then minister to the needs of the deceased.

The iconography and the style of the face date the cartonnage to the second half of the Twenty-second Dynasty. The coffin and the cartonnage were probably prefabricated; certainly it was not made to measure (the woman is nearly 16 cm [6 ½ in.] shorter than the cartonnage), which suggests that her death was sudden and unexpected. If her death was indeed the result of septicemia, it would have followed rapidly (within one or two days) from the onset of systemic inflammation, and the family would not have had much time to prepare. However, there are two other options to consider: cartonnages and coffins were available in standard sizes, and a custom-made set might have been too expensive for the family; or they may have sought to give the deceased woman not only an ideal face, but also an ideal height for her eternal life.

RS

Bibliography

Steindorff 1949, 9–17.

Notes

1. The findings are from a computed axial tomography of the mummy carried out in 2008 in conjunction with the department of diagnostic radiology at the University of Maryland School of Medicine, Baltimore. We thank Dr. Barry Daly, director of the department, and Dr. Warren Tewes of the University of Maryland Dental School for their support and collaboration.
2. According to Lansing; see Steindorff 1949, 11.
3. A small piece that had fallen into the hollows of the cartonnage and was protected from light was found during the reinstallation of the mummy in 2001; the fragment preserves the original yellow color.
4. For a close parallel of the wig, see the mummy cartonnage of Shep-en-Khonsu in the Luxor Museum, J. 106, illustrated in Luxor Museum 1979, 167.

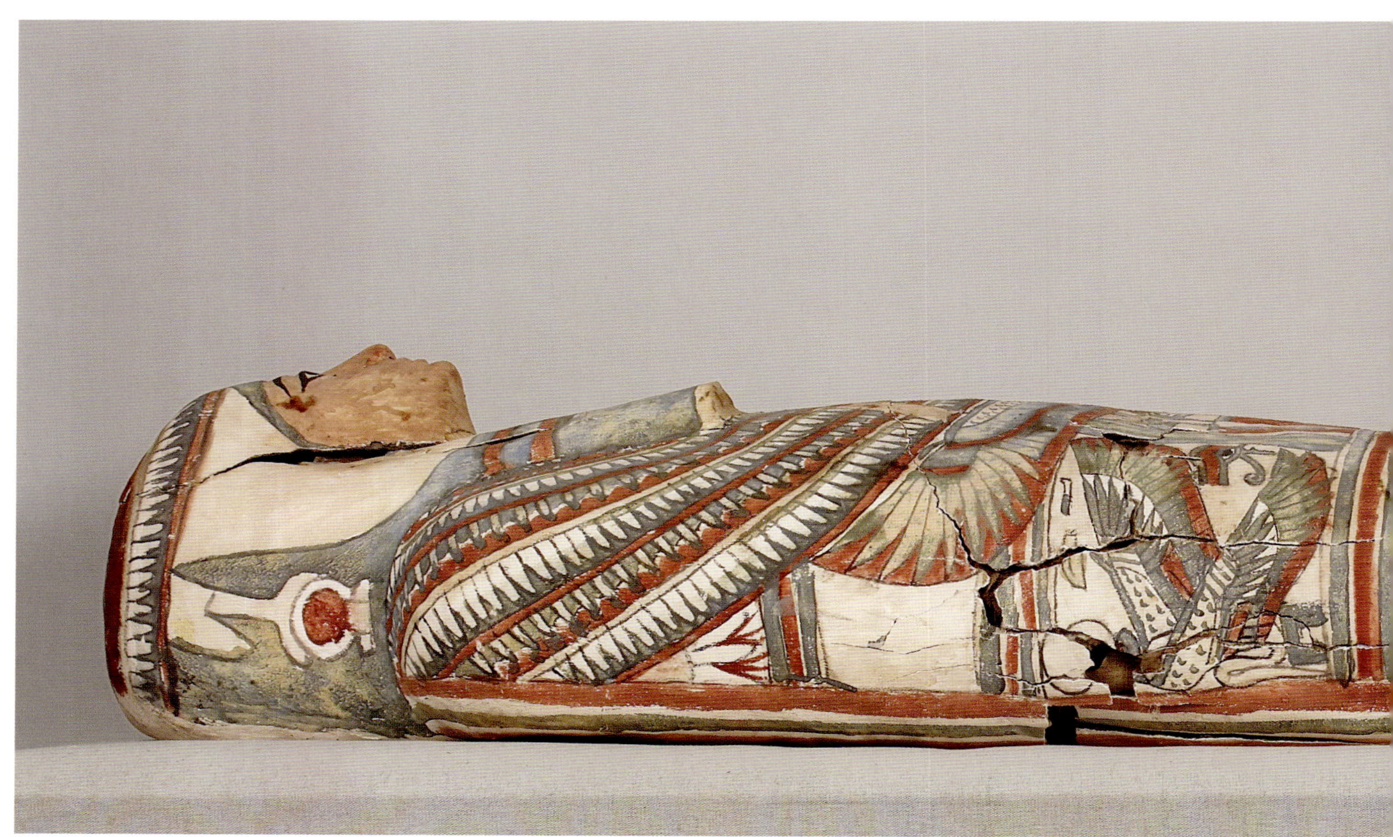

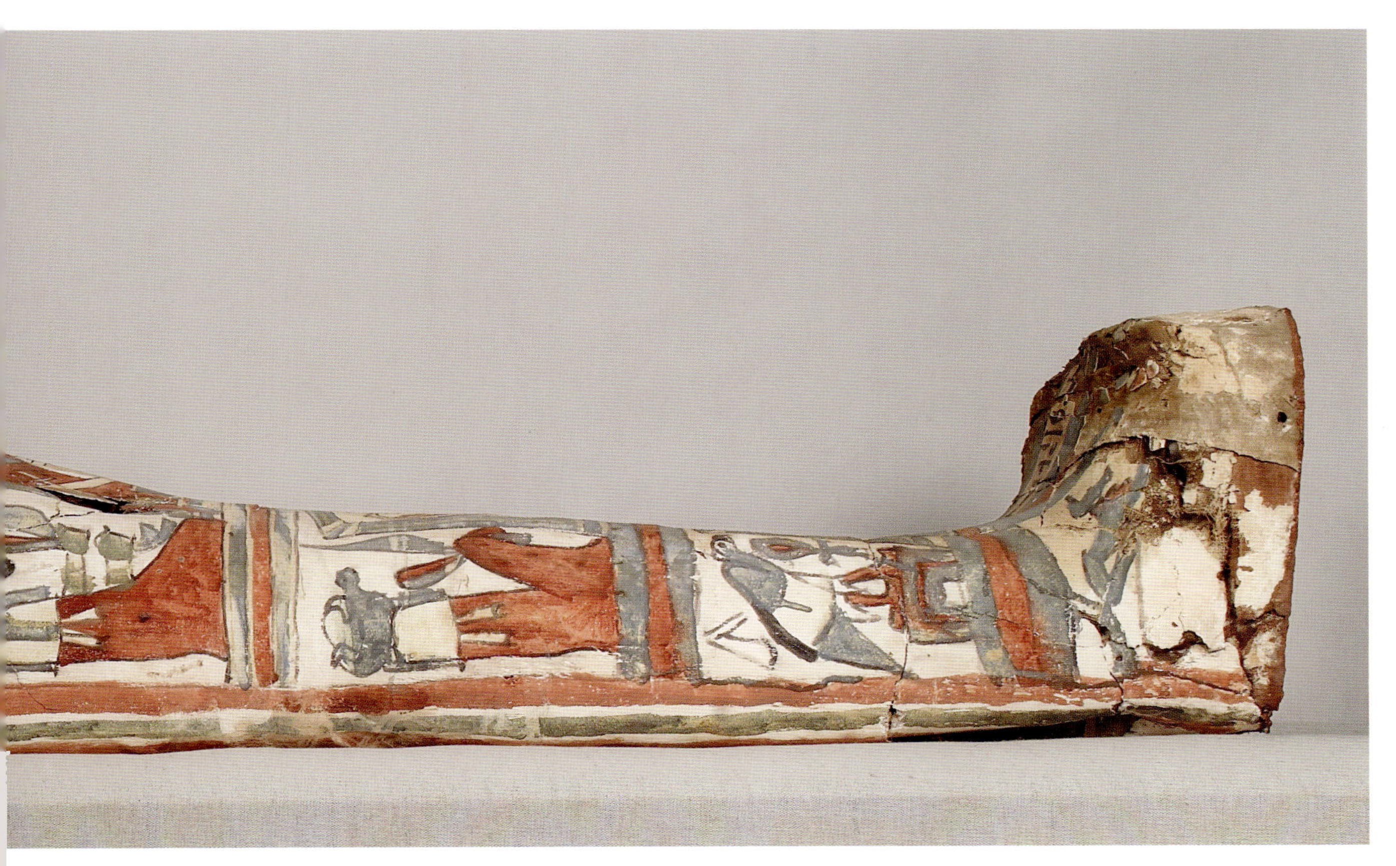

42

Coffin box set

Western Thebes, Deir el-Bahari
Wood, painted plaster, and varnish
Outer coffin (WAM TL.1951.179): 216.2 x 73.9 cm (85 1/8 x 29 1/8 in)
Inner coffin and lid (WAM TL.1951.180); 188.2 x 52 cm (74 1/2 x 20 1/2 in.)
Mummy board (WAM TL.1951.181), 177.8 x 42.3 cm (70 x 15 5/8 in.)
Twenty-first Dynasty, ca. 960–940 B.C.
Provenance: Deir el-Bahari, Tomb 60;[1] The Metropolitan Museum of Art, Egyptian Expedition, 1924–25; The Metropolitan Museum of Art, New York: outer coffin (MMA 25.3.5), inner coffin and lid (MMA 25.3.13A–B), and mummy board (MMA 25.3.14); on loan to the Walters Art Museum from the Metropolitan Museum of Art since 1951.

This coffin box set, together with eight other complete sets, was recovered from the burial chamber of a rock-cut tomb near the precinct of Hatshepsut's temple at Deir el-Bahari, exactly north of the lower court and close to the famous cache of coffins found at the Bab el-Gusus.[2] The crypt, excavated by Herbert Winlock of the Metropolitan Museum of Art Egyptian Expedition in 1924,[3] was originally intended for the burial of family members of a high priest of Amun, Men-kheper-Re, who served in the Theban pontificate of the Twenty-first Dynasty. Over time, intrusive burials of individuals unrelated to the tomb's owner were added to the crypt, including the occupant of the Walters coffin. The interment of this coffin set's owner was one of the last two burials in the crypt. During the excavation, the outer coffin of this set was found jammed into the low entrance to the chamber, too large to fit inside the crypt (fig. 12). The inner coffin, together with its mummy, had been removed in antiquity and placed inside the chamber.

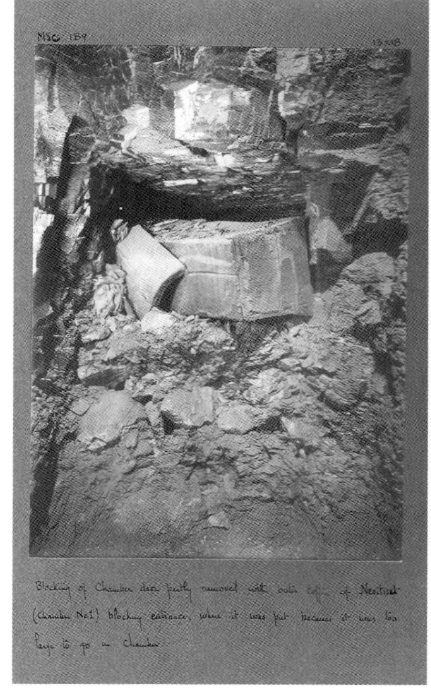

Fig. 12 Deir el-Bahari, tomb 60: door passage blocked by the outer coffin of Nesit-iset. Excavation photograph (1930–31) by the Egyptian Expedition, The Metropolitan Museum of Art, New York

A high incidence of tomb robbery led to drastic changes in burial practices during the Twenty-first Dynasty. Tombs were no longer elaborately furnished and decorated but were replaced by hidden rock caches, which had no interior decoration. The funerary and religious scenes that had earlier decorated the tomb walls were transferred to the coffin surfaces. Hence the coffin became a substitute for the tomb, and iconographic representations essential to securing the passage of the deceased into the afterlife covered every inch of the coffins.

The mummy found in this coffin set was that of an upper-middle-class woman named Nesit-iset. Her name appears on her "Osiris sheet," a special cloth covering the bandaged mummy adorned with a life-size drawing of the god Osiris, and the deceased's name.[4] This set, however, was intended for a woman named Ankh-es-Mut, whose name and title, Chantress of Amun, were never erased from the coffin.[5] It was not unusual in Egyptian burials for funeral equipment to be appropriated for use by others, as was this set.

Coffin sets of the Twenty-first Dynasty normally consisted of five pieces: two anthropoid coffins and a mummy board with a flat underside, placed directly on top of the mummy.[6] The fingertips on this mummy board were cut in antiquity so that they would not extend beyond the board, presumably so that it would fit inside the inner coffin. The set lacks the outer coffin

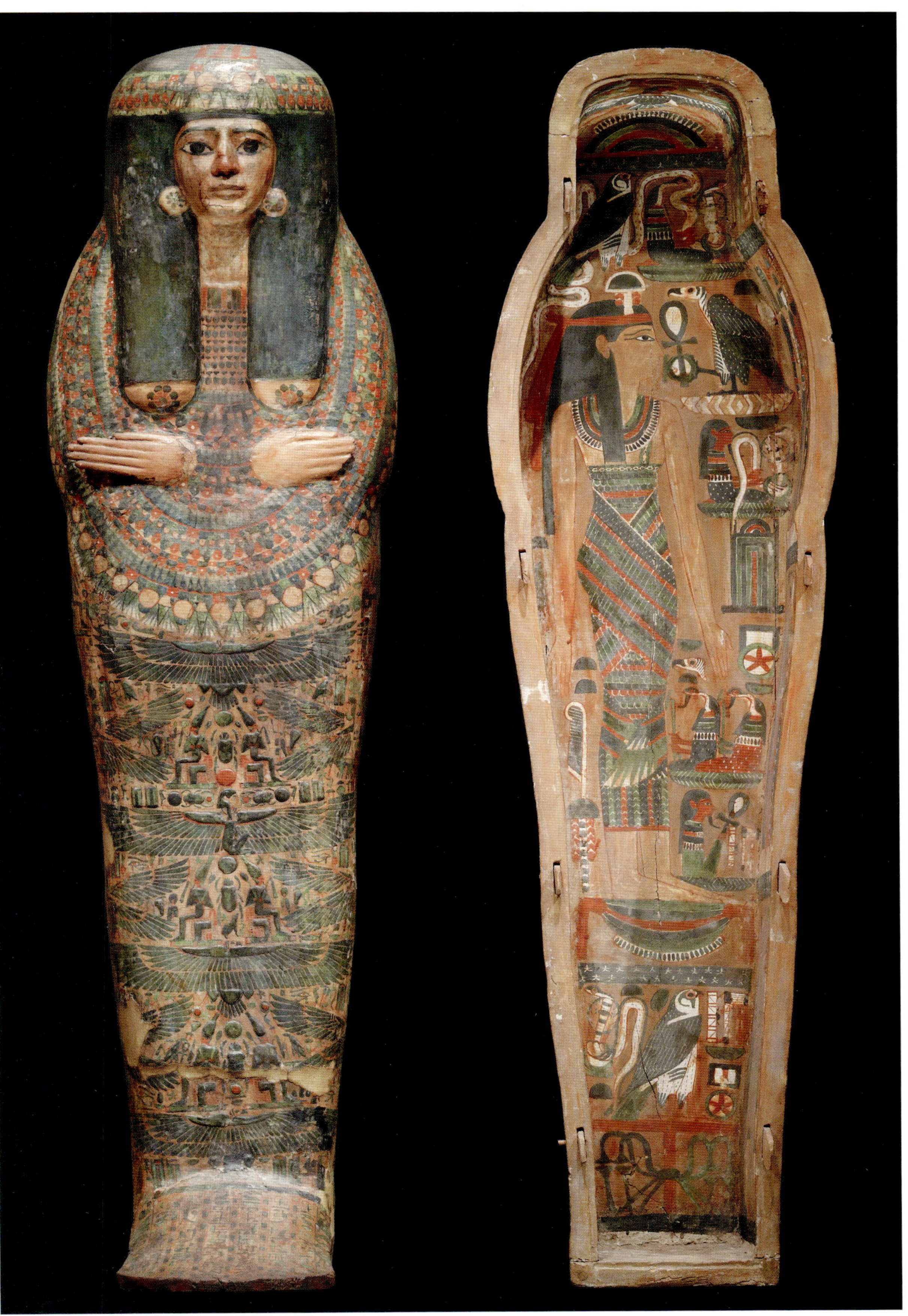

lid, which was severely damaged in antiquity. Typically the colors of the exterior consist of a yellow background with most of the decoration painted in red and light and dark green. This set has raised decoration. After painting, the lids were coated with varnish, which darkened some pigments.

The vivid scenes depict an intricate combination of funerary and religious motifs, linking the deceased to the myths of the underworld god Osiris in the quest to secure resurrection and a glorified afterlife. The cult of the solar deity Re is attested by the many representations of winged deities, such as the sky goddess Nut, the sun disk, and the *kheper* beetle. The combined iconographic repertoire of Osirian and solar deity ornamentation on Twenty-first Dynasty coffin paintings was richer than had ever been produced before.

The lid of the inner coffin depicts the deceased wearing a wig, with sculpted breasts ornamented by rosettes, and a large *wesekh* floral collar covering the torso,[7] from which emerge modeled hands (in raised relief) with extended fingers. The decoration on the lower portion of the lid is composed of horizontal registers containing vignettes and short vertical columns of hieroglyphic inscriptions on the footboard. These distinctive elements indicate a dating that falls within the later pontificate of the high priest Pinedjem II (ca. 980 B.C.) until the end of the reign of his son, Psusennes II (III) (ca. 945 B.C.).[8] The interior embellishment of the coffins features a mixed composition of pictorial units. It conforms to type 3 of Andrzej Niwinski's coffin typology, in which the bottom is divided by horizontal lines into several registers, one of which is much larger than the others, with a vertical central element, usually containing a single figure on which the emphasis is placed. The decoration is painted on a dark, cherry-red ground. On the bottom of both boxes, large figures of the Goddess of the West (guardian of the necropolis) appear, and on the headboard above flies the human-headed *Ba* bird (the spirit of the deceased). The goddess is surrounded on the inner sides by protective deities who ensure the deceased's safe passage into the afterlife.

CH

Bibliography

Winlock 1926, 20, 23, 25–28; Niwinski 1988, 107, no. 17.

Notes

1. Porter and Moss 1964, 629.
2. For a summary of the Bab el-Gusus cache, see Reeves 2000, 81–82.
3. Winlock 1926, 3–32.
4. Illustrated in Winlock 1926, 25, 28, fig. 33.
5. Winlock 1926, 20. Names of the deceased could be inscribed in several places on coffin sets.
6. For Twenty-first Dynasty coffin sets, see Küffer and Renfer 1996, 28–59; Lacovara and Trope 2001a, 47–51, nos. 36–39.
7. Niwinski 1988, 69, no. 28, pl. 10, A–B.
8. For the possible identification of Psusennes II with Psusennes III, see Janssen-Winkeln 2000, 221. For the dating, see Niwinski 1988, 78.

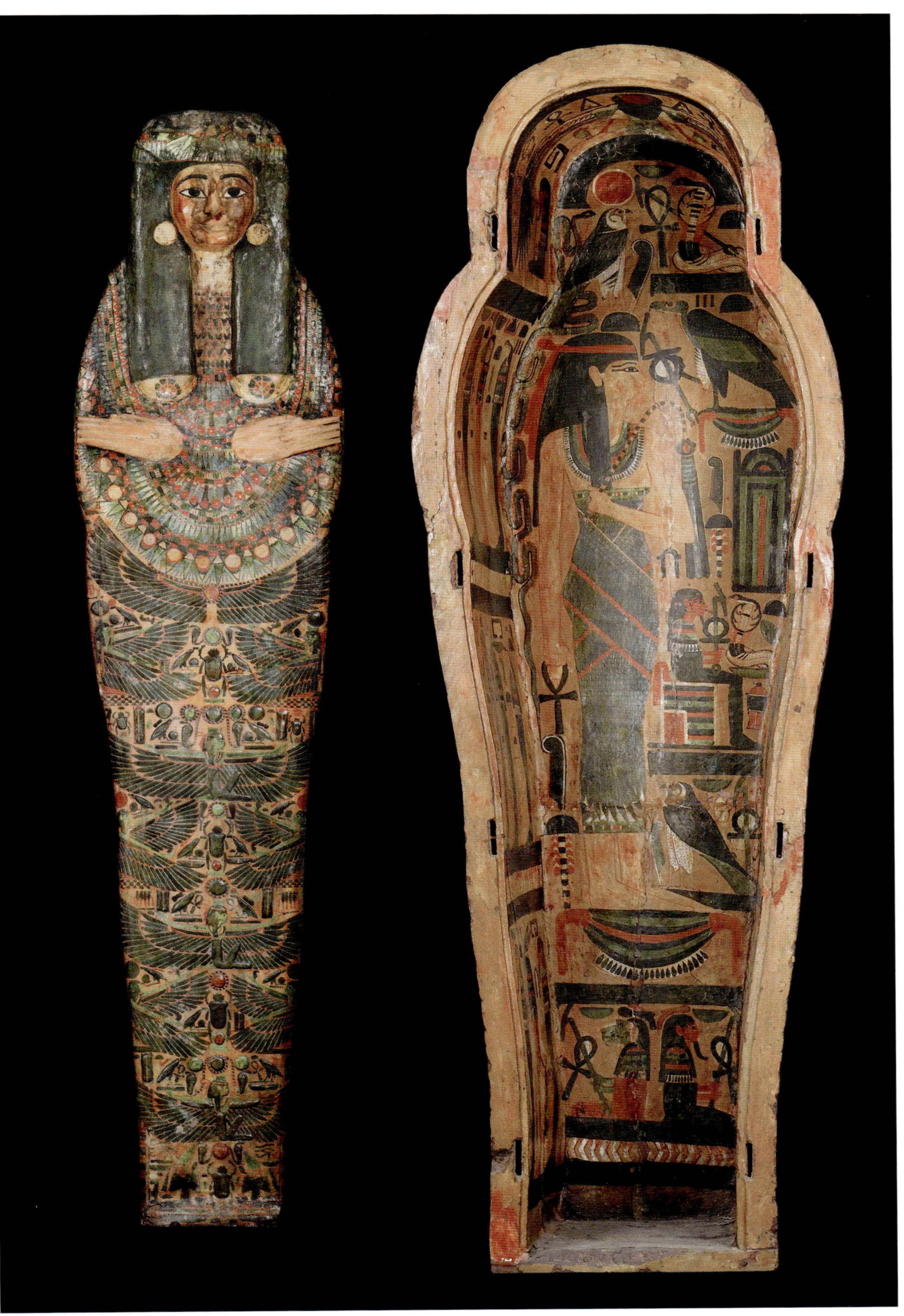

43

Set of four canopic jars

Said to be from Abydos

Limestone, black paint; jars: height 32–36 cm (12 5/8–14 3/16 in.), diameter 13–13.5 cm (5 1/8–5 5/16 in.); lids: height 11.7–14.4 cm (4 5/8–5 11/16 in.), diameter 13–13.5 cm (5 1/8–5 5/16 in.)

Twenty-second–Twenty-third Dynasty, ca. 900–800 B.C.

Provenance: Dikran Kelekian, New York/Paris; Henry Walters, 1912; Walters Art Museum, by bequest, 1931 (41.171–41.174)

As early as the Fourth Dynasty of the Old Kingdom, the internal organs of the deceased were removed from the body during the process of mummification.[1] These organs, the most easily prone to putrefaction, were then placed in special containers, the so-called canopic jars—always a set of four—and buried beside the sarcophagus or coffin with the mummy. The procedure was motivated by the belief that only a complete body, with all of its components, could guarantee an individual's rebirth and the desired afterlife. The earliest known examples were simple stone jars with shallow disklike lids,[2] usually uninscribed. During the First Intermediate Period (the Ninth–Tenth Dynasty, ca. 2100 B.C.), the style changed to lids with human heads, and entire sets of jars were produced from a variety of materials. Somewhat later, the practice arose of storing the jars in an outer box, known as a canopic chest, subdivided into four compartments, one for each jar. Inscriptions described the protection of the internal organs by the Four Sons of Horus: the deities Imsety, Hapy, Duamutef, and Qebehsenuef.

It was not until the late Eighteenth Dynasty (ca. 1300 B.C.) that the lids were carved in the characteristic form of the protective deities' heads, each associated with one of the viscera. Four funerary goddesses, in addition to the canopic deities, protected the jars' contents. Human-headed Imsety guarded the liver (under the protection of the goddess Isis), baboon-headed Hapy guarded the lungs (under the goddess Nephthys), jackal-headed Duamutef guarded the stomach (under the goddess Neith) and falcon-headed Qebehsenuef guarded the intestines (under the goddess Serket). The form and iconography of canopic jars and the chests that contained them remained in use till Greco-Roman times, and they were an indispensable element of standard burials, both royal and private.[3]

Canopic jars nonetheless reflect a diversity of styles, distinguished by their inscriptions, material, and the quality of their craftsmanship. The Walters' fine limestone set has short inscriptions that name the Four Sons of Horus, but not the tomb owner.[4] Colors were used sparingly to highlight only the details of the heads, resulting in the jars' pleasing and expressive appearance.

MS

Bibliography

Unpublished.

Notes

1. For example, in the tomb of Queen Hetepheres I at Giza; see Reeves 2000, 168–71.
2. D'Auria, Lacovara, and Roehrig 1988, 80, no. 10.
3. For the development of the canopic equipment, see Ikram and Dodson 1998, 276–92.
4. For other sets in limestone, see Luxor Museum 1979, 170, no. 263; Scott 1986, 116–17, no. 66.

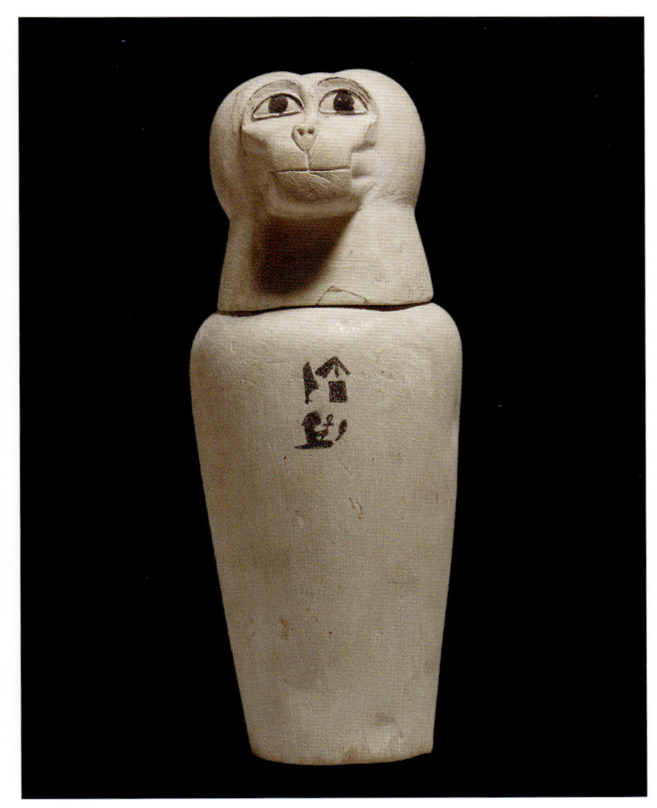
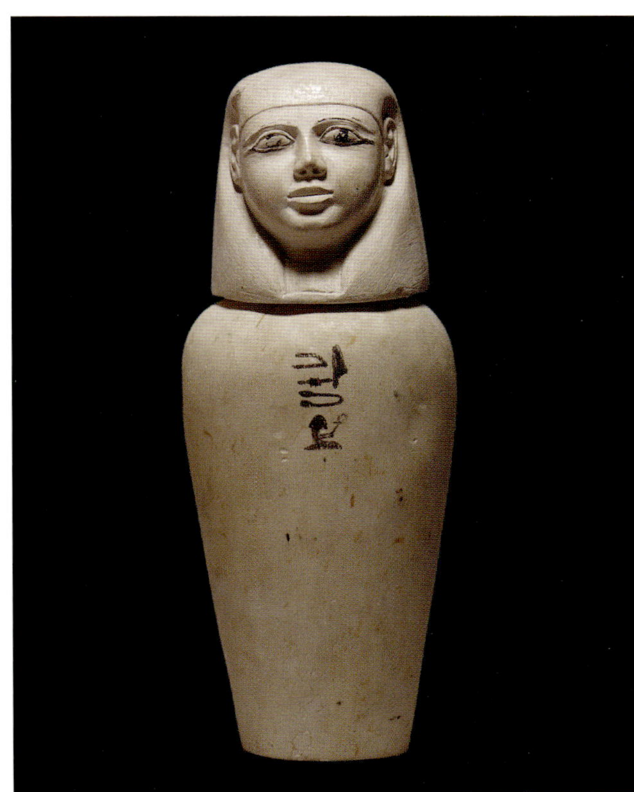
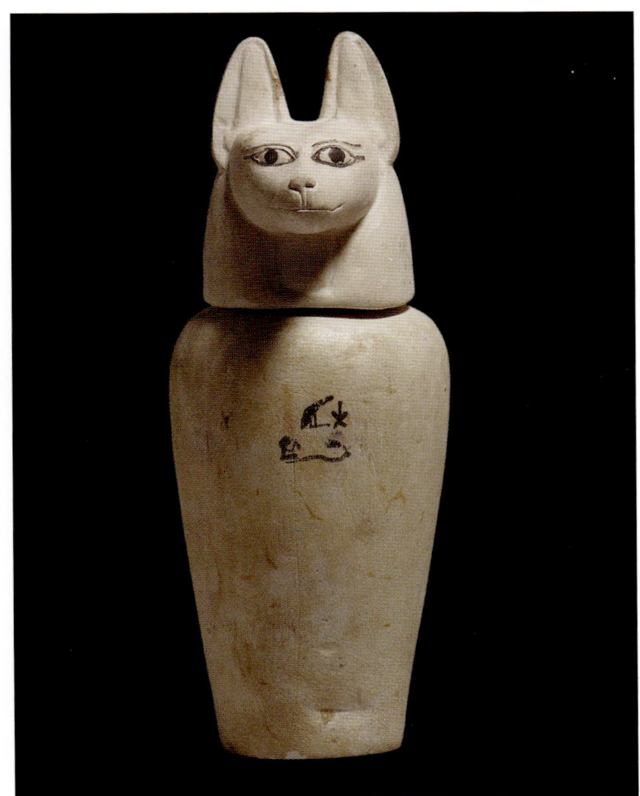
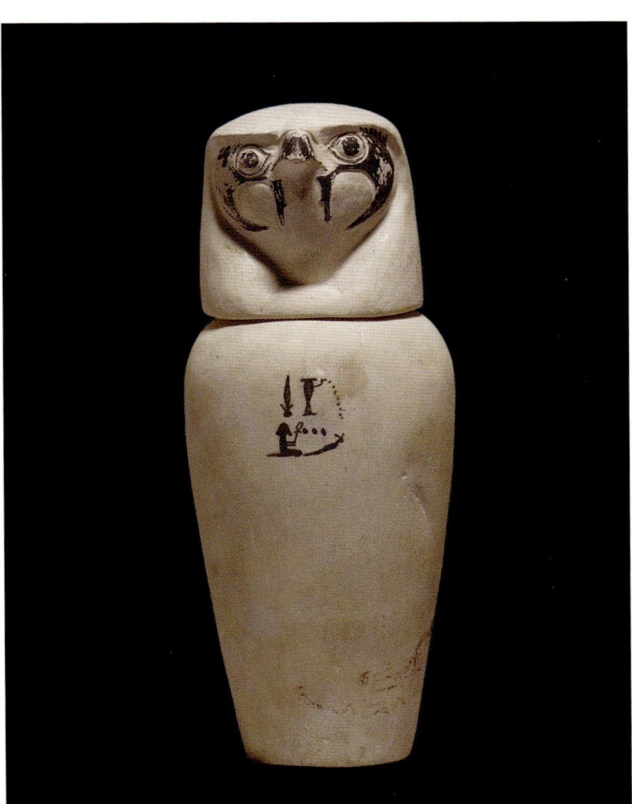

44

"Aegis" with the head of Sakhmet

Gold (weight 46.6 grams); height 7 cm (2 3/4 in.);
length of menat: 6.8 cm (2 5/8 in.)
Twenty-second–Twenty-third Dynasty, ca. 900–750 B.C.
Provenance: Henry Walters, 1924; Walters Art Museum, by bequest, 1931 (57.540)

In the New Kingdom, a new two-part cult object known among Egyptologists as an "aegis" was added to the traditional complement of holy items. The term (in its classical Greek usage) denotes the storm shield of the supreme god Zeus; its usage in Egyptology alludes to the object's ostensible form rather than its actual function.[1] Seen from the front, the aegis resembles a broad collar (named *wesekh* in Egyptian) with falcon-headed terminals and elaborated floral designs, surmounted by the head of a deity. In most examples, the head is that of a human goddess (Hathor or Isis) or a feline goddess (such as Bastet, Sakhmet, Wadjet, or Tefnut).[2] The lioness head of the Walters example, framed by a long wig and crowned by the sun disk with a tall *uraeus*, can be associated with Sakhmet, the principal goddess of the Memphite region. The size of this aegis and the use of gold indicate that it was commissioned by the court, but its function is less easily explained. The aegis might have had a specific function in the temple ritual, as an offering to the goddess.

The back of the collar element is hinged at an angle to a secondary part, a counterweight called the *menat*,[3] which was ordinarily used to balance heavy beaded necklaces. The upper section is decorated at either edge with a small *uraeus* wearing the crowns of Upper (left) and Lower Egypt (right) identified, respectively, as Nekhbet and Wadjet, the two tutelary deities of the united state of Egypt. The chasing shows a standing goddess with a lion's head, crowned with a sun disk and *uraeus*, preparing to suckle the young Horus. To the right of the scene, the metal surface appears to have been carefully abraded in order to eliminate an inscription. No new inscription was added, however, leaving the original ownership of the aegis lost to history. The decoration, with royal-divine motifs, continues in the circular lower part of the *menat*, where two winged *uraei* flank the richly detailed figure of a falcon. It is positioned on top of a palace façade and wears the double crown, an age-old symbol of the king or the first element of his titles. The linear style and slender forms of the engraved figures may also support an even later date for the object than given above, into the Twenty-sixth Dynasty (ca. 650 B.C.).[4]

MS

Bibliography

Canby 1979b, 22, no. 31; Capel and Markoe 1996, 136, no. 66; Schulz 2003b, 123–31, pl. 28.

Notes

1. The use of the term in Egyptology has been questioned by Schulz 2003b, 123.
2. For two unusual examples in bronze, see Delange 2007, 39–49, figs. 20–22.
3. For an aegis with a personified *menat*, see Page-Gasser and Wiese 1997, 256–59, no. 171.
4. For details of the feathers, see Schoske 1995, 63, fig. 67; for the stylistic development of metal figures, see Hill and Schorsch 2007, 130–33.

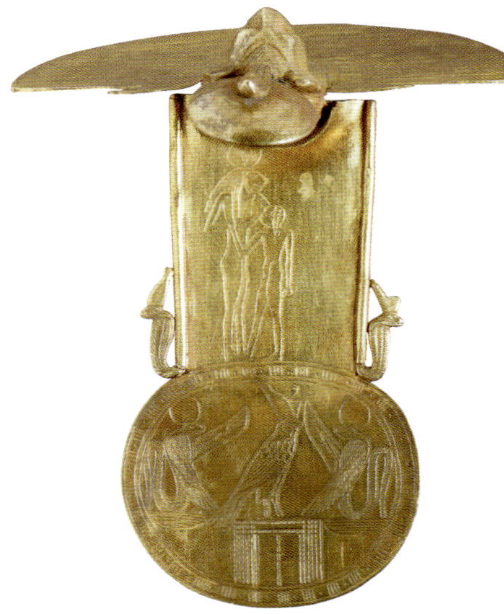

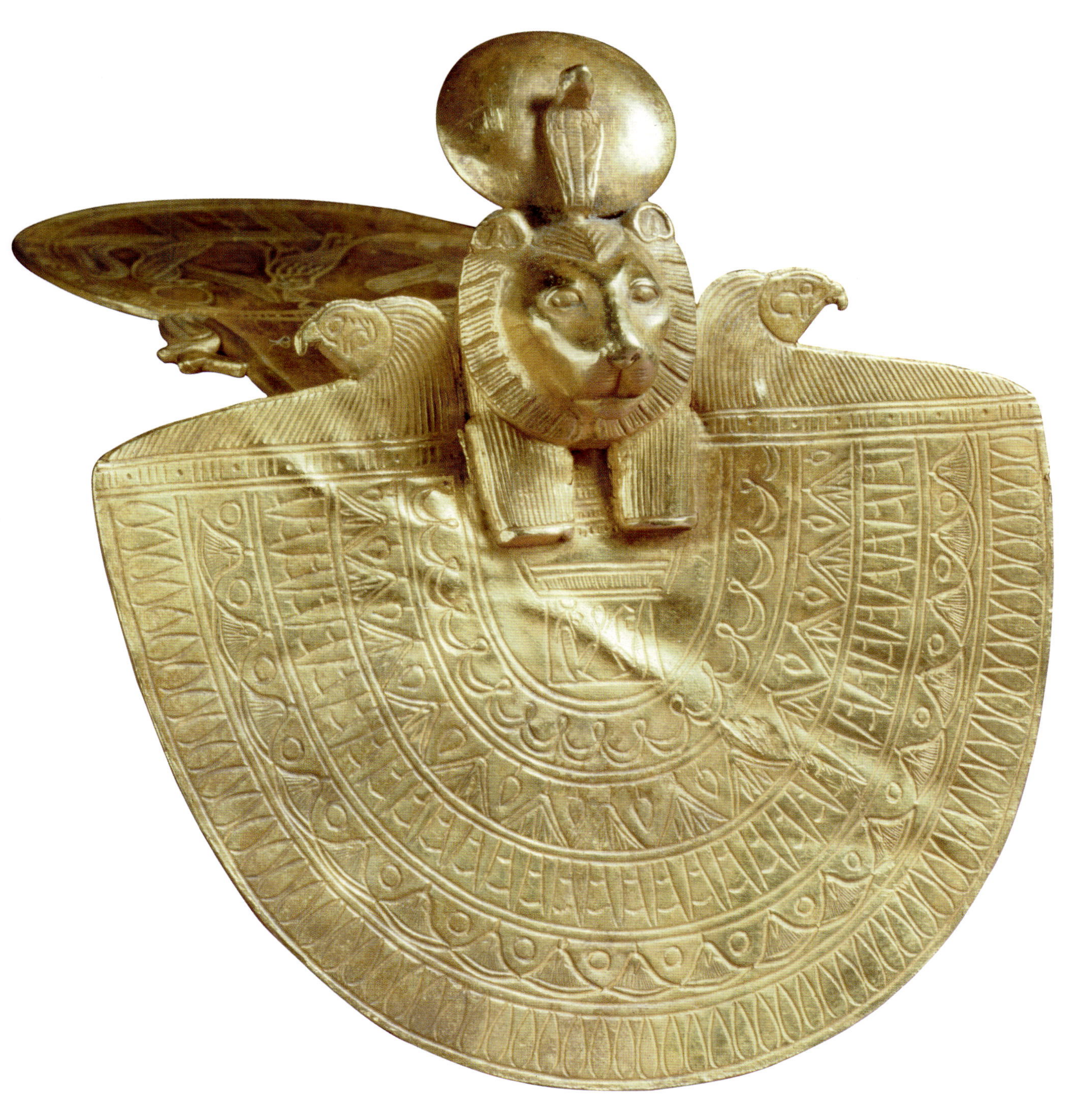

45

Figure of the god Anubis with worshiper

Probably from Karnak, temple of Amun (cachette)
Bronze, gilded; 20.8 x 14.5 cm (8 1/8 x 5 3/4 in.)
Twenty-fifth–Twenty-sixth Dynasty, ca. 680–660 B.C.
Provenance: Egyptian Museum, Cairo (JE 38518), sale; Henry Walters, 1930; Walters Art Museum, by bequest, 1931 (54.400)

Looking at an ancient Egyptian bronze figure of a deity, even the most expert connoisseur would find it difficult to reconstruct the object's original setting. Indeed, we must assume that many surviving single figures were originally part of larger ensembles. Such group configurations could better convey complex mythological meanings or relationships than any single representation of a deity. When the bases of these groups disintegrated, as unfortunately they often did, the components were separated, and the content was lost forever. How many of the larger, multifigured groups were melted down in antiquity in order to recover the precious metals of which they were made remains an open question.

This ensemble consists of three separately cast parts: the standing figure of the god Anubis on its own base; kneeling before him the donor of the group, a certain Wdja-Hor-resnet; and a large pedestal, which unites the two figures.[1] The combination must have been a common one, as attested by the number of surviving complete examples and the even larger number of small figures of worshipers that have lost their original context. Furthermore, the donation of such a group configuration to a temple would have assured the donor of his or her eternal interaction with the deity, for the act of performing the offering ritual secured the god's or goddess's grace and protection.

The jackal-headed Anubis, guardian of the necropolis and master of the mummification process, originally held a *was*-scepter (now lost) in his left hand; in his right hand he grasped an *ankh* symbol. The god is clad in a short kilt, a tripartite wig, and a broad collar and is adorned with carefully engraved armlets and bracelets. Before him are two large *uraei*, wearing the crowns of Upper and Lower Egypt (left and right, respectively) to represent the union of Egypt. The Anubis figure and the two cobras were once entirely gilded. The kneeling worshiper[2] in front of the god stretches both hands forward (palms down) in a gesture of adoration. The inscriptions on the two bases contain a short invocation to Anubis followed by the names of the donor and his parents. The back pillar inscription reads: "Anubis gives life [to] Wdja-Hor-resnet, son of Ankh-pa-khered."

MS

Bibliography

Daressy 1905–6, 138–39, pl. XXX; Steindorff 1946a, 138, no. 588, pl. XC.

Notes

1. The group was once wrapped in cloth; see Hill and Schorsch 2007, 178–80, figs. 76 and 77. The donor's title is not mentioned, although he must have been an important person given the quality of the figure.
2. For another fine example, see Schoske and Wildung 1992, 32–33, no. 17.

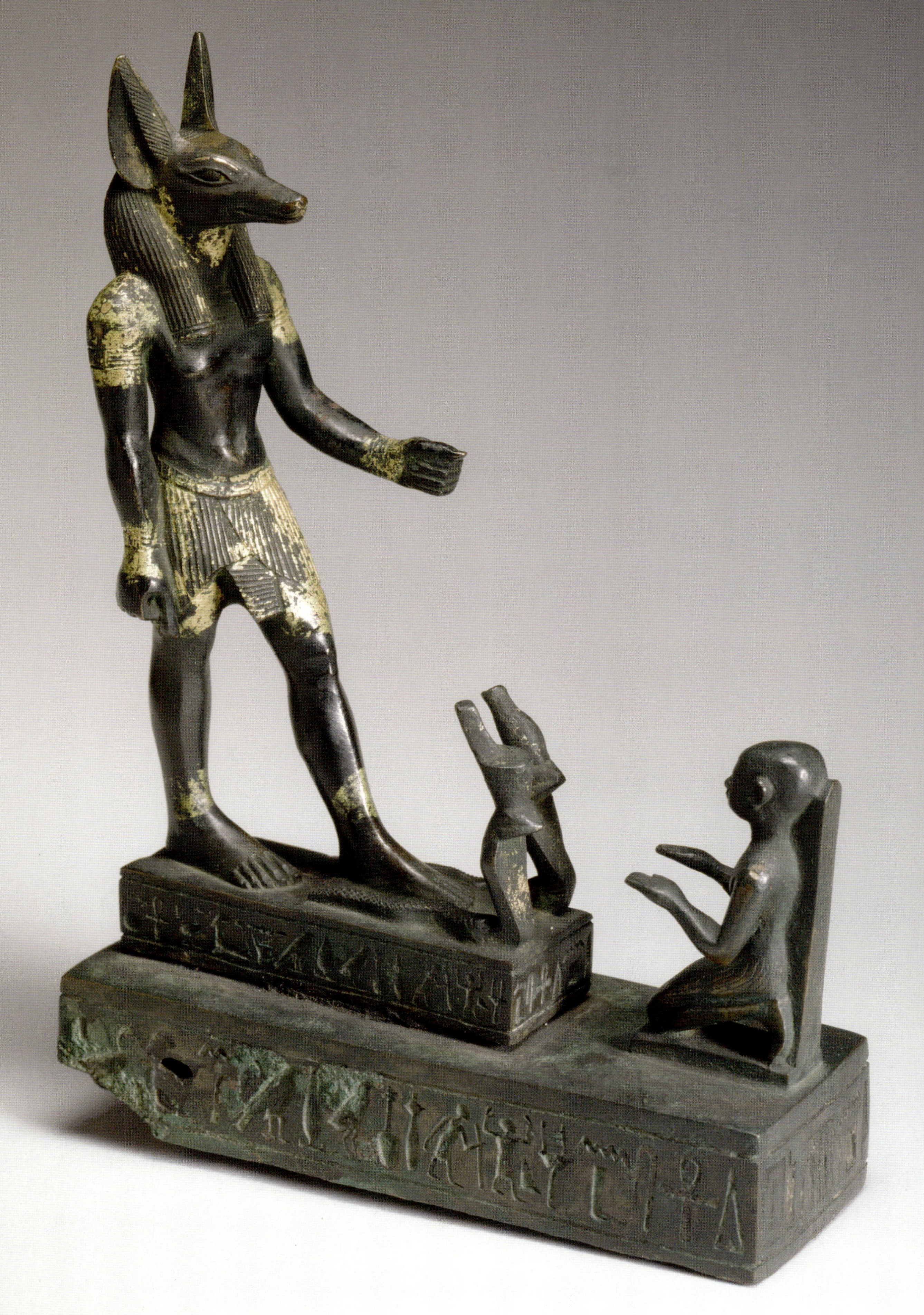

46

Statue of Amun-Re

Probably from Karnak

Bronze alloy, remains of gilding and glass inlay; 47.7 x 10.2 x 13.9 cm (18 3/4 x 4 x 5 3/4 in.)

Twenty-fifth–Twenty-sixth Dynasty, ca. 680–640 B.C.

Provenance: Dikran Kelekian, New York/Paris; Henry Walters, before 1931; Walters Art Museum, by bequest, 1931 (54.413)[1]

The god Amun, whose name means the "hidden one," first appears in the Pyramid Texts of the Old Kingdom, where he is mentioned (in spell 446), together with his female counterpart, Amaunet, as one of the primeval forces; another passage (spell 1540 [P]) refers to the deceased king as "son of Geb [primeval god of earth] on the throne of Amun." It is unlikely that Amun was worshiped as a deity at that time; rather, he was an abstract representation of a hidden, creative force. This concept was modified in the Middle Kingdom, when no fewer than four kings of the Twelfth Dynasty chose the name Amenemhat: "Amun is at the head."

To personalize Amun, and to situate him at Thebes, the theologians incorporated him into mythical and ritual tradition. Amun became the "Lord of Thebes," with his main sanctuary at Karnak on the eastern bank of the Nile, and was conceived as "King of the Gods" and "Lord of the thrones of the Two Lands," of Upper and Lower Egypt. Amun was also worshiped as the fertility god Kamutef—"bull of his mother," an epithet that associated him with the oldest Egyptian fertility god, Min, who created himself and combined with the sun god Re. Amun's incarnation as the god of creation, named Kematef "who has completed his moment" was particularly worshiped at Medinet Habu in Western Thebes. Although most of the aspects of Amun were defined in the Middle Kingdom, Amun's ultimate apotheosis took place during the New Kingdom, when he became the imperial god of Egypt and a universal deity.

This standing bronze figure of Amun was hollow cast and the feathers of the crown worked separately. The surface shows remains of gilding as well as the impression of a textile on the reverse of skirt and crown, indicating that the statue had once been wrapped in fabric. The original base is lost, and a rectangular plate was added under the right foot of the figure in modern times to equalize the different length of the legs.

The god appears in his traditional iconography with double-feather crown and flat, inserted sun disk, divine beard, collar necklace, and a short *shendyt* kilt. In his right hand he holds a staff that has lost its upper part; it may have been a long *was*-scepter (symbolizing "well-being" and "power"). The left hand once grasped an *ankh* sign (symbolizing "life"). This statue of Amun-Re is unusually large;[2] it either stood alone on a base,[3] or was combined with a smaller statuette of a worshiper.[4]

The proportions of the strong body, with muscular arms, broad shoulders, and bull-neck, are typical of the Kushite period (Twenty-fifth Dynasty), when the god Amun was particularly popular. However, the idealized facial features, with the small smiling mouth, are more characteristic of the Saite period (Twenty-sixth Dynasty); therefore, it is possible that the statue was donated to the temple in the early Twenty-sixth Dynasty, perhaps by a high official who came into his position under the Kushite rulers.

RS

Bibliography

Steindorff 1946a, 119, no. 478, pl. LXXIX: Posener 1959, 12 (incl. ill.).

Notes

1. The statue may have been among the bronze figures discovered in the cachette at Karnak in 1905–6, purchased by Henry Walters, together with other statues from the same site, from Dikran Kelekian.
2. With its original base, the height of the statue would have exceeded 50 cm (19 5/8 in.).
3. As does a Twenty-sixth Dynasty statue of Amun-Re donated by King Necho (height 44.4 cm [17 1/2 in.]), Munich, Staatliches Museum Ägyptischer Kunst (ÄS 6978), in Grimm, Schoske, and Wildung 1997, 202, no. 227.
4. See, for example, a Twenty-sixth Dynasty statue of Amun-Re together with the kneeling donor Horu-ir-aa, height 51 cm [20 in.]), Paris, Musée du Louvre (AF 1670), in Monnet 1955.

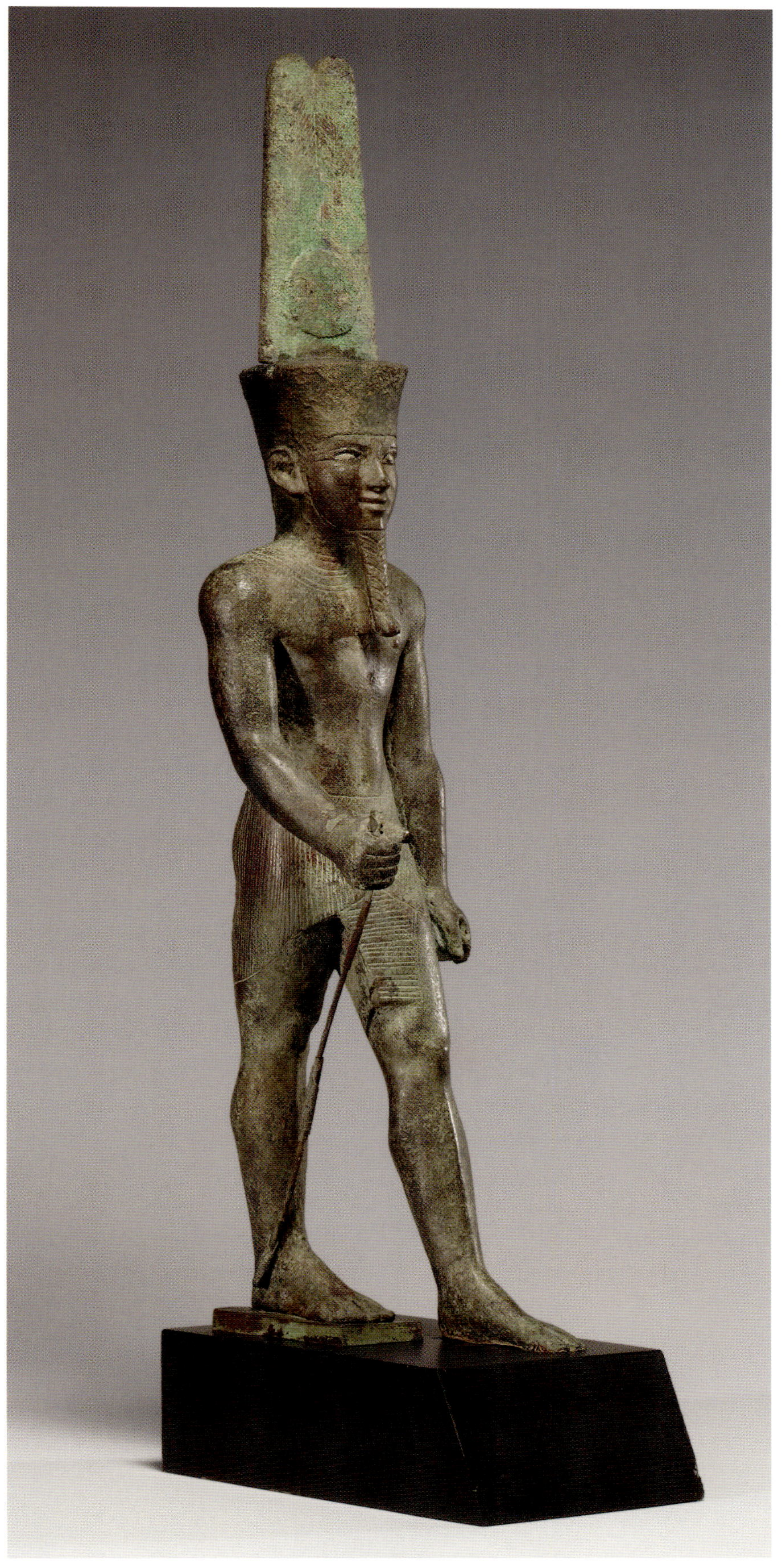

47

Head of King Amasis

Said to be from Memphis

Dark brown-red quartzite; 31.5 x 20 x 23.5 cm (12 x 7 7/8 x 9 1/4 in.)

Twenty-sixth Dynasty, ca. 560 B.C.

Provenance: Dikran Kelekian, New York/Paris; Henry Walters, 1912; Walters Art Museum, by bequest, 1931 (22.415)

The Late Period in Egyptian history can truly be said to have begun when Psamtek I (664–610 B.C.) overthrew his Assyrian masters in 664 B.C. and founded the Twenty-sixth Dynasty. Under the rule of the Saite kings (named for their capital, Sais, in the Nile Delta), the country enjoyed nearly 140 years of political stability and prosperity, accompanied by great achievements in all sectors of the arts. Late Period Egypt reached its apogee under the reign of Amasis (570–526 B.C.), and it remained a strong regional presence until the late dynasties, despite the Persian invasion of 525 B.C.

While archaism is an unmistakable characteristic of Late Period Egyptian art, it would be a rash misjudgment to treat works from that period as dull and weak reworkings of earlier artistic achievements. Evaluating the stylistic development of royal sculpture under the Saite rulers, however, is complicated by the fact that the few works that have survived are fragmentary heads or torsos,[1] and that their provenance is often uncertain or entirely unknown. Each secure identification is therefore a welcome addition, as has happened with the quartzite head of King Amasis at the Walters. The elongated face with distinctive features is unmistakably realistic, unlike the idealizing royal portraits of the past. The small almond-shaped eyes are set very high on the face, leaving barely any space between the thin, horizontal brows and the lower rim of the frontlet of the *nemes* headcloth.[2] Even more striking is the marked elevation of the ridge of the nose, emerging above the brows and causing the broad frontlet to follow the shape of this physical peculiarity. The mouth forms a light smile, the lower lip punctuated by a noticeable groove in the center. In a similar naturalistic way, both ears closely hug the skull.

The subtly modeled head is executed in a very homogeneous variety of quartzite, loaded with fine, sparkling crystals, a stone rarely used for royal statuary in the Twenty-sixth Dynasty. A torso in the Museo Egizio, Florence, from a kneeling figure also identified as Amasis is worked in the same stone,[3] but the similarities are not sufficiently close to conclude with assurance that the two statues constituted a joint commission and donation.

MS

Bibliography

Steindorff 1946a, 70, no. 224, pl. XXXVIII; Josephson 1988, 232–35, pl. XXXII, 1; Josephson 1992, 93–97, pls. 16–19; Seidel and Schulz 1998, 273, pl. 4; Russmann 2001, 37–38, fig. 25.

Notes

1. For a census of Late Period sculpture, see Leahy 1984, 59–76; Myśliwiec 1988, 46–66.
2. For the form of the eyes, compare, for example, Berlin, Ägyptisches Museum, inv. no. ÄM 11864, in Ziegler 2002, 86 (2), 393, no. 21.
3. Florence, Museo Archeologico/Museo Egizio, inv. no. 5625, in Müller 1955, 183–221.

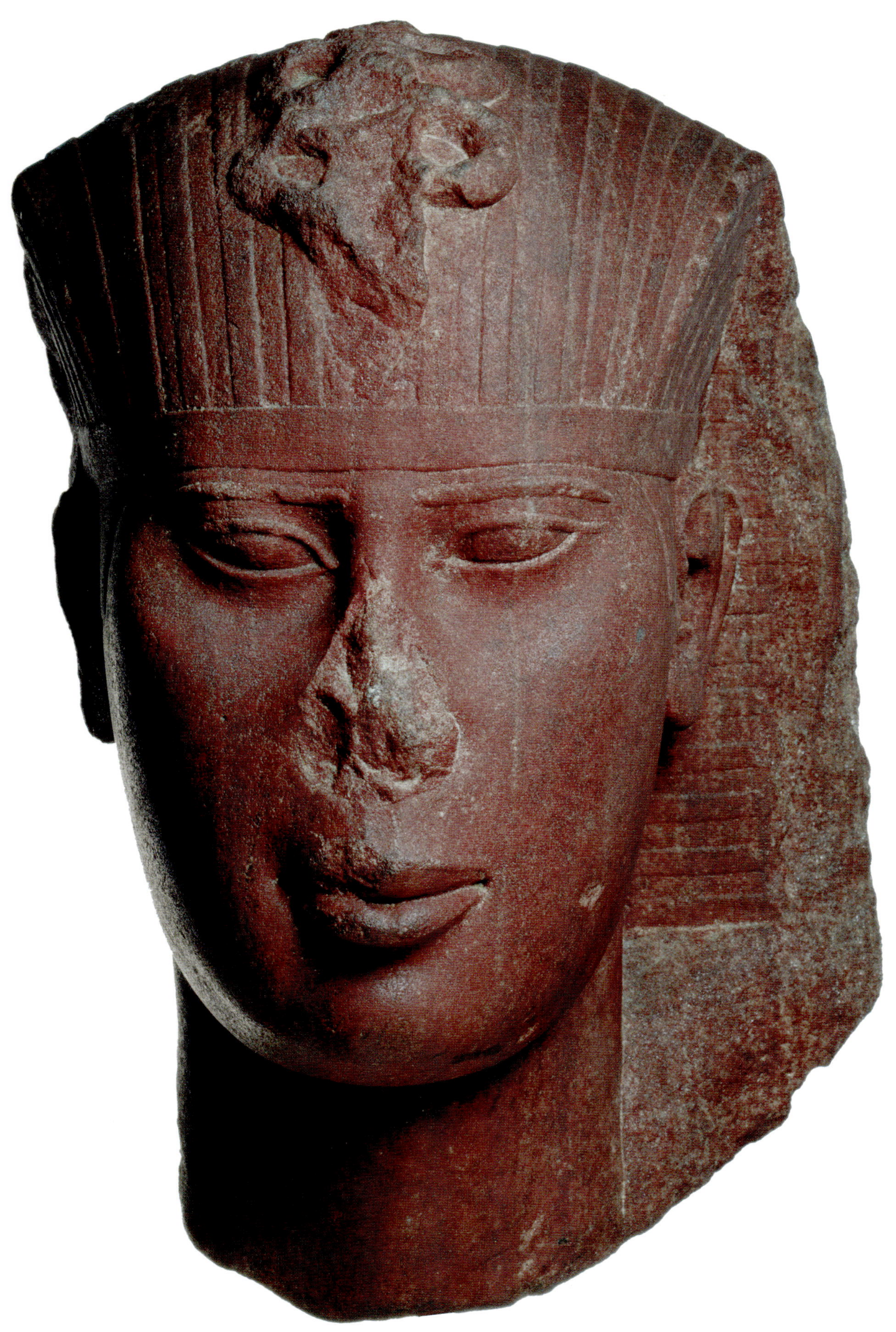

48

Relief of King Necho II

From the western Delta (Kom el-Hisn?)

Limestone, 14.5 x 27.3 cm (5 3/4 x 10 5/8 in.)

Twenty-sixth Dynasty, ca. 600 B.C.

Provenance: Dikran Kelekian, New York / Paris; Henry Walters, 1909; Walters Art Museum, by bequest, 1931 (22.135)

When the long and successful reign of Psamtek I came to an end in 610 B.C., a much less dynamic ruler ascended the throne as Necho II (610–595 B.C.). He was immediately drawn into a constant power struggle against Babylon. Necho II lost control of Syria and Palestine, and barely defeated those enemies on Egypt's borders at the eastern Delta. His failed foreign policy, which consumed much manpower and resources, seems also to have substantially reduced royal building projects and other donations. No large stone statues of the king are documented; and only a few small bronze figures have survived. The meager number of King Necho II's monuments may be due to the *damnatio memoriae*—the deliberate destruction or effacement of monuments and inscriptions—undertaken by Psamtek II, his son and successor. Psamtek II ordered the erasure of his father's name from temple walls as well as from many statues of high officials[1] and refilled the cartouches with his own name.

Under these circumstances, this and another relief of similarly modest size gain in importance.[2] Each limestone block is executed in sunk relief and dated by the royal cartouche of Necho II. No reliable provenance has been established for either of the slabs, but the similarities in their style, workmanship, and dimensions make a common origin most likely. The Walters block preserves the head of the pharaoh on the outer right edge, and the head of the goddess Hathor opposite. Necho wears a short curled wig with a diadem featuring a *uraeus* over the forehead; the royal cartouche appears directly above him. Hathor is represented in her classic iconography with a vulture headdress over her long wig, topped by cow horns and a sun disk. The upper portion of a large *was*-scepter that the goddess once held in her left hand is still recognizable. The facial features, rendered in a plain, linear style, have a somewhat idealizing quality, even though a faint memory of the more realistic Kushite portraits of the Twenty-fifth Dynasty is evident.

The incomplete inscription between the king and Hathor, however, preserves a valuable detail: the name of Hut-ihut, a major city in the western Delta and a former capital of the third nome of Lower Egypt.[3] We can presume with some confidence that these reliefs came from a shrine or temple within that city.

MS

Bibliography

Steindorff 1946a, 77, no. 260, pl. LIII; Bothmer 1960, 49, no. 42, pl. 39, figs. 92, 94; Myśliwiec 1988, 47 (B 2), 55.

Notes

1. See, for one example, Lacovara and Trope 2001b, 46–47, no. 21.
2. The second relief is in Copenhagen, Ny Carsberg Glyptotek, inv. no. ÆIN 46, in Myśliwiec 1988, 47 (B 3), 55, pl. XLVII, b.
3. See W. Helck, "Gaue," in *LÄ* 2 (1977): 394–95.

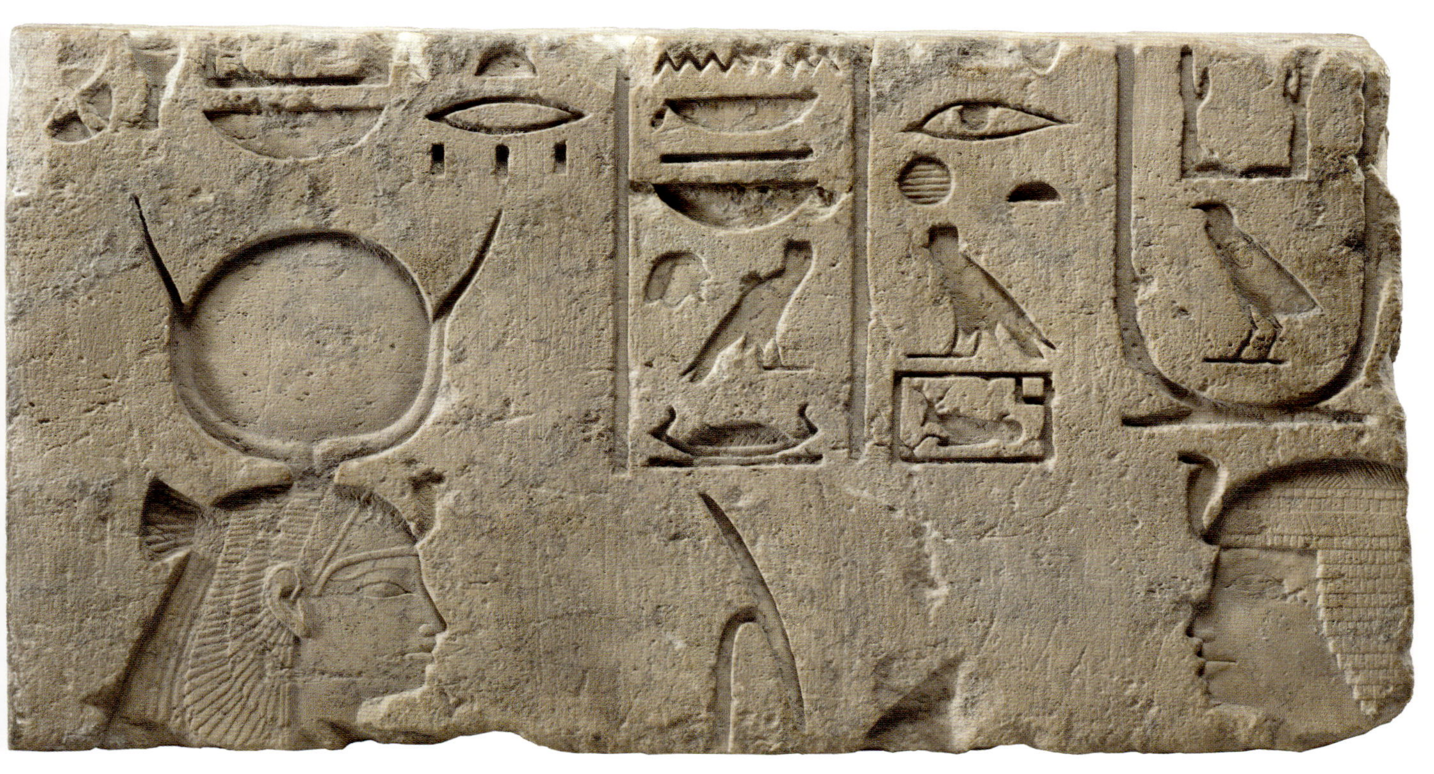

49

Temple relief of Nectanebo II

Sebennytos (present-day Samannud)
Granodiorite; 84.5 x 181 cm (33 ¼ x 71 ¼ in.)
Thirtieth Dynasty, ca. 350 B.C.
Provenance: Dikran Kelekian, New York / Paris; Henry Walters, 1909;
Walters Art Museum, by bequest, 1931 (22.119)

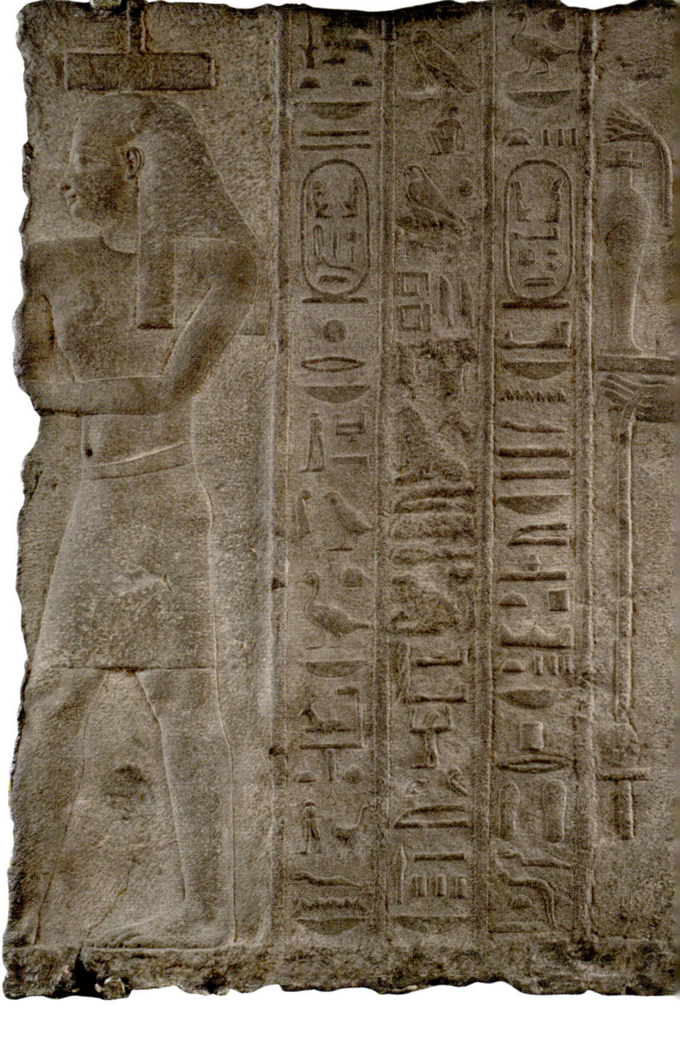

The ancient town of Sebennytos is located on the Damietta branch of the Nile in the central Delta, near the modern city of Samannud. Sebennytos, birthplace of the historian Manetho, who composed a history of Egypt (in Greek) during the reign of Ptolemy II (285–246 B.C.), served as the country's capital for the kings of the Thirtieth Dynasty, Egypt's last native pharaonic rulers. The town's main temple was built by Nectanebo I (380–362 B.C.) and dedicated to Onuris-Shu, the hunter and sky god whose female counterpart was the lion-headed goddess Mehit. The temple's decoration, interrupted by the Persian invasion of 343 B.C., was not completed until the middle of the third century B.C. The temple of Sebennytos was constructed entirely of hard stone: granite, basalt, and quartzite, as was an important temple to Isis at Behbeit-el-Hagar, six miles to the north. The Phersos, as the Greeks called the structure, was essentially intact as late as the fifteenth century of the common era; the Arab historian al-Maqrizi admired its royal statues, which were still standing in its courtyards. Over the ensuing centuries, however, the temple suffered extensive damage, largely as the result of a massive earthquake; when Napoleon Bonaparte's scientific expedition visited the site in the late eighteenth century, they found only piles of stones. Blocks and statues from the temple made their way into European and American collections in the nineteenth and early twentieth centuries.

Since the Old Kingdom the lower registers of friezes in major temples were decorated with processions of fecundity figures, bearing goods that symbolized the nation's prosperity and wealth (see no. 35). This block, carved in raised relief, shows the three male figures, representing individual nomes, walking to the left,[1]

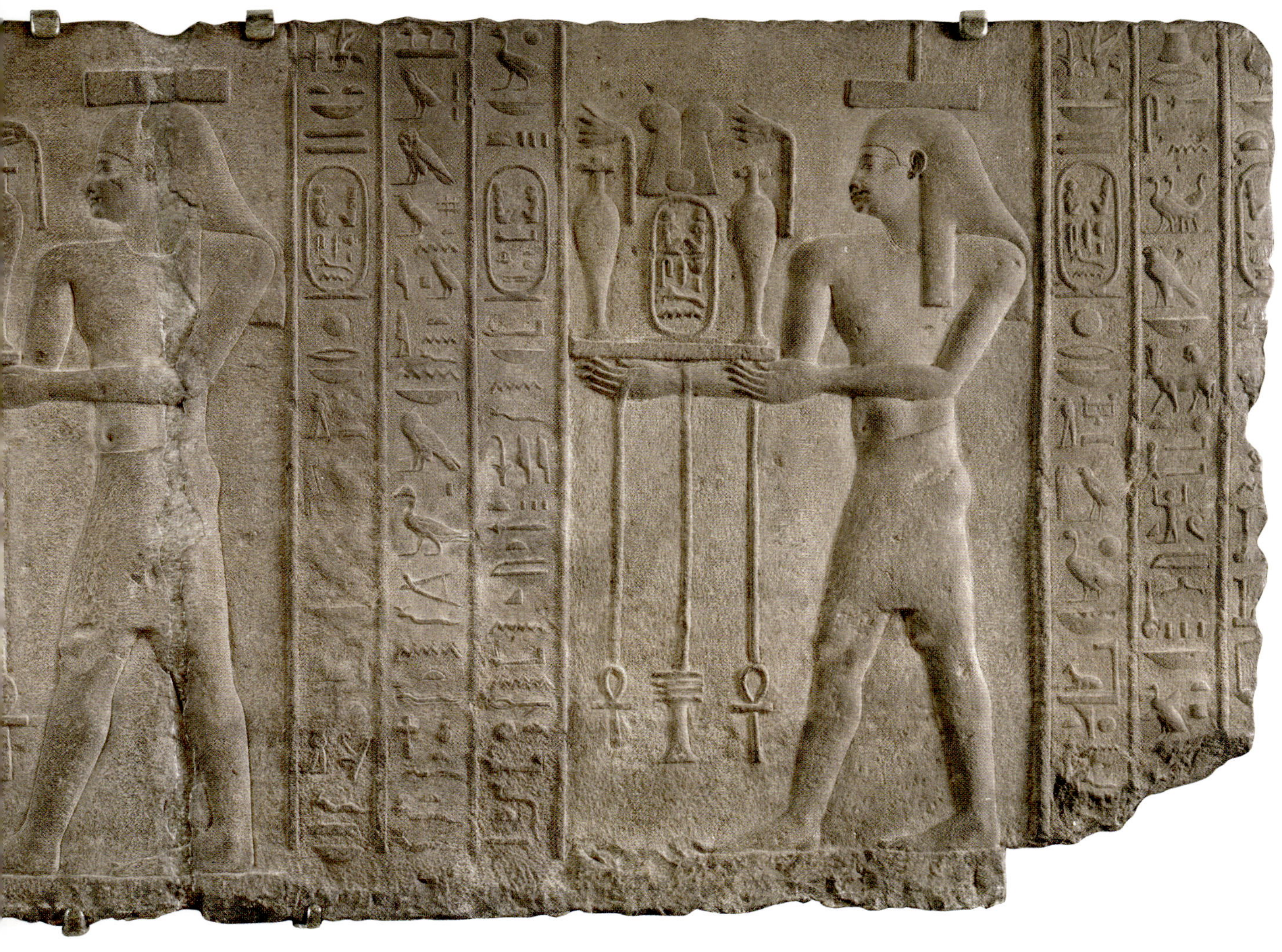

each wearing a long wig and a short kilt. Sadly, no further identification is possible since the nome symbols above their heads are lost. The offering trays in the hands of the figures in the center and on the right are identically loaded with two lotus flowers and *hes*-vases, flanking the central cartouche containing the names of Nectanebo II. In front of each offering-bearer, a three-column inscription conveys a ritualized dialogue between the king and the god Onuris-Shu.[2] The delicate execution of the details is characteristic of the late Thirtieth Dynasty. The dark stone used in this lower register alludes symbolically to the fertility of the soil ensured by the Nile's annual inundations. The temple walls above were contructed of a contrasting stone such as red granite or quartzite, and comparable, symbolically evocative arrangements of colored stone are documented from the New Kingdom forward.

MS

Bibliography

Steindorff 1944–45, 39–59 (no. 5), fig. 6; Steindorff 1946a, 74–75, no. 253, pl. XLVII; Myśliwiec 1988, 71(B, 2b), pl. XCII, d; Spencer 1999, 82, no. 34.

Notes

1. Another block from Sebennytos with the god Hapy looking right, in the Metropolitan Museum of Art, New York (12.182.4 B), is illustrated in Myśliwiec 1988, 71, pl. XCII, d.
2. The unfinished appearance of parts of this inscription is the result of salt efflorescence from groundwater.

50

Bust of a "Libyan" Dignitary

Probably from Thebes

Graywacke; height 37 cm (14 ½ in.)

Early Twenty-sixth Dynasty, ca. 660–650 B.C.

Provenance: Giovanni Dattari Collection, Cairo; sale, Hôtel Drouot, Paris, 17–19 June 1912, no. 293; Dikran Kelekian, New York / Paris; Henry Walters, 1924; Walters Art Museum, by bequest, 1931 (22.398)

Whereas few royal statues survive from the Twenty-sixth Dynasty, private individuals—including courtiers, bureaucrats, and priests—are amply represented, albeit with a noteworthy regional disparity. Most come from Thebes; examples from Lower Egypt, particularly the political centers of Memphis and Sais, are nearly nonexistent. Defining local styles and differentiating between statuary from Upper and Lower Egypt is thus particularly challenging for the transition from Kushite to Saite rule.[1] At least for Thebes, the volume of material and the evident differences in quality among the works suggest the presence of several workshops operating simultaneously.

When Psamtek I was consolidating his power in Lower Egypt,[2] Thebes and its environs were still under the command of Mentuemhat, the old loyalist of the Twenty-fifth Dynasty, who had managed to stay in office under the new Saite regime. Mentuemhat's death in 648 B.C. is the probable point when Upper Egypt finally adopted the classical Saite style; the Walters bust—a highly unusual work—was likely produced within the two decades preceding this event, when artistic styles changed rapidly. The facial features of the official have been tentatively identified as Libyan,[3] but that attribution is implausible; surely a larger number of similar works would have survived, as have Twenty-fifth Dynasty statues, many of which have facial features with ethnic characteristics.

The sculpture, of which only the upper body is preserved, depicts a kneeling official wearing a pleated kilt and a bagwig that leaves both ears free. In the absence of an inscription on the back pillar (it may have been erased in antiquity), the man's identity is unknown, as are the reasons for the evident reworking of the figure's beltline. The striking expression of his face is defined by the high cheekbones, deep nasiolabial furrows, unusual folds around the corners of the mouth,[4] and the protruding chin. A highly skilled artist took the opportunity to create an outstanding portrait of an aged man by fusing realistic features with the inventive spirit of a new artistic era in the making.

MS

Bibliography

Dattari Collection 1912, 36, no. 293, pl. XXXII; Steindorff 1946a, 52, no. 158, pl. XXVII; Bothmer 1960, 20 (no. 18), pl.16 (figs. 38, 39); Simpson 1977, no. 46.

Notes

1. Josephson 1996, 429–38; see also Josephson and Eldamaty 1999.
2. See also Fazzini 2001.
3. See Russmann 2001, 38, 43.
4. For another bust, with less expressive features, see Josephson and Eldamaty 1999, 43–45 (CG 48619), pl. 21 a–d.

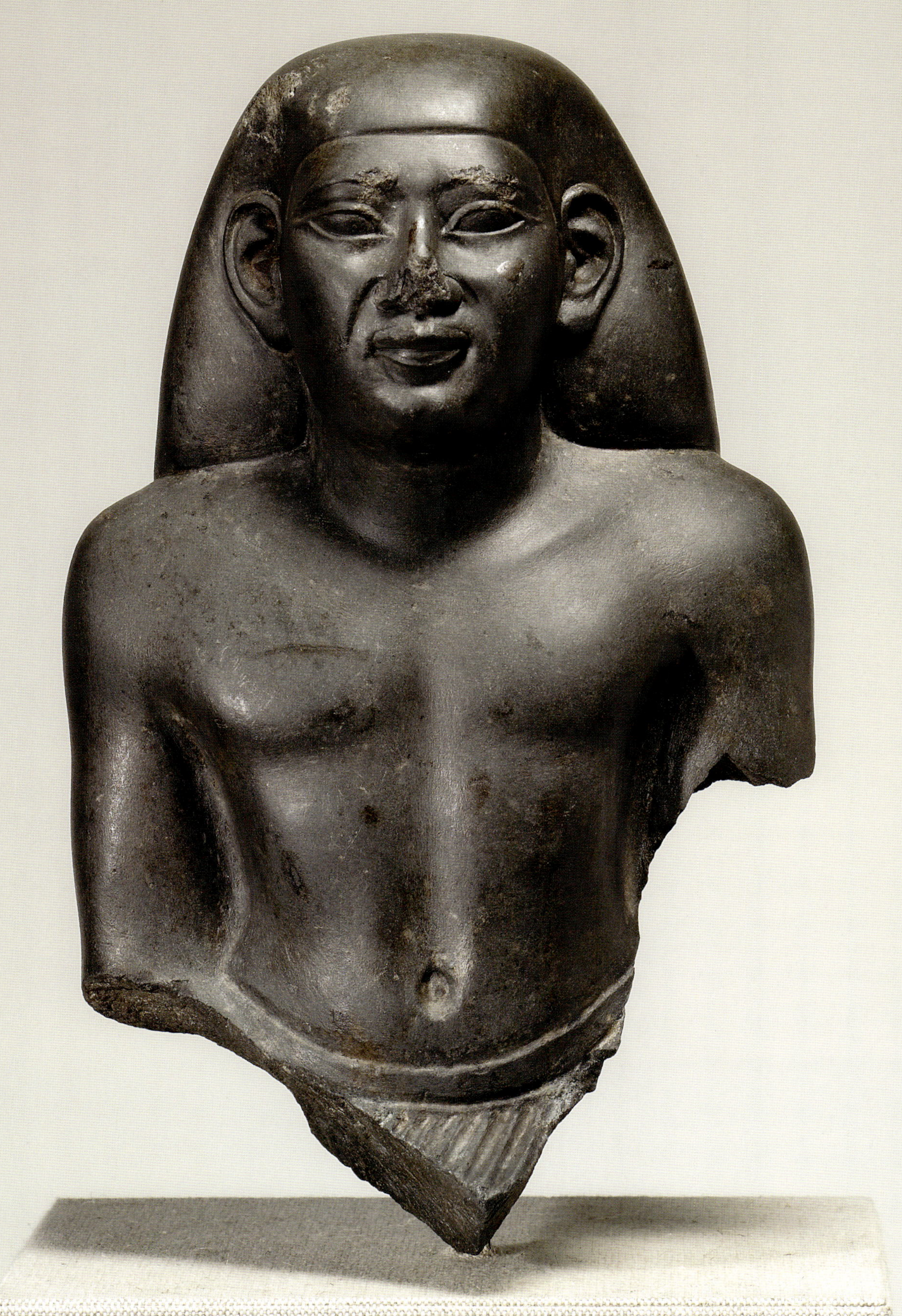

51

Isis with Horus the Child

Bronze, remains of silver inlay; 55 x 15 x 23.5 cm
(21 5/8 x 5 7/8 x 9 1/4 in.)
Twenth-fifth–early Twenty-sixth Dynasty, ca. 680–640 B.C.
Provenance: Henry Walters, before 1931; Walters Art Museum, by bequest, 1931 (54.416)

From the early dynastic period onward, the goddess Isis represented the principle of royal authority,[1] and she is invoked in the Pyramid Texts (the Old Kingdom corpus of religious spells) as the protector of the king and his throne. The Egyptians believed in the divinity of kingship and associated its formation with the creation of the world. After the assassination of Osiris (see no. 52), Isis's brother and spouse, she used her magic powers to impregnate herself by her dead husband and gave birth to Horus, the legitimate heir of the divine kingship. Isis alone raised Horus and protected him from Seth, the murderer of his father.

Isis was also worshiped as a celestial goddess and deity of regeneration. In the Late and Greco-Roman Periods, she was elevated to the status of a universal deity, combining aspects of other Egyptian and foreign divinities. Isis was worshiped throughout the Mediterranean world; even the citizens of Rome built a temple in her honor. The goddess's traditional representation as a mother holding or nursing her child was a prototype for other divine mothers, notably for the Christian veneration of Mary with the Christ Child.[2]

This large bronze figure represents the standard type of the first millennium B.C. The goddess, seated on a separately worked throne (now lost), wears a long sheath-shaped dress and is adorned with a collar necklace. A vulture headdress covers her long wig, and her crown combines a *modius* (disk-shaped base) framed by cobras with a large sun disk flanked by cow horns. These elements symbolize not only her relation to the sun god, but also her celestial qualities, and her status as a divine queen.

Isis sits upright and holds her left breast in her right hand; with her left hand, she supports her reclining son's back. Horus (separately cast and joined to the larger statuette by a prong) is nude (as children were conventionally represented); his royal status is signaled by the *uraeus*, the raised cobra above his forehead. In the typical Egyptian manner, both figures are oriented frontally and do not look at one another.

The style of the piece, particularly the goddess's powerfully built body with a short neck and short waist, suggest a Kushite period manufacture. Although there are thousands of bronzes representing Isis and Horus the Child in museums and collections throughout the world, few statuettes of so large a size have been preserved.[3] It is likely that these figures, some partly inlaid with gold and silver (as are the eyes of Isis in the Walters statue), were donated to the temple by members of the elite for use in temple rituals (see no. 45).

MS

Bibliography

Steindorff 1946a, 107, no. 389, pl. LXIX.

Notes

1. One of many indicators for such an association is the use of the throne character in her name; the character appears in her crown as well; see Schulz 2000, 252–54, with further references.
2. Langner 1996.
3. Most of the bronzes range between 15 and 25 cm (6–9 in.) in height; very few exceed 35 cm (14 in.). A Late Period Isis figure with Horus in the Musée du Louvre, (inv. no. N 5022), which was discovered in the Serapeum at Saqqara, is 56.2 cm (22 1/8 in.) tall. A somewhat smaller Twenty-fifth Dynasty statuette, 44.5 cm (17 1/2 in.) tall, which closely resembles the Walters Isis, is in a private collection in Germany; see Schoske and Wildung 1992, 122, no. 84.

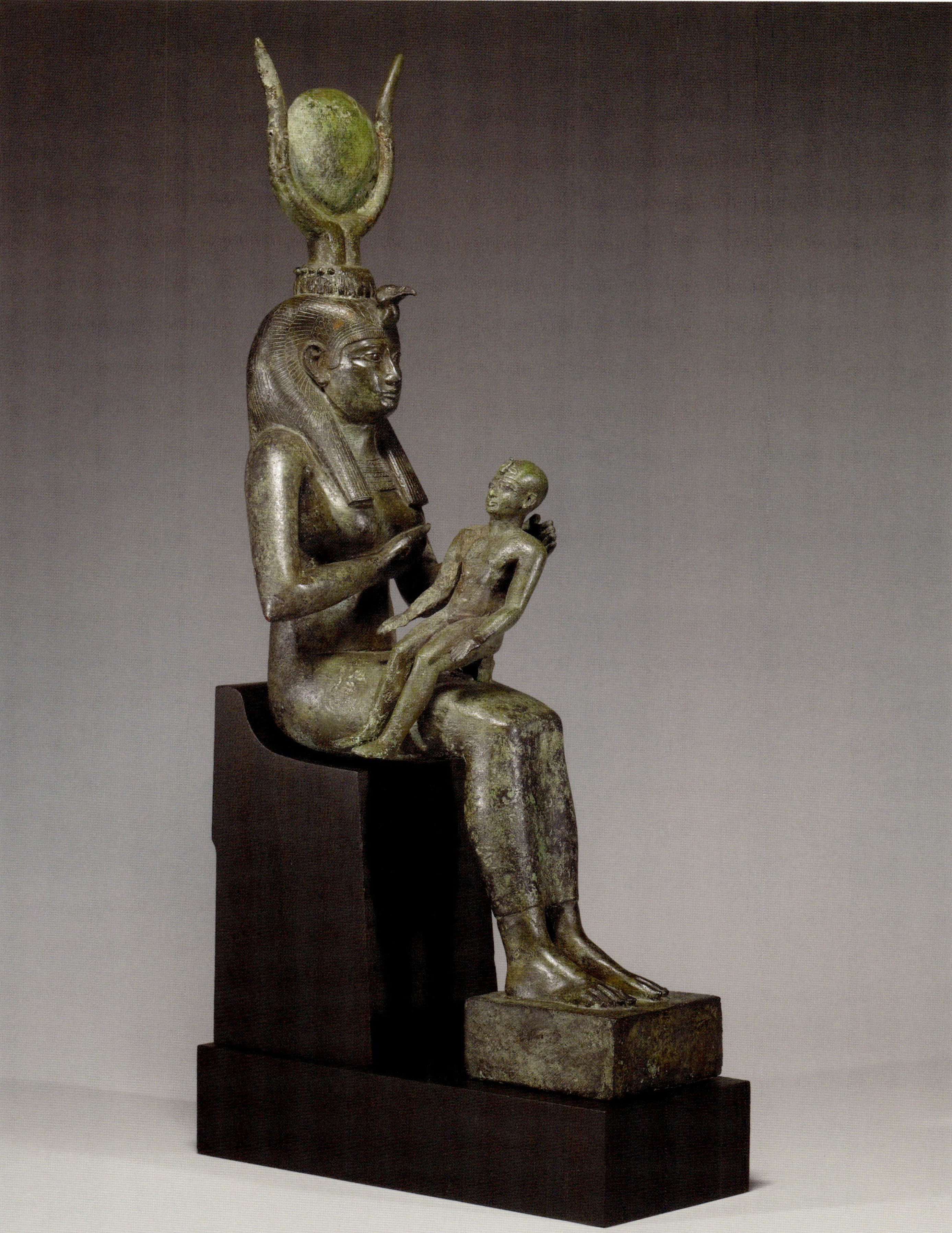

52

Figure of Osiris

From Upper Egypt (?)[1]

Bronze, hollow cast; 61 x 14 cm (25 x 5 ½ in.)

Twenty-sixth Dynasty, ca. 580–550 B.C.

Provenance: Henry Walters, 1914 (Dikran Kelekian as agent); Walters Art Museum, by bequest, 1931 (54.551)

Osiris, the lord of the underworld, associated with death and resurrection, was a central figure in Egyptian myth and kingship ideology. His name may derive from *wsr*, meaning "strong," "mighty," or "powerful." He was probably originally a fertility god, assimilating aspects of other divinities connected to agriculture, kingship, and the afterlife. Osiris figures prominently in the Heliopolitan creation myth, one of the ancient Egyptians' most important ontological models. After the formation of space (the sky, the earth, the upper atmosphere, and the lower moist atmosphere) and cyclical time (created by the passage of the sun through day and night),[2] Osiris and his siblings Isis (see no. 51), Seth, and Nephthys came into being. Whereas Osiris represents order and civilization, Seth represents wild, uncontrolled nature; natural phenomena were construed as a struggle between the two. The assassination of Osiris by Seth, and Osiris's resurrection were at the heart of the Egyptian cosmogony, accounting for the formation of the underworld and the creation of the afterlife and linear time. Osiris's resurrection, which gave hope for human resurrection, would explain the god's popularity in Egypt for over two thousand years and the great number of centers devoted to his cult. Countless statues in stone (particularly graywacke),[3] precious metal, bronze, faience, and painted wood were created in the temple workshops and donated to the god by the people.

This unusually large bronze figure of a standing Osiris depicts the god in his standard iconography.[4] His body is mummified, he wears the *Atef*-crown and the artificial divine beard; a massive *uraeus* rises from his forehead. The funerary sheathing opens at the neck to free the head and reveals a necklace composed of several rows; the high standing edge of the sheathing behind the neck is reminiscent of the collar of the royal *Sed* Festival robe, which signals the renewal of royal power. The god's wrists, emerging from vertical slits at the front of the sheathing, are adorned with bracelets; his hands hold the royal regalia: a crook and flail.[5] The statue's base displays a one-and-a-half-line inscription partly destroyed by the metal's corrosion. It names the god: "Osiris, giving life, Wenen-nefer" (i.e., "the beautiful one"). The title and name of the donor are difficult to identify; the line may read: "the chief of the kitchen Iret-en-Iru (?) son of Iah-(/// born) of Ta-di-aset."

The high quality of the statue, made in the second half of the Twenty-sixth Dynasty (during the reigns of Apries and Amasis), contrasts with the clumsily executed inscription. The present inscription was probably added in its first dedication; the original inscription would likely have appeared on a secondary base, now lost.

RS

Bibliography

Steindorff 1946a, 103, no. 366, pl. LXVI.

Notes

1. According to Dikran Kelekian, who purchased the piece for Henry Walters.
2. Allen 2003, 23–30.
3. Graywacke statues and statuettes of Osiris and Isis were particularly popular in the Twenty-sixth and Twenty-seventh Dynasties; see, for example, Walters Art Museum, acc. nos. 22.207, 22.184, in Steindorff 1946a, 105–6, pl. LXVIII; and for a winged Isis with Osiris, Walters Art Museum, acc. no. 22.199, in Capel and Markoe 1996, 125, no. 57. For other examples and dating criteria, see De Meulenaere and Bothmer 1969, 9–16.
4. Bronze statues of the god on this large a scale are rare; one of the most impressive, also dating to the Twenty-sixth Dynasty, is in the Rijksmuseum van Oudheden, Leiden (inv. no. AB 161). The statue measures 105 cm (33 ⅓ in.) tall and is gilded, symbolizing the union of Osiris with the sun god for their mutual renewal; see Schneider 1998, 118, no. 184.
5. This crook has a long lower end, unlike the short royal crook. This form originates from the crook used to herd cattle, and was the prototype for the royal crook. The royal regalia in the iconography of Osiris vary considerably, combining either a short royal crook and flail, a long crook and flail, or two crooks (long and short) with the flail. The significance of two crooks represented together may allude to Osiris's role as a divine protoking on earth as well as the actual king of the underworld.

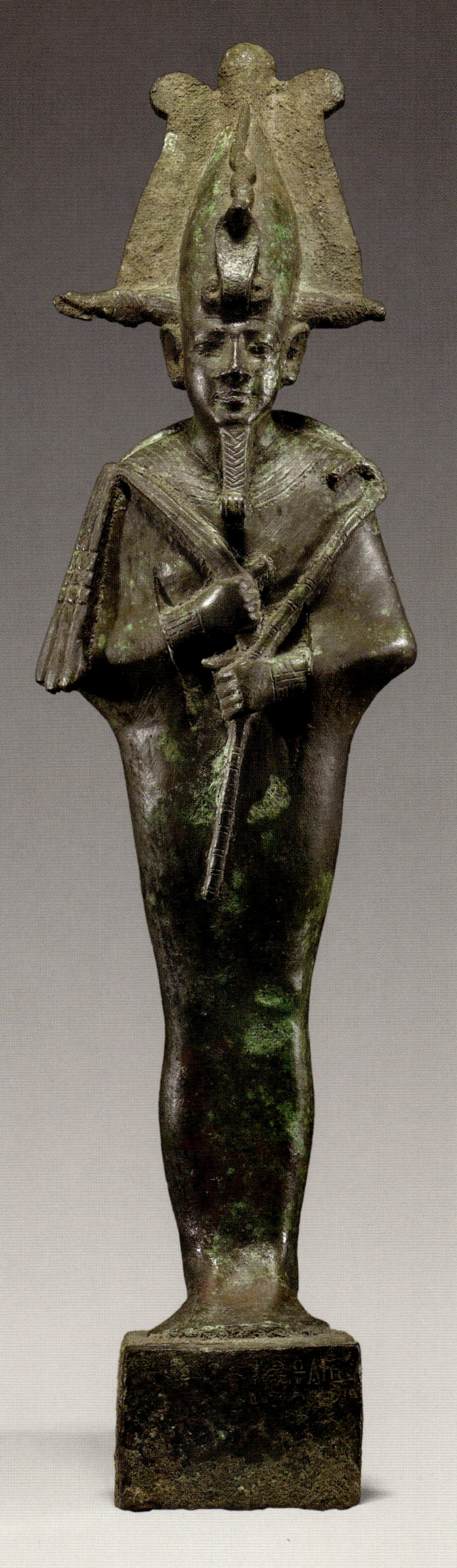

53

Ankh-ef-en-Sakhmet with his family and a harpist

Probably from the Memphite region[1]

Limestone, traces of red paint; 44 x 65 cm (17 5/16 x 25 9/16 in.)

Late Twenty-sixth Dynasty, ca. 550–525 B.C.[2]

Provenance: Khawam Brothers, Cairo (dealers); Henry Walters, 1930; Walters Art Museum, by bequest, 1931 (22.38)

Representations of tomb owners seated in the company of their family while being entertained by musicians, singers, and dancers were common motifs in Egyptian art from the Old Kingdom onward. A special category of scenes depicting harpists singing in praise of the deceased, introduced by the New Kingdom, if not before, calls to mind life's transitory quality.

This scene, once part of a tomb wall, is executed in low relief and would originally have been painted. The elegant carving and clear design of the figures are typical of the Saite period, but the composition and iconography evoke Old Kingdom traditions. While this might reflect the archaizing artistic taste of the Late Period, it may also allude to the tomb owner's privileged status as a member of a priestly elite with access to Old Kingdom tombs, who wanted to show evidence of this in his own tomb.[3]

This tomb owner, named Ankh-ef-en-Sakhmet, sits on a chair with a low back, feet in the shape of cow hooves, and a papyrus blossom attachment. He wears a shoulder-length wig, a collar necklace, and a long apron; in his right hand he holds a handkerchief and, in his left, a long staff. Ankh-ef-en-Sakhmet's chair rests on a mat that elevates him above the other persons depicted.

His wife, Hathor-em-hat, stands behind him, with her left hand on her right shoulder in a respectful gesture of welcome. Her clothing—a long plain sheath dress with shoulder straps, a simple long wig, and a collar necklace—is reminiscent of Old Kingdom fashions; their daughter (Ta-[net]-Nefertem), kneeling on the ground at her father's feet, has a short, slightly teased hairstyle popular in the Late Period. At the extreme right of the scene, a bald harpist faces the family; he is kneeling and rests a shovel-shaped harp against his right shoulder. With his long fingers, he plucks four of the harp's ten strings.[4]

Inscriptions above each of the figures identify the person depicted: the "Priest of Sakhmet of the Acacia Tree, Priest of Ptah: Ankh-ef-en-Sakhmet," "his wife: Hathor-em-hat," "his beloved daughter Ta-[net]-Nefertem," and the harpist and "singer Psamtek-seneb," who is "plucking the harp for your [i.e., Ankh-ef-en-Sakhmet's] *Ka* (life force) every day."

RS

Bibliography

Capart 1938, 15, fig. 4; Steindorff 1946a, 81, no. 275, pl. LVI; Hill 1956–57, 34–41; Bothmer 1960, 110, 112, 114; Leahy 1988, 592–97.

Notes

1. Ankh-ef-en-Sakhmet belonged to a Memphite family and was a priest of the Memphite deities Sakhmet and Ptah; see Schulz 2005, 99–100.
2. The dating is based not only on stylistic and iconographic criteria, but also on the genealogy, derived both from this tomb relief and from a lintel of the same tomb (Walters Art Museum, acc. nos. 22.152 and 22.153), as well as other monuments of relatives; see Schulz 2005, 99–101 with further references.
3. See Schulz 2005, 124.
4. See Krah 1991, 152 (mentioning eight rather than ten strings).

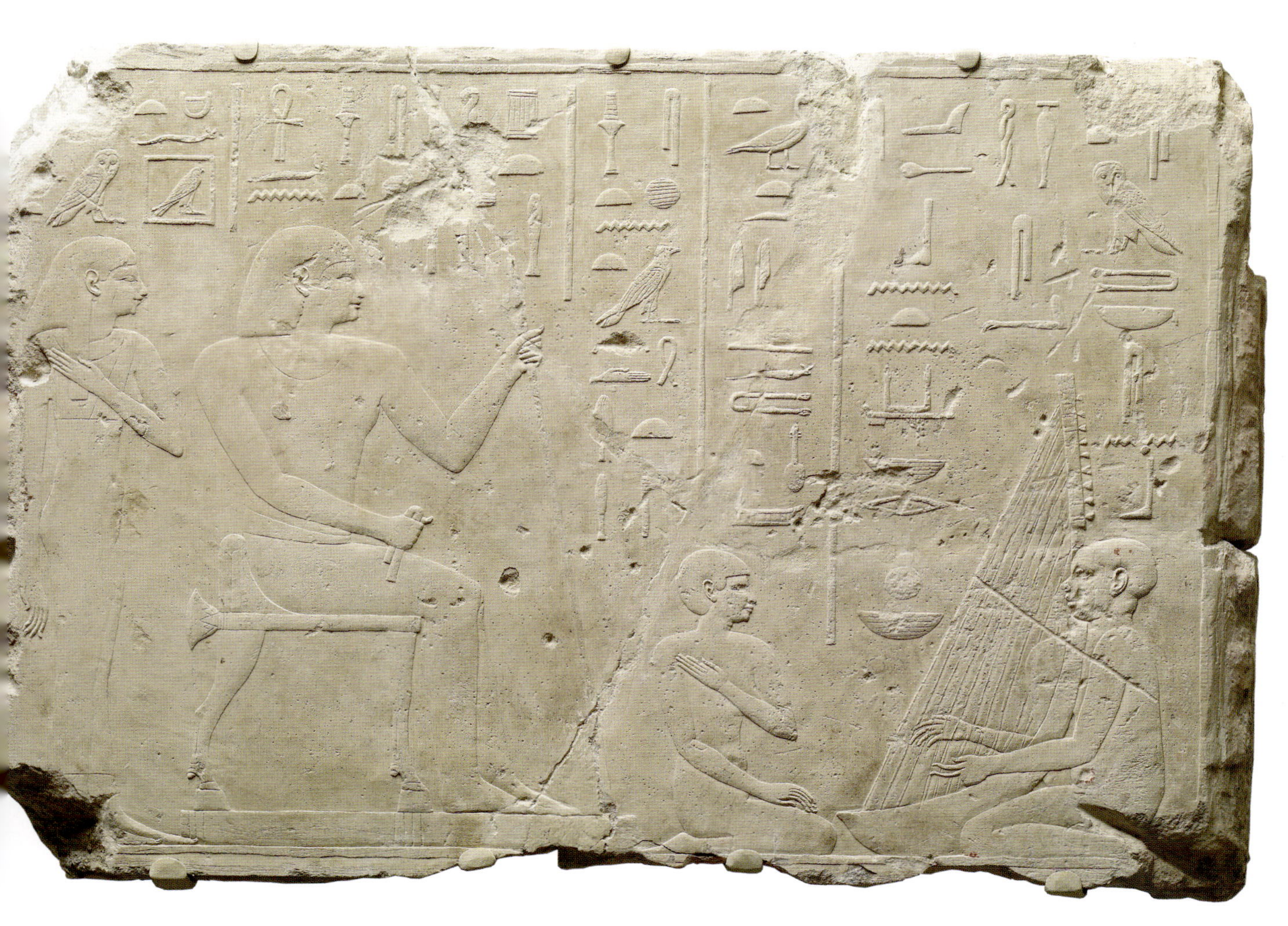

54

Naos-sistrum

Faience, glazed; 15.2 x 7.8 x. 3.5 cm (6 x 3 x 1 3/8 in.)
Second half of the Twenty-sixth Dynasty, ca. 580–525 B.C.
Provenance: Henry Walters, before 1931; Walters Art Museum, by bequest, 1931 (48.465)

A sistrum (from the Greek *seistron*) is a ceremonial percussion instrument made of wood or metal consisting of a handle, a frame, and movable crossbars with threaded loops or disks that jangle when shaken.[1] The Egyptians used two types of sistrum: the arched sistrum with a U-shaped frame, called *sekhem*, and the naos (shrinelike) sistrum, called *sesheshet*. The name of the first (derived from *sekhem*: mighty, powerful) alludes to the instrument's ritual power; that of the second (derived from *seshesh*: to rustle) may refer onomatopoeically to the sound made by the sistrum's precursor: bundles of papyrus plants shaken during rituals. The upper part of the naos-sistrum is in the form of a temple gate; the crossbars passed through holes pierced in the sides.

Both kinds of sistrum were associated with the goddess Hathor, and an image of the goddess's head often links the handle to the frame. Sistrums were used in rituals to call the deities, particularly Hathor and associated goddesses, to beseech them for protection and divine blessing, and to soothe their potentially violent and dangerous tempers. The sistrum also symbolized joy, sexuality, and fertility; it was often represented, in miniature, as an amulet.

Faience sistrums would not have been used as musical instruments; rather, they represented the sacralized ritual object, which was a manifestation of Hathor. The goddess was also the mistress of turquoise and faience; both the medium of this object and the color of its glaze would have associated it with her divinity. Such sistrums were typically donated to the temple by the king or other high officials. Actual sistrums were used predominantly by priestesses (see no. 37), occasionally by the king, and by the god of music: Ihi, son of Hathor.[2] In most instances, statues of men holding sistrums depict the sacralized object rather than the instrument.

This naos-sistrum has lost its handle and with it the inscription that might have named its donor. The preserved upper part shows the head of the goddess Hathor, representing her with a human face, bovine ears, a long wig, and a collar necklace. The head is surmounted by a narrow stand with a cavetto cornice that typically crowned religious buildings, an indication that the head was intended to depict the capital of a Hathor column. This stand, in turn, forms the base of the gate to a shrine similarly surmounted by a cavetto cornice above a torus molding. A *uraeus* serpent spreading its hood occupies the center of the entrance, and two volutes flank the gate. The sistrum's composition, with its references to sacred architecture, may thus be a symbolic allusion to the act of entering a temple.

Temples or shrines with so-called Hathor columns or pillars were common in Egypt from the middle of the second millennium B.C. forward. Their capitals depict the goddess's face, surmounted by a naos (representing the rattle), resting on a column shaft that represents the sistrum's handle. Earlier examples have two Hathor heads, later ones four. Such columns figured as architectural elements in temples and shrines for Hathor but also in those of other goddesses such as the cat goddess Bastet. During the Ptolemaic Period, Hathor columns were also used in so-called birth houses: small temples or chapels, situated in front of larger temples, dedicated to the birth and protection of the divine child.

The style of the face on the Walters sistrum is reminiscent of the Hathor columns found at Sais in a small temple of King Apries (589–570 B.C.).[3] The angular form of the face on the column capitals, with the hairline tapering inward toward the parting, flat cheeks and nose, and squared chin, as well as the carefully rimmed eyes and mouth resemble those of the Walters naos-sistrum, dating the object to the second half of the Twenty-fifth Dynasty.

MS

Bibliography

Capel and Markoe 1996, 123, no. 55a.

Notes

1. For wood sistrums, see an example from the tomb of Tutankhamun (Egyptian Museum, Cairo, JE 62009, 62010) in James 2000, 260; for metal sistrums, see an example in the British Museum, London (EA 36310) in Anderson 1976, 41.
2. One of the earliest representations of Ihi with a sistrum was discovered in the tomb of Tutankhamun, Cairo, Egyptian Museum (JE 60732), in James 2000, 146.
3. Wildung and Schoske 1985, 182, no. 90; for Hathor columns in general, see Bernhauer 2005.
4. Very similar parallels also likely date to the second half of the Twenty-sixth Dynasty, for example, Musée du Louvre, Paris, Ae N 4315 B, in Caubet and Pierrat-Bonnefois 2005, 146–47, no. 393

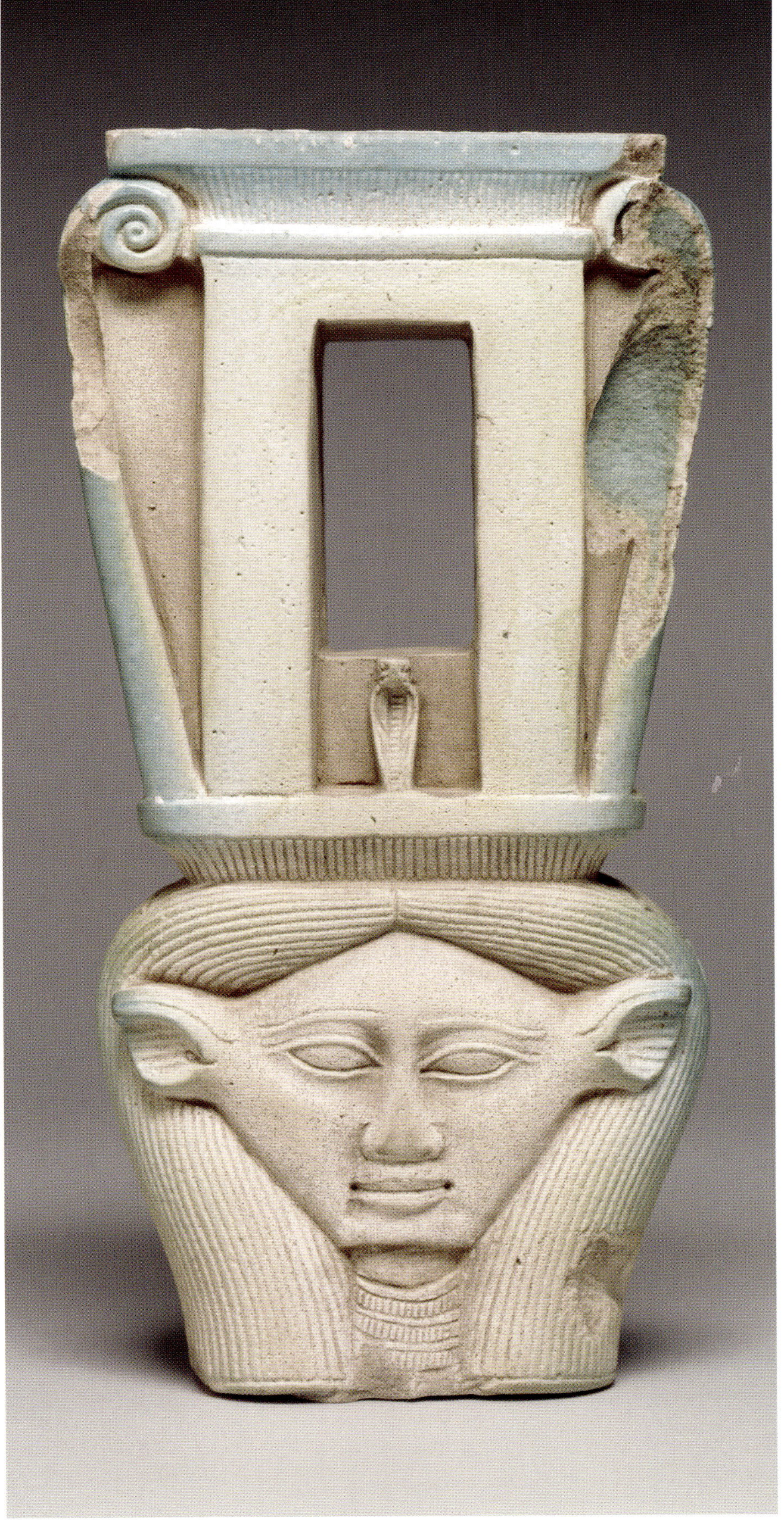

55

Kneeling figure of Hor-wedja

Probably from Memphis

Graywacke; 37.5 x 11.4 x 19.8 cm (14 3/4 x 4 1/2 x 7 13/16 in.)

Twenty-sixth Dynasty, ca. 640–620 B.C.

Provenance: Egyptian Museum, Cairo (CG 669), sale; Henry Walters, before 1931; Walters Art Museum, by bequest, 1931 (22.79)

The traditional typology of private statuary was not expanded during the Late Period, but certain types of statues were particularly favored, and some that had fallen out of use were revived. Such is the case with this statue of an official named Hor-wedja, depicted kneeling with both hands lying flat on his thighs. The gesture, indicating reverence and worship, emerged in the Old Kingdom,[1] but it gained renewed popularity during the Twenty-sixth Dynasty in temple figures, made of various materials and in several sizes.[2]

Hor-wedja kneels on a rectangular base before a back pillar. The well-executed inscriptions in elegantly spaced hieroglyphs give his titles and name his father: Sa-Sobek, vizier of Lower Egypt in the early reign of Psamtek I. According to the short inscription in front of the figure's knees, the statue was commissioned by Hor-wedja's son Mery-Ptah, a priest (as was Hor-wedja) and an estate supervisor. The mention of the deities Ptah-Sokar-Osiris and Hathor (as Mistress of the Southern Sycamore) suggests that the statuette was probably originally placed in a temple in the Memphite region, although Sais, as the new dynasty's capital, cannot be excluded as the sculpture's place of origin. The Walters figure is one of several sculptures in which the kneeling figure's head is slightly raised,[3] a curious detail that has been interpreted as a representation of the owner's apotheosis.

Hor-wedja is depicted wearing a wide wig that more resembles a headscarf than a bagwig, and a narrowly pleated, short kilt with a broad belt. The upper body exhibits a clearly defined collarbone, a strong medial line, and well-defined pectoral muscles with nipples in raised relief. The treatment of the arms and hands is somewhat clumsy, and the work overall has a soft and unarticulated character that is typical of sculpture from the Saite period. The fleshy physiognomy, with lightly protuberant eyes framed by arched brows, the long and slim nose, and mouth with full lips drawn into a slight smile, gives the figure an idealizing, impersonal expression. The satiny finish of the stone is characteristic of sculpture from this period.

MS

Bibliography

Borchardt 1930, 16, CG 669; Steindorff 1946a, 51–52, no. 154, pl. XXIV; De Meulenaere 1957, 83–84, n. 10; Bothmer 1960, 44, no. 37, pl. 34 (figs. 80, 81); Städelsches Kunstinstitut 2006, 518, no. 76 (U. Mandel).

Notes

1. See Saleh and Sourouzian 1986, no. 22.
2. See Russmann 2001, 239–41, no. 131.
3. See Bothmer 1970, 37–48, pl. XIII, 28.

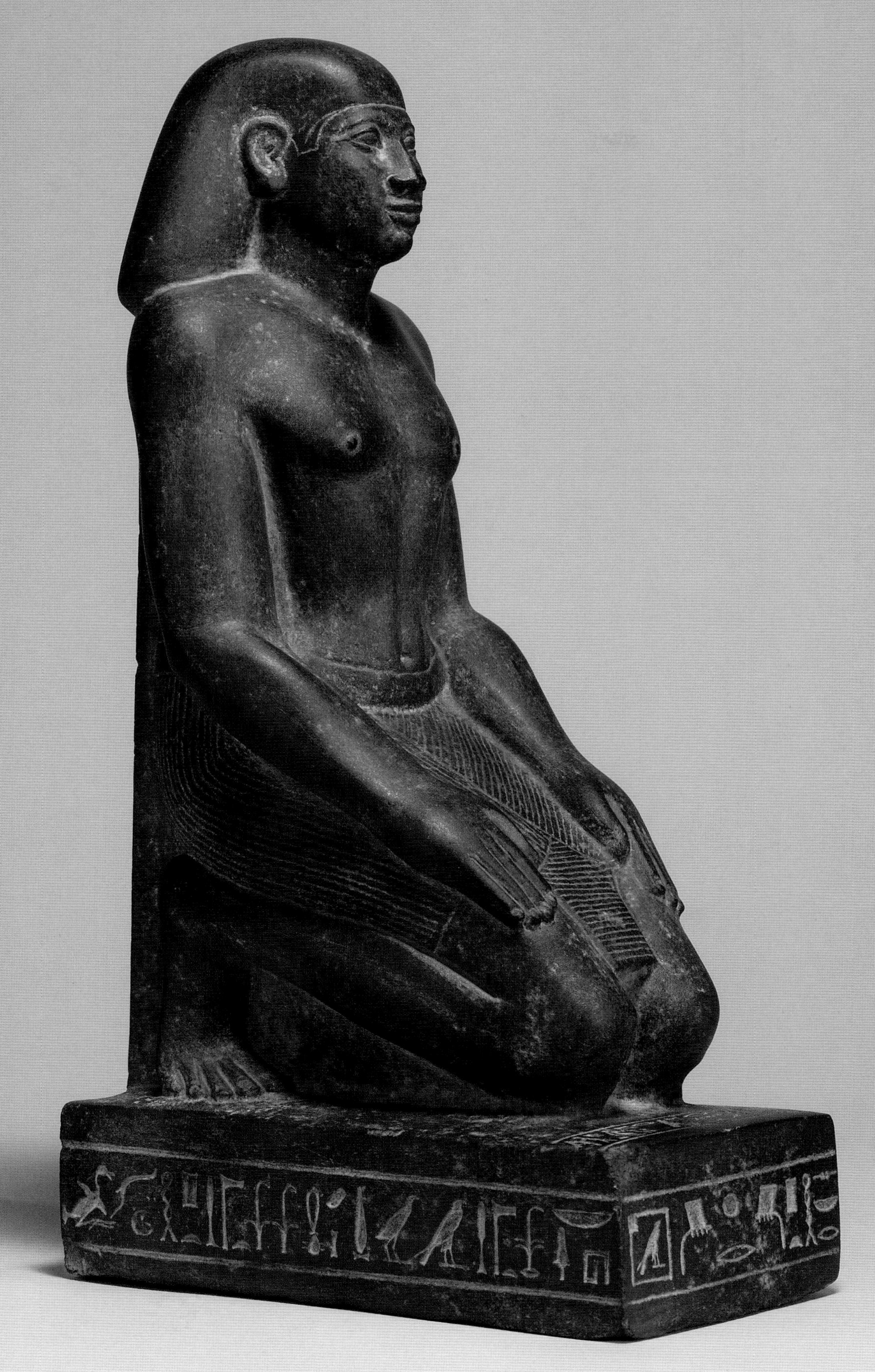

56

Iret-horru with Osiris

From Karnak, temple of Amun (cachette)

Graywacke; 56 x 16 cm (22 x 6 ¼ in.)

Twenty-sixth Dynasty, ca. 595 B.C.

Provenance: Egyptian Museum, Cairo (JE 37890), sale; Dikran Kelekian, New York / Paris; Henry Walters, 1911; Walters Art Museum, by bequest, 1931 (22.215).

In ancient Egypt political upheavals, accompanied by changes in religious practices, were often an occasion for innovations in private sculpture. This was especially evident in the early Eighteenth Dynasty,[1] when new statue types, representing the donor holding a naos or a sistrum, among other objects, came into use for the first time. The representation of a donor (depicted standing, seated, kneeling, or squatting) proffering the figure of a deity or a sacred object ensured the donor's eternal participation in the rituals undertaken in the gods' presence. Representations of the ritual interaction between men and gods were even more highly sought when the high priests of Amun seized power in Thebes during the Twenty-first Dynasty and ruled the country's south. From this point onward, over a period of several centuries, statues depicting the donor squatting (see no. 27) or holding the image of a god were almost the only statue types, dedicated in extraordinary numbers, in the temple of Amun at Karnak.

The vast extent of these dedications was attested early in the twentieth century, when the French architect Georges Legrain discovered a cache of nearly eight hundred stone statues and seventeen thousand bronzes, as well as other artifacts, buried in the courtyard of the temple of Amun in front of the seventh pylon.[2] The standing figure of the priest Iret-horru was one of these statues—the largest Egyptian statue hoard ever recorded—ritually buried by temple priests in the Ptolemaic Period to relieve the crowding of more than two thousand years of private offerings. Iret-horru holds the mummified figure of Osiris,[3] the god of the netherworld, outfitted in his traditional regalia: the tall *Atef*-crown and crook and flail. The priest himself wears a wide wig with narrow striations and an ankle-length pleated garment with a prominent trapezoidal apron. The frontal view exhibits a prominent collarbone and an articulated sternum. Despite its awkward proportions (the arms in particular are clumsily rendered), the statue has a majestic appearance. Statues of donors bearing figures of Osiris were among the most popular types of private statuary in the Late Period; this example was dedicated to Iret-horru by his son Necho,[4] who also served as a priest in Karnak.

MS

Bibliography

Steindorff 1946a, 60–61, no. 174, pl. XXXI; Bothmer 1960, 51–52, no. 44, pls. 40–41 (figs. 97–99); De Meulenaere and Bothmer 1969, 13–14 nn 2, 3; Romano 2002, 29, fig. 17; Schulz and Seidel 2007, 288, fig. 33.

Notes

1. See Bernhauer 2006, 33–49.
2. For the discovery, see De Meulenaere 1998, 334–41.
3. For further examples, see Bothmer 1960, nos. 3, 28, 38, 39, 48.
4. Named for the ruling king, Necho II; for implications, see Bothmer 1960, 51–52.

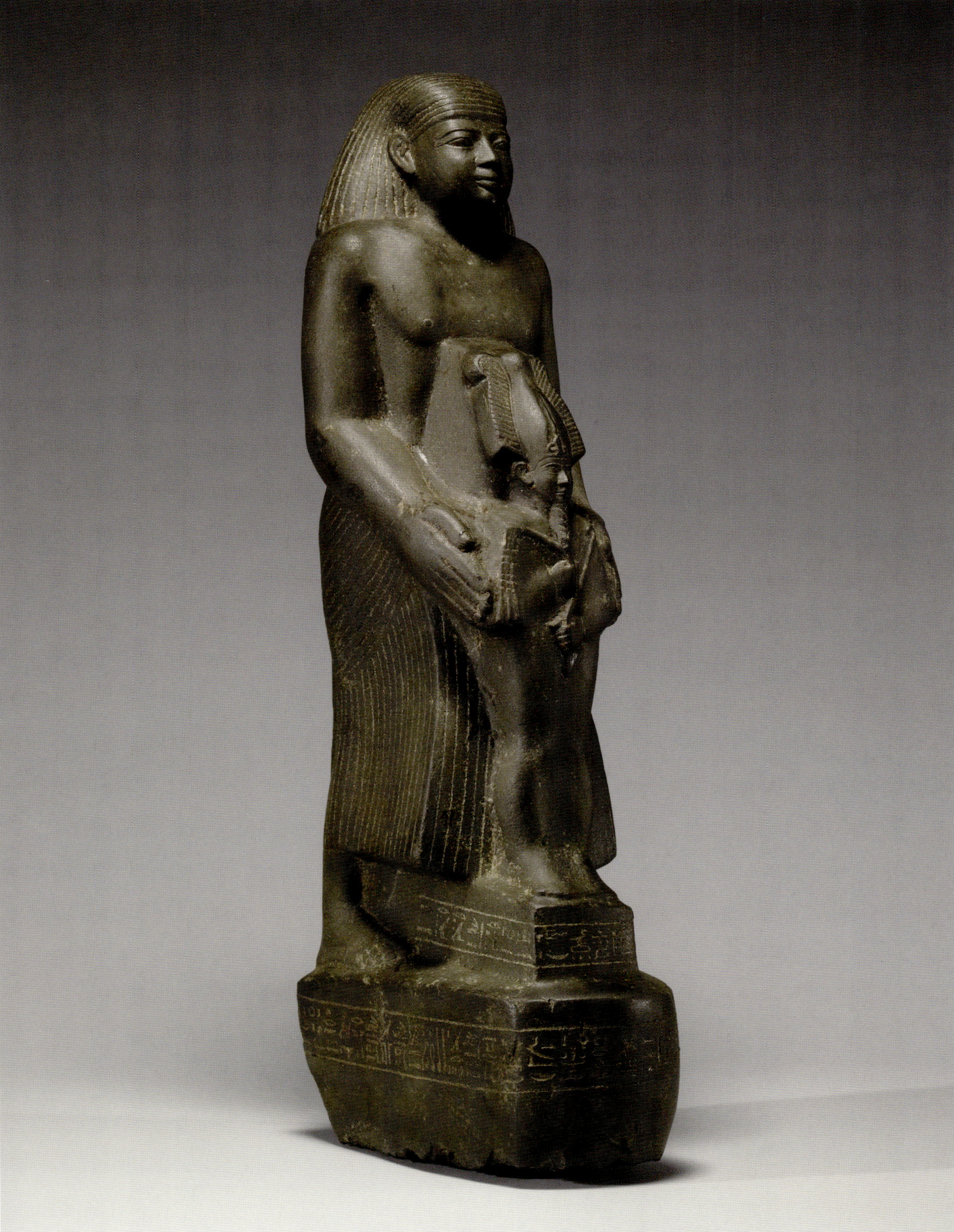

57

Bust of an old man

Probably from the Faiyum region

Graywacke; 19 x 10.3 x 6.9 cm (7 ½ x 4 1/16 x 2 11/16 in.)

Twenty-sixth Dynasty, ca. 660–650 B.C.

Provenance: Dikran Kelekian, New York/Paris; Henry Walters, 1925; Walters Art Museum, by bequest, 1931 (22.145)

Late Period private sculpture is largely idealizing in its portrayal of facial features, but a small group of extraordinary works of outstanding quality survives that follows a truly realistic idiom. This bust of an old man was almost certainly part of a kneeling statuette, depicting the subject holding a naos or with both hands resting on the thighs—a gesture of reverence (see no. 55). The inscription on the back pillar starts in the right column with the appeal to a local god (called the Saite formula),[1] followed by the man's name and titles. The subject is identified as a priest of the goddesses Neith and Bastet, indicating that this figure was likely placed in a temple of the Faiyum region. The suggested completion of the name, of which only the first part remains, to Djed-[bast-iuf-ankh] would accord with such origins but cannot be definitively resolved.[2] The second column describes the act of making offerings in a temple, but the breakage unfortunately leaves the name of the city illegible.

The evocative power of the man's face raises the much-debated question of the dating of this statuette. In the absence of provenance or other information about the work's origins or locality, a dating based exclusively on style is a difficult undertaking.

This striking work, which probably dates from the first decade of the reign of Psamtek I, demonstrates the short-lived artistic realism, known as the new "northern style" which resulted, in part, from the transformation then taking place in political relations between north and south.[3] Some scholars have associated these examples of verism with a group of portraits of aged men dating from the fourth century B.C.[4] In a more general assessment, such impressive rendering of physiognomy could be considered either to constitute portraits of specific individuals or, alternatively, as combinations of diverse facial elements, assembled by the artist to create a highly individualized-looking face conveying qualities such as authority or wisdom.

The wig worn by the Walters figure is unusual, to say the least. It is striated, and each strand is carved in elegant relief, but what is unique is the manner in which the hair tabs are placed above the ears. The subject's body is more subtly modeled than the face, adhering to a standard depiction of youthful elegance.

MS

Bibliography

Steindorff 1946a, 51, no. 152, pl. XXVI; Bothmer 1960, 26–27, no. 23, pl. 21 (figs. 48, 49); Spanel 1988, 118–19, no. 41; Josephson 1997, 7, figs. 6, 7.

Notes

1. The formula appears on male private statues until the Ptolemaic Period, so it does not provide a criterion for dating sculpture; Jansen-Winkeln 2000, 83–124.
2. See Bothmer 1960, 27.
3. See Bothmer 1988, 47–65, and references therein.
4. Kaiser 1966, 5–31; Josephson 1997, 7.

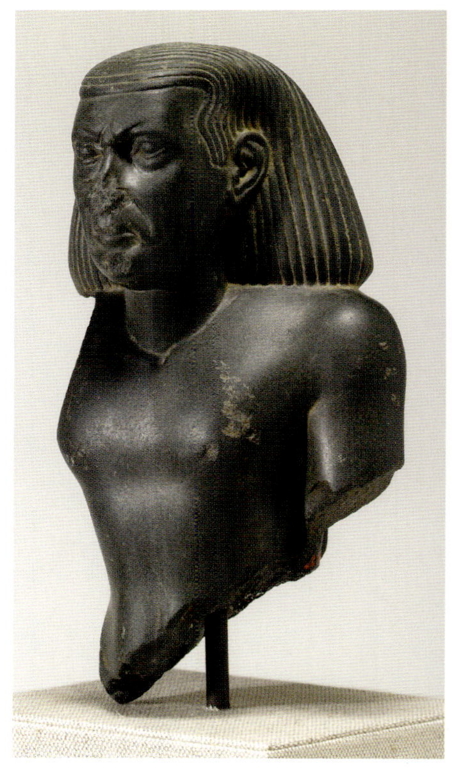

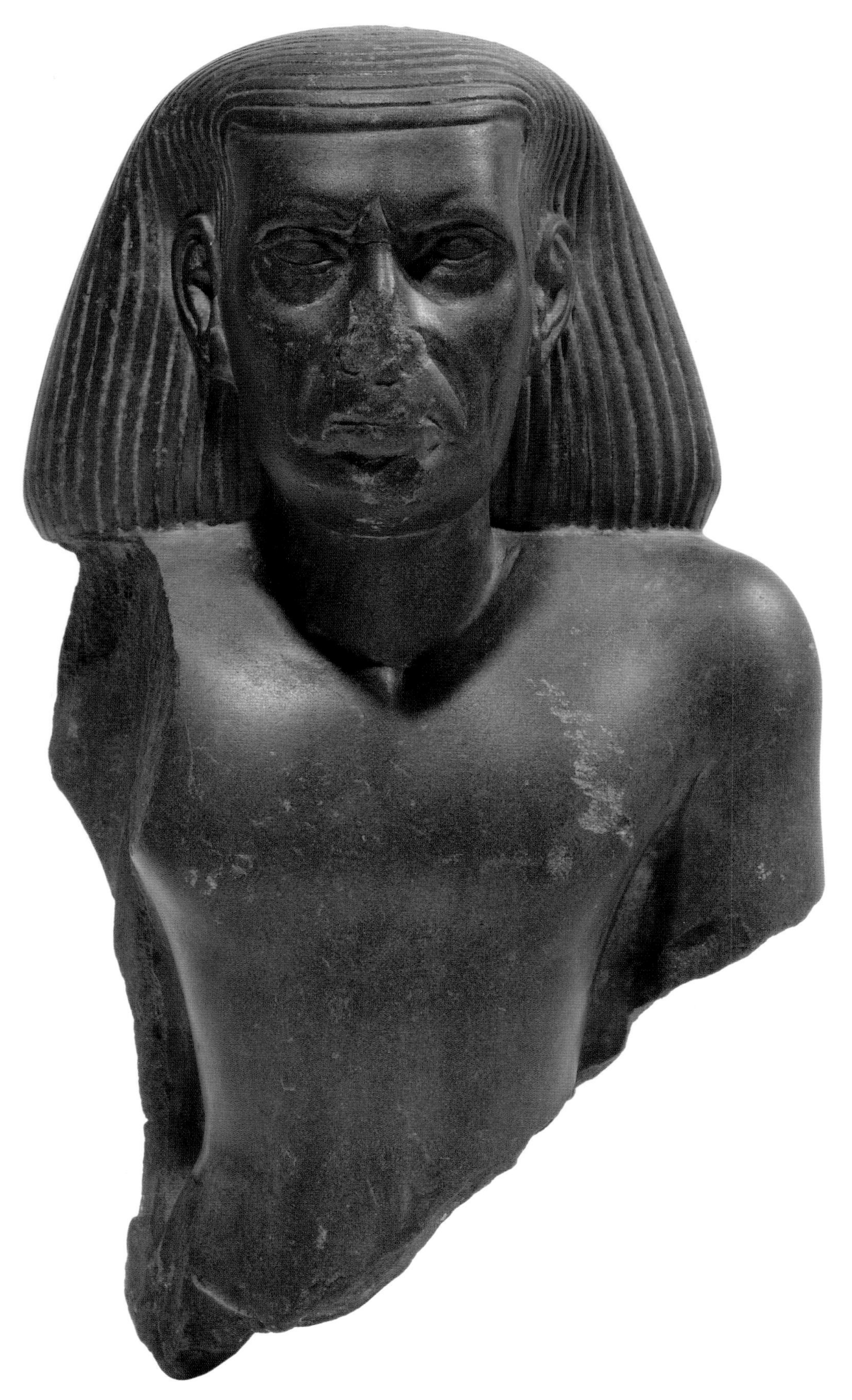

58

The Nile god Hapy holding offerings

Probably from Memphis[1]

Bronze, solid cast; 28 x 10.2 x 0.7 cm (11 x 4 x ¼ in.)

Twenty-fifth–Twenty-sixth Dynasty, ca. 680–650 B.C.

Provenance: Henry Walters, before 1931;

Walters Art Museum, by bequest, 1931 (54.2135)[2]

The male deity Hapy was the personification of the Nile and of the seasonal inundations that brought fertility to the land. As a consequence, he was also linked to the primeval flood and worshiped as a creative force throughout Egypt. A hymn to Hapy, which contains elements of natural history in its account of the inundations and their effects, was so well known that it was used as a student's scientific textbook. Hapy was not exclusively associated with the Nile, however; figures of the god represented the union of Upper and Lower Egypt, as well as the nomes of the country. He is portrayed as a male with a pot belly and pendulous female breasts, which may symbolize fertility and wealth; the attributes that he carries or wears on his head, however, vary considerably.[3]

This bronze plaque was one of several panels that may have covered the doors or the lower part of a wooden shrine. Cast in raised relief with carefully incised details, the panels represented the nomes of Egypt bringing offerings. The god of the Walters panel is dressed in a loincloth that follows the droop of the belly, with three ribbons attached. His shoulder-length bipartite wig is striated, and he wears an artificial, woven divine beard. He is crowned by a bundle of papyrus plants—blossoms flanked by broken buds. The god stands on a mat facing left; he holds an offering tablet in the shape of a *hetep* character (meaning "offering") with two libation vases and lotus plants. More lotuses—blossoms and buds—hang from his right arm, extending downward to an upright cartouche crowned with double-plumes and a sun disk. The original inscription, incised with fine lines, has been erased, probably as an act of *damnatio memoriae*. The style in which the god is represented, particularly his proportions and facial features, date the panel to the late Twenty-fifth or early Twenty-sixth Dynasty. The reasons for the painstaking removal of the royal name may reflect the importance of the temple in which the original shrine was placed. Whatever historical scenario we can imagine for the appropriate time frame, the question as to why the cartouche was not refilled with a new name remains unanswered.

RS

Bibliography

Steindorff 1946a, 170, no. 745, pl. CIX;
Hornung, Loeben, and Wiese 2005, 96, no. 9.

Notes

1. This plaque is associated with several panels that were part of a hoard of bronze objects discovered by Daninos Pasha at Memphis in 1900–1901 (see Daressy 1902, 139–50). Some of these objects came to the Egyptian Museum, Cairo, and others were sold on the international art market. The closest parallels to the Walters' example are in the Museum of Fine Arts, Boston, acc. no. 1982.180 (formerly Ernest Brummer collection; see Simpson in Brovarski 1987, 70–71); the Kunsthistorisches Museum in Vienna, Ägyptisch-Orientalische Sammlung, inv. no. 4194 (see Roeder 1956, 90, no. 130c, formerly Miramar collection), and previously in the Norbert Schimmel collection in New York (see Settgast 1978, no. 253; sold at Sotheby's New York, 16 December 1992). But the most strikingly similar is another panel in the Kestner Museum, Hannover (see Hornung, Loeben, and Wiese 2005, 96, no. 9).
2. No record of the acquisition has been preserved in the Walters Art Museum; however, it is likely that Henry Walters purchased the plaque from Joseph Brummer, who also once owned the Boston panel.
3. For all related aspects, see Baines 1985.

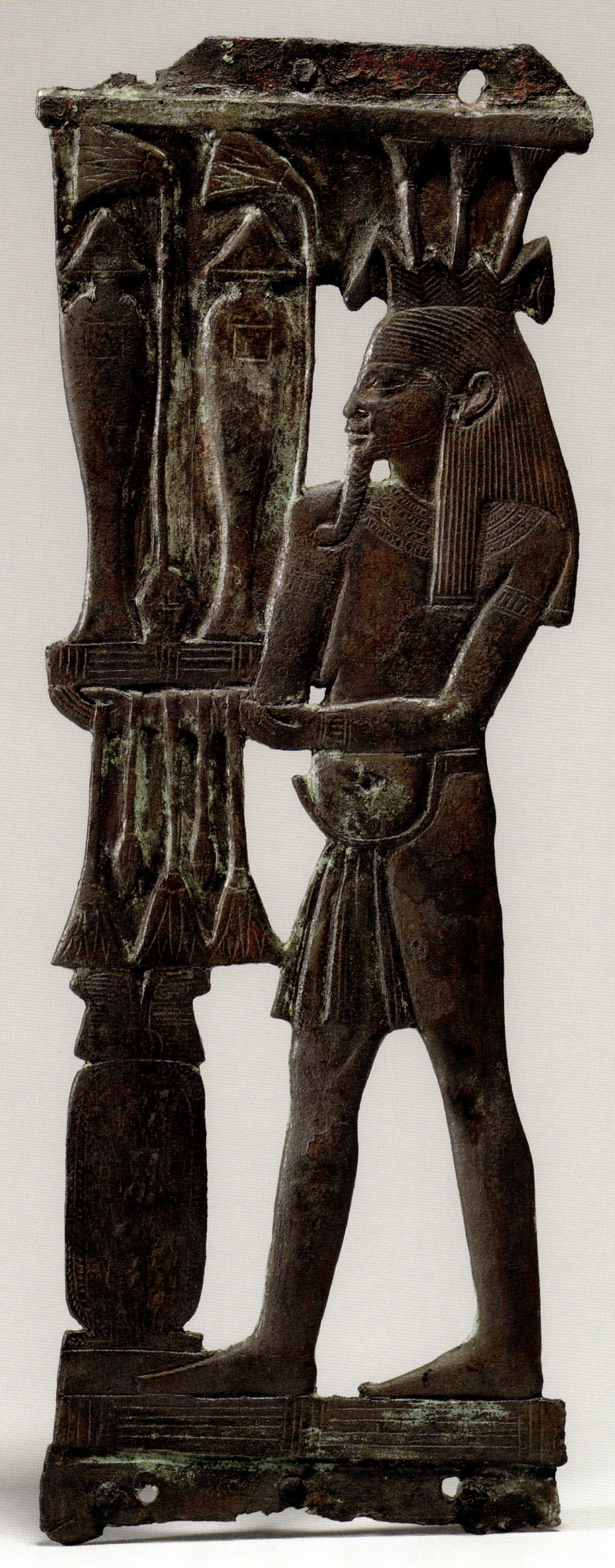

59

Bust of a queen

Said to be from Upper Egypt

Graywacke; 45 x 21 x 13.8 cm (17 11/16 x 8 1/4 x 5 7/16 in.)

Thirtieth Dynasty, ca. 360–330 B.C.

Provenance: Dikran Kelekian, New York / Paris; Henry Walters, 1925; Walters Art Museum, by bequest, 1931 (22.405)

The crook of the preserved right arm indicates that this statuette represented a seated woman, her name lost, together with her throne and base. The heavy Hathor wig that she wears, however, unambiguously signals her royal status. This specific type of wig, characterized by thick plaits curling laterally over the breasts, makes its earliest appearance in Middle Kingdom sculptures of queens,[1] but it appears more frequently in the following periods.[2] The woman's high status is signaled explicitly by the vulture cap, bound with a thin ribbon above the forehead, both wings spreading symmetrically downward over the wig's lappets to meet three bands or rings on either side. The central element of the cap, the head of a vulture or a *uraeus*, is broken off, leaving the wig's frontlet, which spans the forehead, clearly visible.

The vulture headdress was originally an element of the iconography of the goddess Nekhbet, the tutelary deity of Upper Egypt, associated with a city named in her honor (present-day el-Kab). In the late Fourth or Fifth Dynasty, the cap was associated with the queens of Egypt, as an expression of their divine nature.[3] The articulation of the wig on the back of the figure is equally remarkable. Between the two voluminous plaits, the middle part cascades downward in waves, defined by a pattern of alternating horizontal bands, differentiated by two levels of polish, to the top of the back pillar.[4] The queen's form-fitting sheath with shoulder straps would have extended to her ankles.

The anonymous queen of the Walters head is clearly a Late Period work; elements of Middle Kingdom sculpture (the wig, the garment, and the figure's prominent ears) signal an archaizing style, but the treatment of the back of the wig is an innovative feature. To date the bust more precisely, we are reliant on stylistic elements of the facial features. The almond-shaped eyes with thin cosmetic lines and very faintly articulated brows, the elegant modeling of the cheeks, and the smiling mouth with a full, lightly undercut lower lip support the work's assignment to the end of the Thirtieth Dynasty, or even somewhat later.[5]

MS

Bibliography

Steindorff 1946a, 23, no. 31, pl. VII; Vandier 1958, 224, 315, pl. CIII, 5; Lillesø 1975, 141; Sourouzian 1981, 454–55 n 54; Capel and Markoe 1996, 118–20, no. 52.

Notes

1. Saleh and Sourouzian 1986, no. 93.
2. For New Kingdom examples, see Sourouzian 1981, 450–55.
3. For the vulture cap, see Roth 2001, 273–88; for the cap without the Hathor wig, see Roehrig 2005, 29–30, nos. 8, 9.
4. For similar features of earlier statues; see Sourouzian 1981, pls. 69, 72, 74; Wildung 2000, 142–43, nos. 66, 67.
5. For the development of statuary at the end of the Thirtieth Dynasty, see Josephson 1997, 1–32.

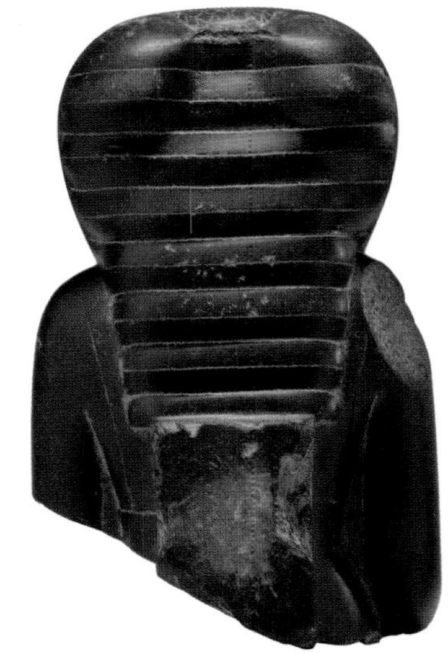

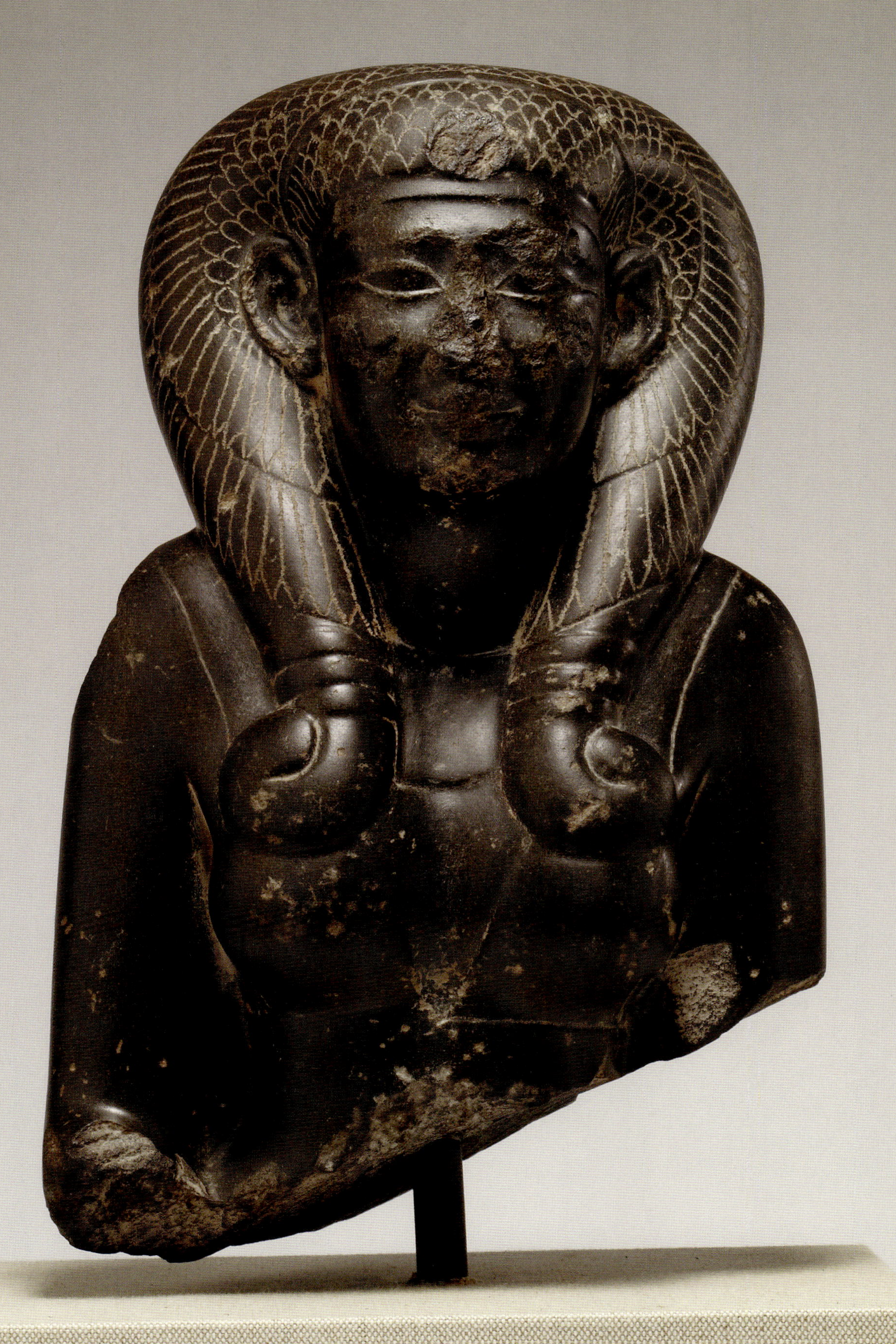

60

Head of a lion

Faience, glazed; 4.7 x 4.2 x 2.2 cm (1 7/8 x 1 5/8 x 7/8 in.)

Thirtieth Dynasty–early Ptolemaic Period, ca. 350–280 B.C.

Provenance: William MacGregor, Tamworth, Staffordshire; sale, Sotheby, Wilkinson & Hodge, London, 26–29 June and 4–6 July 1922, no. 324; Henry Walters, 1923; Walters Art Museum, by bequest, 1931 (48.494)

Representations of lions are common in ancient Egypt from the predynastic period onward, associated with majesty and strength, but also with violence and danger. The lion symbolized kingship, and it was sometimes represented as a manifestation of the ruler or as his companion; scenes of the king leading lion hunts demonstrated his control of nature. Lions were also associated with primeval deities, such as the earth god Aker, or Shu and Tefnut, the gods of the Heliopolitan creation myth, portrayed as a pair of lions, denoting the eastern and western horizon. Several deities, both male (Mahes) and female (Sakhmet: see no. 26), have a human body and a lion's head.

Whereas lions were depicted snarling or roaring throughout much of the ancient Near East (and briefly in Egypt during the first Persian occupation),[1] in Egyptian art, with the exception of battles or hunting scenes, they are usually shown at ease, conveying royal or divine composure.

This plaque with a flat back might have been inlaid in a piece of furniture.[2] Lion heads and legs were common elements of chairs, beds, and headrests; they had a magical as well as a decorative function, and were believed to offer protection and effect regeneration. This lion's head has an elongated face with high hairline and long, pointed snout. The hemispherical eyeballs sit deeply in the carved, rimmed eye sockets; the carved brows meet in a V-shape at the base of the snout, and short circular humps emerge above the inner brows. An incised, vertical forehead-crease runs from the hairline to the bridge of the nose, where it joins the brows. Only the right ear, erect and semicircular, is preserved; the texture of the fur inside the ear is represented by a bipartite pattern of hatching. The fur on the upper side of the muzzle is finely incised, as is the mane, which is composed of striated and unstriated strands.

Although the proportions of the head,[3] and the rendering of the eyes[4] recall Achaemenid-influenced representations of lions in the Twenty-seventh Dynasty, the erect, carefully articulated ears,[5] the style of the mane, and the closed mouth date the work more plausibly to the Thirtieth Dynasty, or slightly later.[6] The high quality of the head, with its carefully executed details, makes it likely that it was produced in a major workshop, perhaps one associated with the court. An unusual feature (perhaps a signature of the artist or his workshop) is the long vertical crease on the forehead. Short lines or depressions are quite common in representations of lions, but no other known example exhibits such a long and deeply incised furrow. It is possible that the Egyptian artist was influenced by Greek representations of lions, which sometimes have a similar furrow.[7]

RS

Bibliography

MacGregor Collection 1922, 46, no. 324.

Notes

1. See Rose 1952, 17–24. Another faience lion head in the Walters Art Museum (acc. no. 48.1386, unpublished) likely served as an attachment to a piece of furniture or a vessel.
2. Killen 1980 and 1996.
3. See Roes 1952, 21; Cooney 1953.
4. See, for example, Cleveland Museum of Art 1974.87, in Berman 1999, 439, no. 340 (K. Boha).
5. Achaemenid-influenced lions typically have ears pinned back against the head; see Boha in Berman 1999, 439, and Bothmer 1987, 52, no. 18 (formerly Christos G. Bastis Collection).
6. Compare a Late Period recumbent limestone lion in the Walters Art Museum (acc. no. 22.40); see Städelsches Kunstinstitut 2006, 473–74, no. 24, with further references; see also the lions of Nectanebo I in the Musei Vaticani, Museo Gregoriano Egizio, 21 and 23, Botti and Romanelli 1951, 14–17, pls. CVI–CVIII.
7. Two examples were in the Mildenberg Collection; see Mildenberg Collection 2004, 5, no. 62, and 137, no. 148.

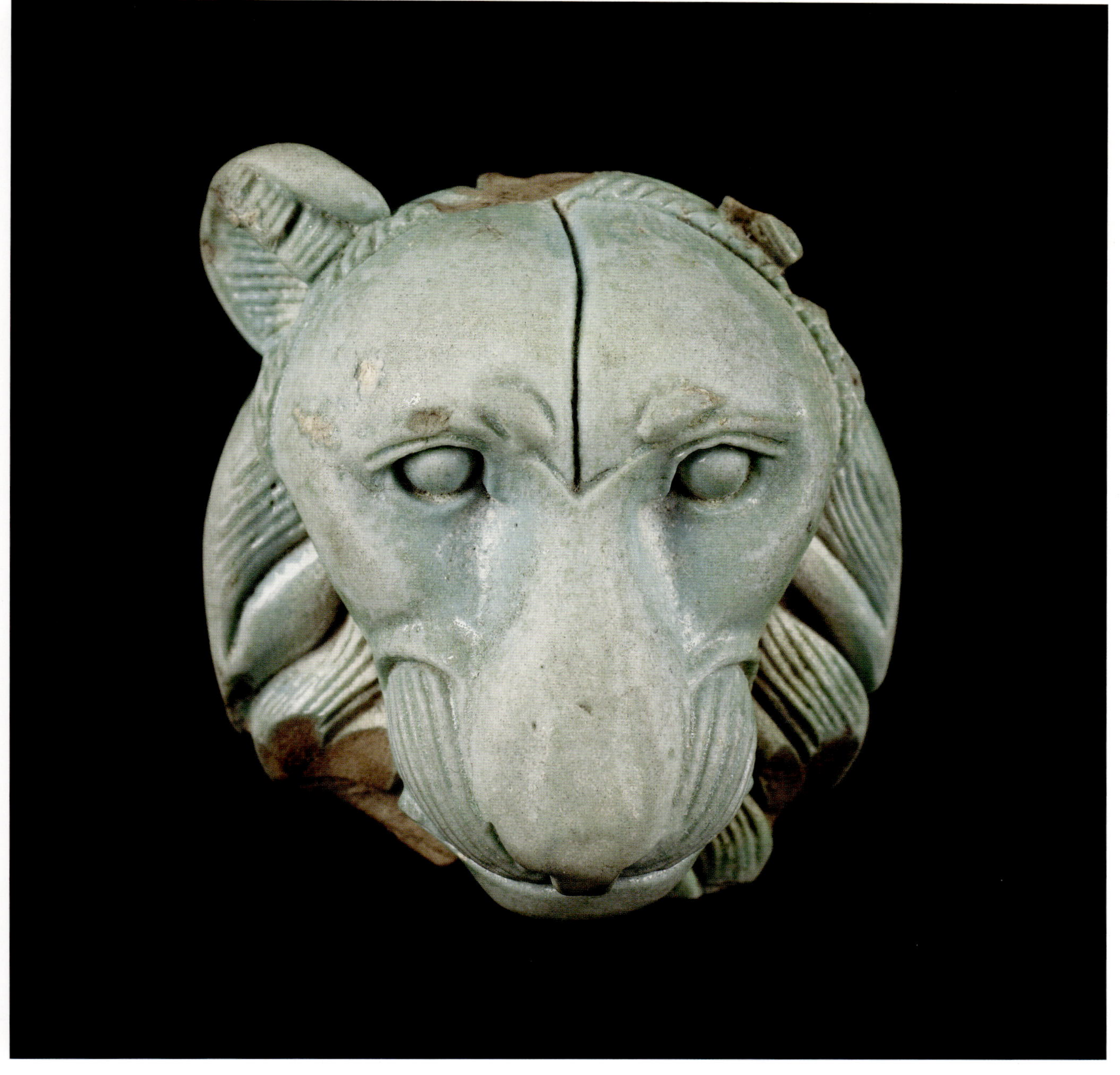

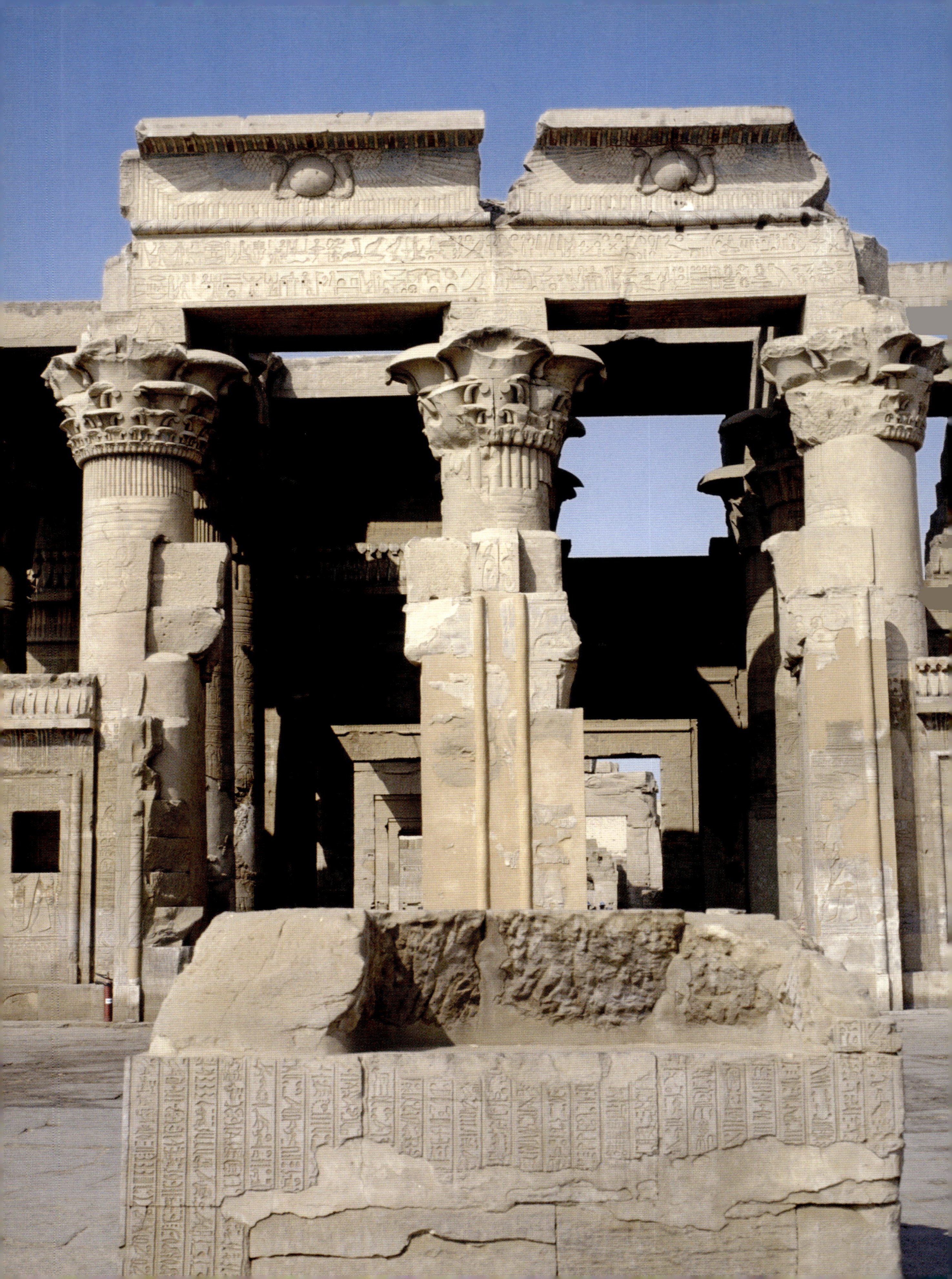

THE PTOLEMAIC PERIOD (332–30 B.C.)

The untimely death of Alexander the Great at Babylon in 323 B.C. created a power vacuum, a realm without a designated successor. Legend has it that on his deathbed, Alexander was asked to whom he would entrust his vast empire and answered, "to the best." Ptolemaios, one of Alexander's generals, became the new *satrap* (governor) of the province of Egypt. Crowned Ptolemy I Soter (305–285 B.C.), he founded a dynasty that would rule Egypt for the nearly three centuries that ensued, developing it into one of the most powerful states of the eastern Mediterranean. Under his reign, Alexandria was transformed into Egypt's political and cultural capital; together with Memphis, it was a center for the cult of Sarapis, the newly created state god of the Ptolemies (see no. 68). To secure their political hegemony, the Ptolemaic rulers allowed local dignitaries and priests to stay in office while filling key positions in the administration and army with loyalists of Greek origin. The long reign of Ptolemy II Philadelphos (285–246 B.C.) and that of his successor, Ptolemy III Euergetes (246–221 B.C.), marked the dynasty's heyday, but ambitious building projects, the costs of nearly permanent warfare against internal and foreign enemies, and the extraordinary pomp and profligacy of the royal court at Alexandria stretched the nation's budget to its limits. Ptolemy II (see no. 61) is credited with the building of the renowned Pharos (lighthouse) in 279 B.C. and completed the construction of the Museion in Alexandria, an academy for teaching and research attached to an immense library that housed hundreds of thousands of papyrus rolls. The Museion was part of the inner Basilea, the nucleus of Alexandria with the fortified royal quarters. The multiple palaces of Ptolemies were interconnected, embellished by inner courtyards and surrounded by groves and gardens. This area also housed the Sema—the as-yet undiscovered burial place of Alexander the Great and all the kings of the Ptolemaic dynasty. Our knowledge of this residence is very limited, most of the evidence having slipped into the rising Mediterreanean or simply lost in time. With his marriage to his sister Arsinoë II, the sibling marriage was institutionalized by Philadelphos, closely linked to the introduction of a dynastic cult of the deified ruler, his family, and his ancestors. The successful religious policies of the early Ptolemies are attested by their diverse building activities, among which the Horus temple at Edfu, whose construction began under Ptolemy III in 237 B.C., was the most prestigious in Upper Egypt. Due to its perfect architecture, this shrine is not only the best-preserved temple of the ancient world, but also enables modern visitors to encounter something of the divine atmosphere that once dwelled in these halls. Against all obstacles, the enormous project was finally completed after 180 years of construction in 57 B.C. under Ptolemy XII Neos Dionysos.

The victory of Ptolemy IV Philopator (221–205 B.C.) over the Seleucid king Antiochos III at the battle of Raphia (near Gaza) in 217 B.C. was the zenith of the dynasty's regional hegemony. Under Ptolemy V Epiphanes (205–180 B.C.), Egypt lost its preeminent position in the Mediterranean as the result of a bitter uprising in Upper Egypt and an intense power struggle within the Alexandrian court. The boy-king Epiphanes was crowned pharaoh in 196 B.C., and the event was recorded in detail by a priests' decree inscribed on one of several stelae, known as the Rosetta Stone, which was the basis for the decipherment of the hieroglyphic writing system by Jean-François Champollion in 1822. The decline of the Ptolemaic state continued through the second century, marked by shifting alliances between members of the royal family that culminated in a civil war lasting from 132 until 124 B.C., with Ptolemy VIII Euergetes II and the queens Cleopatra II (see no. 62) and Cleopatra III leading the conflict. The reliance of the Ptolemaic court on Rome became evident under Ptolemy XII Neos Dionysos (80–58 and 55–51 B.C.), who spent a fortune bribing Roman officials to endorse his claim to the throne; his spending was financed by heavy taxes and loans from Roman bankers. The last of the Ptolemies, Cleopatra VII (51–30 B.C.), was, like her father, entangled with Rome, albeit in a different manner. Famed for her intelligence and charm, she tried to save the doomed empire by forging personal relationships with two of the most powerful Roman politicians of their time: Julius Caesar and Mark Antony. Such political maneuvering, however, ended abruptly in 31 B.C., when the Egyptian fleet under Antony's command was defeated at the battle of Actium by their Roman opponent, Octavian, the later emperor Augustus. Less than a year later, Octavian took Alexandria, Cleopatra and Antony committed suicide, and Egypt was declared a Roman province.

MS

Kom Ombo, Temple of Sobek and Haroëris, courtyard and pronaos (construction begun in the Ptolemaic Period, second century B.C.).
Photo © Dr. Abdel Ghaffar Shedid, Munich

61

Head of Ptolemy II

Probably from the Nile Delta

Gray granite; 28.5 x 22 x 24.2 cm (11 ¼ x 8 11/16 x 9 ½ in.)

Ptolemaic Period, ca. 280 B.C.

Provenance: Dikran Kelekian, New York/Paris; Henry Walters, 1924; Walters Art Museum, by bequest, 1931 (22.109)

Like all of Egypt's previous rulers of foreign extraction, the Ptolemies embraced the Egyptian concept of divine kingship, which placed the all-powerful pharaoh above state and society. The traditional allure and grandeur of such a position in Egypt's long history proved irresistibly attractive to the Ptolemaic rulers, who set their sights on pursuing it politically.[1] To establish their legitimacy as successors within the long line of native pharaohs, the Ptolemaic pharaohs endowed the country with temples and cult statues representing members of the royal family. To this effect, several national synods of priests issued decrees dealing with the production, typology, placement, or ritual function of statuary for the new pharaohs.[2]

Although the sculpture of the Ptolemaic Period embraced a wide variety of types, materials, and sizes, a distinct preference emerged in Lower Egypt under the early Ptolemies for standing figures made of dark hardstone. The facial features of these statues closely resemble those of the Nectanebos, who ruled Egypt during the Thirtieth Dynasty.[3] Indeed, stylistically, the statues of the Nectanebos are almost indistinguishable from the few surviving early Ptolemaic statues; without a decipherable royal name, the identification of these statues remains challenging even for specialists. An assessment of these nearly interchangeable styles raises two points: those workshops that had operated during the later fourth century were still functioning when the early Ptolemies came to power; and the new rulers preferred to emphasize the pharaonic tradition with Egyptian-style statuary and to downplay their Greek origins. The Walters head belongs to a smaller group of sculptures produced for Ptolemy II Philadelphos. The highly stylized, emotionless face is dominated by almond-shaped eyes under weakly articulated brows and a well-formed mouth frozen in a perpetual smile. A large hole drilled into the top of the head suggests that there was formerly a crown, probably made of a combination of precious metals.[4] Likewise, the stripes of the two-color *nemes*-headdress were once gilded, adding further brilliance to this spectacular figure.

MS

Bibliography

Steindorff 1946a, 48, no. 141, pl. XX; Josephson 1997, 25, pl. 8d; Stanwick 2002, 67, 102 (A 25).

Notes

1. For the history of the period, see Hölbl 2001.
2. See Stanwick 2002, 6–14.
3. See Josephson 1997, 23–32.
4. Such crowns were discovered in a hoard excavated at Tukh el-Karamus in the Nile Delta; see Grimm 1998, 56, fig. 55 a–c.

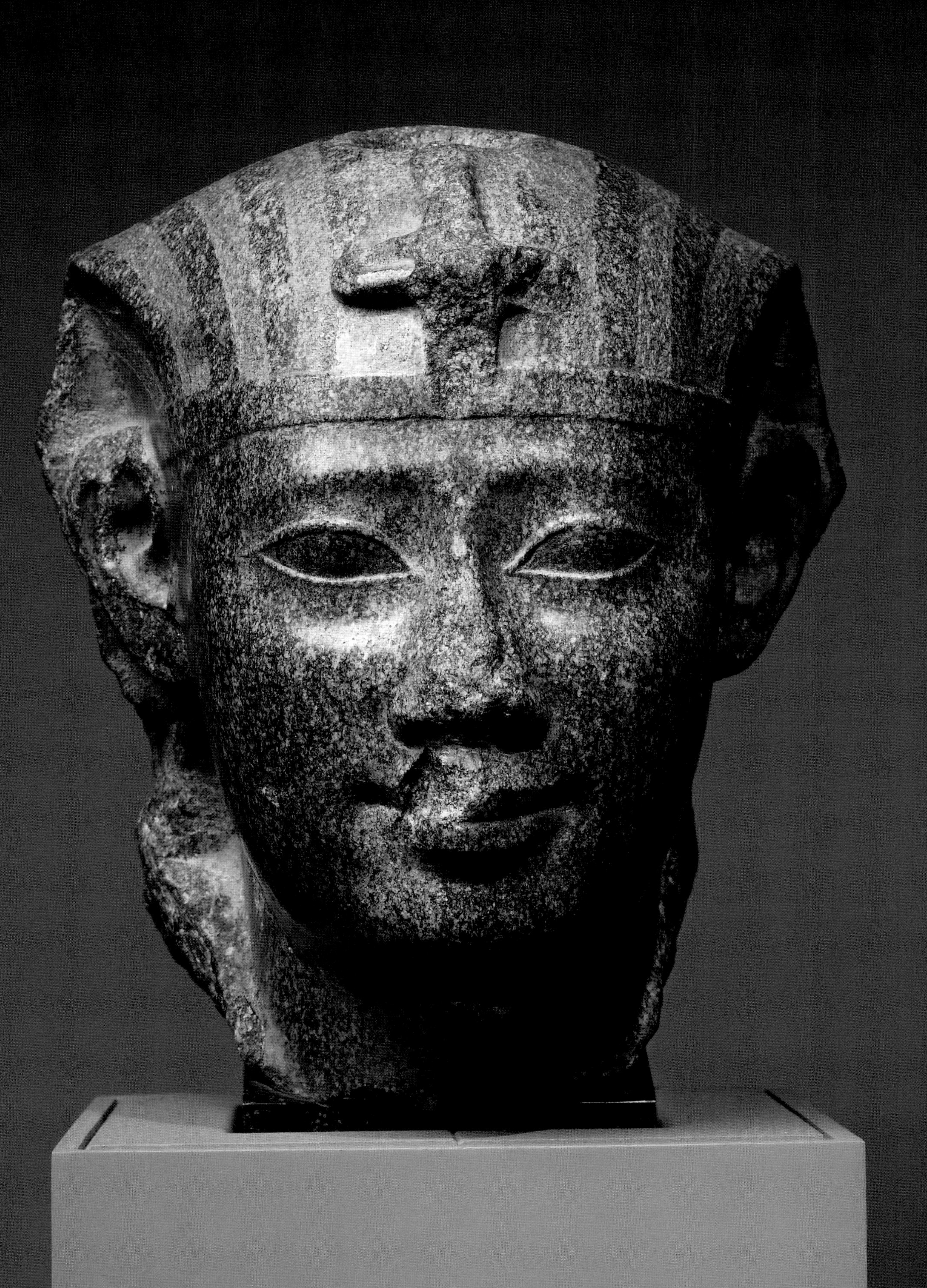

62

Cleopatra II (or Cleopatra III)

Limestone; 24.7 x 17.8 cm (9 3/4 x 7 in.)

Ptolemaic Period, ca. 140–120 B.C.

Provenance: Dikran Kelekian, New York/Paris; Henry Walters, 1928; Walters Art Museum, by bequest, 1931 (22.407)

During the entire pharaonic history of Egypt, the "great royal wife," the principal queen of the ruling king, played an important role in the political makeup of the country. In their capacity as mother of the heir to the throne, some queens wielded considerable influence, as did Tiye, the wife of Amenhotep III in the glorious Eighteenth Dynasty. Under certain circumstances, a well-positioned royal woman could even gain the throne, as did Queen Hatshepsut.[1] Backed by such a tradition, it comes as no surprise to learn that the Ptolemies embraced a concept of divine power that manifested itself both in the king's person and that of his wife.[2] The royal couple were depicted on temple walls, in statuary, and on coins as proof of their legitimate status as Egypt's rulers.[3] The active role of Ptolemaic queens in political affairs was enhanced by their being associated with Isis, who was, beside Sarapis (see no. 68), the leading deity of the Ptolemaic state cult. Indeed, it is often difficult to differentiate between a statue of Isis and that of a queen solely on the basis of iconography or style.[4] That duality was already in place for the cult of the deified Arsinoë II, the wife of Ptolemy II Philadelphos. The so-called Mendes stela informed the reader that images of a queen should be placed near those of the gods in all temples and given equal care.[5]

During the second century, Ptolemaic statuary underwent substantial changes, characterized by the addition of Greek elements, but it was still governed by the traditional principles of Egyptian sculpture. One of these innovations can be observed in the hairstyle of this head of a queen, with its layers of short corkscrew locks.[6] The elaborate masses of hair were held in place by a broad diadem with an attached *uraeus* over the forehead. Identified as either Cleopatra II or her daughter Cleopatra III, both long-lived and power-hungry women, the head offers one of the great female portraits of the Ptolemaic Period, regardless of the fact that we have lost the queen's true identity along with the rest of her statue.

MS

Bibliography

Steindorff 1946a, 70, no. 226, pl. 39; Brunelle 1976, 82; Reeder 1988, 106, no. 29, pls. 29, 1–4; Svenson 1995, 233, no. 117, pl. 46; Stanwick 1999, 514–15, no. G 3; Albersmeier 2002, 210–11, no. 33, pl. 34 a–c.

Notes

1. For a comprehensive account of Hatshepsut's rise to power, see Dorman 2005, 87–89.
2. See Hölbl 2001, 77–123.
3. For statuary, see Ashton 2001, 148–55.
4. Colin 1994, 271–95.
5. For the text, see De Meulenaere and MacKay 1976, 174–77, no. 11, pl. 31.
6. Albersmeier 2002, 67–75, 217–18.

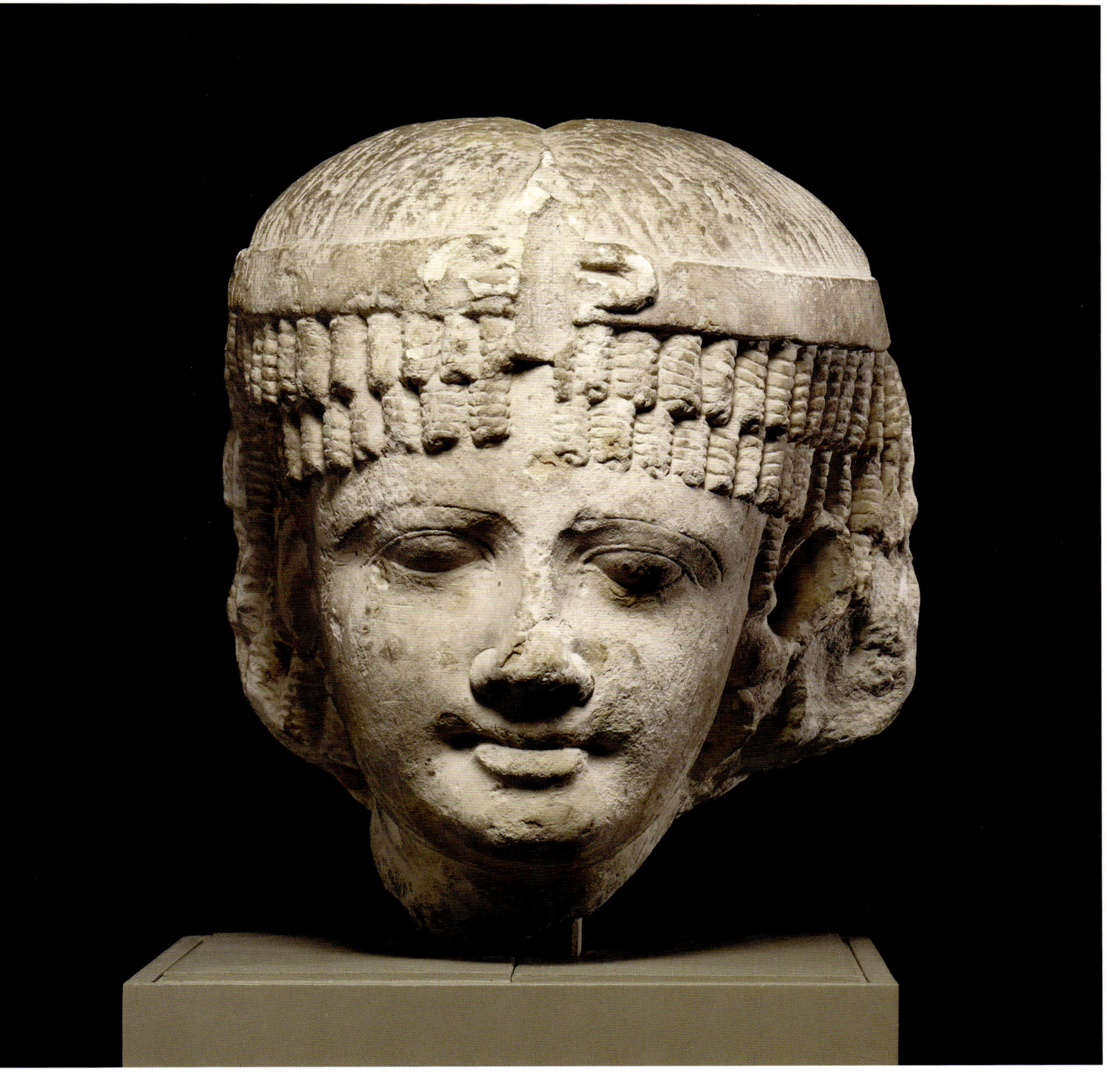

63

Temple relief of Ptolemy II Philadelphos

Sebennytos (present-day Sammanud)

Red granite; 91.2 x 73.5 x 71cm (36 x 29 x 28 in.)

Ptolemaic Period, ca. 270–260 B.C.

Provenance: Henry Walters, before 1931; Walters Art Museum, by bequest, 1931 (22.8)

This block of granite, carved with a relief and an inscription, came from the main temple of the god Onuris-Shu—a hunter and sky deity—in the ancient Egyptian city of Djeb-netjer, the Greek Sebennytos (see no. 49). The temple was built during the Thirtieth Dynasty, when the city was the capital of Egypt, and its reliefs were completed under Ptolemy II. The Macedonian rulers and their successors, the Ptolemaic dynasty, commissioned new temples, but they also reconstructed and enlarged existing shrines to ingratiate themselves with local elites. Ptolemy II in particular was an active builder, and commissioned works throughout Egypt as well as in Greece.

The Walters block was originally a cornerstone, probably from a sanctuary wall.[1] One side depicts a goddess followed by a king; a four-column inscription on the other side contains a solar hymn covered by a stretched-out *pet*-hieroglyph (Egyptian for "sky") filled with stars. The inscription begins with the Horus name (one of five traditional names of the Egyptian king) of the royal reciter of the hymn, which translates as "brave young man." The same Horus name was applied with minor variations to Alexander IV and Ptolemy II.[2] The style of the relief accords with the known reliefs of Ptolemy II from Sebennytos and the nearby temple of Isis at Beheit el-Hagar.[3] An identification with Ptolemy II, the second ruler of the new dynasty, is therefore more likely than Alexander IV.[4]

The goddess on the figurative side of the block wears the traditional sheathlike dress, a long wig, and holds an *ankh* sign in her left hand. Her crown is lost, and only the sticklike lower part, placed under the hair band, is still visible. The form and the mounting are reminiscent of a feather, the familiar symbol of the goddess Maat.

The representation of the king is well preserved, lacking only the upper element of his crown, which can be reconstructed as a double-feather crown with a sun disk above the ram horns and *uraeus* serpents.[5] The king, who wears a short wig, a necklace, and a knee-length kilt with a trapezoidal apron, holds a censer in his right hand; he raises his left hand in a gesture of adoration. A small altar bearing a water jug and a lotus bouquet stands in front of him. Inscribed below his arms is the addressee: "his father," meaning in this context the god Onuris-Shu, "who may give life" in exchange. A standard protective formula is inscribed behind the king's head and back.

RS

Bibliography

Naville 1890, 23–27, pl. VI B; Lepsius 1897, 221; Kamal Bey 1906, 87–94, no. I; Steindorff 1944–45, no. 9, fig. 16: Steindorff 1946a, 77, no. 259, pl. XLV; Hill 1952, 4; Myśliwiec 1988, 127, pl. CIII, a, b; Spencer 1999, 82.

Notes

1. The block is either from the building's front right or back left outer corner, or from one of the interior sides of the entrance.
2. For Alexander IV, see Edgar 1911, 90–96.
3. See Favard-Meeks 1991; a block of this temple depicting Ptolemy II is in the Walters Art Museum (acc. no. 22.200); see Steindorff 1946a, 76, no. 257, pl. XLIV.
4. Bothmer 1953, 2–7.
5. A block from the same temple in the Walters Art Museum (acc. no. 22.176) preserves the crown; see Steindorff 1944–45, 49–50, no. 6, fig. 11.

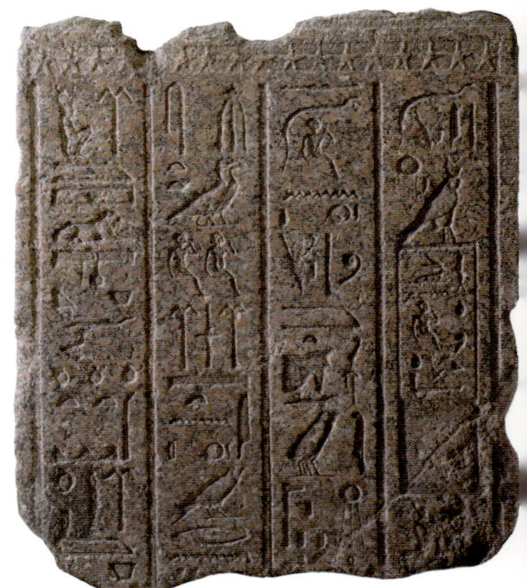

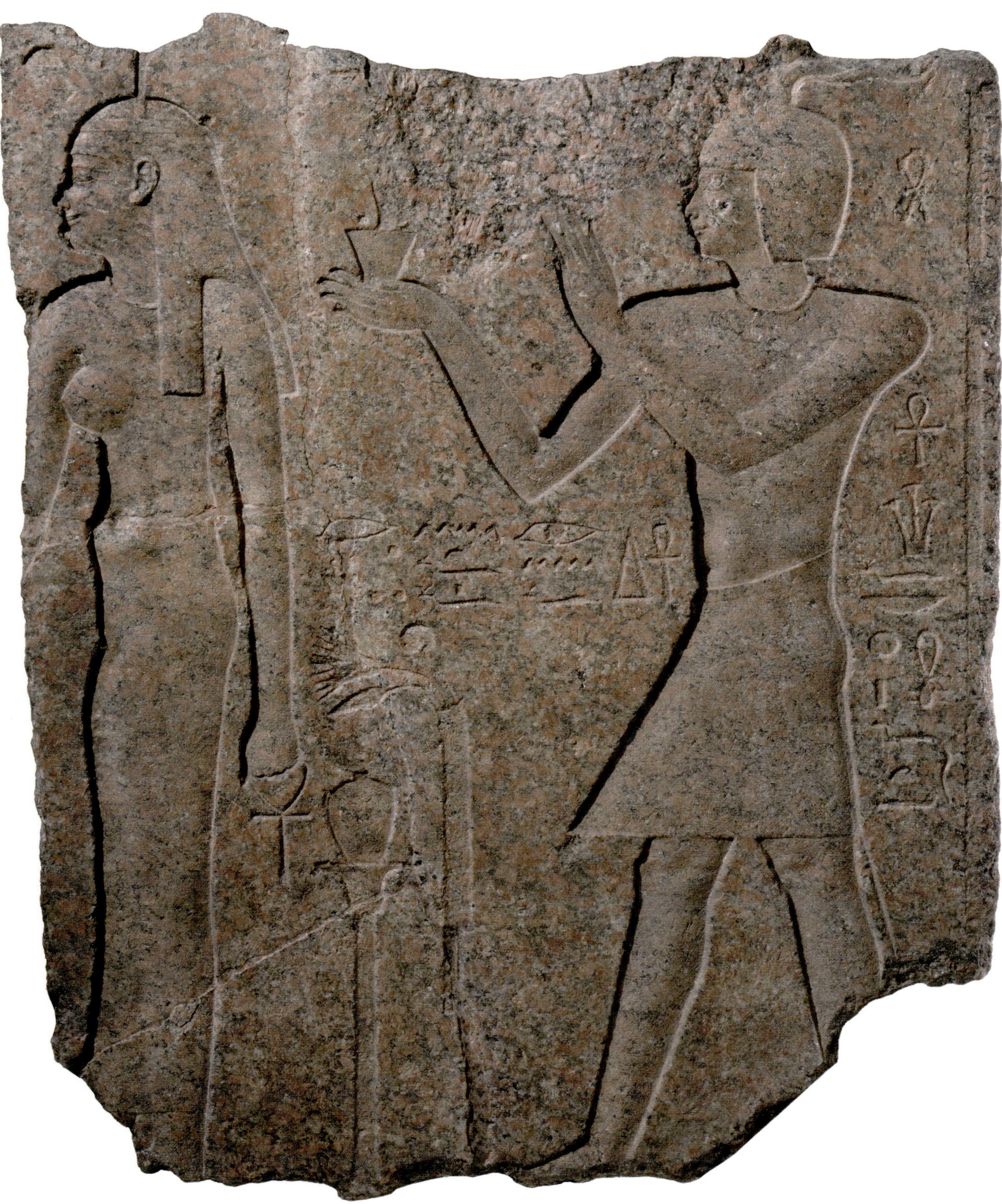

64

Horus stela

Black steatite (soapstone);[1] 23.5 x 14.1 x 5.7 cm
(9 1/4 x 5 9/16 x 2 1/4 in.)
Thirtieth Dynasty, 380–350 B.C.
Provenance: Henry Walters, before 1931; Walters Art Museum, by bequest, 1931 (22.140)

This Horus stela, or cippus, served as a magical apotropaic device. It shows the god Horus as a child together with various wild and dangerous creatures. The stela was intended to be effective against snake and scorpion bites, illnesses, and other manifestations of evil.

Prototypes of such stelae can be traced back to the second half of the New Kingdom, but it was during the Third Intermediate and Late Periods that they developed as standard types. Various materials were used in the manufacture of Horus stelae (dark serpentine was particularly favored during the Late Period), and they were made in several sizes, defined by where they were ultimately placed. Larger examples were made for temples; smaller stelae, such as this one, would have been placed in domestic shrines; miniature stelae were worn or carried as amulets.[2] The object's magical power was released either by touching it,[3] or by trickling water over the surface to absorb the stela's magic energy and then using this water for protection or healing.[4] Underlying the belief in the effectiveness of the stelae were the beliefs that magical forces emanated from the creator,[5] and that reality could be manipulated by images, words, and rituals.

To understand the stela's elaborate composition, the viewer must realize that Horus's strength not only came from the exceptional powers of his mother, Isis, but was also enhanced by various animals, which, though dangerous, were manifestations of primeval or regenerative deities. These creatures included crocodiles, lions, snakes, and scorpions. Even the antelope—linked to Seth, the wild, unpredictable god of untamed nature—can express, when controlled, the transformation of destructive forces into those that may effect desirable results.

The composition, the proportions of the deity, and the deity's facial features date this Horus stela to the Thirtieth Dynasty. Horus wears his hair in a traditional sidelock, and above his forehead is a gazelle's head rather than the more usual *uraeus*.[6] In each hand, he holds various creatures: in his right, two snakes, a scorpion, and a lion; in his left, two snakes, a scorpion, and an antelope. Above his head appears the mask of Bes (see no. 65), who in this context may represent the aged sun god. From the fourth to the first century B.C., when Horus stelae were produced in large quantities, various divine figures, symbols, and scenes appeared on both faces of the stela. On the front of the Walters stela are Serket (Selkis), the scorpion deity who appears three times; and various manifestations of the sun god, who is unified with other gods, including Osiris, Horus, Neith, Nefertem, Thoth, and Khnum, the ram-headed god, who appears twice—once spearing a crocodile, the enemy of the sun god, in front of Taweret (see no. 69) and again protecting with his knives the three squatting Maat figures, who represent the divine order, and the large serpent of the creator god. The deities depicted on the stela symbolize the cyclical process of creation and renewal, as well as the protection of divine order.

Very few Horus stelae name their donor. An inscription on the back of the Walters stela reads, "Tutu, son of Ta-sheret-mehet," suggesting that this stela may have been placed in Tutu's house or in his tomb.

RS

Bibliography

Steindorff 1946a, no. 734, pl. CVIII; Sternberg–el-Hotabi 1999, II, 5; Städelsches Kunstinstitut 2006, 736, no. 350 (F. Hoffmann).

Notes

1. This steatite, analyzed by James Harrell in 1999, is a nearly black chloritic variety.
2. The largest example, measuring 83.5 cm (32 ⅞ in.), is the so-called Metternich Stela in New York, Metropolitan Museum of Art (1950.50.85), see Sternberg–el-Hotabi 1999, II, 72 with further references. One of the smallest examples, at 2.9 cm (1 ⅛ in.) is in the Walters Art Museum (22.380), see Steindorff 1946a, 170, no. 744, pl. CVIII.
3. Many otherwise well-preserved stelae show a much-abraded face of the child; see Sternberg–el-Hotabi 1999, 10–11.
4. Sternberg–el-Hotabi 1999, 12; Satzinger 1987, 189–204.
5. See Ritner1995, 43–62.
6. A very similar composition appears on a Horus stela in the Brooklyn Museum (60.73), see Fazzini et al. 1989, no. 88 (R.S. Bianchi), where the god appears with a *uraeus*.

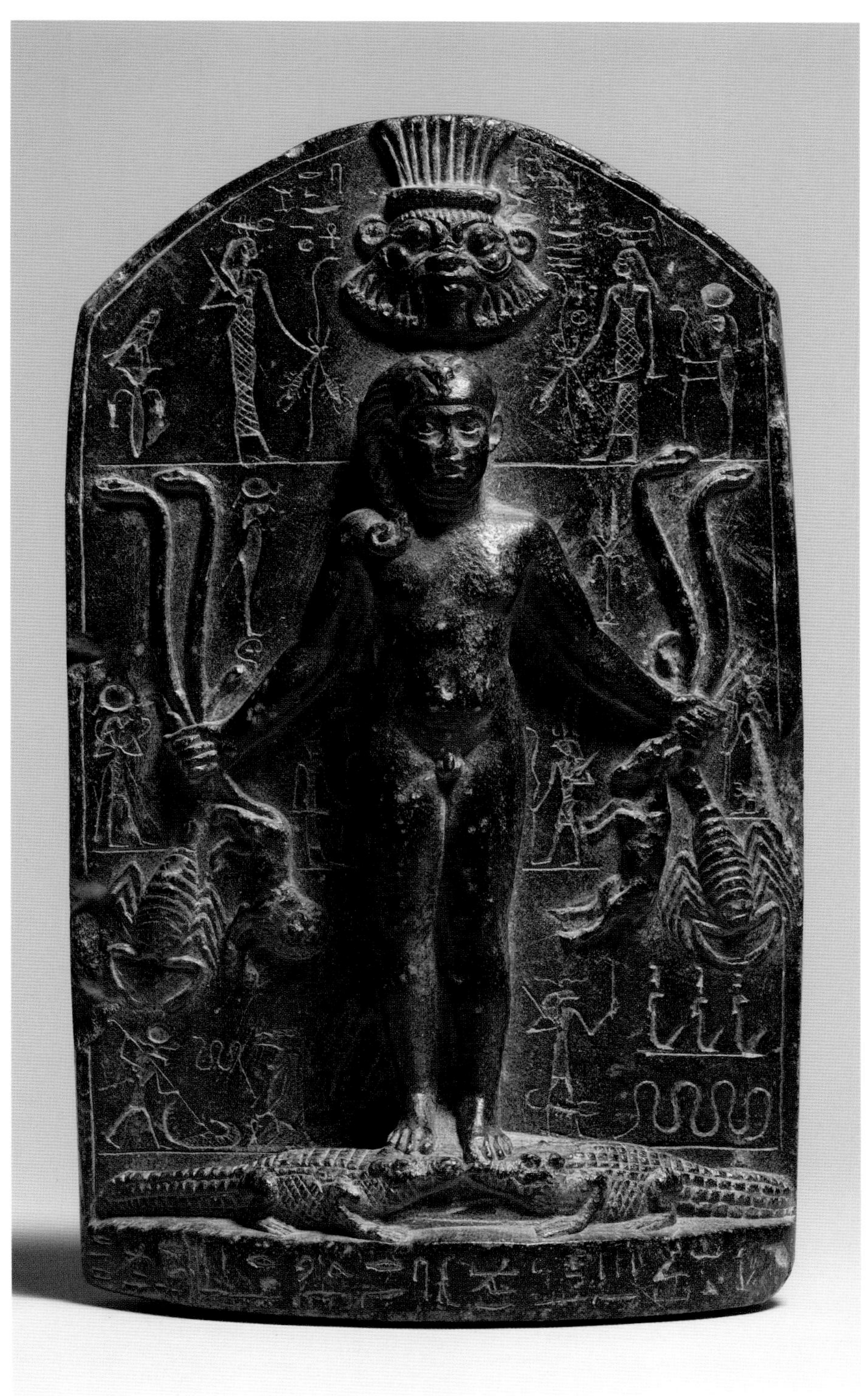

65

Pantheistic Bes figure

Bronze; 24.6 x 13.1 x 9.7 cm (9 5/8 x 5 1/8 x 3 7/8 in.)
Ptolemaic Period, ca. 250–100 B.C.
Provenance: Henry Walters, before 1931, Walters Art Museum, by bequest, 1931 (54.540)

The protective god Bes emerged during the Middle Kingdom at the latest, having been assimilated with other protective deities (notably Aha; see nos. 18 and 19). He is generally represented as a dwarf, most often nude, wearing a lion's mane, with lion's ears, high arched brows, a pug nose, and a full beard; sometimes he is depicted with a protruding tongue, a plumed crown, and a feline skin or tail.

Bes was worshiped as protector of mothers and children, particularly during childbirth, and was also invoked to ward off dangerous creatures and nightmares. He was closely connected to the sun god and may even have been viewed as one of his manifestations (see no. 64). In the Late Period and the Greco-Roman Period, Bes became a pantheistic deity, assimilating characteristics of several gods,[1] perhaps born out of a desire to address requests to an all-inclusive deity who combined aspects of many gods and could thus respond to a multitude of prayers. Representations of such Bes figures appear in magical papyri,[2] on stelae,[3] and as three-dimensional sculptures, particularly bronzes,[4] that were placed in temples and homes to protect the worshipers with Bes's magical skills.

This bronze figure depicts an adult male with the head of Bes from the front and a falcon's body from the back. The god stands on a base encircled by an *uroboros* (a serpent swallowing its own tail, symbolizing eternity), with crocodiles, scorpions, and snakes at his feet. His human arms extend outward at the sides and join two pairs of wings supported by props. His clenched fists would once have held attributes. The god wears a pleated kilt, and bands cross over his chest and back; he has cobras on his knees, a feline head on his genitals, and a human head on his lower back. The head is flanked by four small animal heads on each side (a jackal, a feline, a crocodile, a ram, and a falcon are identifiable), and has a scarab on the back. The crown consists of ram horns combined with two plumes, a sun disk, and cobras. The jackal head of Anubis is attached at the bottom, and the ibis head of Thoth with moon crescent and disk at the top. The back of the crown displays the ram's head appliqué of Amun with an *Atef*-crown. Such a composition of divine elements combines aspects of this and the other world, of earth and sky, of the human and the divine. Bes stands in the center as a link between all these levels of creation, manifesting the magical power of the creator god.

RS

Bibliography

Steindorff 1946a, 157, no. 713, pl. CV.

Notes

1. Other combinations are also documented, such as pantheistic combinations of Amun-Re and Anubis (Walters Art Museum, acc. no. 54.2083, in Steindorff 1946a, 158, no. 714, pl. CV), or an example in a German private collection in Schoske and Wildung 1992, 180–81, no. 119), but they never reached the same level of popularity as the pantheistic Bes.
2. See, for example, the Brooklyn Magical Papyrus 1.1–3.8 and 4.1–5.8, in Sauneron 1970, figs. 2 and 3.
3. See, for example, Cairo, Egyptian Museum, CG 9428 and 9429, in Daressy 1903, pl. X.
4. See, for example, Brussels, Musées Royaux d'Art et d'Histoire, E 7533, in Lefèbvre and van Rinsveld 1990, 197; Paris, Musée du Louvre, N 5141 in Étienne 2000, no. 140a.

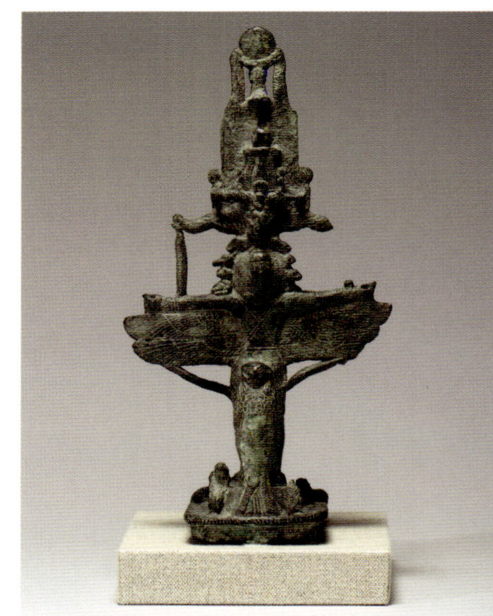

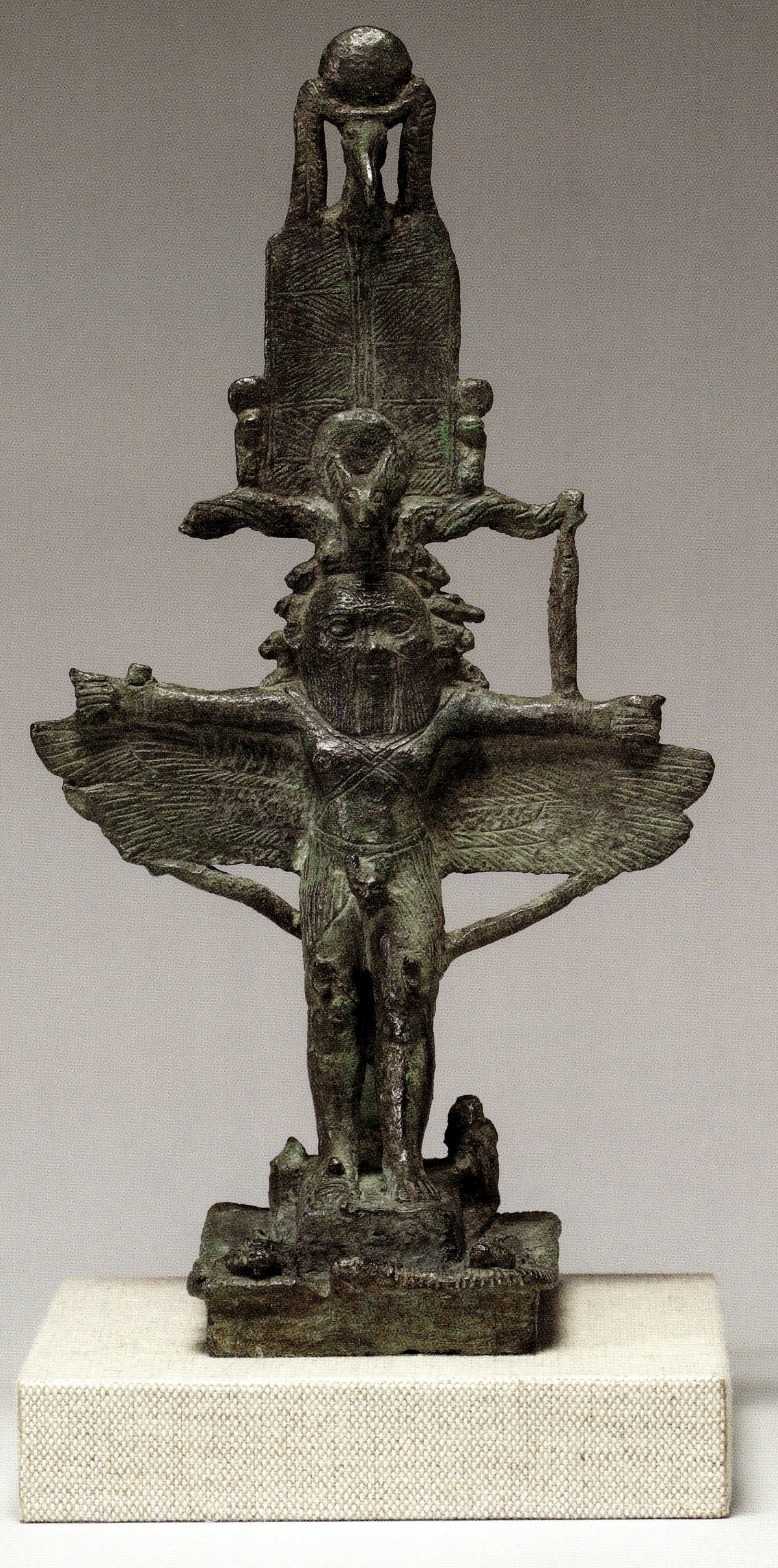

66

The Book of the Faiyum

Probably from the Faiyum oasis

Papyrus, black and red ink: height: 27–31.8 cm (10 5/8–12 1/2 in.)[1]

Ptolemaic Period, third–second century B.C.

Provenance: Collection of Reverend William Frankland Hood (d. 1864) (purchased in Deir el-Bahari); sale, Sotheby, Wilkinson & Hodge London, 11 November 1924, no. 134; William Randolph Hearst; Joseph Brummer, New York; sale, Parke-Bernet Galleries New York,

11–13 May 1949, no. 67; Walters Art Museum, museum purchase, 1949 (W.738)

The Book of the Faiyum is the modern name for a text that describes the Faiyum oasis as the mythical center of creation and ritual. The text was compiled during the Greco-Roman Period, perhaps in the temple of the crocodile god Sobek in Sheded (Greek: Crocodilopolis; Arabic: Medinet el-Faiyum), but it may be based on precedents from the Late Period.[2] It consisted of two papyrus scrolls with hieroglyphic text and illustrations.[3] Besides these hieroglyphic versions, there are also hieratic copies on papyrus,[4] and an unillustrated text is inscribed on the walls of the Sobek temple in Kom Ombo (Upper Egypt).

The illustrated version of the Book of the Faiyum shows a sequence of deities, with short captions identifying them and naming the place where they appeared. The main purpose of the book is to record these locations and to define their role in the ceremonial landscape of the Faiyum. It was created for use by priests; the large number of copies attests to the text's importance.

The book is arranged in sections and subsections; numbers (written in demotic script) indicate the sequence; sections 4–23 are preserved in the Walters papyrus. The text is read from left to right, although the order varies in some of the sections.

The beginning of the book is lost. The early sections depict the "Channel of the Great Waterway," probably the Bahr Yussef—the canal that connects the Nile with Lake Faiyum (modern Birket Qarun)—and the associated wetland; the goddess Mehet-weret, who represents the primeval flood and abundance; and the lake itself as the site of the sun god's creation and re-creation. The next section, the largest of the papyrus, shows an elongated oval enclosing pictures of the lake and its divine forces; the shores are depicted above and below. Forty-two places are mentioned, corresponding in number to the nomes of Egypt. They are represented by anthropomorphic or biomorphic (animal-headed) gods seated on thrones, or zoomorphic gods on bases.

The divine forces within the lake are manifestations of Sobek-Re and related deities. The crocodile Sobek was the god of the water, the marshlands, and riverbanks and was linked to vegetative fertility. When unified with the sun god Re, he received the creative force and was regarded as a primeval deity.

The icons and scenes within the lake's oval are divided into three subsections; the sequence is arranged from right (associated with the west and the setting sun) to left (associated with the east and sunrise). The first subsection comprises four icons and scenes that deal with the re-creation of the sun god and his unification with Osiris for their combined renewal: the first is the manifestation Amun-Re-Sobek, identified by his ram head (surmounted by a *hemhem* crown), lion body and crocodile tail. Next in the sequence is the

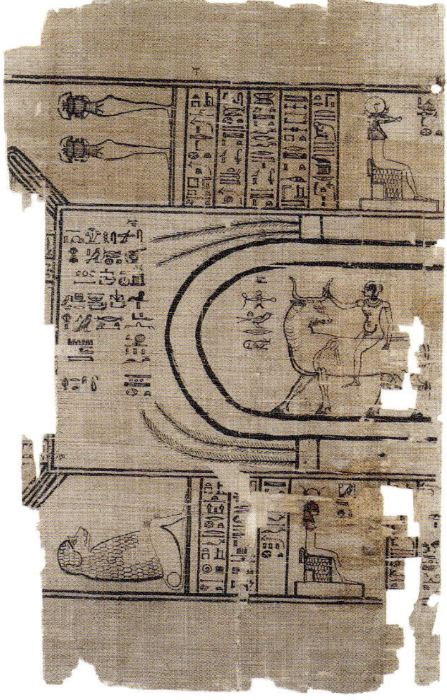

W.738.1B

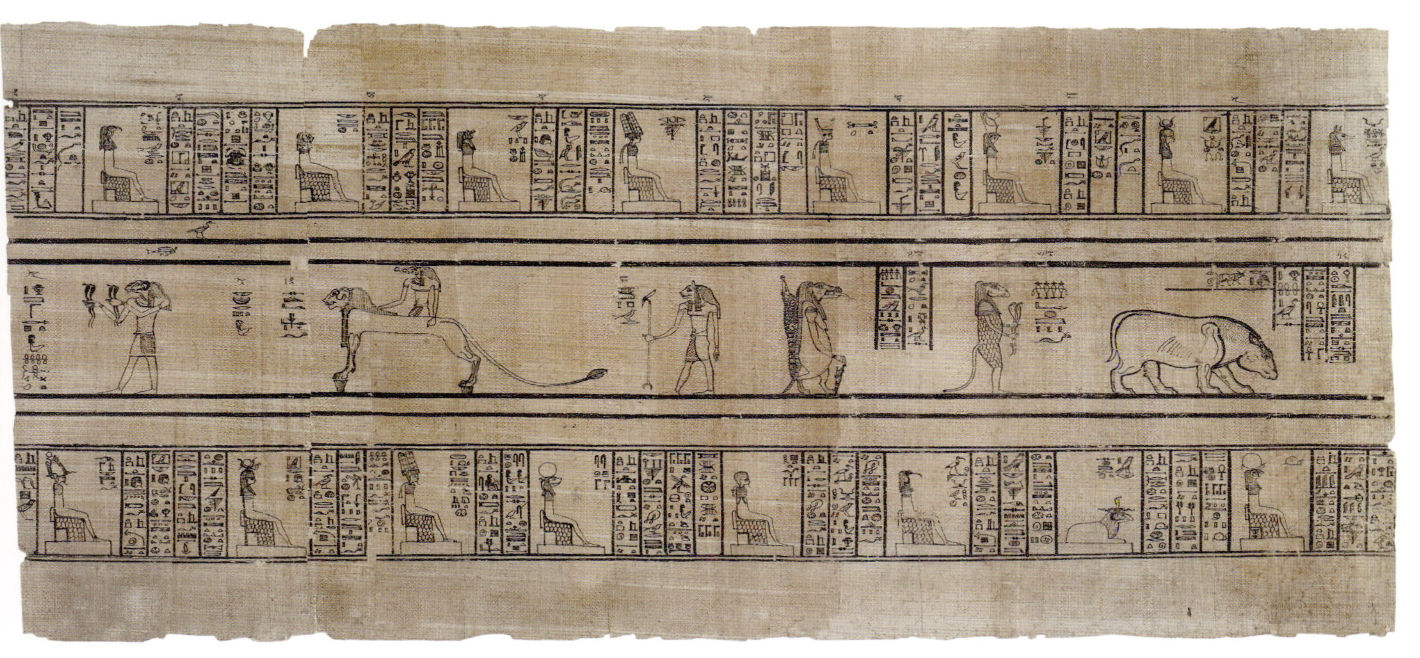

W.738.1C

mummy of Osiris-Sobek-Re in his tomb. The cow head of the goddess Sheded with her solar disk may represent not only the region of the lake, but also the mystery of renewal in the underworld; for that reason, she is named "the Great, whom no one knows." The last scene displays the human goddess Sheded facing a serpent standing on its tail, which may represent the creator god Atum, who is followed by the two legs of Osiris, symbolizing his renewal by the water of the Nile flood.

The second subsection contains six icons and scenes, the first three facing left and the next three right. Their theme is the creation of the world. The sequence starts with the celestial cow who is supported by the god Shu; under her udder sits the sun god Re-Herakhte, waiting to be nourished by her milk. The next figure, the largest of the lake region, is the primeval crocodile god Sobek-Re, who is accompanied by a cryptographic inscription that may express the mystery of creation and eternity. The offering vessel under his front feet and a primeval hill under his back feet may be linked to aspects of ritual and myth. Next in the sequence is a creature composed of a ram's head surmounted by a *uraeus* serpent, a phallus-shaped body, and a crocodile's tail. This figure faces a female goddess that combines elements of a hippopotamus, a cow, and a lion. She is the mother goddess, who is waiting to be sexually united with Sobek-Re—simultaneously father and son, and thus self-creating. The last two figures follow the mother goddess; a juvenile god with a baboon's body, a ramlike head without horns, and cobras in his hands; and a standing hippopotamus goddess with a crocodile on her back, named "Neith, the Great, who protects her son."

The figures of the last section all face left, repeating the orientation of the first. They continue the theme of the sun god's resurrection, assisted by his mother. Reading from right to left are the following deities: the catheaded sun god, a lion bier—representing the celestial mother goddess—from which Sobek-Re emerges, a male ram-headed figure that may refer to the Amun-Re aspect of the god, and the juvenile sun god on the back of the cow-shaped Mehet-weret.

The remaining sections of the two scrolls, which are poorly preserved, deal with the three most important cult places in the Faiyum: Sheded (Crocodilopolis), Ra-sehui, and "acacia tree of Neith," as well as the primeval deities. Displayed in the final scene is Lake Faiyum, which may be interpreted in two ways: as the temple of the god Sobek of Sheded or as the place of regeneration for Re, Osiris, and Horus, as well as for the pharaoh, thus securing in this place the continuity of creation.

RS

Bibliography

Brugsch 1879, 391; Whitehouse 1885, 83–84; Maspero 1898, 63–70 and 81–91; Beinlich 1991 (with further references); Tait 2003, 183–202.

Notes

1. W.738.1B: 29.8 x 29.2 cm (11 3/4 x 11 1/2 in.); W.738.1C: 27 x 28 cm (10 5/8 x 11 in.); W.738.1D: 31.8 x 59.2 (12 1/2 x 23 5/16 in.); W.738.1E: 28.2 x 54.3 cm (11 1/8 x 21 3/8 in.). The remaining fragment (W.738.1A), not illustrated here, measures 29.8 x 10.2 cm (11 3/4 x 4 in.).
2. Three scenes that may have belonged to a version of the book are displayed inside the coffin of Anch-rui from Hawara; see Beinlich 1991, 65.
3. The most famous copy, known as the Boulaq/Hood/Amherst papyrus, was certainly found in the Faiyum, but no reliable records of its origins have been preserved. It was sent to the art market in Thebes, where it was sold in no fewer than three pieces in 1859; one part came to the Boulaq Museum (later the Egyptian Museum), Cairo; a second fragment was bought by the Reverend W. Frankland Hood (Lincolnshire); and a third appeared later in the collection of Lord William Amherst (Hackney) and is today in the Morgan Library (New York); see Beinlich 1991, 15–26.
4. For example, from Tebtunis in the southern Faiyum, see Tait 2003, 201.

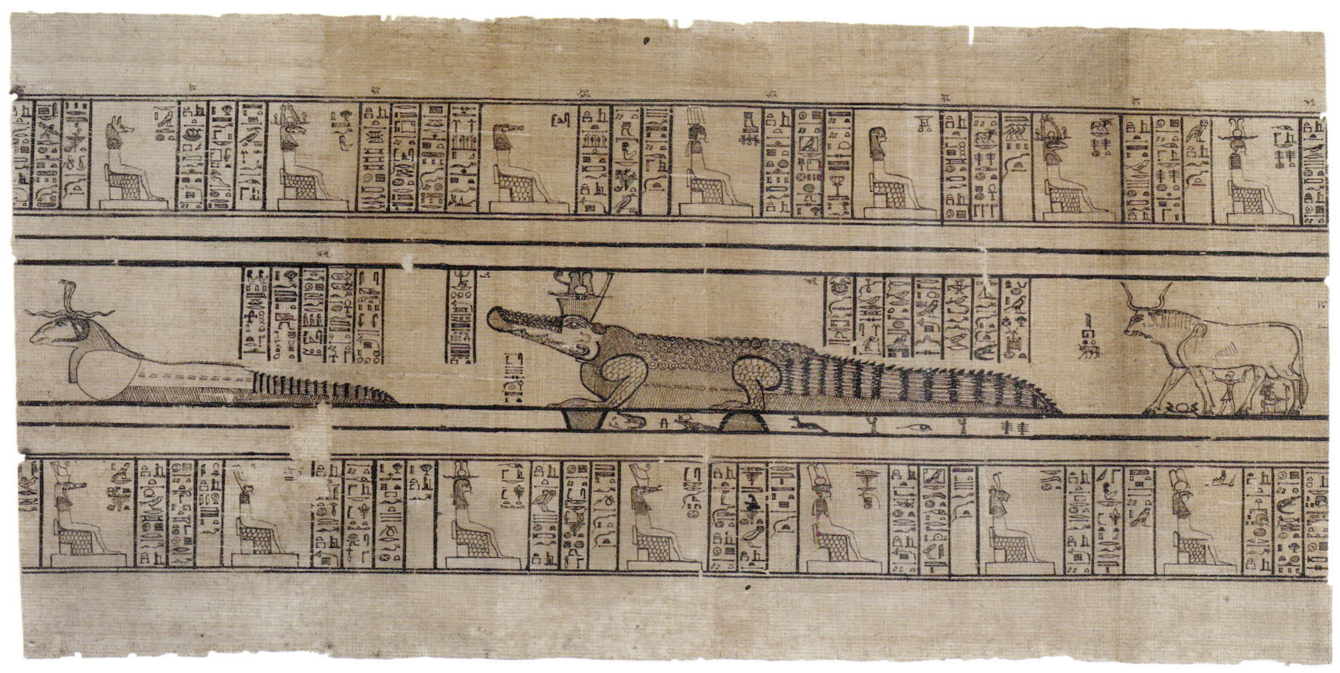
W.738.1D

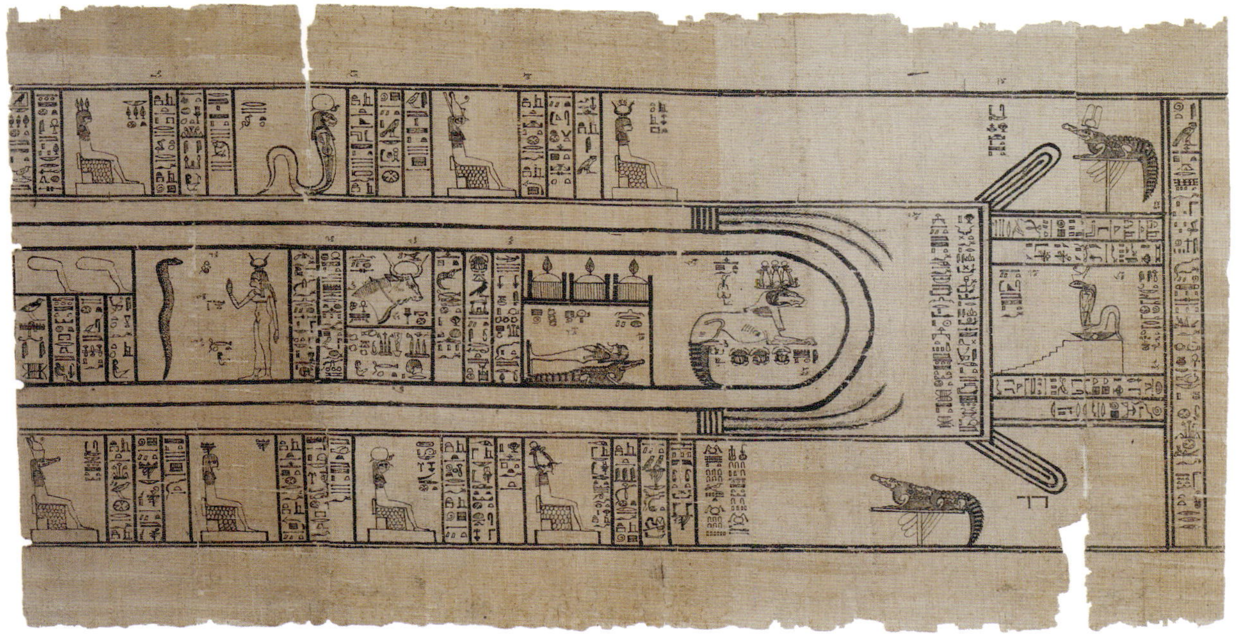
W.738.1E

57

Figure of a Horus falcon

Probably from Alexandria

Gold, blue enamel (glass); 3.8 x 3.45 cm (1 ½ x 1 ⅜ in.)

Early Ptolemaic Period, ca. 300–250 B.C.

Provenance: Joseph Brummer, New York; Henry Walters, 1927;

Walters Art Museum, by bequest, 1931 (57.1484)

This tiny figure of a falcon, probably depicting the god Horus, is particularly interesting for the technique of its manufacture. The object's core, consisting of an unknown material, is covered by a thick sheet of gold, achieving more economically the same visual appearance as casting. The method also allowed for the detailed representation of the bird's feathers using the cloisonné technique, in which thin strips of gold wire were affixed to the surface of the falcon's wings and head; the cavities, or cloisons, thus created were filled with powdered glass.[1] When heated, the molten glass bonded with the metal.

True cloisonné enamel is not documented in Egypt before the Late Period.[2] Previously, jewelry would have been inlaid with small, precisely cut pieces of glass, imitating highly valued stones such as lapis lazuli, turquoise, jasper, and feldspar. The late date of the Walters falcon is confirmed by a small inconspicuous detail: the cloisons vary in size and are oval rather than the traditional U-shape.[3] This feature links the Walters falcon with other gold figures of animals, all of which were made in Alexandria at a time when the arts were reinvigorated under the rule of the early Ptolemies. The little rosette on the falcon's head and the prominent necklace with the floral design connote rites associated with Dionysos, a clear late Hellenic influence.

The falcon is soldered to a gold base and lacks any hook for suspension, an indication that it was not intended to serve as an amulet of the sort cited in chapter 77 of the Book of the Dead: "Spell for being transformed into a golden falcon."[4] The diversity of these gold animals, including, in addition to the Walters falcon, an ibis, two lions, and a falcon-headed sphinx, suggests that their primary function was not governed by religious background but simply to be judged as luxurious possessions of wealthy citizens in a prospering metropolis.

MS

Bibliography

Steindorff 1946a, 151, no. 676 a; Kozloff 1976, 183–85, pl. 32, figs. 4–6; Canby 1979b, 34, no. 79.

Notes

1. See Andrews 1990, 67–99.
2. For a possible precedent, see a Second Intermediate Period pectoral (Boston, MFA, acc. no. 1981.159), in Brovarski 1987, 20–21.
3. For examples from the tomb of Tutankhamun, see James 2000, 202–39.
4. For falcon amulets, see Andrews 1994, 27–29, fig. 25. For a Ptolemaic falcon figure in gold, see Fay 1990, 13–16; for an Egyptian-style example in bronze and gold, see Muscarella 1974, no. 220.

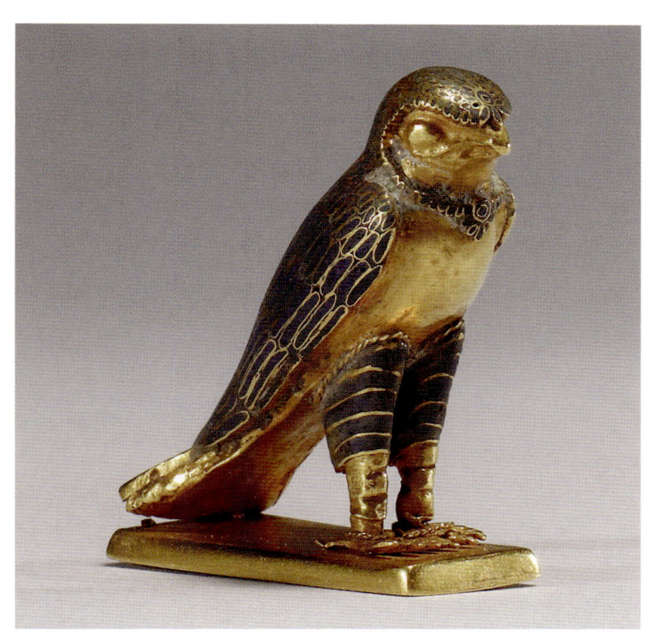

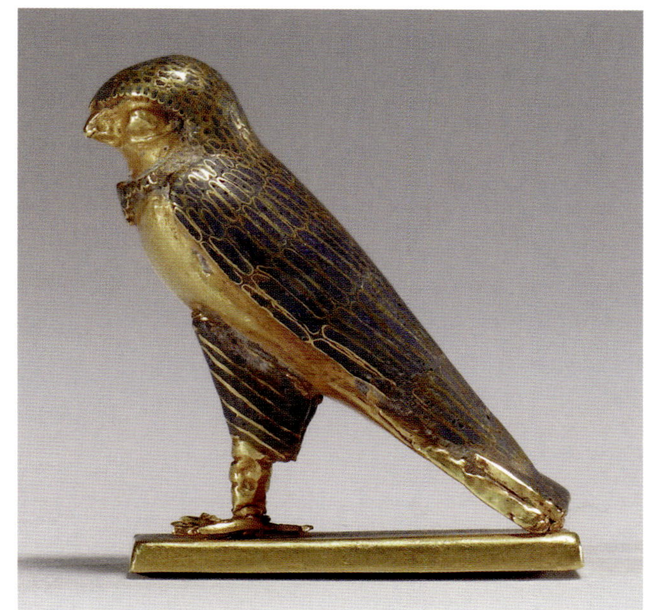

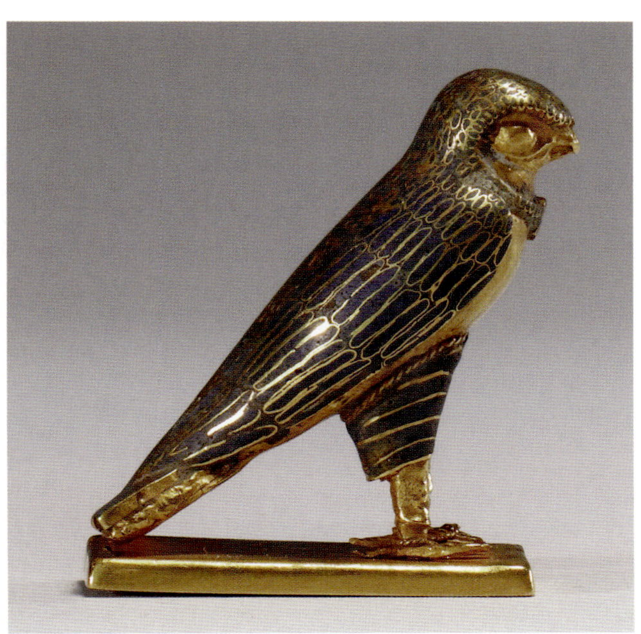

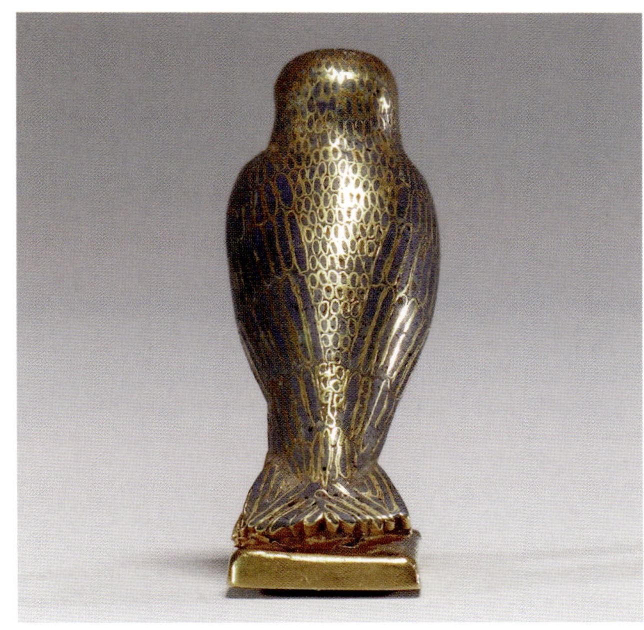

68

Pendant with image of Sarapis

Gold; 4.3 x 3.7 x 0.9 cm (1 11/16 x 1 1/2 x 3/8 in.)

Ptolemaic Period, second–first century B.C.

Provenance: Henry Walters, before 1931; Walters Art Museum, by bequest, 1931 (57.1524)

The god Sarapis emerged in Egypt at the beginning of the Hellenistic era, when the country was occupied by Alexander the Great (332 B.C.) and a dynasty of Macedonian kings, the Ptolemies, ruled Egypt. It was Ptolemy I (305–282 B.C.) who gave the order to develop a new religious cult for his dynasty and the Egyptian state, and he dedicated the first temple to Sarapis at Alexandria for this purpose. For the Greeks, the creation of a new god was something extraordinary, but for the Egyptians the modification of religious concepts to fit new needs was a tradition of long standing.[1] The priests chose the Egyptian god Osiris-Apis (named later also Osorapis), who was a protective deity, a god of oracles, and lord of time and eternity. They modified his name to Sarapis, and gave his visual representation a Hellenistic form, appropriating the shoulder-length hair and full beard of the Greek supreme deity Zeus; the *kalathos*—a woven grain basket—with which Sarapis is often crowned, symbolizes fertility. The companion of the new state god—the goddess Isis—was also depicted in a Hellenistic form, but her name and attributes remained unaltered.

The participation of Egypt's Greek population in rituals for Sarapis and the Hellenized Isis was an expression of their loyalty to the dynasty (native Egyptians clung to their traditional gods), but the worship of Sarapis did not end with the extinction of the Ptolemies. To the contrary: the god became a universal deity in Roman times, venerated throughout the Mediterranean, uniting aspects of Dionysos, Zeus, Helios, Asklepios, and other deities.[2]

This circular pendant, likely the property of a member or protégé of the Ptolemies or a member of the upper class, has a thick wire frame with ball-shaped terminals at the bottom, and a six-part ribbed tube at the top. The ornamental field contains a bust of Sarapis in raised relief.[3] The god wears a *chiton* (tunic) and a folded *himation* (mantle). His *anastole* hairstyle, in which the hair is combed up from the forehead and encircles the crown of the head like a wreath, is characteristic of middle and late Hellenistic representations,[4] and he is crowned by a small *kalathos*. His mustache is long and his full beard curled and parted in the center. The pendant can be dated on the basis of its form and the style of the bust, as well as by virtue of its close similarity to two pendants dating to the first or second century B.C. found at Delos.[5]

RS

Bibliography

Brooklyn Museum 1941, 42, no. 129; Walters Art Gallery 1979, 111, no. 309 (A. Oliver); Reeder 1988, 233, no. 130.3; Schulz and Seidel 2002, 9, no. 11.

Notes

1. Mayr 2004, 27–35.
2. Merkelbach 1995, 74–86.
3. A second–first-century B.C. gold medallion (an attachment to a vase) with busts of Isis and Sarapis is in the Brooklyn Museum (acc. no. 73.85), see Brooklyn Museum 1988, no. 102.
4. See Hornbostel 1973, 133–206.
5. See Reeder 1988, 233, with further references.

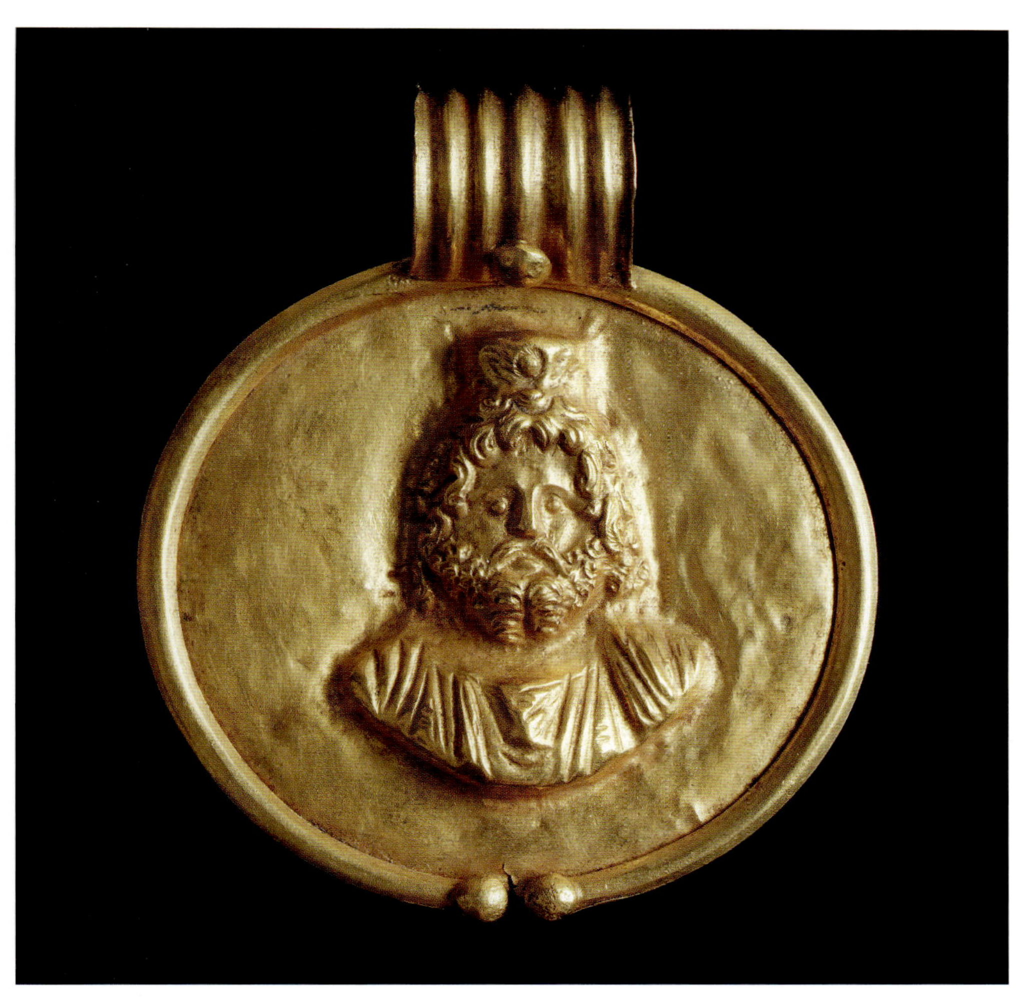

69

Statue of Taweret

Probably from Xoïs (Delta)[1]

Red granite; 53 x 21 x 23 cm (21 1/8 x 8 1/4 x 9 1/16 in.)

Ptolemaic Period, ca. 180–100 B.C.

Provenance: Eddé Collection, Alexandria; sale, Hôtel Drouot, Paris, 31 May–2 June 1911, no. 525; Henry Walters, before 1931; Walters Art Museum, by bequest, 1931 (22.223)

The goddess Taweret, whose name means "the great one," enjoyed immense popularity throughout Egypt's history together with other hippopotamus deities, such as Ipet (meaning "wet-nurse") and Reret ("saw"). Taweret was venerated as a protective deity of women and children, and especially of women in childbirth. Her fearsome appearance, comprising a hippopotamus head and body, pendulous breasts, a swollen belly, limbs terminating in lion paws, and a crocodile tail cascading down the back of the body, was believed to frighten away harmful spirits and demons. Representations of Taweret were widely produced as amulets and worn by women and children in daily life, but such amulets were also used as burial accoutrements. Small figures of the goddess were worshiped in domestic shrines,[2] and her protective likeness appears on furniture, cosmetic tools, jewelry, and vessels.

The imposing size of the Walters Taweret indicates that the statue was placed in a temple area; it is one of very few known large-scale statues of the goddess.[3] The figure has an open mouth with articulated teeth. On the head is a cylindrical flat-topped crown called a *modius*. The wig has vertical striations on the lappets, the endcaps of which have four narrow bands and one wide band (a unique feature). The paws, in an unusual gesture, clutch the hieroglyphic *sa* sign (meaning "protection"); normally Taweret's paws rest on the *sa* sign rather than grasping it. Another large-scale figure of Taweret in the British Museum has a similar feature: the paws grasp *ankh* signs.[4] That element had been a variation specifically associated with the Greco-Roman era, to which both statues are dated.

Another unusual element is the presence of carved cartouches on the arms. They are badly executed, and the indecipherable glyphs do not indicate any known ruler. Compared with the overall high quality of the statue's workmanship, the cartouches are anomalies and were probably added at a later date, perhaps in modern times by a dealer to increase the salability of the statue.

If the statue really comes from Xoïs, it may have been placed in a chapel of the as-yet unexcavated temple of Amun-Re.[5] Ptolemy VIII Euergetes II (170–163 and 145–116 B.C.), in particular, is known to have undertaken works on the Amun temple, and he was also the primary builder of the Ipet temple at Karnak, a cult temple nominally in the service of the god Amun. Its relief decorations invoke the mythic resurrection cycle linking Amun, Ipet (a version of Taweret) and Osiris. This pharaoh's interest in the role of Ipet relative to Amun may have informed his building program at Xoïs, perhaps in connection with the Amun sanctuary.

CH

Bibliography

Eddé Collection 1911, 44, no. 525, pl. 7; Steindorff 1946a, 141, no. 607, pl. XCIII.

Notes

1. According to the entry in the 1911 sales catalogue, the sculpture was reportedly found at Sakha (the ancient Xoïs).
2. For an exquisite example, see Lacovara and Trope 2001b, 152–54, no. 101.
3. Cairo, Egyptian Museum, CG 39145; see Wildung and Schoske 1985, 30, no. 10; and an unpublished limestone Taweret of similar size from the cachette in Karnak (JE 37531); Chicago, Field Museum, 30.822, see Capel and Markoe 1996, 13–32, no. 63a.
4. London, British Museum, EA 35700; see Aston, Harrell, and Shaw 2000, 43, fig. 2.19.
5. Some vestiges of pharaonic material have been recovered from Xoïs, among them an architectural element of Ptolemy VIII Euergetes II; see Porter and Moss 1934, 45.

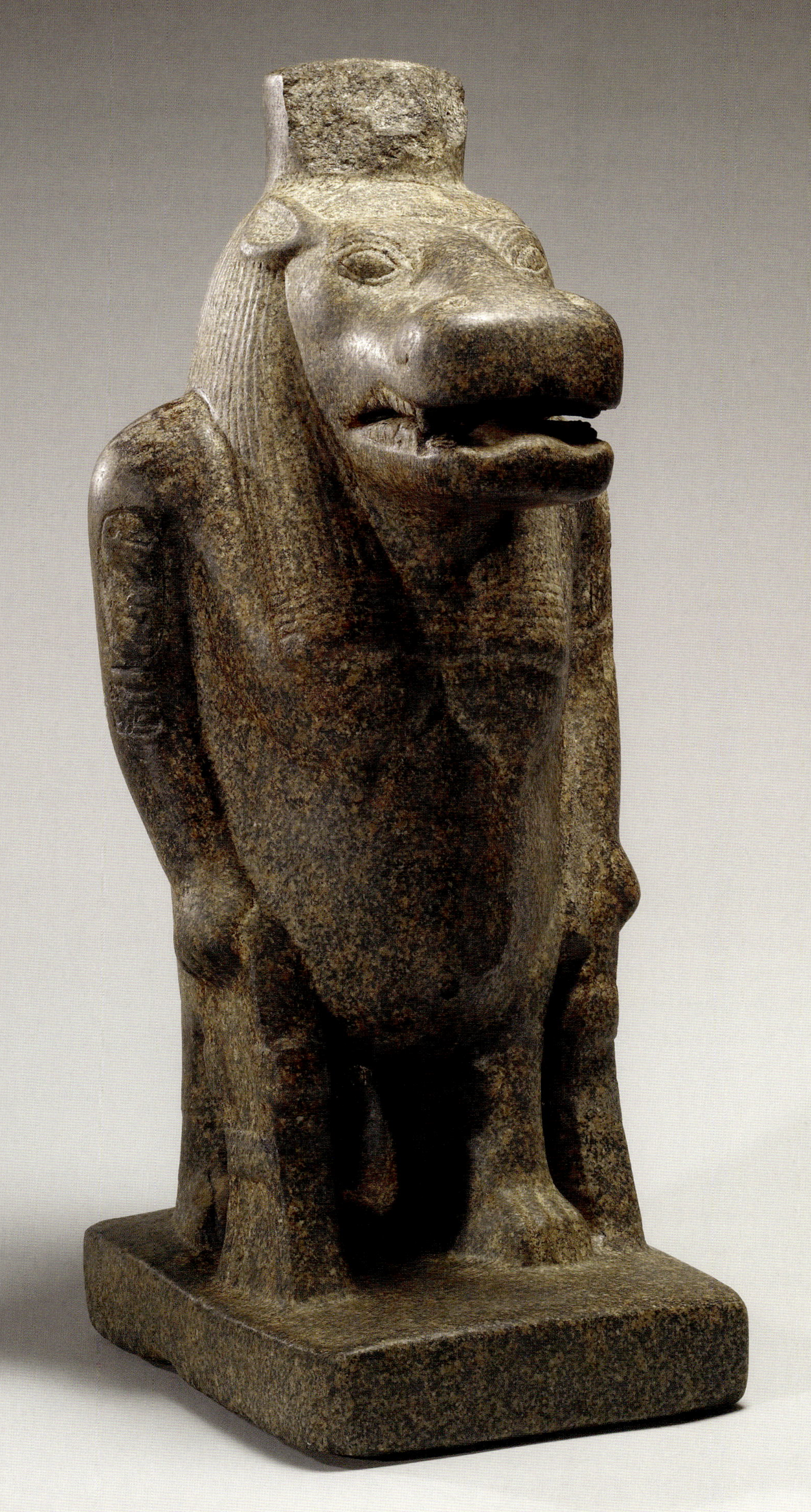

70

Mummy mask

Probably from Meir or Tuna el-Gebel[1]

Painted cartonnage, gold leaf, and glass inlays; 50.9 x 26 x 14.3 cm (20 1/16 x 10 1/4 x 5 5/8 in.)

Late Ptolemaic–early Roman Period, ca. 50 B.C.–A.D. 50

Provenance: Dikran Kelekian, New York/Paris; Henry Walters, 1913; Walters Art Museum, by bequest, 1931 (78.3)

The desire to preserve the idealized face of the deceased led to the development of masks as early as the Old Kingdom. The use of cartonnage (a mixture of linen and plaster) for such masks became common in the Middle Kingdom (see no. 10), and the application of gold leaf from the New Kingdom onward.[2] Widespread use of glass inlays in shrines,[3] coffins,[4] and masks[5] began in the fourth century B.C.

This well-preserved mask was made to cover the head, neck, and chest of a mummy. It was formed of cartonnage, with some of the details carved out of the covering plaster layer in fine raised relief. Next the dark red base color was applied, then the black, and finally the gold leaf. The glass inlays were added last, and inserted in compartments that had been left empty during the modeling.

The wide-open eyes, inlaid with black and white opaque glass, dominate the face, contrasting with the carefully modeled features, which are not accentuated with color. The long headdress frames the face and neck, and reaches down to the chest. It is composed of alternating black and gold strands, with divine figures of jackals at the lappets, and a red and golden border. At the top of the mask, gold wings extend from each side of a cobalt blue glass scarab to cover the head.[6] The space between the headdress and the scarab is painted red to suggest that the beetle is levitating above the deceased. At the center of the headdress is an *ankh* sign, surmounted by a sun disk and flanked by erect cobras, crowned with sun disks. A recumbent jackal, with a winged sun disk hovering over its back, decorates each side of the lower lappets. A golden collar, comprising five rows of rosettes, elongated beads, and teardrop pendants, appears between the headdress's lappets. A pectoral in the form of a shrine hangs from the collar and contains an ibis—the zoomorphic form of the god of wisdom Thoth—inlaid in black, white, and blue glass. Two kneeling goddesses, probably Isis and Nephthys, flank the pectoral. Each has a sun disk on her head and wears a long, curled wig. The two goddesses each hold a fan in one hand; the other hand is raised in the direction of the ibis in a gesture of adoration.

The mask presents the idealized face of an adult. The eyes look slightly upward in a kind of apotheosis.[7] The decoration combines symbolism related to the renewal of the sun god and the protection of the deceased when she enters the underworld. The solar *ankh* sign above the forehead and the golden color of the mask convey the desire to be reborn into the afterlife as a divine being accompanying the sun god.

The proportions, style, and iconography date the mask to the late Ptolemaic or very early Roman Period,[8] and suggest a Middle Egyptian origin, either Meir or Tuna el-Gebel. The choice of the ibis-form Thoth—who represents time and eternity—may link the deceased to the main religious center of the region in the Greco-Roman Period: the temple of Thoth in Hermopolis.

RS

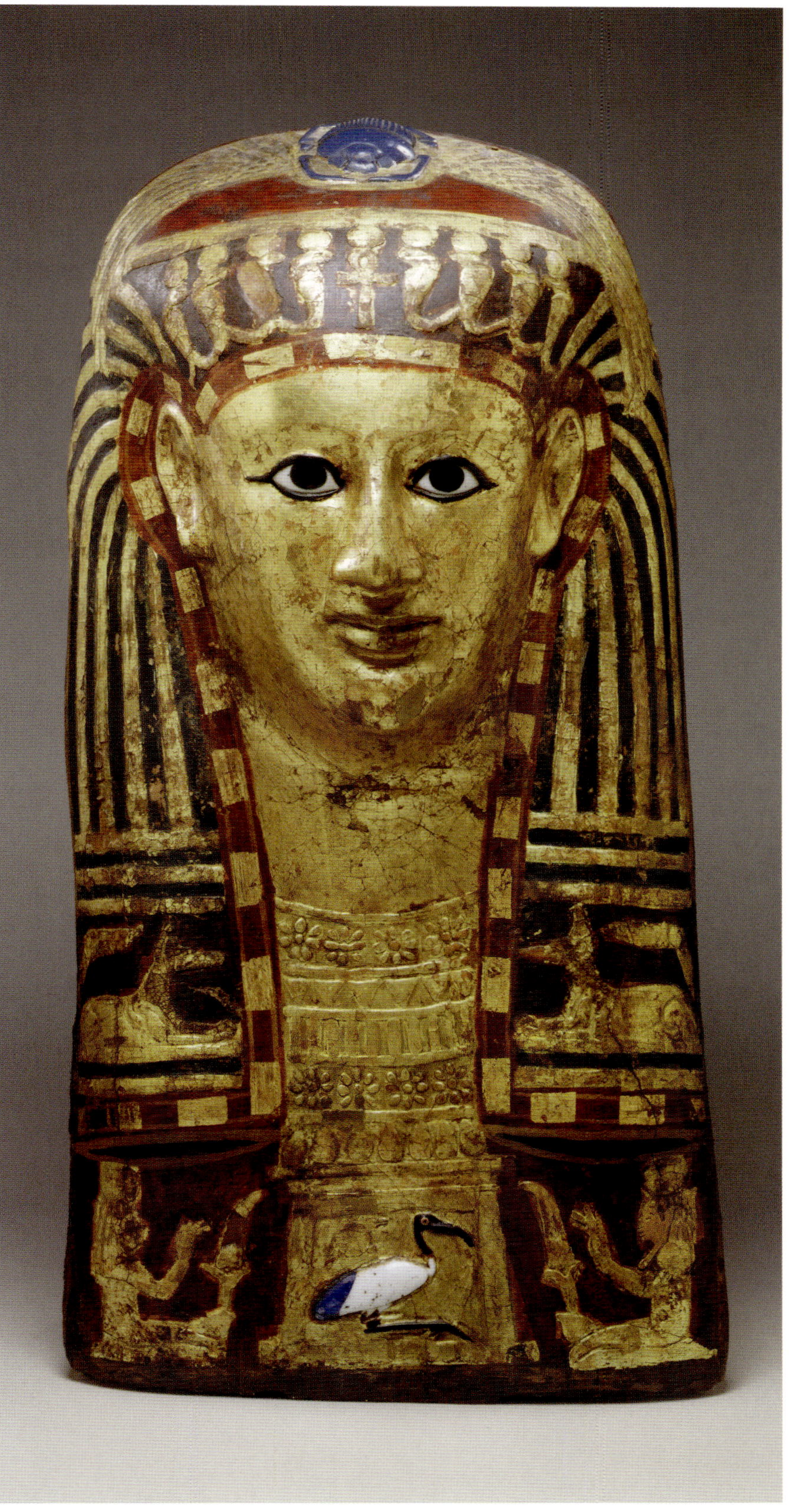

Bibliography

Grimm 1974, 61, 64, pl. 16 no. 2; Walters Art Gallery1982, 4–5 (J.V. Canby); Bianchi 1983, 34–35, fig. 7; Grose 1989, 352, fig. 157.

Notes

1. Dikran Kelekian mentioned Asyut as a place of origin, and it is possible that he bought it there. However, the closest parallels, with an inlaid scarab on top of the head and an ibis in the pectoral, were found in Meir (see Grimm 1974, pl. 16.4) and in Tuna el-Gebel (see Grimm 1974, pl. 18.2); either of those sites seems a more plausible place of origin for the Walters mask.
2. For example, the mummy mask of Sat-Djehuty (London, British Museum, EA 29770) in Russmann 2001, 204, no. 106.
3. For example, a shrine found at Tebtynis (Faiyum) (Turin, Museo Egizio, 1734), in Müller and Thiem 1998, 234–35.
4. For example, the coffin of Petosiris found at Tuna el-Gebel (Cairo, Egyptian Museum JE 46592) in Saleh and Sourouzian 1986, no. 260l; and the coffin of Seuta in Tuna el-Gebel, for which see Kessler and Brose 2007, 84–89.
5. See Grimm 1974, pls. 16.4, 18.2; Ikram and Dodson 1998, 187–188.
6. For a close parallel of a scarab beetle made from blue glass dating to the Ptolemaic Period, see Hornung and Bryan 2002, 210, no. 106 (I. El-Nawawy).
7. For the association of an upward gaze with apotheosis, see Bothmer 1970, 37–48.
8. The closest stylistic and iconographic parallel, found at Meir, is a mask that belonged to a man named Hierax dating to the late first century B.C. (Cairo, Egyptian Museum, JE 42951); see Grimm 1974, 61, pl. 16.4, a.

71

Mummy portrait of a young man

From the Faiyum (er-Rubayat?)

Encaustic on wood panel; 38.7 x 17.4 cm (15 3/4 x 7 3/4 in.)

Roman Period, reign of Marcus Aurelius, ca. A.D. 170–180

Provenance: Dikran Kelekian, New York/Paris; Henry Walters, 1912; Walters Art Museum, by bequest, 1931 (32.6).

Mummy portraits represent one of the most intriguing body of objects from Roman Egypt. The vast majority of the nearly one thousand known examples were found in the Faiyum oasis south of Cairo, hence their alternative name: "Faiyum portraits." They were first systematically excavated by the British archeologist Flinders Petrie, who started digging at the site of Hawara in the Faiyum in 1888.[1] During the course of his excavations, he recovered nearly a hundred and fifty such portraits. They range in date from the reign of the emperor Tiberius (A.D. 14–37) to the late third century, when they fell into decline for reasons that are still debated.[2]

The portraits of the deceased were painted on thin wooden panels using either encaustic (wax) or tempera pigments; the former are generally more sophisticated. They were then placed over the mummy's face and carefully integrated into the outer wrappings. The subjects depicted—men, women, and children—were members of a social elite in the oasis communities, of which several were founded during the Greco-Roman Period. Their wealth would have come from trade or agriculture. That such portraits were a luxury can be deduced from the fact that they were used only in a very small percentage of Roman burials (1–2 percent).[3] Since life expectancy at the time was less than forty years, it was usually younger or middle-aged citizens who were portrayed, although a youthful portrait of one Demetrios, whose death at the remarkable age of 89 is recorded in an inscription, indicates an all-too-human desire to be remembered in his prime.

The Walters portrait shows a young man with a closely trimmed full beard and a luxuriant head of hair edged by a row of corkscrew locks falling over his forehead. His eyebrows are thick and his expression is somewhat melancholic. He wears a conventional whitish tunic rendered with a few cursory strokes of the brush, leaving the lower part of the panel free. The fashionable hairstyle and the trim of the beard confirm a dating from the later years of the reign of Marcus Aurelius.[4] The single most significant criterion in establishing the chronological sequence of male portraits is the hairstyle, which invariably was that of the ruling emperor. For female images, an additional clue is the style of the jewelry.[5]

MS

Bibliography

Parlasca 1969, no. 201; Parlasca et al. 1985, 90–91; Borg 1996, 78–80, pl. 27,2.

Notes

1. For this material, see Walker and Bierbrier 1997, 37–75, nos. 11–53.
2. See Borg 1996, 196-208.
3. For several aspects of the portraits, see Bierbrier 1997, 1–53.
4. On the beards, see Frenz 1999.
5. See Seipel 1998, 221–39, nos. 142–90.

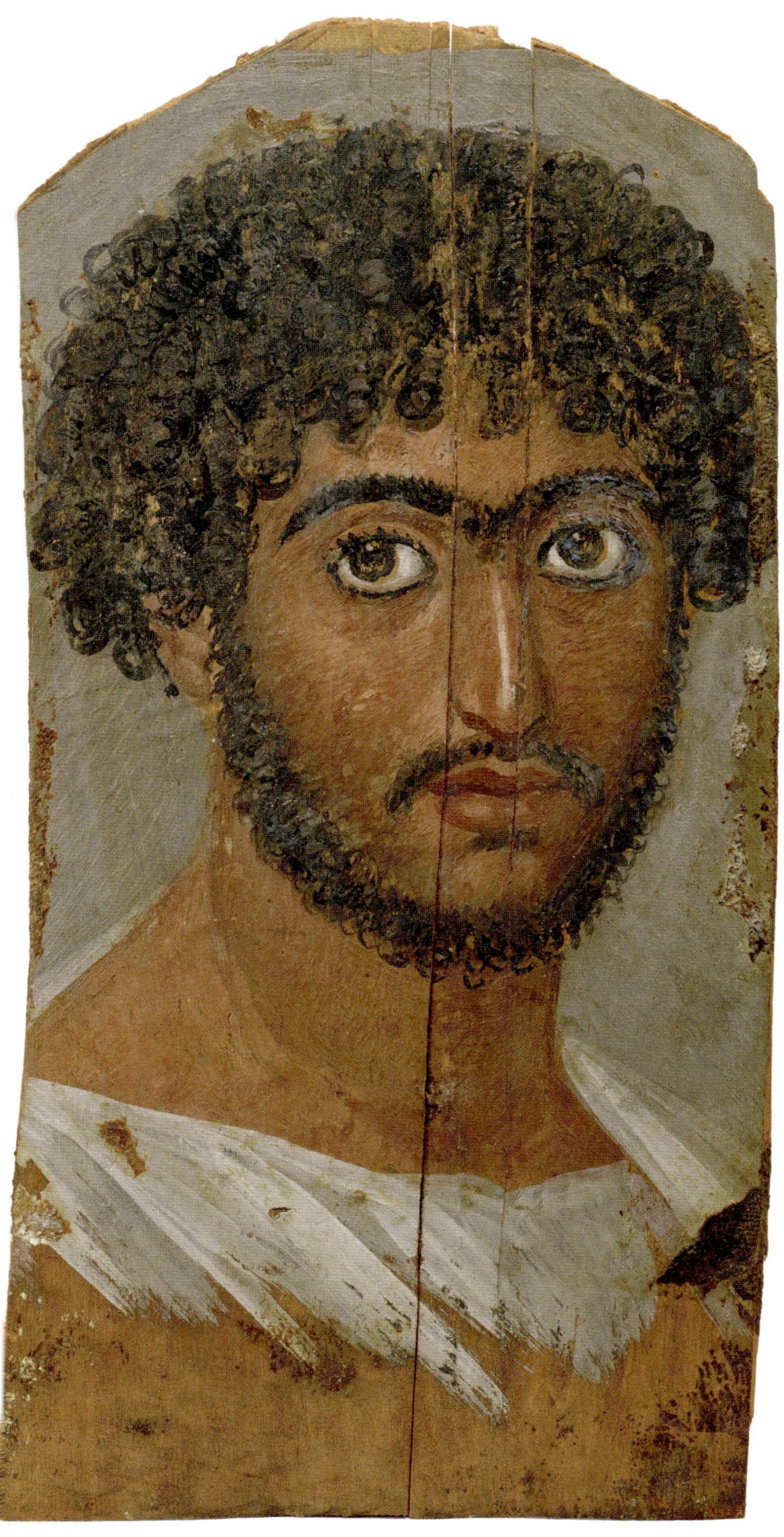

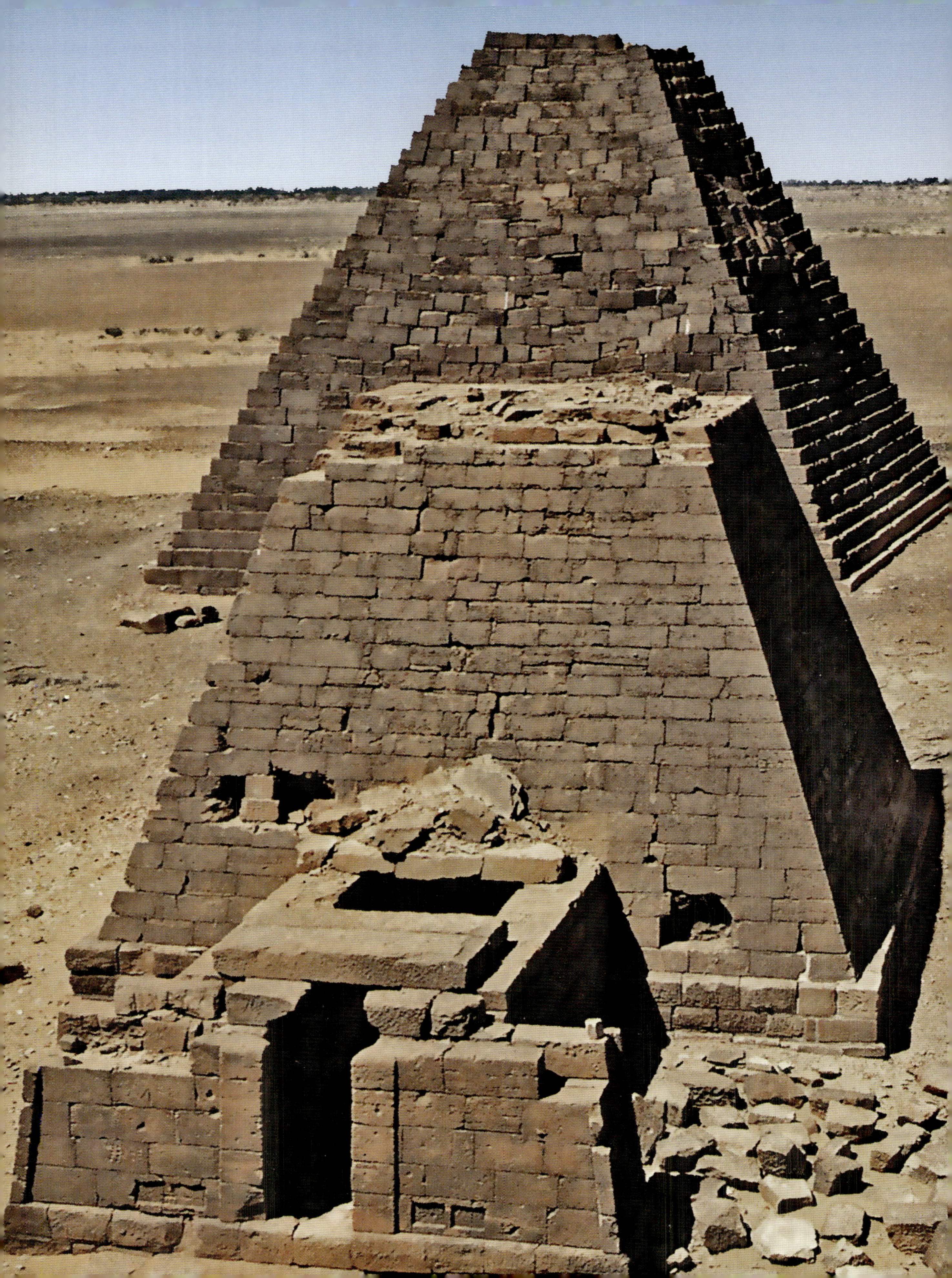

ANCIENT NUBIA (KUSH): THE MEROITIC PERIOD (275 B.C.–A.D. 350)

The final defeat of Tanutamani (664–656 B.C.), the last king of the Twenty-fifth Dynasty, by the Assyrians in 663 B.C. marked the end of Kushite dominion over Egypt. Driven back to their homeland in the region of the Middle Nile, the rulers of Kush (Nubia) turned to domestic affairs, only to be challenged by Psamtek II (595–589 B.C.), who invaded Nubia in 593/92 B.C. After a victorious battle near the Third Cataract, the Egyptians took forty-two hundred prisoners, and marched south as far as Napata. The city, close to the holy site of Gebel Barkal, had served as the residence for the Kushite court since the ninth century; the royal cemetery was situated nearby at Nuri. As the religious center for the cult of Amun, the most important god in the Kushite pantheon, the city continued to thrive even when the capital was relocated to Meroë in the seventh or sixth century. The Napatan Period came to an end around 275 B.C. with the transfer of the royal burial ground to Meroë, ordered by King Arkamani I. At around the same time, the Egyptians under Ptolemy II Philadelphos started a successful military action against Kush, which secured Egypt's control of Lower Nubia between the First and Second Cataracts. Despite persistent political tensions, the two powers developed a mutually beneficial trading partnership. The seemingly insatiable demands of the Ptolemaic rulers for luxurious raw materials from Nubia and southern territories, such as ivory, exotic woods, spices, and animals (including war elephants) were balanced by the Kushites' need for manufactured goods. Trading was concentrated in the Dodekaschoinos, the region of the Nile Valley immediately south of Aswan. The shared economic and strategic interests in this area are attested by the joint presence of the Ptolemies and the Meroitic rulers at the religious centers. The involvement of the Kushite kings Arkamani II and Adikhalamani (ca. 218–185 B.C.) in the construction of temples at Philae, Dakka, and Debod is well documented by inscriptions, including their collaboration with Ptolemy IV Philopator (221–205 B.C.). When the Romans fully occupied Egypt in 28 B.C., they controlled the Dodekaschoinos as well, ensuring access to the gold mines in the Wadi el-Allaqi. Four years later, the Meroites exploited a strategic weakness of the Romans to ransack Elephantine and Philae, taking bronze figures of the emperor Augustus as booty, but their triumph was short-lived. In 23 B.C. the Roman prefect of Egypt, Gaius Petronius, defeated the Meroitic army decisively and conquered Napata. A peace treaty from 21/20 B.C. ended the hostilities and established a new frontier at Maharraqa, leaving the northern part of Lower Nubia under Roman control and ceding the southern territories to Meroë.

For a long period thereafter, trade was advanced by stable relations between north and south, but social and religious matters remained rooted in indigenous traditions. Nevertheless, Egyptian influence was still evident, especially in the arts and architecture. Royal figures, statues of deities, and temple reliefs from the great shrines at Meroë, Naga, and Musawwarat es-Sufra clearly reflect pharaonic traditions, although the style is distinctively Meroitic. The extraordinary mixture of local and Greco-Roman elements is particularly evident in the first-century A.D. "kiosk" at Naga. Our knowledge of Meroitic culture remains circumscribed by our limited understanding of the written language, which may have been formulated as late as the second century B.C. (see no. 72); outside of names and standard funerary formulae, Meroitic texts remain largely unintelligible.

The Meroitic pantheon was still dominated by Egyptian deities, with Amun as the most important god. Existing shrines dedicated to Amun were enlarged and new temples were built at Meroë and elsewhere. In contrast, deities like the ferocious lion-god Apedemak or the divine pair of Arensnuphis and Sebiumeker were of true Nubian origin. An even clearer African influence can be discerned in representations of elephants (reliefs and three-dimensional sculptures) in the Great Enclosure at Musawwarat es-Sufra, the holy site south of Meroë. There, a whole complex of temples, courtyards, and adjoining rooms served the most prestigious place of pilgrimage in the country.

The slow and progressive decline of the Meroitic state began around A.D. 200 at the latest, and ended shortly after 350/60, when the dynastic kingdom of Meroë vanished from the historical record. Already weakened by the loss of its economic power as a result of altered trading routes, the state was no longer strong enough to resist the constant incursions of nomadic tribes. To what extent a campaign about this time led by Ezana, king of Axum (present-day northern Ethiopia), contributed to the demise of Meroë remains a matter of considerable debate.

MS

Meroë, royal pyramids of the northern cemetery (third century B.C.–fourth century A.D.) Photo © Christianne Henry, Havre de Grace, Maryland

72

Votive plaque of King Tanyidamani

Meroë (Sudan), temple of Apedemak

Dark red siltstone; 17.7 x 8.8 cm (7 x 3 ½ in.)

ca. 100 B.C.

Provenance: William MacGregor, Tamworth, Staffordshire; sale, London, Sotheby, Wilkinson & Hodge, 26–29 June and 4–6 July 1922, no. 469; Dikran Kelekian, New York / Paris, 1922; Henry Walters, 1923; Walters Art Museum, by bequest, 1931 (22.258 a–b)

This votive plaque and a stela naming the same king (Boston, Museum of Fine Arts, acc. no. 23.736) are the earliest royal historical texts displaying the cursive Meroitic script. Carved skillfully in sunk relief in a fine-grained siltstone, the Walters double-sided plaque was at some point split longitudinally; it was in two fragments when it entered Henry Walters' collection.[1] The two sides were subsequently rejoined. The obverse depicts the figure of King Tanyidamani (ca. 110–90 B.C.), facing right, with inscribed rectangular text panels in cursive Meroitic script flanking his head. The reverse depicts the lion-headed god Apedemak, facing left, with a rectangular text panel also inscribed with Meroitic script above his face. The irregular and careless rendering of both text panels has none of the masterful carving evident in the figures of the king and the deity. Most likely part of a stela, the plaque was probably rounded at the top; decorated on both sides, it might have been intended to be displayed sitting upright in a socket within a temple setting.

The ancient city of Meroë, the southern capital of the Kushite kingdom, was excavated between 1909 and 1914 by the British archeologist John Garstang. This plaque (found during the 1909–10 season) was recovered from one of several temples in Nubia dedicated to the lion god Apedemak, whose cult was centered in steppes between the Nile and its eastern tributary, the Atbara River in the present-day region of Butana in northern Sudan.[2] The Meroë lion temple (M6) underwent two building campaigns: one in the late second or early first century B.C. and the other in the late first or early second century A.D.[3] The plaque is associated with the first of these constructions, sponsored by King Tanyidamani, but the date of the plaque's dedication is not recorded.

The king's features are rendered in the traditional style of Nubian rulers; high cheekbones, the "Kushite fold" extending from the nostrils to the corners of the mouth,[4] full lips, and a fleshy nose. The king's attire is noteworthy. He wears a *hemhem* crown—an extremely elaborate crown composed of twisted ram's horns, ostrich plumes, sun disks, *uraei* perched on the horns and at the king's forehead, and two streamers. Such special crowns were probably worn on solemn ritual occasions when the monarch wished to be associated with an important deity. His earrings consist of a sun disk flanked by *uraei* with pendant ram's heads. Around his neck he wears a broad collar, a cord with three pendant ram's heads (mostly effaced), and a necklace of ball beads. The prominence of ram elements, symbolic of the god Amun, in the crown and jewelry of the king, associates Tanyidamani with that deity's cult. The long ceremonial robe has a crisscross pattern and features a tasseled band extending from his right shoulder.

The tasseled band or cord, derived from the lasso used in hunting by both Egyptian and Nubian gods,[5] represents the legitimate right of the king to rule, bestowed on him at his investiture by the god Amun. It symbolically represents reciprocity between the king and god, the deference shown by the king to his divine father (Amun), and the protection given in return to the monarch by the deity. The tasseled cord was introduced during the Twenty-fifth Dynasty, when Nubian kings ruled Kush and Egypt. It both identified the king as high priest and was an insignia of the Nubian hunter deities: Apedemak, Arensnuphis, and Sebiumeker. Its evolution in the royal costume of Kushite rulers exemplifies how elements of Egyptian religion were reinterpreted to accommodate indigenous customs and beliefs.

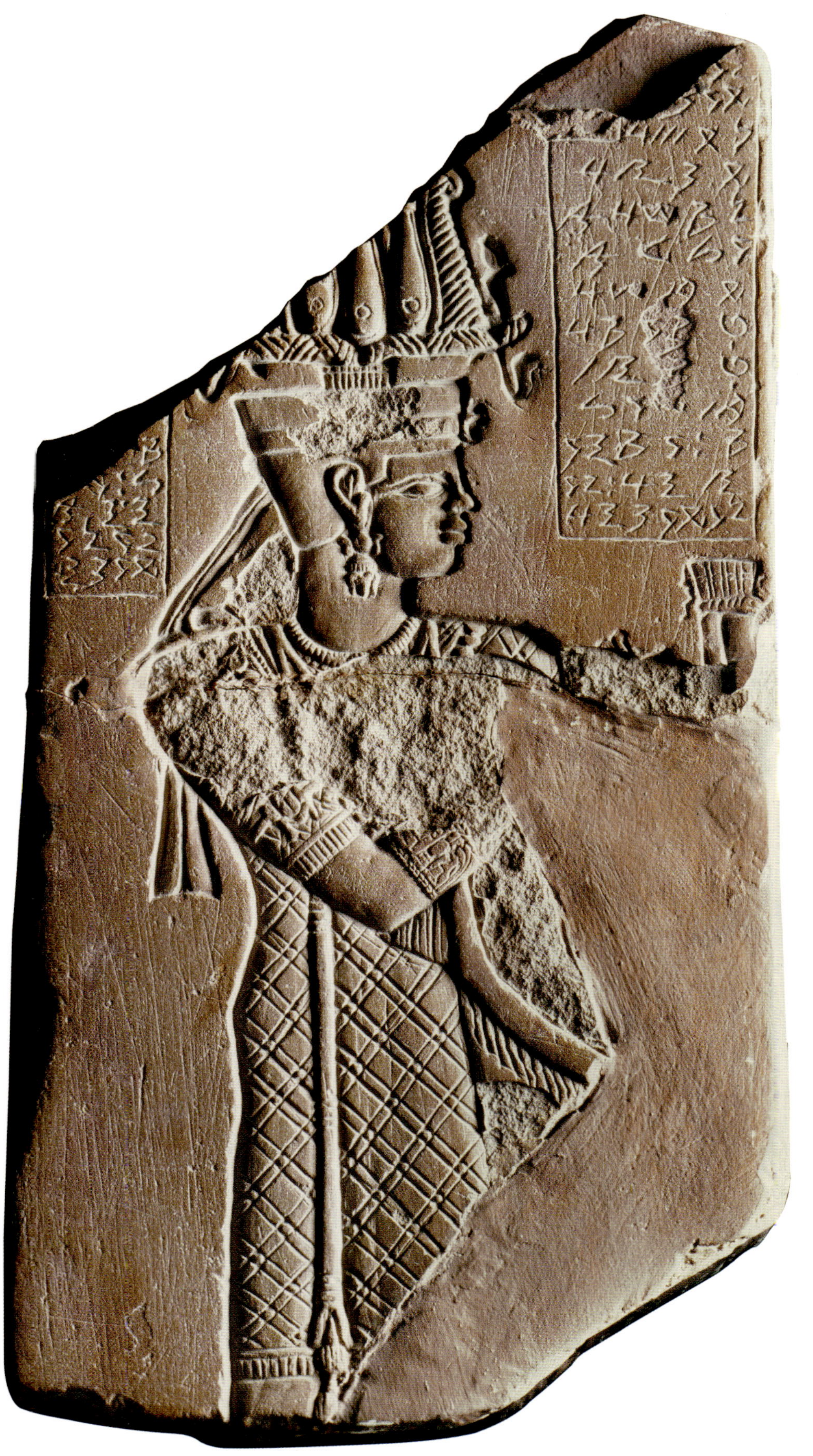

The king is wearing elaborate armlets and bracelets. He holds a scepter in his left hand and is probably holding or offering something in his missing right hand. The Meroitic cursive script in the text panels is still not completely understood. The god's name appears in the last two lines of the panel behind the king. The text is thought to be a short hymn that the king is reciting to the deity as he makes an offering in worship.[6]

The Nubian lion god Apedemak was the most important of the non-Egyptian gods in the Nubian pantheon. He is represented as a human figure with a lion's head and was both a war god and a fertility deity. Temple reliefs at Musawwarat es-Sufra show him holding a bow and arrows and smiting enemies, and at Naqa he appears as a three-headed figure, holding bouquets of durra, a variety of sorghum cultivated in the Butana. His warrior costume—a scalelike patterned garment held up by or affixed to suspenders, a pleated ceremonial kilt, and wide armlets and bracelets—is known from other reliefs. On his head is an echeloned wig with narrow lappets resting on a broad collar, and a pectoral around his neck. He also wears the *hemhem* crown. The god clutches a staff in his right hand with two bunches of durra (a symbol of fertility), the staff topped by a small seated lion. In his left hand he holds a looped cord terminating in an *ankh* sign. The looped cord may be symbolically associated with the lasso of the hunter-warrior aspect of the god, whereby he binds his enemies, and tethers wild animals (lion and elephant), as seen in reliefs at Musawwarat es-Sufra. The open loop of the cord in the god's hand on the plaque has the same rendering as in the temple scenes. In this image the god appears to be offering the *ankh* (i.e., life), to the king. The Meroitic text panel may indicate the god's reply or confirmation to the king in response to his worship.

CH

Bibliography

MacGregor Collection 1922, 59, no. 469; Steindorff 1946a, 90, no. 293, pl. LI; Shinnie 1967, 101, 105, 220, fig. 31; Zabkar 1975, 11, 60, pl. XXIII; Wenig 1978, 1: 97, fig. 70, 2: 200, no. 1; Celenko 1996, 67; Török 1997b, 1:46.

Notes

1. See MacGregor Collection 1922, 59, no. 469. The figure of the king has suffered losses in the relief areas of the chest and arms. Both sides of the plaque are chipped along the edges, and both figures are missing portions of stone on the crowns and below the knees.
2. The oldest lion temple, dating to 220 B.C., is at Musawwarat es-Sufra; the lion temple at Naqa dates to the first century A.D.
3. For Garstang's excavations of M6, See Török 1997b, 1:46–48, 2: figs. 1, 11.
4. Russmann 1974, 11, 13; Török 1997a, 195.
5. See Török 1997a, 440–42.
6. Zabkar 1975, 11.

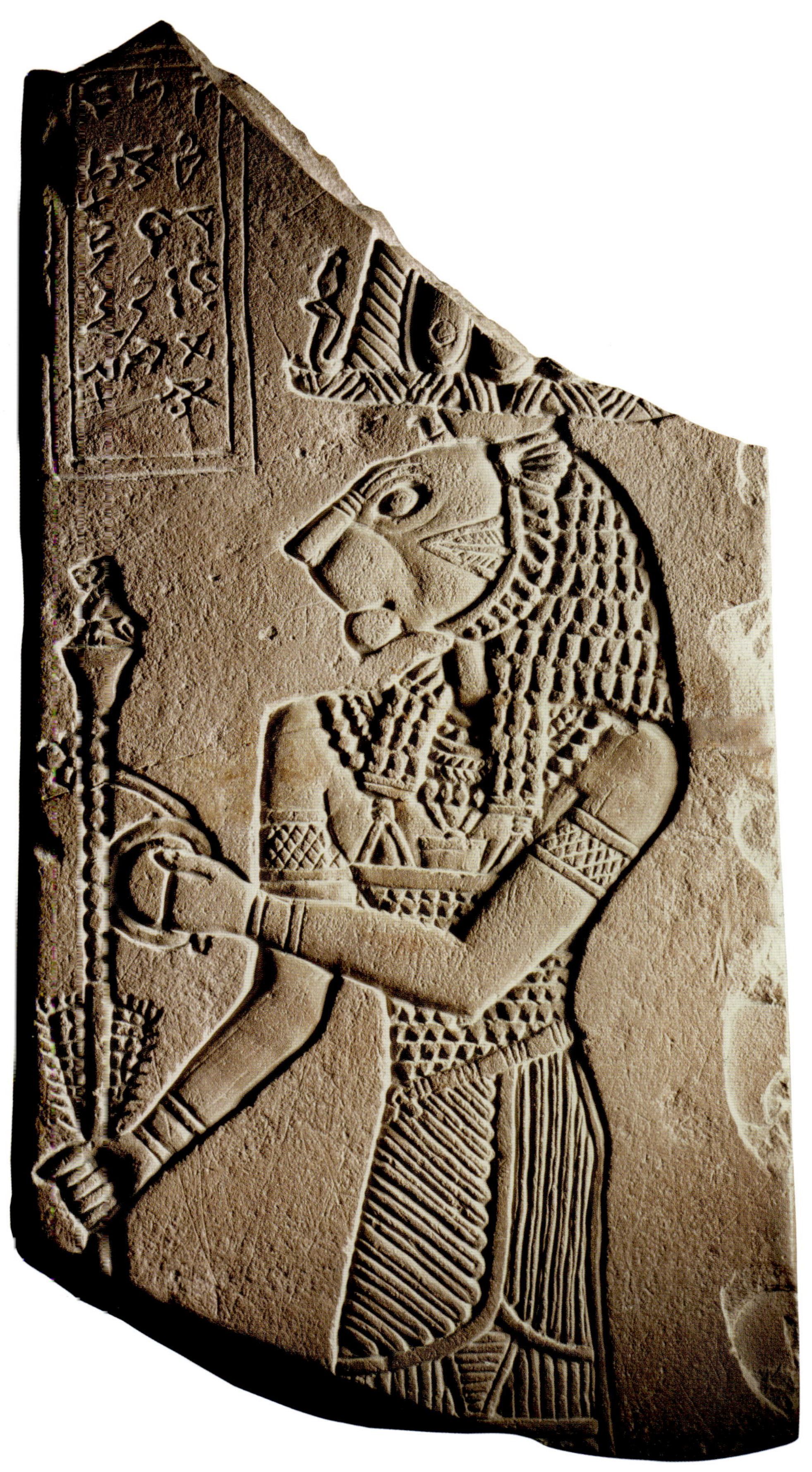

MAPS OF EGYPT AND NUBIA

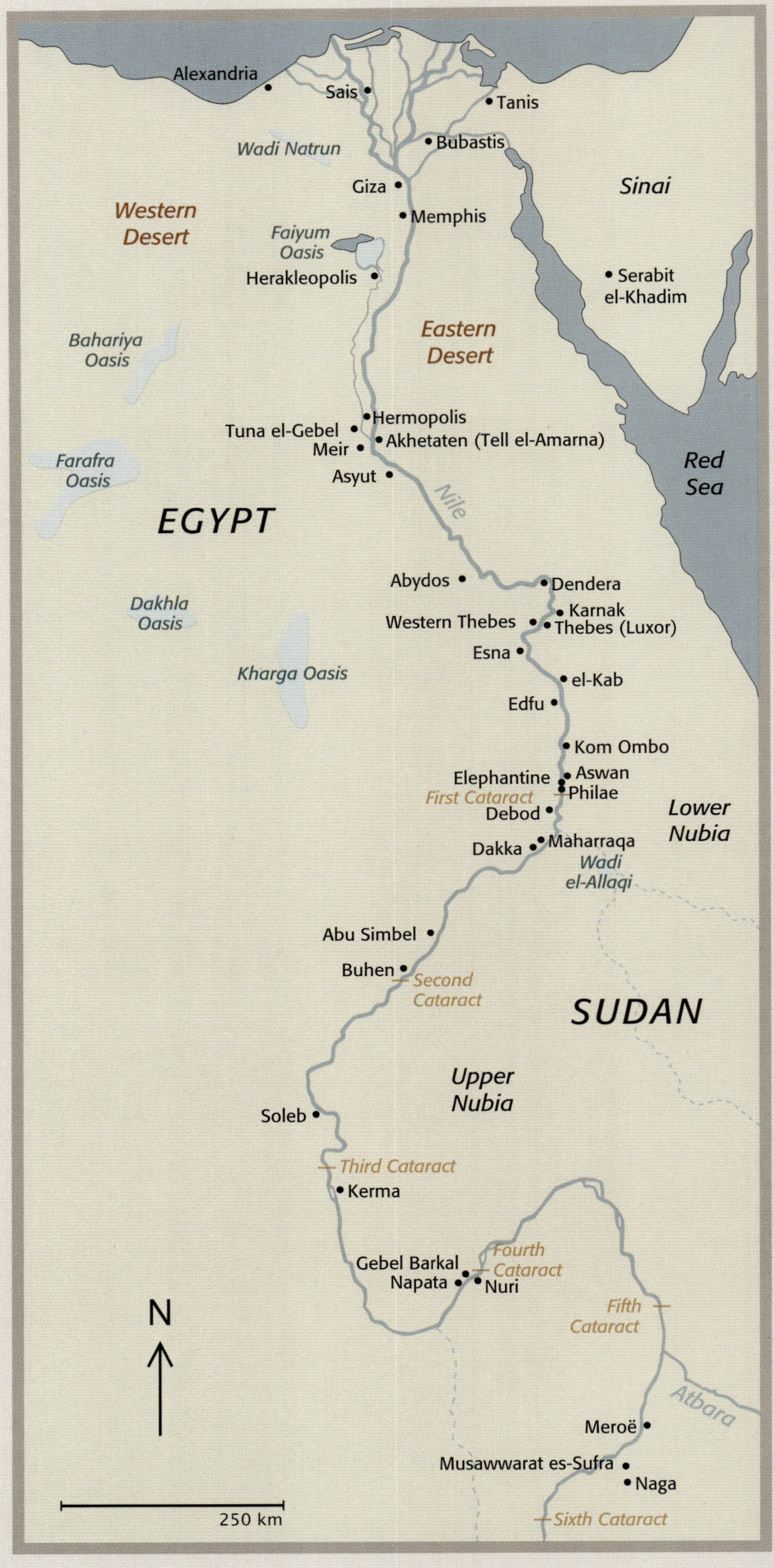

Egypt and Nubia

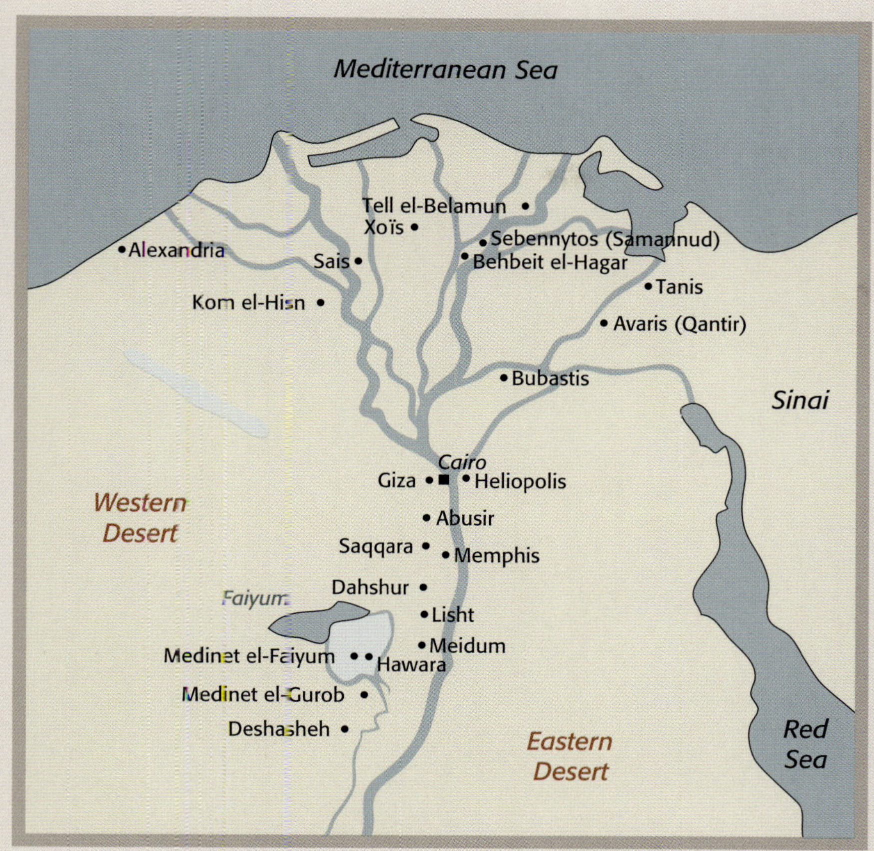

Lower Egypt and the Memphite region

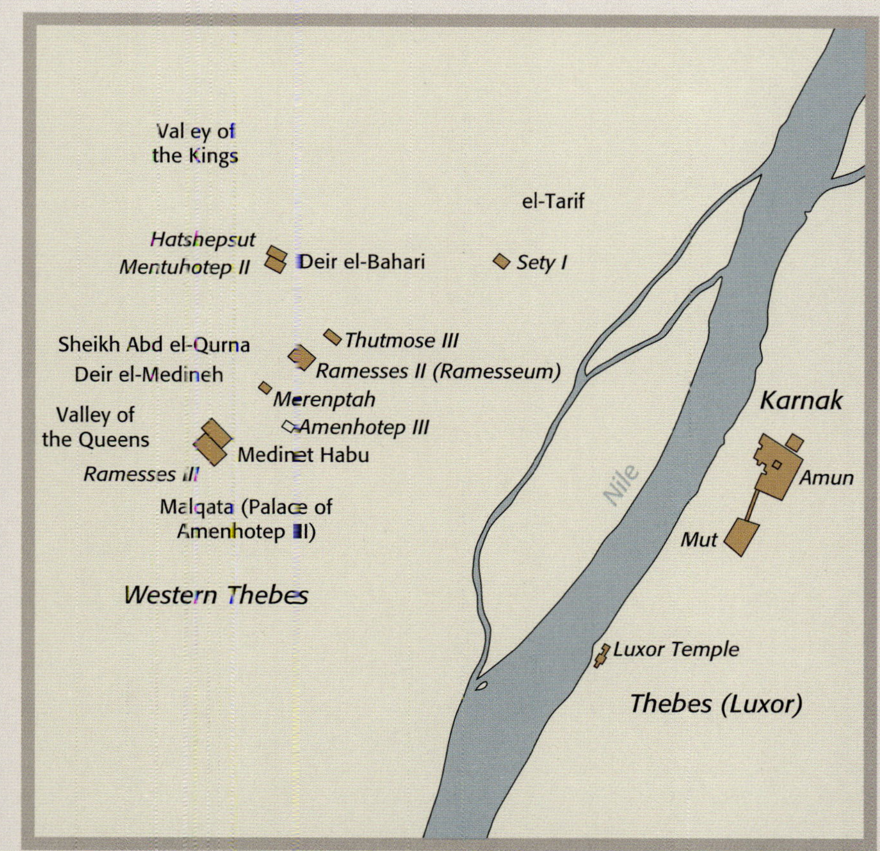

Thebes

CHRONOLOGY

A variety of different records are used to establish chronological data for the pharaonic history of Egypt. Ancient king lists such as the Turin Royal Canon, dated inscriptions of specific events, or astronomical phenomena have enabled Egyptologists to formulate a chronology that is more complete and reliable than for any other of the ancient Near Eastern civilizations. However, only the dates from the Twenty-sixth Dynasty (664 B.C.) forward are precise in nature. As we go back in history, the margin of error ranges from a decade to in excess of a hundred years. The structuring of the history of ancient Egypt into "dynasties," the grouping of several mostly related rulers, was first realized by the priest Manetho of Sebennytos (Delta), who wrote around 280 B.C. a history of the country based on older documents. The additional grouping into "kingdoms" or "periods" is an effort to explain the basic division of thousands of years. Modern-language spellings of rulers' names sometimes impede clarity, but Sesostris, Senwosret or Senusret, designate the same pharaoh, as do Amenophis or Amenhotep. The following chronological table (in general based on Ian Shaw, *The Oxford History of Ancient Egypt* [New York and Oxford, 2000]) is limited to the most significant rulers. Ultimately many of these dates are still under discussion, and new evidence, as well as better evaluation of already known sources, continuously helps to refine the historical landscape of Egypt.

PREDYNASTIC PERIOD ca. 5200–3000 B.C.

Badarian Culture	ca. 4500–4000 B.C.
Naqada I Culture	ca. 4000–3500 B.C.
Naqada II Culture	ca. 3500–3150 B.C.
Naqada III Culture ("Dynasty 0")	ca. 3150–3000 B.C.

EARLY DYNASTIC PERIOD ca. 3000–2686 B.C.

First Dynasty	***ca. 3000–2860 B.C.***
Aha	
Djer	
Djet	
Den	
Queen Merneith	

Second Dynasty	***ca. 2860–2686 B.C.***
Hetepsekhemwy	
Raneb	
Ninetjer	
Peribsen	
Khasekhemwy	

OLD KINGDOM 2686–2181 B.C.

Third Dynasty	***2686–2613 B.C.***
Djoser	2667–2648 B.C.
Sekhemkhet	2648–2640 B.C.
Huni	2637–2613 B.C.

Fourth Dynasty	***2613–2494 B.C.***
Sneferu	2613–2589 B.C.
Khufu (Cheops)	2589–2566 B.C.
Djedefre (Radjedef)	2566–2558 B.C.
Khafre (Chephren)	2558–2532 B.C.
Menkaure (Mykerinos)	2532–2503 B.C.
Shepseskaf	2503–2498 B.C.

Fifth Dynasty	***2494–2345 B.C.***
Userkaf	2494–2487 B.C.
Sahure	2487–2475 B.C.
Neferirkare	2475–2455 B.C.
Niuserre	2445–2421 B.C.
Menkauhor	2421–2414 B.C.
Djedkare	2414–2375 B.C.
Unas	2375–2345 B.C.

Sixth Dynasty	***2345–2181 B.C.***
Teti	2345–2323 B.C.
Pepy I	2321–2287 B.C.
Nemtyemsaf I (Merenre)	2287–2278 B.C.
Pepy II	2278–2181 B.C.

Seventh and Eighth Dynasties	***2181–2160 B.C.***
Ephemeral rulers	

FIRST INTERMEDIATE PERIOD 2160–2055 B.C.

Ninth and Tenth Dynasties	***2160–2025 B.C.***
(Herakleopolis)	
Khety I–III	

Eleventh Dynasty	***2125–2055 B.C.***
(Thebes only)	
Intef I (Sehertawy)	2125–2112 B.C.
Intef II (Wahankh)	2112–2063 B.C.
Intef III (Nakhtnebtepnefer)	2063–2055 B.C.

MIDDLE KINGDOM 2055–1650 B.C.

Eleventh Dynasty	***2055–1985 B.C.***
(all Egypt)	
Mentuhotep II	2055–2004 B.C.
Mentuhotep III	2004–1992 B.C.
Mentuhotep IV	1992–1985 B.C.

Twelfth Dynasty	***1985–1773 B.C.***
Amenemhat I	1985–1956 B.C.
Sesostris I	1956–1911 B.C.
Amenemhat II	1911–1877 B.C.
Sesostris II	1877–1870 B.C.
Sesostris III	1870–1831 B.C.
Amenemhat III	1831–1786 B.C.
Amenemhat IV	1786–1777 B.C.
Queen Sobekneferu	1777–1773 B.C.

Thirteenth Dynasty	***1773–after 1650 B.C.***
Hor	
Amenemhat V	
Sobekhotep II	
Khendjer	
Sobekhotep III	
Neferhotep I	

Fourteenth Dynasty	***1773–1650 B.C.***
Minor rulers contemporary with the Thirteenth Dynasty	

SECOND INTERMEDIATE PERIOD 1650–1550 B.C.

Fifteenth Dynasty (Hyksos)	***1650–1550 B.C.***
Khyan	ca. 1600 B.C.
Apepi	ca. 1555 B.C.
Khamudi	

Sixteenth Dynasty	***1650–1550 B.C.***
Early Theban rulers contemporary with the Fifteenth Dynasty	

Seventeenth Dynasty	***ca. 1585–1550 B.C.***
Rahotep	
Intef VI	
Taa I (Senakhtenre)	
Taa II (Seqenenre)	ca.1560 B.C.
Kamose	1555–1550 B.C.

NEW KINGDOM
1550–1069 B.C.

Eighteenth Dynasty	***1550–1295 B.C.***
Ahmose	550–1525 B.C.
Amenhotep I	525–1504 B.C.
Thutmose I	504–1492 B.C.
Thutmose II	492–1479 B.C.
Thutmose III	479–1425 B.C.
Queen Hatshepsut	473–1458 B.C.
Amenhotep II	427–1400 B.C.
Thutmose IV	400–1390 B.C.
Amenhotep III	390–1352 B.C.
Amenhotep IV/Akhenaten	352–1336 B.C.
Tutankhamun	336–1327 B.C.
Ay	1327–1323 B.C.
Horemheb	323–1295 B.C.

Nineteenth Dynasty	***1295–1186 B.C.***
Ramesses I	295–1294 B.C.
Sety I	1294–1279 B.C.
Ramesses II	1279–1213 B.C.
Merenptah	1213–1203 B.C.
Amenmessu	203–1200 B.C.
Sety II	1200–1194 B.C.
Siptah	1194–1188 B.C.
Queen Tausret	1188–1186 B.C.

Twentieth Dynasty	***1186–1069 B.C.***
Sethnakht	1186–1184 B.C.
Ramesses III	1184–1153 B.C.
Ramesses IV	1153–1147 B.C.
Ramesses VI	1143–1136 B.C.
Ramesses IX	1126–1108 B.C.
Ramesses XI	1099–1069 B.C.

THIRD INTERMEDIATE PERIOD
1069–664 B.C.

Twenty-first Dynasty	***1069–945 B.C.***
Smendes	1069–1043 B.C.
Psusennes I	1039–991 B.C.
Siamun	978–959 B.C.
Psusennes II	959–945 B.C.

Twenty-second Dynasty	***945–715 B.C.***
Sheshonq I	945–924 B.C.
Osorkon I	924–889 B.C.
Takelot I	889–874 B.C.
Sheshonq III	825–773 B.C.
Osorkon IV	730–715 B.C.

Twenty-third Dynasty	***818–715 B.C.***

Several kings, ruling in different centers. Contemporary with epochs until the early Twenty-fifth Dynasty.

Twenty-fourth Dynasty	***727–715 B.C.***
Tefnakhte	727–720 B.C.
Bakenrenef (Bocchoris)	720–715 B.C.

Twenty-fifth Dynasty	***747–656 B.C.***
Piy	747–716 B.C.
Shabaqo	716–702 B.C.
Shabitqo	702–690 B.C.
Taharqo	690–664 B.C.
Tanutamani	664–656 B.C.

LATE PERIOD
664–332 B.C.

Twenty-sixth Dynasty	***664–525 B.C.***
Psamtek I	664–610 B.C.
Nekau (Necho) II	610–595 B.C.
Psamtek II	595–589 B.C.
Apries	589–570 B.C.
Amasis	570–526 B.C.
Psamtek III	526–525 B.C.

Twenty-seventh Dynasty (First Persian Period)	***525–404 B.C.***
Cambyses	525–522 B.C.
Darius I	522–486 B.C.
Xerxes I	486–465 B.C.
Artaxerxes I	465–424 B.C.
Artaxerxes II	405–359 B.C.

Twenty-eighth Dynasty	***404–399 B.C.***
Amyrtaios	404–399 B.C.

Twenty-ninth Dynasty	***399–380 B.C.***
Nepherites I	399–393 B.C.
Hakor (Achoris)	393–380 B.C.
Nepherites II	380 B.C.

Thirtieth Dynasty	***380–343 B.C.***
Nectanebo I	380–362 B.C.
Teos	362–360 B.C.
Nectanebo II	360–343 B.C.

Second Persian Period	***343–332 B.C.***
Artaxerxes Ochos	343–338 B.C.
Darius III Codoman	336–332 B.C.

HELLENISTIC PERIOD
332–30 B.C.

Macedonian Dynasty	***332–305 B.C.***
Alexander the Great	332–323 B.C.
Philip Arrhidaeus	323–317 B.C.
Alexander IV	317–310 B.C.

Ptolemaic Dynasty	***305–30 B.C.***
Ptolemy I Soter	305–285 B.C.
Ptolemy II Philadelphos	285–246 B.C.
Ptolemy III Euergetes I	246–222 B.C.
Ptolemy IV Philopator	221–205 B.C.
Ptolemy V Epiphanes	205–180 B.C.
Ptolemy VI Philometor	180–145 B.C.
Ptolemy VII–Ptolemy XI	145–80 B.C.
Ptolemy XII Neos Dionysos	80–51 B.C.
Cleopatra VII	51–30 B.C.

EARLY ROMAN PERIOD
30 B.C.– A.D. 68

Augustan-Julio-Claudian Era	
Augustus	30 B.C.– A.D. 14
Tiberius	A.D. 14–37
Caligula	A.D. 37–41
Claudius	A.D. 41–54
Nero	A.D. 54–68

ANCIENT NUBIA (KUSH): THE MEROITIC PERIOD
275 B.C.– A.D. 350

Arkamani I (Ergamenes)	ca. 275–260 B.C.
Arnekhamani, Arkamani II, Adikhalamani	ca. 235–185 B.C.
Tanyidamani	ca. 110–90 B.C.
Queen Amanishakheto	ca. 10 B.C.–1 B.C./A.D.
Natakamani	ca. A.D. 12–20
Shorkaraor	ca. A.D. 20–30
Teqerideamani II	ca. A.D. 250–265

ABBREVIATED REFERENCES

Adams 1992
Adams, B. "Two More Lions from Upper Egypt: Hierakonpolis and Koptos." In *The Followers of Horus: Studies Dedicated to Michael Allen Hoffman, 944–1990*, ed. R. Friedman and B. Adams, 69–76. ESA Publication 2 / Oxbow Monograph 20. Oxford, 1952.

Albersmeier 2002
Albersmeier, S. *Untersuchungen zu den Frauenstatuen des Ptolemäischen Ägypten.* Aegyptiaca Treverensia 10. Mainz, 2002.

Aldred 1973
Aldred, C., ed. *Akhenaten and Nefertiti.* Exh. cat., New York: Brooklyn Museum, 1973.

Allen 2003
Allen, J. "The Egyptian Concept of the World." In *Mysterious Lands: Encounters with Ancient Egypt*, ed. D.B. O'Connor and S. Quirke, 23–30. London, 2003.

Alt 1952
Alt, A. "Ein Gesandter aus Palästina in Ägypten." *Bibliotheca Orientalis* 9 (1952): 163–64.

Altenmüller 1986
Altenmüller, H. "Ein 'Zaubermesser' des Mittleren Reiches." *Studien zur Altägyptischen Kultur* 13 (1986): 1–27.

Altenmüller 2007
Altenmüller, H. "Zur Herkunft und Bedeutung der Schiffe mit Igelkopf." *Bulletin of the Egyptian Museum* 4 *(Commemorative Publication for Mohamed Ibrahim Morsi)* (2007): 13–22

Anderson 1976
Anderson, R.D. *Catalogue of Egyptian Antiquities in the British Museum*, 3: *Musical Instruments*. London, 1976.

Andrews 1990
Andrews, C. *Ancient Egyptian Jewellery.* London, 1990.

Andrews 1994
Andrews, C. *Amulets of Ancient Egypt*. London, 1994.

Arnold 1996
Arnold, D. *Royal Women of Amarna: Images of Beauty from Ancient Egypt.* Exh. cat., New York: The Metropolitan Museum of Art, 1997.

Arnst 1991
Arnst, C.B. "Die Aussagekraft unscheinbarer Motive: Vier memphitische 'NN'-Reliefs aus der Zeit Tutanchamuns und ihre mögliche Zuordnung zum Grab des Haremhab." *Bulletin de la Société d'Égyptologie de Genève* 15 (1991): 5–30.

Ashton 2001
Ashton, S.-A. "Identifying the Egyptian-style Ptolemaic Queens." In *Cleopatra of Egypt: From History to Myth*, ed. S. Walker and P. Higgs, 148–88. Exh. cat., London: British Museum, 2001.

Aston 1994
Aston, B.G. *Ancient Egyptian Stone Vessels: Materials and Forms.* Studien zur Archäologie und Geschichte Altägyptens 5. Heidelberg, 1994.

Aston, Harrell, and Shaw 2000
Aston, B., J. Harrell, and I. Shaw. "Stone." In *Ancient Egyptian Materials and Technology*, ed. P.T. Nicholson and I. Shaw, 5–77. Cambridge, 2000.

Aufrère 2000
Aufrère, S.H. "La 'stèle aux chiens': Testament politique d'Antef l'ancien." *Égypte, Afrique & Orient* 18 (2000): 35–40.

Baines 1985
Baines, J. *Fecundity Figures: Egyptian Personification and the Iconology of a Genre.* Warminster, 1985.

Baines 2003
Baines, J. "On the Genre and Purpose of the 'Large Commemorative Scarabs' of Amenhotep III." In *Hommage à Fazya Haikal*, ed. N.C. Grimal, 29–43. Bibliothèque d'études 138. Cairo, 2003.

Beinlich 1991
Beinlich, H. *Das Buch vom Fayum: Zum religiösen Eigenverständnis einer ägyptischen Landschaft.* Ägyptologische Abhandlungen 51. Wiesbaden, 1991.

Berman 1999
Berman, L.M., ed. *Catalogue of Egyptian Art: The Cleveland Museum of Art.* New York, 1999.

Bernhauer 2005
Berhauer, E. *Hathorsäule und Hathorpfeiler: Altägyptische Architekturelemente vom Neuen Reich bis zur Spätzeit.* Philippika Marburger altertumskundliche Abhandlungen 8. Wiesbaden, 2005.

Bernhauer 2006
Bernhauer, E. "Zur Typologie rundplastischer Menschendarstellungen." *Studien zur Altägyptischen Kultur* 34 (2006): 33–49.

Bianchi 1983
Bianchi, R.S. "Those Ubiquitous Glass Inlays from Pharaonic Egypt: Suggestions about Their Function and Dates." *Journal of Glass Studies* 25 (1983): 29–35.

Bierbrier 1997
Bierbrier, M.L., ed. *Portraits and Masks: Burial Customs in Roman Egypt*. London, 1997.

Blankenberg van Delden 1969
Blankenberg van Delden, C. *The Large Commemorative Scarabs of Amenhotep III.* Documenta et Monumenta Orientis Antiqui 15. Leiden, 1969.

Bochi 1996
Bochi, P.A. "Of Lines, Linen, and Language: Study of a Patterned Textile and Its Interweaving with Egyptian Beliefs." *Chronique d'Égypte* 71 (1996): 221–53.

Borchardt 1911
Borchardt, L. *Der Porträtkopf der Königin Teje im Besitz von Dr. James Simon in Berlin.* Leipzig, 1911.

Borchardt 1930
Borchardt, L. *Statuen und Statuetten von Königen und Privatleuten im Museum von Kairo, Nr. 1–1294*, 3: *Text und Tafeln zu Nr. 654–950.* Berlin, 1930.

Borg 1996
Borg, B. *Mumienporträts: Chronologie und kultureller Kontext*. Mainz, 1996.

Bothmer 1953
Bothmer, B.V. "Ptolemaic Reliefs, III: Deities from the Time of Ptolemy Philadelphus." *Bulletin of the Museum of Fine Arts, Boston* 51.2, no. 283 (1953): 2–7.

Bothmer 1960
Bothmer, B.V., with H. de Meulenaere and H.W. Müller. *Egyptian Sculpture of the Late Period, 700 B.C. to A.D. 100.* Exh. cat., New York: Brooklyn Museum, 1960.

Bothmer 1970
Bothmer, B.V. "Apotheosis in Late Egyptian Sculpture." *Kêmi* 20 (1970): 37–48.

Bothmer 1987
Bothmer, B.V., et al. *Antiquities from the Collection of Christos G. Bastis*, ed. E.S. Hall. Mainz, 1987.

Bothmer 1988
Bothmer, B.V. "Egyptian Antecedents of Roman Republican Verism." *Quaderni de la ricerca scientifica* 116 (1988): 47–65.

Botti and Romanelli 1951
Botti, G., and P. Romanelli. *Le sculture del Museo Gregoriano Egizio*. Vatican City.

Bourriau 1988
Bourriau, J. *Pharaohs and Mortals: Egyptian Art in the Middle Kingdom*. Exh. cat., Cambridge: Fitzwilliam Museum, 1988.

Brand 2000
Brand, P. *Monuments of Seti I.* Probleme der Ägyptologie 16. Leiden and Boston, 2000.

Brooklyn Museum 1941
Pagan and Christian Egypt: Egyptian Art from the First to the Tenth Century A.D. Exh. cat., New York: Brooklyn Museum and Brooklyn Institute of Arts and Sciences, 1941.

Brooklyn Museum 1988
Cleopatra's Egypt: Age of the Ptolemies. Exh. cat., New York: Brooklyn Museum, 1988.

Brovarski 1987
Brovarski, E., ed. *A Table of Offerings: Seventeen Years of Acquisitions of Egyptian and Near Eastern Art*. Exh. cat., Boston: Museum of Fine Arts, 1987.

Brovarski et al. 1982
Brovarski, E., et al. *Egypt's Golden Age: The Art of Living in the New Kingdom, 1558–1085 B.C.* Exh. cat., Boston: Museum of Fine Arts, 1982.

Brugsch 1879
Brugsch, H. *Dictionnaire géographique de l'ancienne Égypte*. Leipzig, 1879.

Brunelle 1976
Brunelle, H.E. "Die Bildnisse der Ptolemäerinnen." Doctoral diss., Johann Wolfgang Goethe-Universität, Frankfurt am Main, 1976.

Bryan 1987
Bryan, B., "Portrait Sculpture of Thutmose IV." *Journal of the American Research Center in Egypt* 24 (1987): 3–20.

Bryan 1990
Bryan, B.M., "Private Relief Sculpture Outside Thebes and Its Relationship to Theban Relief Sculpture." In *The Art of Amenhotep III*, ed. L. Berman, 65–80. Exh. cat., Cleveland Museum of Art, 1990.

Bryan 2007
Bryan, B., "A 'New' Statue of Amenhotep III and the Meaning of the Khepresh Crown." In *The Archaeology and Art of Ancient Egypt: Studies in Honor of David O'Connor*, ed. Z. Hawass and J. Richards, 151–67. Cairo, 2007.

Burlington Fine Arts Club 1895
Exhibition of the Art of Ancient Egypt. Exh. cat., London: Burlington Fine Arts Club, 1895.

Burlington Fine Arts Club 1921
Catalogue of an Exhibition of Ancient Egyptian Art. Exh. cat., London: Burlington Fine Arts Club, 1921.

Burlington Fine Arts Club 1922
Catalogue of an Exhibition of Ancient Egyptian Art. Exh. cat., London: Burlington Fine Arts Club, 1922.

Canby 1979a
Canby, J.V. *Gallery Guide to the Art of Egypt, Walters Art Museum*. Baltimore, 1979.

Canby 1979b
Canby, J.V. "The Jewelry of Ancient Egypt." In Walters Art Gallery, *Jewelry: Ancient to Modern*, 20–51. New York, 1979.

Canby 1985
Canby, J.V. "Ancient Egypt and the Near East." In *Masterpieces of Ivory*, ed. R.H. Randall, 33–53. New York and Baltimore, 1985.

Capart 1938
Capart J. "A Neo-Memphite Bas-Relief." *Journal of the Walters Art Gallery* 1 (1938): 13–17.

Capel and Markoe 1996
Capel, A.C., and G.E. Markoe. *Mistress of the House, Mistress of the Heaven: Women in Ancient Egypt*. Exh. cat., Cincinnati Art Museum. New York, 1996.

Caubet and Pierrat-Bonnefois 2005
Caubet., A., and G. Pierrat-Bonnefois. *Faïences de l'antiquité: De l'Égypte à l'Iran*. Exh. cat., Paris: Musée du Louvre, 2005.

Celenko 1996
Celenko, T., ed. *Egypt in Africa*. Exh. cat., Indianapolis Museum of Art, 1996.

Černý 2001
Černý, J. *A Community of Workmen at Thebes in the Ramesside Period*, 2nd ed. Bibliothèque d'Études 50. Cairo, 2001.

Chadefaud 1982
Chadefaud, C. *Les statues porte-enseignes de l'Égypte ancienne (1580–1085 avant J.C.): Signification et insertion dans le culte du Ka royal*. Paris, 1982.

Chassinat 1901
Chassinat, E. "Un interprète égyptien pour les pays chananéens?" *Bulletin de l'Institut Français d'Archéologie Orientale* 1 (1901): 98–100.

Cherpion 1995
Cherpion, N. "Sentiment conjugal et figuration à l'Ancien Empire." In *Kunst des Alten Reiches: Symposium im Deutschen Archäologischen Institut Kairo am 29. und 30. Oktober 1991*, 33–47. Sonderschriften des Deutschen Archäologischen Instituts, Abteilung Kairo 28. Mainz, 1995.

Christie's New York 2001
Christie's New York. *Antiquities*, Wednesday, 5 December 2001, and Thursday, 6 December 2001. New York.

Colin 1994
Colin, F. "L'Isis 'dynastique' et la mère des dieux phrygienne." *Zeitschrift für Papyrologie und Epigraphik* 102 (1994): 271–95.

Cooney 1953
Cooney, J.D. "The Lions of Leontopolis." *Brooklyn Museum Bulletin* 15, no. 2 (Winter 1953): 17–31.

Cooney 1967
Cooney, J. "Gods Bearing Gifts for the King." *Bulletin of the Cleveland Museum of Art* 54 (1967): 286–88.

Daressy 1902
Daressy, M.G. "Une trouvaille de bronzes à Mit Rahineh." *Annales du Service des Antiquités de l'Égypte* 3 (1902): 139–50.

Daressy 1903
Daressy, G. *Textes et dessins magiques.* Catalogue général des antiquités égyptiennes du Musée du Caire, nos. 9401–9449. Cairo, 1903.

Daressy 1905–6
Daressy, G. *Statues de divinités.* Catalogue général des antiquités égyptiennes du Musée du Caire, nos. 38001–39384. 2 vols. Cairo, 1905–6.

Dasen 1993
Dasen, V. *Dwarfs in Ancient Egypt and Greece*. Oxford Monographs on Classical Archaeology. Oxford and New York, 1993.

Dattari Collection 1912
Antiquités égyptiennes, grecques and romaines: Collections de feu M. Jean P. Lambros d'Athènes et de M. Giovanni Dattari du Caire, vente à Paris, Hôtel Drouot, salles nos. 9 et 10, le lundi 17, mardi 18, et mercredi 19 juin 1912. Paris.

D'Auria, Lacovara, and Roehrig 1988
D'Auria, S., P. Lacovara, and C.H. Roehrig. *Mummies and Magic: The Funerary Arts of Ancient Egypt*. Exh. cat., Boston: Museum of Fine Arts, 1988.

Davies 1913
Davies, N. de G. *Five Theban Tombs*. Archaeological Survey of Egypt 21. London, 1913.

Davis 1981
Davis, W.M. "An Early Dynastic Lion in the Museum of Fine Arts." In *Studies in Ancient Egypt, the Aegean, and the Sudan: Essays in Honor of Dows Dunham on the Occasion of his Ninetieth Birthday*, ed. W.K. Simpson, 34–42. Boston, 1981.

Delange 1987
Delange, E. *Catalogue des statues égyptiennes du Moyen Empire, 2060–1560 avant J.-C.* [Musée du Louvre]. Paris, 1987.

Delange 2007
Delange, E. "The Complexity of Alloys: New Discoveries about Certain 'Bronzes' in the Louvre." In *Gifts for the Gods: Images from Egyptian Temples*, ed. M. Hill and D. Schorsch, 39–49. New York and New Haven, 2007.

De Meulenaere 1957
De Meulenaere, H. "Notes d'onomastique tardive." *Revue d'Égyptologie* 11 (1957): 77–84.

De Meulenaere 1998
De Meulenaere, H. "The Karnak Cachette." In *The Cairo Museum: Masterpieces of Egyptian Art*, ed. F. Tiradetti, 334–55. London, 1998.

De Meulenaere and Bothmer 1969
De Meulenaere, H. and B.V. Bothmer, "Une tête d'Osiris au Musée du Louvre." *Kêmi* 19 (1969): 9–16.

De Meulenaere and MacKay 1976
De Meulenaere, H., and P. MacKay. *Mendes II*. Warminster, 1976.

Detroit Institute of Arts 1963
Life and Art in Ancient Egypt. Exh. cat., Detroit Institute of Arts, 1963.

Donohue 1988
Donohue, V.A. "The Vezir Paser." *Journal of Egyptian Archaeology* 74 (1988): 103–23.

Dorman 2005
Dorman, P.F. "Hatshepsut: Princess to Queen to Co–Ruler." In *Hatshepsut: From Queen to Pharaoh*, ed. C.H. Roehrig, 87–90. Exh. cat., New York: The Metropolitan Museum of Art, 2005.

Drenkhahn 1986
Drenkhahn, R. *Elfenbein im Alten Ägypten*. Exh. cat., Hannover: Kestner-Museum, 1986.

von Droste zu Hülshoff 1980
von Droste zu Hülshoff, V. *Der Igel im Alten Ägypten*. Hildesheimer Ägyptologische Beiträge 11. Hildesheim, 1980.

Eaton-Krauss 1981
Eaton-Krauss, M. "Miscellanea Amarnensia." *Chronique d'Égypte* 56, no. 112 (1981): 245–64.

Eaton-Krauss and Graefe 1985
Eaton-Krauss, M., and E. Graefe. *The Small Golden Shrine from the Tomb of Tutankhamun*. Oxford, 1985.

Eddé Collection 1911
Collection de M. le Docteur Eddé, d'Alexandrie: Antiquités égyptiennes et grecques, vente à Paris, Hôtel Drouot, 31 mai–2 juin 1911. Paris.

Edgar 1911
Edgar, C.C. "The Temple of Samanoud." *Annales du Service des Antiquités de l'Égypte* 11 (1911): 90–97.

Edwards 1971
Edwards, I.E.S. "Bill of Sale for a Set of Ushabtis." *Journal of Egyptian Archaeology* 57 (1971): 120–24.

Eichler 1993
Eichler, E. *Untersuchungen zum Expeditionswesen des ägyptischen Alten Reiches*. Göttinger Orientforschungen, ser. 4. Ägypten 26. Wiesbaden, 1993.

Ertman 2000
Ertman, E.L. "Scribe Behind a Chair: Analysis of the Walters Art Gallery Relief No. 22.128." *Amarna Letters* 4 (2000): 112–19.

Étienne 2000
Étienne, M. *Heka: Magie et envoûtement dans l'Égypte ancienne*. Exh. cat., Paris: Musée du Louvre, 2000.

Favard-Meeks 1991
Favard-Meeks, C. *Le temple de Behbeit el-Hagara: Essai de reconstruction et d'interprétation*. Studien zur Altägyptischen Kultur, Beiheft 6. Hamburg, 1991.

Fay 1990
Fay, B. *Ancient Egyptian Jewellery in the Collection of the Verein zur Förderung des Ägyptischen Museums in Berlin-Charlottenburg*. Berlin, 1990.

Fay 1996
Fay, B. "The 'Abydos Princess'." *Mittelungen des Deutschen Archäologischen Instituts, Abteilung Kairo* 52 (1996): 115–41.

Fay 2008
Fay, B. "Tell Me, Richard—Did the Ancient Egyptians Really Wear Suspenders? Thoughts on the Vizier's Insignia and One of the Men Who Wore It during Amenhotep III's Reign." In *Servants of Mut: Studies in Honor of Richard A. Fazzini*, ed. S.H. D'Auria, 89–101. Probleme der Ägyptologie 28. Leiden and Boston, 2008.

Fazzini 2001
Fazzini, R. "Recumbent Sphinx." In *The Collector's Eye. Masterpieces of Egyptian Art from the Thalassic Collection*, ed. P. Lacovara and B.T. Trope, 39–42. Atlanta, 2001.

Fazzini et al. 1989
Fazzini, R.A., et al. *Ancient Egyptian Art in the Brooklyn Museum*. New York, 1989.

Fischer 1958
Fischer, H.G. "Eleventh Dynasty Relief Fragments." *Yale University Art Gallery Bulletin* 24, no. 2 (1958): 28–38.

Fischer 1974
Fisher, H.G. "The Mark of a Second Hand on Ancient Egyptian Antiquities." *Metropolitan Museum Journal* 9 (1974): 5–34.

Freed, Markowitz, and D'Auria 1999
Freed, R.E., Y.J. Markowitz, and S.H. D'Auria. *Pharaons of the Sun: Akhenaten, Nefertiti, Tutankhamen*. Exh. cat., Boston: Museum of Fine Arts, 1999.

Frenz 1999
Frenz, H.C. "Bemerkungen zu den Datierungsmöglichkeiten und zur individuellen Ähnlichlkeit bei Mumienporträts." In *Augenblicke: Mumienporträts und ägyptische Grabkunst aus römischer Zeit*, ed. K. Parlasca and H. Seemann, 71–73. Exh. cat., Frankfurt: Kunsthalle Schirn, 1999.

Friedman 1998
Friedman, F.D., ed. *Gifts of the Nile: Ancient Egyptian Faience*. Exh. cat. Providence: Rhode Island School of Design, 1998.

Froehner 1903
Froehner, W. *Catalogue of the Collection of Julien Gréau*. Paris, 1903.

Gauthier 1920
Gautier, H.M. "Les statues thébaines de la déesse Sakhmet." *Annales du Service des Antiquités de l'Égypte* 20 (1920): 177–207.

Germond 1981
Germond, P. *Sekhmet et la protection du monde*. Aegyptiaca Helvetica 9. Geneva, 1981.

Glanville 1972
Glanville, S.R. *Catalogue of Egyptian Antiquities in the British Museum*, 2: *Wooden Model Boats*. London, 1972.

Grimm 1974
Grimm, G. *Die römischen Mumienmasken aus Ägypten* Wiesbaden 1974.

Grimm 1998
Grimm, G. *Alexandria: Die erste Königsstadt der hellenistischen Welt: Bilder aus der Nilmetropole von Alexander der Grossen bis Kleopatra VII*. Mainz 1998.

Grimm, Schoske, and Wildung 1997
Grimm, A., S. Schoske, and D. Wildung. *Pharao: Kunst und Herrschaft im Alten Ägypten*. Exh. cat., Kunsthaus Kaufbeuren, 1997.

Grose 1989
Grose, D.F. *Early Ancient Glass*. Exh. cat., Toledo Museum of Art, 1989.

Gundlach 2002
Gundlach, R. "Die Gedenkskarabäen Amenophis' III.—Ihre Ideologie und historische Bedeutung." In *Festschrift Arne Eggebrecht, zum 65. Geburtstag am 12. März 2000*, ed. B. Schmitz, 31–46. Hildesheimer Ägyptologische Beiträge 48. Hildesheim, 2002.

Hardwick 2003
Hardwick, T. "The Iconography of the Blue Crown in the New Kingdom." *Journal of Egyptian Archaeology* 89 (2003): 117–41.

Harpur 1981
Harpur, Y.M. "Two Old Kingdom Tombs at Giza." *Journal of Egyptian Archaeology* 67 (1981): 24–35.

Harrell 1990
Harrell, J. "Misuse of the Term 'Alabaster' in Egyptology." *Göttinger Miszellen* 119 (1990): 37–42.

Hill 1951
Hill, D.K. "Model Boat from Egypt." *Bulletin of the Walters Art Gallery* 3, no. 4 (1951): 3–4.

Hill 1952
Hill, D.K. "Ptolemy II." *Bulletin of the Walters Art Gallery* 5, no. 1 (1952): 4.

Hill 1956–57
Hill, D.K. "Notes on Some Neo-Memphite Reliefs." *Journal of the Walters Art Gallery* 19–20 (1956–57): 35–40.

Hill 1958
Hill, D.K. "Chairs and Tables of the Ancient Egyptians." *Archaeology* 11, no. 4 (1958): 276–80.

Hill 1960
Hill, D.K. "Daily Life in Ancient Egypt." *Bulletin of the Walters Art Gallery* 13, no. 1 (1960): 2–4.

Hill 2004
Hill, M. *Royal Bronze Statuary from Ancient Egypt*. Leiden, 2004.

Hill and Schorsch 2007
Hill, M., and D. Schorsch, eds. *Gifts for the Gods: Images from Egyptian Temples*. Exh. cat., New York: The Metropolitan Museum of Art. New York and New Haven, 2007.

Hilton-Price 1897
Hilton-Price, F. *A Catalogue of the Egyptian Antiquities in the Possession of F.G. Hilton-Price*. London, 1897.

Hodjash and Berlev 1982
Hodjash, S., and O. Berlev. *The Egyptian Reliefs and Stelae in the Pushkin Museum of Fine Arts, Moscow*. Leningrad, 1982.

Hölbl 2001
Hölbl, G. *A History of the Ptolemaic Empire*. London, 2001.

Hopfner 1921/1924
Hopfner, T. *Griechisch-ägyptischer Offenbarungszauber*. 2 vols. Studien zur Palaeographie und Papyruskunde 21, 23. Leipzig, 1921/1924.

Hornbostel 1973
Hornbostel, W. *Sarapis: Studien zur Überlieferungsgeschichte, den Erscheinungsformen und Wandlungen der Gestalt eines Gottes*. Études préliminaires aux religions orientales dans l'empire romain 32. Leiden, 1973.

Hornung and Bryan 2002
Hornung, E., and B. Bryan, eds. *The Quest for Immortality: Treasures of Ancient Egypt*. Exh cat., Washington, D.C.: National Gallery of Art, 2002.

Hornung, Krauss, and Warburton 2006
Hornung, E., R. Krauss, and D. Warburton, eds. *Ancient Egyptian Chronology*. Handbook of Oriental Studies / Handbuch der Orientalistik, Section 1: The Near and Middle East, vol. 83. Leiden and Boston, 2006.

Hornung, Loeben, and Wiese 2005
Hornung, E., C.E. Loeben, and A. Wiese, eds. *Immortal Pharaoh: The Tomb of Thutmose III*. Exh. cat., Edinburgh: City Arts Centre. Madrid, 2005.

Hornung and Stähelin 1976
Hornung, E., and E. Stähelin, eds. *Skarabäen und andere Siegelamulette aus Basler Sammlungen*. Mainz, 1976.

Ikram and Dodson 1998
Ikram, S., and A. Dodson. *The Mummy in Ancient Egypt*. London, 1976.

James 2000
James, T.G.H. *Tutankhamun*. Vercelli, Italy, 2000.

Jansen-Winkeln 2000
Jansen-Winkeln, K. "Zum Verständnis der 'Saitischen Formel'." *Studien zur Altägyptischen Kultur* 28 (2000): 83–124.

Jansen-Winkeln 2006
Jansen-Winkeln, K. "The Third Intermediate Period." In *Ancient Egyptian Chronology* (Handbook of Oriental Studies / Handbuch der Orientalistik, Section 1: The Near and Middle East, vol. 83), ed. E. Hornung, R. Krauss, and D. Warburton, 258–59. Leiden and Boston, 2006.

Johnston 1999
Johnston, W.R. *William and Henry Walters, the Reticent Collectors*. Baltimore, 1999.

Josephson 1988
Josephson, J.A. "An Altered Royal Head of the Twenty-sixth Dynasty." *Journal of Egyptian Archaeology* 74 (1988): 232–35.

Josephson 1992
Josephson, J.A. "Royal Sculpture of the Later XXVI Dynasty." *Mitteilungen des Deutschen Archaeologischen Instituts, Abteilung Kairo* 48 (1992): 93ff.

Josephson 1996
Josephson, J.A. "A Portrait Head of Psamtik I?" In *Studies in Honor of William Kelly Simpson*, 2, ed. P. Der Manuelian, 429–38. Boston, 1996.

Josephson 1997
Josephson, J.A. "Egyptian Sculpture of the Late Period Revisited." *Journal of the American Research Center in Egypt* 34 (1997): 1–20.

Josephson and Eldamaty 1999
Josephson, J., and M.M. Eldamaty. *Statues of the XXVth and XXVIth Dynasties*. Catalogue général des antiquités égyptiennes du Musée du Caire, nos. 48601–48649. Cairo, 1999.

Junker 1941
Junker, H. *Die Mastaba des Snb (Seneb) und die umliegenden Gräber.* Giza V. Vienna, 1941.

Kahl et al. 2005
Kahl, J., et al. "The Asyut Project: Field Work Season 2004." *Studien zur Altägyptischen Kultur* 33 (2005): 153–76.

Kahl et al. 2006
Kahl, J., et al. "Third Season of Field Work." *Studien zur Altägyptischen Kultur* 34 (2006): 241–49.

Kahl 2008
Kahl, J. *Ancient Asyut: The First Synthesis after Three Hundred Years of Research*. Wiesbaden 2008.

Kaiser 1966
Kaiser, W. *Ein Statuenkopf der ägyptischen Spätzeit*, Jahrbuch der Berliner Museen 8. Berlin, 1966.

Kamal Bey 1906
Kamal Bey, A. "Sébennytos et son temple." *Annales du Service des Antiquités de l'Égypte* 7 (1906): 87–94.

Kayser 1973
Kayser, H. *Die ägyptischen Altertümer im Roemer-Pelizaeus-Museum in Hildesheim*. Hildesheim, 1973.

Kessler and Brose 2007
Kessler D., and P. Brose, eds. *Ägyptens letzte Pyramide: Das Grab des Seuta(s) in Tuna el-Gebel*. Munich, 2007.

Killen 1980
Killen, G. *Ancient Egyptian Furniture*, 1: *4000–1300 B.C.* Warminster, 1980.

Killen 1996
Killen, G. *Ancient Egyptian Furniture*, 2: *Boxes, Chests and Footstools.* Warminster, 1996.

Klemm and Klemm 1991
Klemm, D., and R. Klemm. "Calcite-Alabaster oder Travertine?" *Göttinger Miszellen* 122 (1991): 57–70.

Kormyschewa 2001
Kormyschewa, E.Y. "Report on the Activity of the Russian Archaeological Mission at Giza, Tomb G 7948." *Annales du Service des Antiquités Égyptiennes* 74 (2001): 23–37.

Kormyschewa 2003
Kormyschewa, E.Y. "Report on the Activity of the Russian Archaeological Mission at Giza, Tomb G 7948." *Annales du Service des Antiquités Égyptiennes* 77 (2003): 91–130.

Kozloff 1976
Kozloff, A.P. "A New Species of Animal Figure from Alexandria." *American Journal of Archaeology* 80 (1976): 183–85.

Kozloff and Bryan 1992
Kozloff, A., and B.M. Bryan. *Egypt's Dazzling Sun: Amenhotep III and His World*. Exh. cat., Cleveland Museum of Art, 1992.

Krah 1991
Krah, K. *Die Harfe im pharaonischen Ägypten*. Orbis Musicarum 7. Göttingen, 1991.

Küffer and Renfer 1996
Küffer, A., and M. Renfer. *Das Sargensemble einer Noblen aus Theben*. Bern, 1996.

Kuhlmann 1982
Kuhlmann, K.P. "Der Tempel Ramses II. in Abydos: Zweiter Bericht über die Neuaufnahme." *Mitteilungen des Deutschen Archäologischen Instituts, Abteilung Kairo* 38 (1982): 355–62.

LÄ
Lexikon der Ägyptologie, ed. W. Helck and E. Otto. 7 vols. Wiesbaden, 1972–92.

Lacovara and Trope 2001a
Lacovara, P., and B.T. Trope. *The Realm of Osiris: Mummies, Coffins, and Ancient Egyptian Funerary Art in the Michael C. Carlos Museum*. Atlanta, 2001.

Lacovara and Trope 2001b
Lacovara, P., and B.T. Trope, eds. *The Collector's Eye. Masterpieces of Egyptian Art from the Thalassic Collection*. Exh. cat., Atlanta: Michael C. Carlos Museum, 2001.

Langner 1996
Langner, L. *Isis lactans—Maria lactans: Untersuchungen zur koptischen Ikonographie*. Arbeiten zum spätantiken und koptischen Ägypten 9. Altenberg, 1996.

Leahy 1984
Leahy, A. "Saite Royal Sculpture: A Review." *Göttinger Miszellen* 80 (1984): 59–76.

Leahy 1988
Leahy, L.M. "Private Tomb Reliefs of the Late Period from Lower Egypt." Doctoral thesis, University of Oxford, 1988.

Leitz 2002
Leitz, C., ed. *Lexikon der ägyptischen Götter und Götterbezeichnungen*, 7. Orientalia Lovaniensia Analecta 116. Leuven, 2002.

Lefèbvre and van Rinsveld 1990
Lefèbvre, F., and B. van Rinsveld. *L'Égypte: Des pharaons aux Coptes*. Brussels, 1990.

Lepsius 1897
Lepsius, K. R., ed. R. Naville. *Denkmäler aus Aegypten und Aethiopien, Texte* 1: *Unteraegypten und Memphis.* Leipzig, 1897.

Lichtheim 1975
Lichtheim, M. *Ancient Egyptian Literature*, 1: *The Old and Middle Kingdom*. London and Los Angeles, 1975.

Lilyquist and Brill 1993
Lilyquist, C., and R.H. Brill. *Studies in Early Egyptian Glass.* New York, 1993.

Lillesø 1975
Lillesø, E. "Two Wooden Uraei." *Journal of Egyptian Archaeology* 61 (1975): 137–46.

Luxor Museum 1979
The Luxor Museum of Ancient Egyptian Art. Mainz, 1979.

MacGregor Collection 1922
Sotheby, Wilkinson & Hodge. Sales catalogue, June–July 1922. London, 1922.

Málek 1997
Málek, J. "The Temples at Memphis. Problems Highlighted by the EES Survey." In *The Temple in Ancient Egypt: New Discoveries and Recent Research*, ed. S. Quirke, 90–101. London, 1997.

Málek 1999
Málek, J. *Topographical Bibliography of Ancient Egyptian Hieroglyphic Texts, Statues Reliefs, and Paintings*, 8: *Objects of Provenance Not Known*, part 2: *Private Statues: Dynasty XVIII to the Roman Period; Statues of Deities.* Oxford, 1999.

Martin 1975
Martin, G.T. "Discovery of the Memphite Tomb of Horemheb." *Illustrated London News* 263, no. 6925 (1975): 73–75.

Martin 1989
Martin, G.T. *The Memphite Tomb of Horemheb, Commander-in-Chief of Tut'ankhamun*, 1: *The Reliefs, Inscriptions, and Commentary*. London, 1989.

Martin 1991
Martin, G.T. *The Hidden Tombs of Memphis: New Discoveries from the Time of Tutankhamin and Ramesses the Great.* London, 1991.

Maspero 1883
Maspero, G. "Rapport sur une mission en Italie." *Recueil de traveaux relatifs à la philologie et à l'archéologie égyptiennes et assyriennes* 4 (1883): 125–51.

Maspero 1898
Maspero, G. "Le Papyrus du Fayoum." *Bibliothèque d'études* 7 (1898): 81–91.

Mayr 2004
Mayr. P. "Serapis: Göttliche Integrationshilfe. Ein neuer Gott als Mittler zwischen zwei Hochkulturen." *Antike Welt* 35.3 (2004): 27–35.

McDonald 1982
McDonald, J.K. "Baskets and Basketry." In *Egypt's Golden Age: The Art of Living in the New Kingdom, 1558–1085 B.C.*, ed. E. Brovarksi, 133–39. Exh. cat., Boston: Museum of Fine Arts. 1982.

Merkelbach 1995
Merkelbach, R. *Isis regina—Zeus Sarapis: Die griechisch-ägyptische Religion nach den Quellen dargestellt.* Stuttgart and Leipzig, 1995.

Mildenberg Collection 2004
Christie's London. *A Peaceable Kingdom: The Leo Mildenberg Collection of Ancient Animals*, Tuesday, 26–Wednesday, 27 October 2004.

Monnet 1955
Monnet-Saleh, J. "Un monument de la corégence des Divines Adoratrices Nitocris et Ankhenesneferibrê." *Revue d'Égyptologie* 10 (1955): 37–47.

Müller 1955
Müller, H.W. "Der Torso einer Königsstatue im Museo Archeologico zu Florenz: Ein Beitrag zur Plastik der ägyptischen Spätzheit." In *Studi in memoria di Ippolito Rosellini nel primo centenario della morte (4 giugno 1843)*, 2, Università di Pisa, 183–221. Pisa, 1955.

Müller and Thiem 1998
Müller, H.W., and E. Thiem. *Die Schätze der Pharaonen*. Augsburg, 1998.

Muscarella 1974
Muscarella, O.W., ed. *Ancient Art: The Norbert Schimmel Collection*. Mainz, 1974.

Myśliwiec 1988
Myśliwiec, K. *Royal Portraiture of the Dynasties XXI–XXX*. Mainz, 1988.

Naville 1890
Naville, E. *The Mound of the Jew and the City of Onias*. Memoirs of the Egypt Exploration Fund 7. London, 1890.

Needler 1984
Needler, W. *Predynastic and Archaic Egypt in the Brooklyn Museum.* Wilbour Monographs 9. New York, 1984.

Nibbi 1989
Nibbi, A. *Canaan and Canaanite in Ancient Egypt*. Oxford, 1989.

Nicholson and Shaw 2000
Nicholson, P.T., and I. Shaw, eds. *Ancient Egyptian Materials and Technology.* Cambridge, 2000.

Niwinski 1988
Niwinski, A. *Twenty-First Dynasty Coffins from Thebes: Chronological and Typological Studies*. Theben 5. Mainz, 1988.

Nolte 1968
Nolte, B. *Die Glasgefäße im alten Ägypten.* Münchner Ägyptologische Studien 14. Berlin, 1968.

Oppenheim et al. 1973
Oppenheim, A., et al. *Glass and Glassmaking in Ancient Mesopotamia: An Edition of the Cuneiform Texts Which Contain Instructions for Glassmakers.* Corning Museum of Glass Monographs 3. Corning, N.Y., 1973.

Page-Gasser and Wiese 1997
Page-Gasser, M., and A. Wiese. *Ägypten: Augenblicke der Ewigkeit. Unbekannte Schätze aus schweizer Privatbesitz.* Exh. cat., Antikenmuseum Basel und Sammlung Ludwig. Mainz, 1997.

Parke-Bernet Galleries 1949
Parke-Bernet Galleries, New York, auction catalogue, 9 June 1949, third session. New York.

Parlasca 1969
Parlasca, K. *Repertorio d'arte dell'Egitto greco-romano*, serie B, 1: *Ritratti di mummie*, 1. Palermo, 1969.

Parlasca et al. 1985
Parlasca, K., J.-E. Berger, and R. Pintaudi. *El-Fayyum*. Segni dell'uomo 35. Milan, 1985.

Peck 1978
Peck, W.H. *Drawings from Ancient Egypt*. London, 1978.

Petrie 1898
Petrie, W.F. *Deshasheh*. Memoirs of the Egypt Exploration Fund 15. London, 1898.

Petrie 1903
Petrie, W.F. *Abydos II*. Memoirs of the Egypt Exploration Fund 24. London, 1903.

Petschel and von Falck 2004
Petschel, S., and M. von Falck, eds. *Pharao siegt immer: Krieg und Frieden im alten Ägypten.* Exh. cat., Hamm: Gustav-Lübcke-Museum. Bönen, 2004.

Piccione 1990
Piccione, P.A. "Mehen, Mysteries, and Resurrection from the Coiled Serpent." *Journal of the American Research Center in Egypt* 27 (1990): 43–52.

Pinch 1993
Pinch, G. *Votive Offerings to Hathor.* Oxford, 1993.

Polz 1995
Polz, F. "Die Bildnisse Sesostris'III. und Amenemhets III: Bemerkungen zur königlichen Rundplastik der späten 12. Dynastie." *Mitteilungen des Deutschen Archäologischen Instituts, Abteilung Kairo* 51 (1995): 227–54.

Porten 1981
Porten, B. "The Identity of King Adon." *Biblical Archaeologist* 44, no. 1 (1981): 36–52.

Porter and Moss 1934
Porter, B., and R.L.B. Moss. *Topographical Bibliography of ancient Egyptian Hieroglyphic Texts, Reliefs and Paintings*, 4: *Lower and Middle Egypt*. Oxford, 1934 (repr. 2004).

Porter and Moss 1964
Porter, B., and R.L.B. Moss. *Topographical Bibliography of Ancient Egyptian Hieroglyphic Texts, Reliefs and Paintings*, 1, part 2: *The Theban Necropolis: Royal Tombs and Smaller Cemeteries*. Second ed. Oxford, 1964.

Porter and Moss 1974
Porter, B., and R.L.B. Moss. *Topographical Bibliography of Ancient Egyptian Hieroglyphic Texts, Reliefs and Paintings*, 3, part 1: *Memphis: Abû Rawâsh to Abûsîr*. Second ed., ed. J. Málek. Oxford, 1974.

Porter and Moss 1994
Porter, B., and R.L.B. Moss. *Topographical Bibliography of Ancient Egyptian Hieroglyphic Texts, Reliefs and Paintings*, 2: *Theban Temples.* Oxford, 1994.

Porter and Moss, ed. Málek, Magee, and Miles 2008
Porter, B., and R.L.B. Moss, rev. J. Málek, D. Magee, and E. Miles. *Topographical Bibliography of Ancient Egyptian Hieroglyphic Texts, Reliefs and Paintings*, 8: *Objects of Provenance Not Known,* parts 1 and 2: *Statues of the New Kingdom and the Third Intermediate Period.* Oxford, 2008.

Posener 1959
Posener, G. *Dictionnaire de la civilisation égyptienne*. Paris, 1959.

Raedler 2004
Raedler, C. "Die Wesire Ramses'II.—Netzwerke der Macht." In *Das ägyptische Königtum im Spannungsfeld zwischen Innen- und Außenpolitik im 2. Jahrtausend v. Chr.*, ed. R. Gundlach and A. Klug, 277–416. Wiesbaden, 2004.

Ranke 1939
Ranke, H. "An Egyptian Stela of the Early Eighteenth Dynasty." *Journal of the Walters Art Gallery* 2 (1939): 19–23.

Reeder 1988
Reeder, E.D. *Hellenistic Art in the Walters Art Museum.* Baltimore and Princeton, 1988.

Reeves 2000
Reeves, N. *Ancient Egypt: The Great Discoveries.* London, 2000.

Reisner 1913
Reisner, G.A. *Models of Ships and Boats.* Catalogue général des antiquités égyptiennes du Musée du Caire, nos. 4798–4976 and 5034–5200. Cairo, 1913.

Ritner 1995
Ritner, R.K. "The Religious, Social, and Legal Parameters of Traditional Egyptian Magic." In *Ancient Magic and Ritual Power*, ed. M. Meyer and P. Mirecki, 43–63. Leiden, New York, and Cologne, 1995.

Robins 2000
Robins, G. *Ancient Egyptian Art*. London, 2000.

Roccati and Silotti 1987
Roccati, A., and A. Silotti, eds. *La magia in Egitto ai tempi dei faraoni: Atti del Convegno Internazionale di Studi, Milano, 29–31 ottobre 1985*. Milan, 1987.

Roeder 1956
Roeder, G. *Ägyptische Bronzefiguren.* Staatliche Museen zu Berlin. Mitteilungen aus der Ägyptischen Sammlung 6. Berlin, 1956.

Roehrig 2005
Roehrig, C.H., ed. *Hatshepsut: From Queen to Pharaoh*. Exh. cat. New York: The Metropolitan Museum of Art, 2005.

Roes 1952
Roes, A. "Achaemenid Influence upon Egyptian and Nomad Art." *Artibus Asiae* 15 (1952): 7–30.

Rogers 1982
Rogers, J. D. "Egypt's Golden Age." *Walters Art Gallery Bulletin* 35, nos. 4, 5 (1982).

Romano 2002
Romano, J.F. *In the Fullness of Time: Masterpieces of Egyptian Art from American Collections*. Exh. cat., Salem, Oregon: Hallie Ford Museum of Art, 2002.

Roth 2001
Roth, S. *Die Königsmütter des Alten Ägypten*. Ägypten und Altes Testament 46. Wiesbaden, 2001.

Russmann 1974
Russmann, E.R. *The Representation of the King in the XXVth Dynasty.* Monographies Reine Élisabeth 3. Brussels and Brooklyn, 1974.

Russmann 2001
Russmann, E.R. *Eternal Egypt: Masterworks of Ancient Art from the British Museum*. Exh. cat., New York: Brooklyn Museum, 2001.

el-Saghir 1992
el-Saghir, M. *Das Statuenversteck im Luxortempel*. Zaberns Bildbande zur Archaologie 6. Mainz, 1992.

Saleh and Sourouzian 1986
Saleh, M., and H. Sourouzian. *Das Ägyptische Museum Kairo.* Mainz, 1986.

Satzinger 1981
Satzinger, H. "Der Heilige Stab als Kraftquelle des Königs." *Jahrbuch der Kunsthistorischen Sammlungen in Wien* 77 (1981): 9–43.

Satzinger 1987
Satzinger, H. "Acqua guaritrice: Le statue e le stele magiche e il loro uso magico-medico nell'Egitto faraonico." In *La magia in Egitto ai tempi dei faraoni: Atti del Convegno Internazionale di Studi, Milano, 29–31 ottobre 1985*, ed. A. Roccati and A. Silotti, 189–204. Milan, 1987.

Sauneron 1970
Sauneron, S. *Le papyrus magique illustré de Brooklyn.* Wilbour Monographs 3. New York, 1970.

Schäfer (ed. Baines) 1986
Schäfer, H. *Principles of Egyptian Art*, ed. and trans. J. Baines. Oxford, 1986.

Schipper 1999
Schipper, B.U. *Israel und Ägypten in der Königszeit: Die kulturellen Kontakte von Salomo bis zum Fall Jerusalems.* Orbis Biblicus et Orientalis 170. Freiburg (Switzerland) and Göttingen, 1999.

Schneider 1977
Schneider, H.D. *Shabtis: An Introduction to the History of Ancient Egyptian Funerary Statuettes with a Catalogue of the Collection of Shabtis in the National Museum of Antiquities at Leiden.* 3 vols. Leiden, 1977.

Schneider 1998
Schneider, H. *Life and Death under the Pharaohs: Egyptian Art from the National Museum of Antiquities in Leiden.* Exh. cat., Leiden: Rijksmuseum van Oudheden, 1998.

Schoske 1995
Schoske, S., ed. *Staatliche Sammlung Ägyptischer Kunst München*. Mainz, 1995.

Schoske and Wildung 1992
Schoske, S., and D. Wildung. *Gott und Götter im Alten Ägypten*. Mainz, 1992.

Schulman 1964
Schulman, A.R. *Military Rank, Titles, and Organisation in the Egyptian New Kingdom.* Münchner Ägyptologische Studien 6. Berlin, 1964.

Schulz 1992
Schulz, R. *Die Entwicklung und Bedeutung des kuboiden Statuentypus: Eine Untersuchung zu den sogenannten "Wurfelhockern."* Hildesheimer Ägyptologische Beiträge 33/34. Hildesheim, 1992.

Schulz 2000
Schulz, R. "Warum Isis? Gedanken zum universellen Charakter einer ägyptischen Göttin im Römischen Reich." In *Ägypten und der östliche Mittelmeerraum im 1. Jahrtausend v. Chr.: Akten des Interdisziplinären Symposions am Institut für Ägyptologie der Universität München 25.–27.10.1996*, ed. M. Görg and G. Hölbl, 251–80. Ägypten und Altes Testament 44. Wiesbaden, 2000.

Schulz 2003a
Schulz, R. "Colors of the Heavens." Exh. brochure, Baltimore: Walters Art Museum, 2003.

Schulz 2003b
Schulz, R. "Ein Löwenkopf-Usech mit Menit." In *Das Alte Ägypten und seine Nachbarn: Festschrift zum 65. Geburtstag von Helmut Satzinger*, ed. M.R. Hasitzka, J. Diethart, and G. Dembski. Kremser wissenschaftliche Reihe 3. Krems, 2003.

Schulz 2005
Schulz, R., "Musikanten und Brettspieler: Gedanken zur Bild-und Textanalyse eines bekannten Reliefs." *Imago* 1 (2005): 98–124.

Schulz 2006
Schulz, R. "Dog Is Missing His Master: Reflections on an Old Kingdom Tomb Relief." In *The Old Kingdom Art and Archaeology: Proceedings of the Conference Held in Prague, 31 May–4 June 2004*, ed. M. Barta, 315–24. Prague, 2006.

Schulz 2008
Schulz, R. "Small but Beautiful: The Block Statue of Khaemwaset." In *Servant of Mut: Studies in Honor of Richard A. Fazzini*, ed. S.H. D'Auria, 216–22. Probleme der Ägyptologie 28. Leiden and Boston, 2008.

Schulz and Seidel 2002
Schulz R., M. Seidel, and C. Henry. "Serapis: The Creation of a God." Exh. brochure, Baltimore: Walters Art Museum, 2002.

Schulz and Seidel 2007
Schulz, R., and M. Seidel. *Khepereru—Scarabs: Scarabs, Scaraboids, and Plaques from Egypt and the Ancient Near East in the Walters Art Museum.* Baltimore, 2007.

Scott 1986
Scott, G.D., III. *Ancient Egyptian Art at Yale*. New Haven, 1986.

Seidel 1996
Seidel, M., *Die königlichen Statuengruppe, 1: Die Denkmäler vom Alten Reich bis zum Ende der 18. Dynastie*. Hildesheimer Ägyptologische Beiträge 42. Hildesheim, 1996.

Seidel 2002–3
Seidel, M. "A Mummy Mask from the Middle Kingdom." *Journal of the Walters Art Museum* 60/61 (2002–3): 109–10.

Seidel and Schulz 1998
Seidel, M., and R. Schulz, eds. *Egypt. The World of the Pharaohs*. Cologne, 1998.

Seipel 1989
Seipel, W., ed. *Ägypten Götter, Gräber und die Kunst: 4000 Jahre Jenseitsglauben.* Kataloge des OÖ. Landesmuseums, n.s. 22. Linz, 1989.

Seipel 1992
Seipel, W., ed. *Gott, Mensch, Pharao: Viertausend Jahre Menschenbild in der Skulptur des Alten Ägypten.* Exh. cat., Vienna: Kunsthistorisches Museum, 1992.

Seipel 1998
Seipel, W., ed. *Bilder aus dem Wüstensand: Mumienporträts aus dem Ägyptischen Museum Kairo*. Exh. cat., Vienna: Kunsthistorisches Museum, 1998.

Settgast 1978
Settgast, J. *Von Troja nach Amarna*. Exh. cat., Berlin: Ägyptisches Museum 1978.

Shaw and Nicholson 1995
Shaw, I., and P.T. Nicholson. *British Museum Dictionary of Ancient Egypt*. London, 1995.

Shinnie 1967
Shinnie, P.L. *Meroë: A Civilization of the Sudan.* London, 1967.

Simpson 1974a
Simpson, W.K. *The Terrace of the Great God at Abydos: The Offering Chapels of the Dynasties 12 and 13*. Publications of the Pennsylvania–Yale Expedition to Egypt 5. New Haven and Philadelphia, 1974.

Simpson 1974b
Simpson, W.K. "The Middle Kingdom in Egypt: Some Recent Acquisitions." *Boston Museum Bulletin* 72, no. 368 (1974): 100–16.

Simpson 1977
Simpson, W.K., *The Face of Egypt: Permanence and Change in Egyptian Art*. Exh. cat., Dallas Museum of Fine Arts. Katonah, N.Y., 1977.

Smith 1946
Smith, W.S. *A History of Egyptian Sculpture and Painting in the Old Kingdom*. Oxford, 1946.

Sourouzian 1981
Sourouzian, H. "Une tête de la reine Touy à Gourna." *Mitteilungen des Deutschen Archäologischen Instituts, Abteilung Kairo* 37 (1981): 445–55.

Sourouzian 1989
Sourouzian, H. *Les monuments du roi Merenptah*. Mainz, 1989.

Spanel 1988
Spanel, D. *Through Ancient Eyes: Egyptian Portraiture.* Exh. cat., Birmingham [Alabama] Museum of Art, 1988.

Spencer 1999
Spencer, N.A. "The Epigraphic Survey of Samanud." *Journal of Egyptian Archaeology* 85 (1999): 55–83.

Spurr, Reeves, and Quirke 1999
Spurr, S., N. Reeves, and S. Quirke. *Egyptian Art at Eton College: Selections from the Myers Museum.* Exh. cat., New York: The Metropolitan Museum of Art, 1999.

Städelsches Kunstinstitut 2006
Städelsches Kunstinstitut und Städische Gallerie. *Ägypten Griechenland Rom: Abwehr und Berührung*. Exh. cat., Frankfurt, 2006.

Stanwick 1999
Stanwick, P.E. "Egyptian Royal Sculptures of the Ptolemaic Period." Ph.D. diss., New York University, Institute of Fine Arts, 1999.

Stanwick 2002
Stanwick, P.E. *Portraits of the Ptolemies: Greek Kings as Egyptian Pharaohs*. Austin, 2002.

Steindorff 1939
Steindorff, G. "The Statuette of an Egyptian Commissioner in Syria." *Journal of Egyptian Archaeology* 25 (1939): 30–33.

Steindorff 1940
Steindorff, G. "A Portrait Statue of Sesostris III." *Journal of the Walters Art Gallery* 3 (1940): 42–53.

Steindorff 1942
Steindorff, G. "Two Egyptian Statues of the Ramesside Period." *Journal of the Walters Art Gallery* 5 (1942): 9–17.

Steindorff 1944–45
Steindorff, G. "Reliefs from the Temples of Sebennytos and Iseion in American Collections." *Journal of the Walters Art Gallery* 7/8 (1944–45): 39–59.

Steindorff 1946a
Steindorff, G. *Catalogue of the Egyptian Sculpture in the Walters Art Gallery.* Baltimore, 1946.

Steindorff 1946b
Steindorff, G. "Magical Knives of Ancient Egypt." *Journal of the Walters Art Gallery* 9 (1946): 41–51, 106–7.

Steindorff 1947
Steindorff, G. "Fates and Fakes of Egyptian Antiquities." *Journal of the Walters Art Gallery* 10 (1947): 53–59.

Steindorff 1949
Steindorff, G. "The Walters Art Gallery Mummy." *Journal of the Walters Art Gallery* 12 (1949): 9–17.

Stern and Schlick-Nolte 1994
Stern, E.M., and B. Schlick-Nolte. *Early Glass of the Ancient World, 1600 B.C.–A.D. 50: Ernesto Wolf Collection.* Ostfildern and New York, 1994.

Sternberg–el-Hotabi 1999
Sternberg–el-Hotabi, C. *Untersuchungen zur Überlieferungsgeschichte der Horusstelen: Ein Beitrag zur Religionsgeschichte Ägyptens im 1. Jahrtausend v. Chr.* Wiesbaden, 1999.

Strauß 1974
Strauß, E.-C. *Die Nun-Schale: Eine Gefäßgruppe des Neuen Reiches.* Münchner Ägzptologische Studien 30. Berlin, 1974.

Svenson 1995
Svenson, D. *Darstellungen hellenistischer Könige mit Götterattributen.* Archäologische Studien 10. Frankfurt, 1995.

Tacke 1996
Tacke, N. "Die Entwicklung der Mumienmaske im Alten Reich." *Mitteilungen des Deutschen Archäologischen Instituts Abteilung Kairo* 12 (1996): 307–36.

Tait 2003
Tait, J. "The 'Book of the Fayum': Mystery in a Known Landscape." In *Mysterious Lands: Encounters with Ancient Egypt*, ed. D.B. O'Connor and S. Quirke, 183–202. London, 2003.

Te Velde 1982
Te Velde, H. "Ptah." In *Lexikon der Ägyptologie* 4:1177–80. Wiesbaden, 1982.

Tiradritti 1998
Tiradritti, F. *The Cairo Museum: Masterpieces of Egyptian Art*. London, 1998.

Török 1997a
Török, L. *The Kingdom of Kush: Handbook of the Napatan-Meroitic Civilization*. Leiden, New York, and Cologne, 1997.

Török 1997b
Török, L. *Meroe City, an Ancient African Capital: John Garstang's Excavations in the Sudan*. London, 1997.

Ullmann 2002
Ullmann, M. "Der Tempel Ramses' II. in Abydos als 'Haus der Millionen an Jahren'." *5. Ägyptologische Tempeltagung, Würzburg, 23–26 September 1999*, ed. H. Beinlich, 179–200. Akten der Ägyptologischen Tempeltagungen 3/Ägypten und Altes Testament 33. Wiesbaden, 2002.

Valloggia 1976
Valloggia, M. *Recherche sur les "Messagers" (wpwtyw) dans les sources égyptiennes profanes*. Hautes études orientales 6. Geneva and Paris, 1976.

Vandier 1958
Vandier, J. *Manuel d'archéologie égyptienne*, 3: *La statuaire*. Paris, 1958.

Vandier d'Abbadie 1937
Vandier d'Abbadie, J. *Catalogue des ostraca figurés de Deir el Medineh.* Documents de fouilles de l'Institut français d'archéologie orientale du Caire 2.23. Cairo, 1937.

van Dijk 1992
van Dijk, J. "The New Kingdom Necropolis of Memphis: Historical and Iconographical Studies." Doctoral thesis, Rijksuniversiteit, Groningen, 1992.

Vassilika 2006
Vassilika, E. *Art Treasures from the Museo Egizio*. Turin, 2006.

Vernus 1969
Vernus, P. "Un fragment de bas-relief trouvé à Tanis." *Kêmi* 19 (1969): 93–101.

Vernus 1971
Vernus, P. "Encore une fois le titre *wab Hrt*." *Kêmi* 22 (1971): 7–9.

Vittmann 2003
Vittmann, G. *Ägypten und die Fremden im ersten vorchristlichen Jahrtausend.* Kulturgeschichte der antiken Welt 97. Mainz, 2003.

Walker and Bierbrier 1997
Walker, S., and M.L. Bierbrier. *Ancient Faces: Mummy Portraits from Roman Egypt.* Catalogue of Roman Portraits in the British Museum, part 4. London, 1997.

Wallis 1898
Wallis, H. *Egyptian Ceramic Art: The MacGregor Collection. A Contribution towards the History of Egyptian Pottery.* London, 1898.

Wallis 1900
Wallis, H. *Egyptian Ceramic Art: Typical Examples of the Art of the Egyptian Potter Portrayed in Colour Plates.* London, 1900.

Walters Art Gallery 1979
Jewelry, Ancient to Modern. New York, 1979.

Walters Art Gallery 1982
Three Thousand Years in Glass: Treasures from the Walters Art Gallery. Baltimore, 1982.

Walters Art Gallery 1997
The Walters Art Gallery: Guide to the Collection. London and Baltimore, 1997.

Ward 1986
Ward, W.A. *Essays on Feminine Titles of the Middle Kingdom and Related Subjects*. Beirut, 1986.

Weill 1914
Weill, R. "Monuments égyptiens diverses, IV." *Recueil de travaux rélatifs à la philologie et à l'archéologie égyptiennes et assyriennes* 36 (n.s.), no. 4 (1914): 85–87.

Welsby 1998
Welsby, D.A. *The Kingdom of Kush: The Napatan and Meroitic Empires.* Princeton, 1998.

Wenig 1978
Wenig, S. *Africa in Antiquity: The Arts of Ancient Nubia and the Sudan.* Exh. cat., New York: Brooklyn Museum, 1978.

Westendorf 1966
Westendorf, W. *Altägyptische Darstellungen des Sonnenlaufes auf der abschüssigen Himmelsbahn.* Münchner Ägyptologische Studien 10. Munich, 1966.

Whitehouse 1885
Whitehouse, F.C. "Five Hieroglyphic Inscriptions Completing the Papyrus of the Fayoum." In *Études archéologiques, linguistiques, et historiques dédiées à Mr. le Dr. C. Leemans à l'occasion du cinquantième anniversaire de sa nomination aux fonctions de directeur du Musée archéologique des Pays-Bas*, 83–84. Leiden, 1885.

Wiese 2001
Wiese, A.B. *Antikenmuseum Basel und Sammlung Ludwig: Die Ägyptische Abteilung.* Mainz, 2001.

Wildung 1972
Wildung, D. "Two Representations of Gods from the Early Old Kingdom." *Miscellanea Wilbouriana*, 1, 145–60. New York, 1972.

Wildung 2000
Wildung, D., ed. *Ägypten 2000 v. Chr.: Die Geburt des Individuums.* Munich, 2000.

Wildung and Schoske 1985
Wildung, D., and S. Schoske, eds. *Nofret, die Schöne: Die Frau im Alten Ägypten.* 2 vols. Exh. cat., Munich: Haus der Kunst. Mainz, 1985.

Winlock 1926
Winlock, H.E. "The Egyptian Expedition 1924–1925." *Bulletin of the Metropolitan Museum of Art* 21, no. 3, part 2 (1926).

Zabkar 1975
Zabkar, L.V. *Apedemak, Lion God of Meroë: A Study in Egyptian-Meroetic Syncretism.* Warminster, 1975.

Ziegler 1997
Ziegler, C. *Les statues égyptiennes de l'Ancien Empire*. Paris, 1997.

Ziegler 1998
Ziegler, C. "À propos de quelques ivoires." In *Les critères de datation stylistiques à l'ancien empire*, ed. N. Grimal, 407–19. Bibliothèque d'études 120. Cairo, 1998.

Ziegler 1999
Ziegler, C. "Nonroyal Statuary." In *Egyptian Art in the Age of the Pyramids*, ed. J.P. O'Neill, 57–71. Exh. cat., New York: The Metropolitan Museum of Art, 1999.

Ziegler 2002
Ziegler, C., ed. *The Pharaohs.* Exh. cat., Milan: Palazzo Grassi. London, 2002.

INDEX

Concordance of accession and loan numbers

22.8: 152–53 (no. 63)
22.11: 32–33 (no. 8a)
22.12: 32–33 (no. 8b)
22.16: 38–39 (no. 11)
22.18: 34–35 (no. 9)
22.19: 34–35 (no. 9)
22.38: 130–31 (no. 53)
22.58: 18–19 (no. 2)
22.68: 72–73 (no. 27)
22.79: 134–35 (no. 55)
22.87: 20–21 (no. 3)
22.92: 58–59 (no. 20)
22.93: 88–89 (no. 35)
22.100: 88–89 (no. 35)
22.105: 94–95 (no. 38)
22.106: 92–93 (no. 37)
22.107: 68–69 (no. 25)
22.109: 148–49 (no. 61)
22.111: 82–83 (no. 32)
22.114: 86–87 (no. 34)
22.115: 44–45 (no. 14)
22.119: 122–23 (no. 49)
22.128: 80–81 (no. 31)
22.135: 120–21 (no. 48)
22.140: 154–55 (no. 64)
22.145: 138–39 (no. 57)
22.163: 66–67 (no. 24)
22.177: 98–99 (no. 40)
22.197: 46–47 (no. 15)
22.203: 50–51 (no. 17)
22.215: 136–37 (no. 56)
22.223: 166–67 (no. 69)
22.225: 34–35 (no. 9)
22.258a–b: 174–76 (no. 72)
22.325: 30–31 (no. 7)
22.349: 48–49 (no. 16)
22.373: 42–43 (no. 13)
22.398: 124–25 (no. 50)
22.405: 142–43 (no. 59)
22.407: 150–51 (no. 62)
22.415: 118–19 (no. 47)
22.422: 22–23 (no. 4)
22.425: 24–25 (no. 5)

32.1: 90–91 (no. 36)
32.6: 170–71 (no. 71)

41.28: 26–27 (no. 6)
41.171–174: 110–11 (no. 43)

42.206: 74–75 (no. 28)
42.85: 96–97 (no. 39)

47.31: 64–65 (no. 23a)
47.32: 64–65 (no. 23b)

48. 457: 84–85 (no. 33)
48.400: 60–61 (no. 21)
48.403: 76–77 (no. 29)
48.420: 54–55 (no. 19)
48.426a–b: 62–63 (no. 22)
48.465: 132–33 (no. 54)
48.494: 144–46 (no. 60)

54.400: 114–15 (no. 45)
54.406: 78–79 (no. 30)
54.413: 116–17 (no. 46)
54.416: 126–27 (no. 51)
54.540: 156–57 (no. 65)
54.551: 128–29 (no. 52)
54.2135: 140–41 (no. 58)

57.540: 112–13 (no. 44)
57.1484: 162–63 (no. 67)
57.1524: 164–65 (no. 68)

71.509: 40–41 (no. 12)
71.510: 52–53 (no. 18)
71.622: 16–17 (no. 1b)
71.623: 16–17 (no. 1a)

78.3: 168–69 (no. 70)
78.4: 36–37 (no. 10)

79.1: 102–5 (no. 41)

IL.2001.1.1, IL2001.1.12 (British Museum EA 63, EA 37), 70–71 (nos. 26a, 26b)
TL.1951.179 (MMA 25.3.5): 106–9 (no. 42)
TL.1951.180 (MMA 25.3.13A–B): 106–9 (no. 42)
TL.1951.181 (MMA 25.3.14): 106–9 (no. 42)

W.738: 158–60 (no. 66)